"SHAKESPEARE" IDENTIFIED

What a wounded name,
Things standing thus unknown, shall live behind me.
Hamlet, V.2

Dear son of memory, great heir of fame,
What need'st thou such weak witness for thy name?
Thou in our wonder and astonishment
Hast built thyself a livelong monument.
MILTON, *On Shakespeare*

EDWARD DE VERE, SEVENTEENTH EARL OF OXFORD—AGE 25—

FROM THE PORTRAIT AT WELBECK ABBEY BY AN UNKNOWN ARTIST.
REPRODUCED BY PERMISSION OF
THE NATIONAL PORTRAIT GALLERY.

[Original size: 29.25" x 25"]

"SHAKESPEARE" IDENTIFIED

in Edward de Vere
the Seventeenth Earl of Oxford

BY

J. Thomas Looney

CENTENARY EDITION
JAMES A. WARREN, Editor

Published by

FOREVER PRESS

SOMERVILLE, MASSACHUSETTS

Published by

Forever Press
PO Box 263
Somerville MA 02143
www.foreverpress.org

ISBN 978-0998928937

The cover is a re-creation of the dust jacket of the 1920 Cecil Palmer edition of *"Shakespeare" Identified.*

Images in this publication all reproduced by permission of the National Portrait Gallery.

EDITOR'S NOTE

J. Thomas Looney's *"Shakespeare" Identified* introduced the idea that Edward de Vere, 17th Earl of Oxford, was the man behind the pseudonym "William Shakespeare." Published almost a century ago, it remains the most revolutionary book on Shakespeare ever written. Since its appearance, several generations of scholars have deepened and extended Looney's original findings, further substantiating his claim that Edward de Vere was indeed the author of the dramatic and poetic works widely regarded as the greatest in the English language.

Yet, incredibly, *"Shakespeare" Identified* has long been out of print. All unsold copies of the first British edition (1920, Cecil Palmer) were destroyed during a bombing raid on London in 1940. The first two U.S. editions (1920, Frederick A. Stokes Company; 1949, Duell, Sloan and Pearce) sold out decades ago. The third edition (1975, Kennikat Press, edited by Ruth Loyd Miller) is no longer being marketed by the publisher. In recent decades the book has been obtainable only as rare and expensive copies of older editions, or as bound photocopies of them sold through the print-on-demand market.

With this Centenary edition bringing the book back into print, readers can once again experience Looney's fascinating account of how he, shining light from a new perspective on facts already known to Shakespeare scholars of his day, uncovered the true story of who "Shakespeare" really was and how he came to write his works.

This edition has the first new layout of the book since the original U.S. edition in 1920. In this modern formatting, titles such as "Romeo and Juliet" which had been in quotation marks, are now italicized, as in *Romeo and Juliet*, and longer quotes are indented and in smaller font. Those aspects of punctuation that grate most on modern eyes—such as a blank space between a word and a punctuation mark—have been modernized, and the many inconsistencies in formatting in the previous editions have been standardized. A complete list of changes is included at the end of the book.

At the same time, I have retained as many aspects of the original edition as possible. Looney's British spelling of words such as "theatre," "apologise," "labours," and "realise" remain un-Americanized, and antiquated words such as "whilst" and "amongst" have been kept to convey the flavor of Looney's singular manner of expressing himself. The font, though changed, has been carefully chosen to give the text a stylish appearance that still conveys the gravitas of the book's weighty subject.

Perhaps most importantly of all for scholars, I have reverse-engineered more than two hundred and thirty passages Looney quoted from other works, providing readers for the first time with accurate information on the books and papers he consulted in his research. The quotes themselves have been verified, and any corrections to them explained in footnotes. Those notes are supplemented by a Bibliography at the end of the book for easy reference to Looney's sources.

The most difficult decision I faced as editor was whether to allow the new layout to work itself out naturally, which would have resulted in a text thirty pages shorter than the 1920 New York edition, or whether to force this edition's pagination to conform to that of the earlier editions.

Because the 1949 and 1975 editions matched the layout and pagination of the 1920 edition, that pagination scheme is well established in the minds of those who have studied the book, and I felt it best not to abandon it. At the same time, matching it exactly while using the new font and typesetting, and inserting footnotes rather than endnotes, would result in the text stopping in the middle of the last line on most pages.

The compromise solution I found, after selecting the most appropriate header and left and right margins, was to alter the bottom margin as needed to remain in sync with the older pagination. Thus, although the bottom margins of pages facing each other (pages 4 and 5, for instance) are the same, bottom margins on other pairs of pages vary. This compromise means that the text of this edition, while not matching the pagination of the earlier editions exactly, rarely differs from it by more than a line or two at the bottom of the odd numbered pages.

The content of the text is the same as the first U.S. edition published by Stokes in 1920. No text has been deleted from the numbered pages, as was the case with the second and third U.S. editions, making this edition the first since 1920 to include the full text. More than a dozen of the subject indicators, which were placed in the margins of Cecil Palmer's 1920 London edition and embedded in the text of the editions published in the United States, were omitted from the U.S. editions. I have restored them, making this the first U.S. edition to include all the material that Looney approved for publication. No other material has been added to the text, except for footnotes. Additions to the prefatory material include this "Editor's Note" and the list of images on page xii. A List of Changes and a Bibliography have been added to the supplementary material at the end.

Substantive examinations of how Looney came to write *"Shakespeare" Identified*, of his continuing efforts to promote awareness of Edward de Vere's authorship of "Shakespeare's" works until his death in 1944, and of how the book has changed public and academic understanding of Shakespeare and his works have been deferred to a separate volume, where they can be examined at length. That book, *J. Thomas Looney and "Shakespeare" Identified: The 100th Anniversary of the Book that is Revolutionizing Shakespeare Studies*, is forthcoming, and will be released before March 4, 2020, the hundredth anniversary of the publication of *"Shakespeare" Identified*.

I'd like to thank the Gentlemen of the Green Room—they know who they are—for encouragement in preparing this new edition. And I'm grateful to Alex McNeil for his careful proofreading of the entire book.

JAMES A. WARREN
Sept. 15, 2018

PREFACE

THE solution to the Shakespeare problem, which it is the purpose of the following pages to unfold, was worked out whilst the Great European War was in progress; and my wish was to give the matter full publicity immediately upon the cessation of hostilities. As this was found to be impracticable, steps had to be taken, both to ensure that the results achieved should not be lost, and also to safeguard what I believed to be my priority of discovery. With these objects, an announcement of the mere fact of the discovery, omitting all details, was made in November, 1918, to Sir Frederick Kenyon, Librarian of the British Museum, and he very readily undertook to receive, unofficially, a sealed envelope containing a statement on the subject. As more than a year has passed since the deposition was made, and as no one else has come forward with the same solution, the question of priority is not likely now to arise, and therefore, with the publication of the present work, the purpose of the deposited document naturally lapses. My first duty, then, must be to express my deep sense of indebtedness to Sir Frederick Kenyon for the freedom from anxiety that I have enjoyed whilst further developing the argument and carrying through its publication.

It was to my brother-in-law, Mr. M. Gompertz, B.A., Head Master of the County High School, Leytonstone, and to my friend Mr. W. T. Thorn that I first submitted a statement of evidences; and their complete acceptance of my solution has been the source of much confidence and encouragement. To them I am also under large obligations for practical assistance; to the former specially for the revision of proofs, and to the latter for valuable work on the Index.

PREFACE

The relationship of Mr. Cecil Palmer to the undertaking has been much more than that of publisher. When the case was laid before him he adopted its conclusions with enthusiasm and made the cause his own. My personal obligations to him are therefore very considerable.

One of the greatest debts I have to acknowledge is more impersonal: namely, to the Library of the Literary and Philosophical Society, Newcastle-upon-Tyne. The unique system upon which this institution is conducted has rendered possible an ease and rapidity of work that would probably have been impossible in any other institution in the country.

I have also gratefully to acknowledge indebtedness respecting the portraits it was important the work should contain: to His Majesty the King for permission to reproduce the miniature of Sir Philip Sidney in Windsor Castle; to His Grace the Duke of Portland, not only for permission to reproduce, but also for facilities, spontaneously and graciously offered, for securing a good copy of his portrait of Edward de Vere at Welbeck Abbey; to the Trustees of the National Portrait Gallery for similar permission respecting the portraits of Lord Burleigh and Sir Horace Vere; and to Mr. Emery Walker, F.S.A., for kindly granting the use of several photographs and blocks of these portraits.

I now send forth the results of my investigations to face the ordeal of a public examination. Although I have tried to regard all schools of thought as so many agencies in the one cause of truth, it is too much to expect that, in dealing with such controversial matters, I have avoided hurting susceptibilities. For any shortcomings of this kind I throw myself on the generosity of my readers. I have no wish, however, to be spared fair and helpful criticism; nor can I hope to escape criticism of the less kindly type: but if in the end I can see the truth prevail and an act of reparation done to a great Englishman, I shall be content.

J. THOMAS LOONEY.

December 15th, 1919.

vi

CONTENTS

CHAPTER 1

Growing scepticism; Ignatius Donnelly; Anti-Stratfordian authorities; "Shakespeare" and law; "Shakespeare's" education; Halliwell-Phillipps; William Shakspere's early life; Shakespeare and Burns; William Shakspere's three periods; Closing period; The Will; Ben Jonson; Hemming and Condell; Penmanship; The "Shakespeare" manuscripts; The First Folio; Obituary silence; William Shakspere's middle period; No participation in publication; Uncertain duration; Uncertain habitation; The great *alibi*; William Shakspere's silence; Character of contemporary notices; The Stratfordian impossibility; Absence of incidents; No letters; William Shakspere as actor; Municipal records; As London actor; Accounts of Treasurer of Chamber; Missing Lord Chamberlain's books; Notable omissions; Summary.

CHAPTER II

Authorship a mystery; A solution required; Literary authorities; "Shakespeare's" voluntary self-effacement; Genius; Maturity and masterpieces; A modern problem; The method of solution; Stages outlined.

CHAPTER III

Recognized genius and mysterious; Appearance of eccentricity; A

CONTENTS

CONTENTS

CONTENTS

CONTENTS

LIST OF ILLUSTRATIONS

PRELIMINARY NOTE

IN discussing the authorship of the Shakespeare plays and poems it is necessary to guard against the ambiguity attaching to the name "Shakespeare."

Following the example of the Baconians and Sir George Greenwood, I have spelt the word with an "e" in the first syllable, and an "a" in the final syllable—"Shakespeare"—when referring to the author, whoever he may have been; and without these two letters—"Shakspere"—when referring to the person hitherto credited with the authorship. By the addition of the Christian name in the latter case, and in other ways, I have tried to accentuate the distinction.

In immaterial connections the former is usually employed, and in quotations the spelling of the original is generally followed.

INTRODUCTION

As a much graver responsibility attaches to the publication of the following pages than is usual in the case of treatises on literary subjects, it is impossible to deal with the matter as impersonally as one might wish. The transference of the honour of writing the immortal Shakespeare dramas from one man to another, if definitely effected, becomes not merely a national or contemporary event, but a world event of permanent importance, destined to leave a mark as enduring as human literature and the human race itself. No one, therefore, who has a due sense of these things is likely to embark upon an enterprise of this kind in a spirit of levity or adventure; nor will he feel entitled to urge convictions tending to bring about so momentous a change as if he were merely proposing some interesting thesis. However much the writer of a work like the present might wish to keep himself in the background he is bound to implicate himself so deeply as to stake publicly his reputation for sane and sober judgment, and thus to imperil the credit of his opinion on every other subject. It would therefore have been more discreet or diplomatic to have put forward the present argument tentatively at first, as a possible or probable, rather than an actual solution of the Shakespeare problem. The temptation to do this was strong, but the weight of the evidence collected has proved much too great and conclusive to permit of this being done with even a fair measure of justice either to the case or to my own honest convictions. Only one course then was open to me. The greater responsibility had to be incurred; and therefore some remark upon the circumstances under which the investigations came to be undertaken is not only justifiable but necessary.

For several years in succession I had been called upon to go through repeated courses of reading in one particular play of Shakespeare's, namely *The Merchant of Venice*. This long continued familiarity with the contents of one play induced a peculiar sense of intimacy with the mind and disposition of its author and his outlook upon life. The personality which seemed to run through the pages of the drama I felt to be altogether out of relationship with what was taught of the reputed author and the ascertained facts of his career. For example, the Stratford Shakspere was untravelled, having moved from his native place to London when a young man, and then as a successful middle-aged man of business he had returned to Stratford to attend to his lands and houses. This particular play on the contrary bespoke a writer who knew Italy at first hand and was touched with the life and spirit of the country. Again the play suggested an author with no great respect for money and business methods, but rather one to whom material possessions would be in the nature of an encumbrance to be easily and lightly disposed of: at any rate one who was by no means of an acquisitive disposition. This was hardly the type of man to have risen from poverty to affluence by his own efforts when but little more than thirty years of age, nor was such a man likely to have been responsible for some of the petty money transactions recorded of the Stratford man. Other anomalies had forced themselves upon my attention and had done much to undermine my faith in the orthodox view. The call of other interests, however, prevented my following up the question with any seriousness.

A recurrence of the old doubts under new circumstances led me at length to look more closely into the problem and to consult writers who had dealt with it. These convinced me that the opponents of the orthodox view had made good their case to this extent, that there was no sufficient evidence that the man William Shakspere had written the works with which he was credited, whilst there was a very strong prima facie presumption that he had not. Everything seemed to point to his being but a mask, behind which some great genius, for inscrutable reasons, had elected to work out his own destiny. I do not maintain that any single objection, to what for convenience sake we must call the Stratfordian view, afforded by itself sufficient grounds for regarding it as untenable; for most of these objections have been stoutly combated severally, by men whose opinions are entitled to respect. It was rather the cumulative effect of the many objections which, it appeared to me, made it impossible to adhere with any confidence to the old view of things, and so gave to the whole situation an appearance of inexplicable mystery.

Here, then, were the greatest literary treasures of England, ranked by universal consent amongst the highest literary achievements of mankind, to all intents and purposes of unknown origin. The immediate effect of such a conviction was the sense of a painful hiatus in the general outlook upon the supreme accomplishments of humanity; a want much more distressing than that which is felt about the authorship of writings like the Homeric poems, because the matter touches us more directly and intimately. It was impossible, I felt, to leave things thus, if by any means the problem could be solved and the gap filled up. I resolved, therefore, notwithstanding the extreme boldness, or rather presumption, of the undertaking to attempt a solution of the problem.

At the beginning it was mainly the fascination of an interesting enquiry that held me, and the matter was pursued in the spirit of simple research. As the case has developed, however, it has tended increasingly to assume the form of a serious purpose, aiming at a long overdue act of justice and reparation to an unappreciated genius who, we believe, ought now to be put in possession of his rightful honours; and to whose memory should be accorded a gratitude proportionate to the benefits he has conferred upon mankind in general, and the lustre he has shed upon England in particular.

That one who is not a recognized authority or an expert in literature should attempt the solution of a problem which has so far baffled specialists must doubtless appear to many as a glaring act of overboldness; whilst to pretend to have actually solved this most momentous of literary puzzles will seem to some like sheer hallucination. A little reflection ought, however, to convince anyone that the problem is not, at bottom, purely literary. That is to say, its solution does not depend wholly upon the extent of the investigator's knowledge of literature nor upon the soundness of his literary judgment. This is probably why the problem has not been solved before now. It has been left mainly in the hands of literary men, whereas its solution required the application of methods of research which are not, strictly speaking, literary methods. The imperfection of my own literary equipment, of which I was only too conscious, was therefore no reason why I should not attempt the task; and if the evidence collected in support of any proposed solution should of itself prove satisfactory, its validity ought not to be in any way affected by considerations purely personal to the investigator.

I proceeded accordingly to form plans for searching for the real author of Shakespeare's plays. These plans were outlined before taking any step, and will be fully explained in due course. Personally, I have not the slightest doubt as to their having succeeded. Whether I shall be able to so present the case as to establish an equally strong conviction in the minds of others, is, of course, a vastly different matter. The force of a conviction is frequently due as much to the manner in which the evidence presents itself, as to the intrinsic value of the evidence. For example, when a theory, that we have formed from a consideration of certain facts, leads us to suppose that certain other facts will exist, the later discovery that the facts are actually in accordance with our inferences becomes a much stronger confirmation of our theory than if we had known these additional facts at the outset. We state this principle in matters of science when we affirm that the supreme test and evidence of the soundness of a scientific theory is its power of enabling us to foresee some events as a consequence of others. The manner, therefore, in which facts and ideas have been arrived at becomes itself an important element in the evidence; and it is this consideration which has decided for me the method most suitable for presenting the case.

Though it is impossible ever to carry the minds of others through precisely the same processes as those by which one's own settled beliefs have been reached, it has seemed to me that in this instance some attempt of the kind should be made in order that the reader, in seeing how readily newly discovered particulars have arranged themselves in a clear order around an original hypothesis, may come to feel something of the same certainty which these things have produced in my own mind. As a matter of fact, some of the most convincing evidence presented itself after my theory of the authorship had already assumed the form of a settled conviction, and indeed after this work was virtually completed; thus rendering my receding from the theory practically impossible. To others, however, who might only see it in the general mass of accumulated evidence, it could not appeal with anything like the same compelling force. These considerations have decided me to present the case as far as possible in the form of a representation of the various stages through which the enquiry was pursued, the manner in which the evidence was collected, and the process by which an accumulating corroboration transformed a theory into an irresistible conviction.

What at first blush may appear a pedantic description of a method ought, therefore, to be viewed as in itself a distinctive form of evidence. I would ask, then, that it be regarded as such, and that what would otherwise be an unseemly obtrusion of personality be excused accordingly.

The reader's indulgence must also be sought on another score. The first steps in an enquiry pursued according to the method I had to adopt were inevitably slow, and this may import a measure of tediousness into the introductory stages of an exposition following on the same lines. Yet without a patient attention to the various steps of the enquiry the unity and conclusiveness of the argument as a whole might be missed. Although these pages are addressed to the general reader rather than to literary scholars, I am obliged to assume a serious desire to discover the truth and a willingness to take some trouble to arrive at it. Especially must I ask for that concentrated individual reflection by which alone the various parts of the argument may be seen as a whole: a practice which, we are afraid, is somewhat alien to the purely literary mind.

In one or two instances I have no doubt made use of books that are somewhat rare, the most critical chapter of the work, in fact, depending wholly upon a work, copies of which are not readily accessible to everyone: nevertheless it will be found that nothing important in the argument rests upon newly unearthed data. Everything has been accessible for years to anyone who might have been on the lookout for the facts, and was prepared to take trouble to ascertain them. Even where personal judgments constitute important elements in the evidence, as is natural in enquiries of this nature, the case has been made to rest at almost every critical stage, not upon my own judgment alone, but upon the statements of writers of recognized standing and authority whose works have for some time been before the public. In most cases it will be found that the authorities quoted are writers of the Stratfordian school. Great as are my obligations specially to Sir George Greenwood's work,[1] I have purposely refrained from quoting from it when I might often have done so with advantage to my own argument, and preferred resting upon the authority of

---

[1] See, for instance, Greenwood's *The Shakespeare Problem Restated* and *Is There a Shakespeare Problem?*

writers of the opposite school. How completely these writers support my thesis, will I trust be apparent in the sequel. This being so, the question might reasonably be asked: how comes it that the discovery which is claimed has not been made before now? The answer to this question is to be found in the history of almost all the important advances that man has made. The basic facts of his discoveries have usually been well known for some time before. What has been of special consequence has been the perception, sometimes purely accidental, of a relationship amongst these facts hitherto not noticed. Once detected, however, other facts have become grouped and coordinated by it, and the resultant discovery, for which mankind had probably waited long, appears at last so natural and obvious, that men wonder that it had not been thought of before. This may be taken as a compendium of human discovery generally.

In almost every such case there has been a preparatory movement towards the discovery; a movement in which many minds have participated; and the one who has been fortunate enough to make the discovery has frequently been, in important respects, inferior to those into whose labours he has entered. Now, I have no doubt that Shakespearean study has of late years been making surely towards the discovery of the real author of the works. I can detect two distinct currents of literary interest, which, it seems to me, were bound ultimately to converge, and in their converging disclose the authorship. The first of these has been the tendency to put aside the old conception of a writer creating everything by the vigour of his imagination, and to regard the writings as reflecting the personality and experiences of their author. The result has been the gradual rise of a conception of the personality of "Shakespeare," differing very widely from the conventional figure: an outstanding expression of this tendency being Mr. Frank Harris's work on *The Man Shakespeare*. The second current, only faintly perceptible as yet, has been slowly forcing from obscurity, into our knowledge of

Elizabethan literature and drama, the name and figure of one still quite unknown to the vast mass of his countrymen. These two movements, if continued, had in them the possibility of the discovery; though how long that discovery might have been deferred, no one can say.

What I have to propose, however, is not an accidental discovery, but one resulting from a systematic search. And it is to the nature of the method, combined with a happy inspiration and a fortunate chance, that the results here described were reached.

In presenting a thesis the strength of which must depend largely upon the convergence of several separate lines of argument, a certain amount of repetition of particular facts is unavoidable, and in this matter I have preferred to risk an unnecessary reiteration rather than an incomplete statement of any particular argument. The reason for such repetition it is hoped will not be overlooked. My object being to solve an important problem rather than to swell the supply of literature, all merely literary considerations have been kept subordinate to the central purpose.

One other matter affecting the general presentation of the argument remains to be mentioned. As originally written the work contained no special examination of Stratfordianism, but merely incidental observations scattered throughout the various chapters. My feeling was that sufficient had already been written by others upon the subject; that short of absolute proof of the negative, the anti-Stratfordians had established their case, and that what was wanted was not more evidence but a serious attention to what had already been written, and above all a reasonable positive hypothesis to put in the place of the old one. From this point of view it seemed possible to begin my argument at the point where others had left off. I was, however, advised by friends, more capable than myself of judging the needs of readers, to make my argument complete in itself, by presenting first of all the case for the negative view, and thus clearing the way for my own special investigations. This change of plan is bound to involve what might appear like wanton and pointless repetition in several instances, and may interfere with the unity of the constructive scheme of exposition. I would, however, urge the reader not to linger unduly over the things that are destined to pass away, but to press on to a consideration of those matters which, if there be truth in my thesis, will endure, at least so long as the English language is understood.

CHAPTER I

THE STRATFORDIAN VIEW

Ex nihilo nihil fit

I.

Growing Skepticism.

IN spite of the efforts of orthodox Stratfordians to belittle the investigations that have been made into the question of the authorship of the Shakespeare dramas; perhaps indeed because of the very manner they have chosen to adopt, the number of Britons and Americans, to say nothing of the non-English speaking nationalities, who do not believe that William Shakspere of Stratford produced the literature with which he is credited is steadily on the increase. Outside the ranks of those who have deeply committed themselves in print it is indeed difficult nowadays to find anyone in the enjoyment of a full and assured faith. At the same time the resort of the faithful few to contemptuous expressions in speaking of opponents is clearly indicative of uneasiness even amongst the most orthodox littérateurs.

The unfortunate "cryptogram" of Ignatius Donnelly, whilst tending to bring the enquiry into disrepute with minds disposed to serious research, has been unable altogether to nullify the effects of the negative criticism with which his work opens. The supplementing of this by writers of the calibre of Lord Penzance, Judge Webb, Sir George Greenwood, and Professor Lefranc has raised the problem to a level which will not permit of its being airily dismissed without thereby reflecting adversely on the capacity and judgment of the controversialists who would thus persist in giving artifice instead of argument. That, however, is their concern. The common sense of the rank and file of Shakespeare students, when unhampered by past committals, leads irresistibly towards the rejection of the old idea of authorship; and only the doctors of the ancient literary cult hang in the rear.

Nevertheless, much remains to be done before the Stratfordian hypothesis will be sufficiently moribund to be neglected. And although this work is addressed mainly to those who are either in search of a more reasonable hypothesis, or, having become awakened to a sense of the existence of the "Shakespeare Problem" are willing to take the trouble to examine impartially what has already been written by others on the subject, the present argument would probably be incomplete without a more explicit treatment of the Stratfordian point of view than has been given in the main body of the treatise. At the same time it is impossible to present the anti-Stratfordian argument completely without adding enormously to the bulk of the work. Moreover, as we have a very definite positive argument to unfold we wish to avoid the dangers of diverting attention from it by giving an unnecessary prominence to the negative argument so ably treated by previous writers. That negative argument, like its present constructive counterpart, is cumulative; and, like every sound cumulative argument, each of these is receiving additional corroboration and confirmation with almost every new fact brought to light in respect to it. How much of this accumulated material it is necessary to present before the case can be considered amply and adequately stated must needs depend largely upon the preparedness and partialities of those addressed.

Ignatius Donnelly.

Although the thirty years which have passed since Ignatius Donnelly's work appeared have witnessed marked developments of the critical argument, the full force of the first hundred pages of his first volume[2] has not yet been fully appreciated. To allow a

---

[2] Ignatius Donnelly, *The Great Cryptogram*, Part I: William Shakspere Did Not Write the Plays, pp. 1-120.

justifiable repugnance to his "cryptogram" work to stand in the way of a serious examination of the material he has brought together from untainted sources, like Halliwell-Phillipps and others of recognized capacity and integrity, is to fall behind the times in the spirit of dispassionate scientific research. A few hours spent, therefore, in leisurely weighing the material contained in his opening chapters, notwithstanding its incompleteness, will probably convince most people that the Stratfordian hypothesis rests upon the most insecure foundations: differentiating it entirely from all other outstanding cases of English authorship in historic times, as for example, Chaucer, Spenser and Milton. The exceptional character of many of the facts he has collected, the multiplicity of the grounds for rejecting the hypothesis, and the general consistency of the various arguments, all combine to form a single justification for a negative attitude towards the conventional view. A mere repetition in these pages of what others have written will not add much to its force; to spend time in expounding its unity is to attempt to do for others what any reflecting mind pretending to judge the case ought to do for itself.

Anti-Stratfordian Authorities.

What is true of the case as presented by Ignatius Donnelly has probably still greater force as applied to the work of men who have treated this problem in more recent years. It would be perfectly gratuitous to insist upon the analytical acumen of Lord Penzance,[3] and therefore scarcely short of an impertinence to brush aside lightly his opinions in matters involving the weighing of evidence. Consequently, when such new arguments as he advances, and the new bearings he is able to point out in former arguments, are marked by the same unity and lead to the same general conclusions as those of other capable writers both before and since his time, we may claim that a measure of what may be called authoritative research has been accomplished, liberating

---

[3] Judge James P. Wilde, First Baron Penzance. See, for instance, *Lord Penzance on the Bacon-Shakespeare Controversy.*

subsequent investigators from repeating all the particulars by means of which these general results have been reached. In other words, a certain basis of authority has been established: not, of course, an absolute and infallible authority, but a relative, practical, working authority such as we are obliged to accept in the theoretical no less than in the active affairs of life.

"Shakespeare" and law.

When, for example, three eminent English lawyers tell us that the plays of Shakespeare display an expert knowledge of law such as William Shakspere could hardly be expected to possess, it would be extreme folly on the part of one who is not a lawyer to spend himself and use up space in putting together evidence to prove the same point. No amount of evidence which he might collect would have the same value as the authoritative statement of these men. He may, if he cares to, claim that the lawyers have not made good their point, or he may agree with the general conclusion, and dispute the theory that the author was an active member of the legal profession. But if he agrees with them on the main issue he cannot serve his cause in any way by traversing again the ground that these experts have already covered.

"Shakespeare's" education.

Again, when, in addition to these writers we have authorities of the opposite school agreeing that the author of the plays possessed a first-hand knowledge of the classics, including a knowledge of passages which would not come into a schoolboy's curriculum, it would be affectation upon the part of a writer laying no claim to expert knowledge of the classics to restate the particulars, or attempt to add to what has already been said some little fragment from his own scanty stores. In the same way we are now entitled to affirm, without adducing all the evidence upon which it has been determined, that the author of "Shakespeare's" plays and poems possessed a knowledge of idiomatic French, and most probably a reading familiarity with the Italian language, such as William Shakspere could not have learnt at Stratford: and, what is perhaps of as great importance as anything else, he employed as the habitual vehicle of his mind an English of the highest educated type completely free from provincialism of any kind.

The "Shakespeare Problem," we maintain, has now reached a stage at which such summarized results may be placed before readers with the assurance that these conclusions have behind them the sanction of men of unquestioned probity and capacity: thus relieving the modern investigator from the labour of repeating all the particulars from which the conclusions are drawn. And although these compendious dogmatic statements cannot be expected to convince the man who claims to have studied the writers we have named and yet preserved his orthodoxy unshaken, they will probably suffice for the average or the generality of mankind. Orthodox faiths, however, are usually intrinsically weakest when most vehemently asserted; and the persistence of the Stratfordian faith has probably been due much less to its own inherent strength than to the want of a better to put in its place.

Halliwell-Phillipps.

Those who have had occasion to study Shakespearean problems will, we believe, agree that the most trustworthy work for particulars respecting the life of William Shakspere of Stratford is Halliwell-Phillipps's *Outlines.* Writing in 1882, six years before the appearance of Donnelly's work, the problem of Shakespearean authorship seems never to have touched him; and therefore, undoubting Stratfordian though he was, he writes with perfect freedom and openness, glozing over nothing, and not shrinking from making admissions which some later Baconian or sceptic might use against the subject of his biography. Without wishing to imply anything against subsequent biographies, written in the refracting atmosphere of controversy, we may describe Halliwell-Phillipps's *Outlines* as the most honest biography of William Shakspere yet written.

II.

William Shakspere's early life.

As, then, the main root of the Shakespeare problem has always been the difficulty of reconciling the antecedents of William Shakspere (so far as they are known or can be reasonably inferred) with the special features of the literary work attributed to him, it ought to suffice that the contention from which most anti-Stratfordian argument starts is abundantly supported by Halliwell-Phillipps. Dirt and ignorance, according to this authority, were outstanding features of the social life of Stratford in those days and had stamped themselves very definitely upon the family life under the influence of which William Shakspere was reared. Father and mother alike were illiterate, placing their marks in lieu of signatures upon important legal documents: and his father's first appearance in the records of the village is upon the occasion of his being fined for having amassed a quantity of filth in front of his house, there being "little excuse for his negligence." So much for the formative conditions of his home life. On the other hand, so far as pedagogic education is concerned there is no vestige of evidence that William Shakspere was ever inside of a school for a single day: and, considering the illiteracy of his parents and the fact that ability to read and write was a condition of admission to the Free School at Stratford, it is obvious that there were serious obstacles to his obtaining even such inferior education as was offered by schools in small provincial places in those days. Respecting this difficulty of meeting the minimum requirements for admission to the school Halliwell-Phillipps remarks: "There were few persons living at Stratford-on-Avon capable of initiating him into these preparatory accomplishments . . . but it is as likely as not that the poet received his first rudiments of education from older boys."[4] Later generations of schoolboys have preferred more exciting pastimes.

---

[4] J. O. Halliwell-Phillipps, *Outlines of the Life of Shakespeare*, p. 39.

Shakespeare and Burns.

It is impossible to deny that the general educational advantages of Robert Burns, including, as we must, the intellectual level of peasant life in Scotland in his day, family circumstances and character of parents, were altogether superior to what existed at Stratford and in the home of William Shakspere two centuries before. The following remark of Ruskin's, whom it is impossible to suspect of "heterodoxy," will therefore not be out of place at this point.

> There are attractive qualities in Burns and attractive qualities in Dickens, which neither of those writers would have possessed, if the one had been educated and the other had been studying higher nature than that of Cockney London; but those attractive qualities are not such as we should seek in a school of literature. If we want to teach young men a good manner of writing we should teach it from Shakespeare, not from Burns; from Walter Scott and not from Dickens.[5]

This statement of Ruskin's, made without reference to anything controversial, furnishes a special testimony to the fact that the distinctive literary qualities of Shakespeare are the direct antithesis of those which belong to a great poetic genius, such as Burns, whose genius enables him to attain eminence in spite of homely beginnings. It is hardly possible, moreover, to pick up the slightest biographical sketch of Scotland's poet without meeting testimony to the same fact. The following, for example, we take from the first such sketch which comes to hand.

> Burns was essentially 'one of the people' in birth, breeding, and instincts . . . he has been taken more to men's bosoms than any [other] if we except, perhaps, the bard of Avon, *whose admirers* belong *more exclusively to the educated classes.*[6]

Spontaneously this comparison between the two poets rises in the mind of almost any writer who deals specially with either one of them, and leads always to a contrast upon the particular point with which we are dealing.

---

[5] John Ruskin, *The Two Paths*, p. 63.
[6] *The Complete Poetical Works of Robert Burns*, edited by Wm. Gunnyon, p. xix.

Shakspere and books.

Shakespeare's work if viewed without reference to any personality would never have been taken to be the work of a genius who had emerged from an uncultured milieu. The only conditions which could have compensated in any degree for such initial disabilities as those from which William Shakspere suffered would have been a plentiful supply of books and ample facilities for a thorough study of them. It is generally agreed, however, that even if he attended school he must have had to leave at an early age in order to assist his father, whose circumstances had become straitened: and that he had to engage in occupations of a non-intellectual and most probably of a coarsening kind. And, so far from being able to compensate for all this by means of books the place is spoken of as "a bookless neighbourhood."[7] "The copy of the black-letter English History . . . in his father's parlour, never existed out of the imagination."[8] Even after his London career was over, and as the supposed greatest writer in England he retired to Stratford, the situation was probably no better. "Anything like a private library, even of the smallest dimensions, was then of the rarest occurrence, and that Shakespeare [William Shakspere] ever owned one, at any time of his life, is exceedingly improbable."[9] Dr. Hall—Shakspere's son-in-law—however, possessed in 1635 what he called his "study of books,"[10] which probably included any that had belonged to Shakespeare. If the latter were the case, the learned doctor did not consider it worthwhile to mention the fact.[11]

Burns and books.

In contrast with all this take the following passages from the

---

[7] Halliwell-Phillipps, *Outlines*, p. 88.
[8] Halliwell-Phillipps, *Outlines*, p. 57.
[9] Halliwell-Phillipps, *Outlines*, p. 245. Text in brackets was added by Looney.
[10] Halliwell-Phillipps, *Outlines*, p. 245.
[11] In the 1920 editions of *"Shakespeare" Identified*, the passage "which probably included . . . to mention the fact" is in quotation marks and is followed by "(Halliwell-Phillipps's 'Outlines')." It does not appear in Halliwell-Phillipps's book, however; Looney apparently mistakenly put quotation marks around his own comment. They have been removed.

short biographical sketch already quoted, of the poet who, in purely educational matters, is placed so much below "Shakespeare."

> When he was six years of age the poet [Burns] was sent to a school at Alloway Mil . . . [Later, his father], in conjunction with several neighbours, engaged a young man, John Murdock, agreeing to pay him a small quarterly salary, and to lodge him alternately in their houses. The boys were taught by him reading, writing, arithmetic and grammar. . . . Mr. Murdock left for another situation [and] the father undertook to teach his sons arithmetic by candle light in the winter evenings. . . . Burns went [to Murdock] one week before harvest and two after it to brush up his learning. . . . The first week was devoted to English grammar, and the other two to a flirtation with French. . . . Burns laboured at this new study with such eagerness and success that he could, according to his brother, translate any ordinary prose author; and we know that to the last he loved to interlard his correspondence with phrases from that language. And when he bethought himself of attempting, in later life, a dramatic composition, among the books he ordered from Edinburgh was a copy of Molière. . . . Besides he had read and digested at an early age many valuable and some ponderous books. His father had borrowed for his reading, in addition to his own scanty stock; and wealthy families in Ayr, as well as humble families nearer home, gave him free access to what books of theirs he wished to read. [Amongst the books he read in this way were] . . . *The Life of Hannibal*, Salmon's *Geographical Grammar*, Derham's *Physico-Theology*, *The Spectator*, Pope's *Homer*, Hervey's *Meditations*, Locke's *Essay on the Human Understanding*, and several plays of Shakespeare.
>
> In his nineteenth summer he was sent to Kirkoswald Parish School to learn mensuration, surveying, etc. . . . In these he made good progress. . . . The teacher had great local fame as a mathematician . . . [The poet's] sojourn at Kirkoswald had much improved him. He had considerably extended his reading; he had exercised himself in debate, and laid a firm foundation for fluent and correct utterance . . . For three or four years after this . . . at Lochlea . . . he still extended his reading and indulged occasionally in verse making.[12]

---

[12] *Poetical Works of Robert Burns*, p. xxiv. Text in brackets was added by Looney.

The Stratford paradox.

Needless to say the particulars given in this sketch are not the generous inferences of modern admirers, but are supplied by the properly authenticated utterances of Burns himself, his brother, his teachers, and other contemporaries. Yet, with such a preparation at a time when books had become so accessible; with his quickness of apprehension, his genius, and his respect for the good things that books alone could give him, Robert Burns remains the type of uncultured genius; whilst Shakspere, whose supposed work has become the fountain head of cultured English, fixing and moulding the language more than any other single force, emerges from squalor and ignorance without leaving a trace of the process or means by which he accomplished the extraordinary feat. Burns dies at the age of thirty-seven, leaving striking evidence of his genius, but no masterpiece of the kind which comes from wide experience and matured powers. Shakspere, before reaching the age of thirty, is credited with the authorship of dramas and great poetic classics evincing a wide and prolonged experience of life. Even in such a detail as mere penmanship the contrast is maintained. Burns leaves us specimens of calligraphy which ought to have satisfied the exacting demands of Hamlet, and won the praise which the first editors of "Shakespeare's" works bestowed upon the author of the plays. William Shakspere leaves specimens of penmanship so malformed that Sir E. Maunde Thompson is obliged to suppose that before the writing of his first great works and during the whole of his early Stratford life he had had but little opportunity for exercising his handwriting.

The exceptional kind of life necessary to have evolved a "Shakespeare" under such unhappy conditions would most certainly have marked him off from his fellows. No single record or even tradition of his early life is, however, suggestive of the student, or of a youth intellectually distinguished from those about him. Traditions of the oratorical flourishes with which as a butcher he would kill a sheep, and of his poaching exploits and misadventures, survive; definite records of marriage under compulsion at the age of eighteen to a woman eight years his senior, and grave suggestions that on the birth of twins a few years later, he deserted her: these things sum up the record of the formative years of his life. After narrating the very commonplace traditions and records of William Shakspere's early life, Sir Walter Raleigh, the eminent professor of literature at Oxford, remarks: "It is the very vanity of scepticism to set all these aside in favour of a tissue of learned fancies."[13]

III

William Shakspere's three periods.

The contrast between the coarse and illiterate circumstances of his early life, and the highly cultured character of the work he is supposed to have produced, is not, however, the strongest aspect of this particular argument: although quite alone it is enough to have created serious misgivings. The compelling force of this argument from contrast is only fully felt when it is clearly realized that the career of William Shakspere divides naturally into three periods: not two. We have the opening period at Stratford just indicated; we have a middle period during which he is supposed to have resided mainly in London and produced the remarkable literature to which he owes his fame; and we have a closing period spent, like the first, in the unwholesome intellectual atmosphere of Stratford. And it is the existence of this series of three periods which furnishes the data for a sound scientific examination of the problem.

The closing period.

The fact which, once grasped, will carry us forward most quickly to a final settlement of this question is that the closing period of his life at Stratford stands in as marked contrast to the supposed middle period in London as does the first, and under precisely the same aspect, but very much less explicably. The

---

[13] Sir Walter Raleigh, *Shakespeare*, p. 44.

operation of hidden forces and agencies might partly account for the obscure youth, blossoming out as the most cultured writer of his day. But with the literary fame he is supposed to have won, how can we explain the reversion to the non-intellectual record of his closing Stratford period? For it is as destitute of an aftermath of literary glory as the first period was devoid of promise. Having it is supposed by virtue of an immeasurable genius forced himself out of an unrefined and illiterate milieu into the very forefront of the literary and intellectual world, he returns whilst still in his prime, and probably whilst relatively still a young man, to his original surroundings. For the last eighteen years of his life he has himself described as "William Shakspere, of Stratford-upon-Avon"; yet, with so prolonged a residence there, such intellectual gifts as he is supposed to have possessed, such force of character as would have been necessary to raise him in the first instance, he passes his life amongst a mere handful of people without leaving the slightest impress of his eminent powers or the most trifling fruits of his attainments and educational emancipation upon anyone or anything in Stratford. In the busy crowded life of London it is possible to conceal both the defects and qualities of personality, and men may easily pass there for what they are not; but one man of exceptional intellectual powers, improved by an extraordinary feat of self-culture, could hardly fail to leave a very strong impression of himself upon a small community of people, mostly uneducated, such as then formed the population of Stratford. When, then, we are told that that man was living at one time at the rate of £1,000 a year (£8,000 of today)[14]—and Sir Sidney Lee sees nothing improbable in the tradition—the idea that such a man could live in such a place, in such style, and leave no trace of his distinctive powers and interests in the records of the community is the kind of story which, we are convinced, practical men will refuse to believe once they are fairly confronted with it.

---

[14] £1 in 1920 has a value of £44 in 2018. The £1,000 in Shakespeare's time would thus have a value of £352,000, or US$465,000, in 2018.

Shakspere and letters.

Had he walked out of Stratford an ignorant boor in 1587 and returned ten years later having learnt nothing more during his absence than how to get hold of money and keep it, there is absolutely nothing in the records of all his affairs at Stratford that need have been in the slightest degree different from what it is. There was at least one man in Stratford who could write in a good style of penmanship, and he addressed a letter to Shakspere while in London. This is the only letter that has been preserved of any that may have been addressed to Shakspere in the whole course of his life, and the reader may see a facsimile of it in the book *Shakespeare's England*.[15] Its only purpose, however, is to negotiate a loan of £30 and it contains no suggestion of any intellectual community between the two men. This letter reappears under circumstances which would quite justify a suspicion that Shakspere himself had been unable to read it. No suggestion of its having been answered has been discovered, nor is there the faintest trace of any letter from his pen to any other person in Stratford. We do not mean merely that no autograph letter has been preserved, but there is no mention of any letter, no trace of a single phrase or word reported as having been addressed to anyone during all these years, as a personal message from what we are asked to believe was the most facile pen in England. According to every Stratfordian authority he lived and worked for many years in London whilst directing a mass of important business in Stratford. Then he lived for many years in retirement in Stratford whilst plays from his pen were making their appearance in London. In all, he followed this divided plan of life for nearly twenty years (1597-1616); a plan which, if ever in this world a man's affairs called for letters, must have entailed a large amount of correspondence, had he been able to write; yet not the faintest suggestion of his ever having written a letter exists either in authentic record or in the most imaginative tradition. And the people who believe this still stand out for a monopoly of sane judgment.

---

[15] By William Winter.

Shakspere's occupations.

He returns to this "bookless neighbourhood" one of the most enlightened men in Christendom it is supposed, yet even Rumour, whose generous invention has created so much "biography" for him, has not associated his years of retirement with a single suggestion of a book or bookish occupations. Possessing, it is presumed, a mind teeming with ideas, and coffers overflowing, there is no suggestion of any enterprise in which he was interested for dispelling the intellectual darkness of the community in which he lived. Having, it is supposed, performed a great work in refining and elevating the drama in London, and having thus ready to his hands a powerful instrument for brightening and humanizing the social life of the fifteen hundred souls that at the time formed the population of Stratford, he is never once reported to have filled up his own leisure with so congenial an occupation as getting up a play for the people of Stratford or in any way interesting himself in the dramatic concerns of the little community: nor even, when plays were banned, raising his voice or using his pen in protest.

On the other hand there are records of his purchasing land, houses and tithes: of his carrying on business as a maltster: of his money-lending transactions: of his prosecution of people for small debts at a time when according to Sir Sidney Lee his yearly income would be about £600 (or £4,800 in money of today).[16] We have particulars of his store of corn; of his making an orchard; "a well-authenticated tradition that he planted a mulberry tree with his own hands";[17] but not the slightest record of anything suggestive of what are supposed to have been his dominating interests. On the contrary he appears, even in his choice of a home, quite regardless of those things that press upon the senses and sensibilities of esthetic natures. For in picturing his last moments Halliwell-Phillipps refers to "the wretched sanitary conditions surrounding his residence," and adds, "If truth and not romance is to be invoked, were the woodbine and sweet

---

[16] £211,000, or US$279,000, in 2018 values. See footnote 14, p. 22.
[17] Sir Sidney Lee, *A Life of William Shakespeare*, p. 210.

honeysuckle within reach of the poet's deathbed, their fragrance would have been neutralized by their vicinity to middens, fetid water-courses, mud walls and piggeries."[18] It is to this his biographer attributes the last illness of the great dramatist, rather than to conviviality.

IV

The Will.

No relief from this kind of record is met with through all the years of his final residence at Stratford. At last the end approaches. The great genius is facing death and making arrangements for the direction of his affairs when his own hand shall have been removed. He is evidently looking anxiously into the future, making the most careful provision for the transmission of his property through his daughter "Susanna Hall . . . and after her decease to the first sonne of her bodie . . . and to [his] heires males, . . . and for defalt . . . to the second sonne and [his] heires . . . and the third sonne . . . and the fourth sonne . . . and the fifth sonne . . . and the sixth sonne . . . and the seaventh sonne . . . and . . . for defalt to [his] daughter Judith, and the heires males of her bodie . . . and for defalt to the right heires of the saied *William Shackspeare, for ever.*" Then he carefully disposes of his "second best bed," his "broad silver gilt bole," his "goodes, chattels, leases, plate, jewels and household stuff."[19]

No provision for unpublished plays.

Here, then, he stands dipping "into the future far as human eye can see" ("for ever"): this supposed author of England's most valuable spiritual treasures. The greater part of the works, to the production of which his life and genius had been devoted, had never yet appeared in print. According to the accepted view these invaluable works, which were to secure the fame of "William Shackspeare, for ever" were drifting about, scattered amongst actors and theatre managers; in danger therefore of being

---

[18] Halliwell-Phillipps, *Outlines*, p. 231.
[19] Halliwell-Phillipps, *Outlines*, p. 240, 455.

permanently lost.

Whilst then he was arranging the distribution of his wealth, it was the most natural thing in the world that his mind should have turned to these important productions and that some part of his wealth should have been set aside to ensure the publication of his dramas. With his name and fame there was little fear but what the publishing venture could be made to succeed, and that the possible grandchildren, whose interests he was considering so carefully, would have gained rather than lost by his providing for the publication. From the first word of this will to the last, however, there is nothing which suggests that the testator ever had an interest either in the sixteen plays that had already appeared in print or in the twenty that had yet to be published or in anything else of a literary nature: a perfectly appropriate end to the whole series of the Stratford records of him, from the day of his baptism to the day of his death, but in flat contradiction to the supposition that the greatest achievement of his life had been the production of those immortal dramas beside which his lands and houses become of insignificant value.

Any supposition that he had already provided for the publication of the dramas is contradicted by the manner in which these works were published in the First Folio edition of 1623. Hardly any terms of reproof could be too severe for a writer who with a knowledge of the introductory pieces of the First Folio edition should maintain that that work appeared as a result of previous arrangements made by William Shakspere of Stratford. And this fact taken along with the total absence of any mention in his will of the unpublished documents ought many years ago to have disposed of the idea that he was their author. The disappearance of the manuscripts themselves, combined with the absence of any mention of them in the will, has given rise to an almost insistent demand for a "Shakespeare" manuscript, and of this Sir E. Maunde Thompson's book on the subject is but the outward and visible sign.[20] For no third-rate writer passing the

---

[20] Sir Edward Maunde Thompson, *Shakespeare's Handwriting: A Study*.

closing years of his life in destitution could have been more completely dissociated from his own literary products than was this the supposed greatest writer in England as he passed the last years of his life in leisure and affluence.

Heminge and Condell.

One entry alone in the will connects the testator with his London career—as actor, however, not as dramatist. He left to his "fellowes" Heminge, Burbage, and Condell £1 6s. 8d. each, to buy rings. Halliwell-Phillipps in reproducing the will gives in italics the parts which had not been in the will at first, but which were subsequently interlined: and this bequest to his "fellowes" is one of the interlineations. Like his wife, to whom he left his "second best bed," the actors with whom he had been associated only came in as an afterthought, if not as a result of direct suggestion from other quarters. This is the connection which was put to service in publishing the First Folio edition of "Shakespeare's" works, resulting in what has been recognized as a purely fictitious claim for the responsibility for the publication on the part of the two survivors. Albeit no one, not even Ben Jonson, whose part in the publication has been made so much of, ventured to suggest that he had been entrusted by the reputed author with the publication of the works. If such a task had been entrusted to them it is inconceivable that they should have omitted to mention the fact. They assert, however, that out of regard for his memory they had, on their own initiative, gathered together the manuscripts of the plays and published them. They, moreover, so bungle their account with inconsistencies that Sir Sidney Lee admits the inaccuracy of their story. "John Heming and Henry Condell," he says, "were *nominally* responsible for the venture, but it seems to have been suggested by [others] . . . the two actors made pretensions to a larger responsibility than they really incurred, but their motives . . . were doubtless irreproachable."[21]

---

[21] Lee, *Life*, p. 315.

To this false pretension, be it observed, "honest Ben Jonson" was party. The camouflage was, of course, as legitimate as any other method of concealing authorship: but when it is urged that Ben was too honest deliberately to deceive the public, we can only answer that the fact is there and cannot be gainsaid. We may also add, what cannot be said of all those who would use Ben's name to prop up Stratfordianism, that Ben was a humorist. His motives also, like Heminge's and Condell's, "were doubtless irreproachable." The point that matters here, however, is that the manner of the publication places beyond doubt the fact that William Shakspere of Stratford had made no arrangement for it. The entire absence of any mention either of his executors or a single member of his much-cared-for family amongst the ten names appearing in connection with the publication, reveals the same completely negative relationship of everything Stratfordian towards the Shakespearean literature.

No memento for Ben Jonson.

Seeing that mention has been made of Ben Jonson, the forlorn hope of the Stratfordians, it is remarkable, or rather it would have been astounding, if there had been any truth in Stratfordianism, that the only literary contemporary of Shakspere's with whom the latter is supposed to have been on intimate terms, the kindred spirit who, accompanied by Drayton, is supposed to have paid the one visit that relieved the intellectual isolation of his self-imposed exile—with fatal results, however, for the tradition is that Shakspere drank to excess and died in consequence—this boon comrade and kindred wit, has no mention whatever in a will bequeathing a number of memorial rings and other mementos to friends.

In addition to the bequests to his family and what is probably remuneration to the two overseers of the will, he leaves his sword to Mr. Thomas Combe, and money to buy memorial rings is left to Hamlett Sadler, William Raynolds, John Hemynges, Richard Burbage and Henry Condell. Every one of these bequests of memorial rings appears, however, as an interpolation into the will:

as an afterthought at best. But even in his afterthoughts dear old Ben has no place. We are assured that these interlineations would be made during his last illness. At any rate they must have been made during the last three months of his life, for the original document bears the date January 25th, 1616. "January" is then struck out and "March" substituted, so that alterations were being made up to within a month of his death. Surely, then, if there is any shred of truth in these traditions, Ben Jonson would be in his mind at the time.

Shakspere ignores reputed godson.

Another tradition has it that Shakspere was godfather to Ben's son, and even traditional particulars of friendly repartee on the subject have been preserved. Amongst the bequests, however, is one of twenty shillings to a godson named William Walker, but no mention whatever is made of the other godson, Ben's boy. Obviously Ben Johnson and his son, the reputed literary comrade and godson, respectively, of the great poet dramatist, counted for nothing in the eyes of William Shakspere; and the Stratfordianism that rests upon a belief in the personal intimacy of the two men is quite out of touch with realities: precisely the same absence of "reality" which marks Jonson's facetious tribute to "Shakespeare" in the now famous lines which face the so-called portrait of "Shakespeare" in the First Folio edition of the plays.

If, then, there be any truth in the tradition of Jonson's visit to William Shakspere just before the latter's death, it quite bears the appearance, in view of the respective parts which Jonson, Heminge, and Condell played in the publication of the First Folio edition, of having had something to do with the projected publication: the interlineation of the actor's names into a will that had already been drawn up being possibly one of the results of the visit. The non-appearance of Jonson's own name in the will was, under this assumption, a serious defect in the arrangement: the principals were evidently not experts at subterfuge. It was the loss of the last chance of bringing into the Stratford records of William Shakspere anything or anyone connected with contemporary literature: a loss which all Jonson's efforts years after Shakspere's death could not make good. The respective roles which Ben Jonson and William Shakspere had to play in this final comedy had evidently been badly adjusted.

The actual part played by Jonson in this business hardly comes within the province of the present stage of our argument. The important fact is that there was subterfuge in the manner of publishing the First Folio edition, and to this subterfuge Ben Jonson was a party. There are substantial reasons for believing that the introduction signed by the actors Heming and Condell was Jonson's own composition. The general inconsequence of his attitude has been exposed by Sir George Greenwood; and any argument based upon an assumed literal historic accuracy and unambiguity of Jonson's statements has no *locus slandi*; the literal applicability to William Shakspere of those statements being refuted by Shakspere's own will.

A bookless Shakspere.

The significance of the omission from the will of all mention of books, still further strengthened by Dr. Hall's silence respecting any books of Shakspere's that had passed into his possession, confirms the impression that William Shakspere had never owned any; notwithstanding the fact already pointed out that only by an unusual resort to books could he have made up for his initial disadvantages.

Shakspere's "Un-Shakespeare" will.

Turning finally to the actual text of the will as a literary document, the question naturally arises as to traces of "Shakespeare's" craftsmanship. "Shakespeare's" knowledge of law and interest in its subtleties and technique makes it impossible to suppose that such a document could have been executed on his behalf without his participation in its composition. Yet the entire document is just such as a lawyer, in the ordinary way of business, would have drawn up for any other man. The only part in which the personality of the testator might have been exposed is the opening passage, which is as follows:

In the name of God, amen! I, William Shackspeare, of
Stratford upon Avon, in the county of Warr. gent. in perfect health
and memorie, God be praysed, doe make and ordayne this my last
will and testament in manner and forme followeing, that ys to saye,
First, I comend my soule into the handes of God my Creator,
hoping and assuredlie beleeving, through thonelie merittes of Jesus
Christe my Saviour, to be made partaker of lyfe everlastinge, and
my bodie to the earth whereof yt ys made. [22]

The remainder is purely business.

From the first word of this document to the last there is not
the faintest trace either of the intellect or of the literary style of
the man who wrote the great dramas.

Shakspere's penmanship.

Needless to say the penmanship of the will is the work of the
professional lawyers; but at the end we meet the only instance on
record of his ever having put his pen to paper in Stratford. For all
these years he had lived in Stratford, buying and selling, lending
money, prosecuting debtors, dealing in single transactions
involving the turnover of sums of money equivalent to thousands
of pounds in modern values, resulting in the preservation of the
signatures or "marks" of people with whom he dealt, but no
single signature of Shakspere in connection with these Stratford
dealings has ever been unearthed. Not until we come to the
signing of his will, in the last year of his life, do we meet with an
example of his penmanship in his Stratford records. He signed his
will. There are three signatures, each on a separate page of the
document; and, with the exception of part of one of them, they
constitute probably as striking a freak in handwriting as can be
found anywhere. Sir E. Maunde Thompson, whose work on
Shakespeare's Penmanship[23] testifies abundantly to his faith in the
Stratford man, admits that if these three signatures had appeared
on separate documents we should have been justified in
supposing that they were written by three different hands. With
the one exception, of which we shall presently treat, the whole of

---

[22] Shakespeare will is transcribed in Halliwell-Phillipps, *Outlines*, pp. 236-240.
[23] The correct title is *Shakespeare's Handwriting: A Study*.

the work is so wretchedly executed that it might well be taken for the work of a child trying to copy writing of which he had only an imperfect appreciation. It is most like the effort of an illiterate man who had attempted to learn how to write his own name, and had not wholly succeeded, but who was struggling through the process, probably with a copy in front of him.

Writing experts.

So outrageous is it to suppose that this is the normal handwriting of the great dramatist that recent apologists have suggested the explanation that in his later years he suffered from paralysis: ignoring the fact that the opening words of his will are an assertion of his "perfect health and memory," and the further fact that though he managed to produce some kind of signature whilst afflicted with paralysis, he seems to have produced none at all without the affliction. Paralysis had evidently been good for him. Sir E. Maunde Thompson does not, however, propound the paralysis theory; and with very good reason: for the exceptional part, to which reference has already been made, could not possibly have been done by anyone so afflicted. This part consists of three words, "By me William," which precede the name "Shakspeare" in the principal signature to the will. Here we have a single example of expert penmanship standing in such overwhelming contrast to all the other Shakspere writing as to be most perturbing to the orthodox Stratfordian.

To admit frankly that the words "By me William" were not written by the same hand that wrote the rest of the signature and signatures would be to send the whole structure of Stratfordianism toppling into chaos. Sir E. Maunde Thompson's theory is that the testator was very ill at the time, that he began the writing in a moment of temporary revival and fell off when he came to the writing of "Shackspeare." Not only is the contrast between the two parts of the one signature too great for such an explanation, but the contrast is just as great between this particular piece of expert penmanship and the whole of the remainder. This is a point, however, in which mere discussion can do little. Photographic reproductions of these signatures may be seen in Sir Sidney Lee's *Life of William Shakespeare*; in Sir E. Maunde Thompson's *Shakespeare's Penmanship*;[24] in Sir Edwin Durning-Lawrence's *Bacon is Shakespeare*; and in *Shakespeare's England*;[25] and the most casual examination of them will convince anyone, we believe, that the contrast agrees more readily with the theory that there were at least two hands at work upon these signatures than with any other theory. This does not, of course, prove that there were actually two hands at work; for the writers just named, with one exception, would naturally refuse their assent to such an inference, notwithstanding the suspicious appearances.

Missing signatures.

One other point must be mentioned in connection with these will signatures. Halliwell-Phillipps indicates that in the first draft of the will, arrangements were made only for Shakspere's "seal": not for his signature at all. The word "seal" was afterwards struck out and "hand" substituted. By itself this might not have counted for much; but, taken in conjunction with the fact that on no previous Stratford document had a signature appeared, considerable colour is given to the supposition that the lawyers who prepared his documents were not accustomed to his signing them. Considering, too, the looseness of the times with respect to wills—a looseness to which the various uninitialled erasures and interlineations of this will bear testimony—along with the peculiar character of the signatures when at last they appeared, the whole of this "signature" work might easily have been done after the document had passed quite out of the lawyer's hands; there being no witnesses to the signatures.

> With regard to the erasures and interlineations, a few may have been the work of the scrivener . . . but some are obviously the result of the testator's subsequent personal directions. . . . In those days there was so much laxity in everything connected with

---

[24] The correct title is *Shakespeare's Handwriting: A Study.*
[25] By William Winter.

testamentary formalities that no inconvenience would have arisen
from such expedients. No one, excepting in subsequent litigation,
would ever have dreamt of asking . . . any questions at all. The
officials thought nothing of admitting to probate a mere copy of a
will that was destitute of the signatures both of testator and
witnesses.[26]

Although not actually written at Stratford there are three
other Shakspere signatures which belong to his closing Stratford
period. The first of these was written in London in 1612, and the
other two in connection with his purchase of the Blackfriars
property in 1613: so that no stroke from his pen has been
unearthed prior to the close of his supposed literary period. Of
the first, Sir E. Maunde Thompson says that it is clearly the work
of an able penman. Of the second he says that it might be taken
for the work of an uncultivated man: this he attributes to
nervousness. The third is done in a style so entirely different from
the others that he considers it useless for the purpose of expert
examination of handwriting: this he seems disposed to attribute
to "wilful perversity."[27] Although, then, he does not actually
assert that they might be taken for the work of three different
writers, his remarks are tantamount to this. And so we may sum
up the whole of the writing that has come to us from the hand of
one who is supposed to have been the greatest of our English
writers. All we have are six signatures in no way connected with
any literary matter.   All these were executed in the last years of
his life, after his great literary tasks were finished; and are so
written that, when examined by our leading expert on the subject,
who is quite orthodox in his views of authorship, they look as if
they might have been the work of six different men. At the same
time there is amongst this writing some that appears like the effort
of an uneducated person, and only one signature (1612) of any
real value for the study of penmanship. To this we would add as
an unshakable personal conviction, supported by the opinions of
many to whose judgment we have appealed, that the signatures

---

[26] Halliwell-Phillipps, *Outlines*, p. 364.
[27] Thompson, *Handwriting*, p. 0.

bear witness to his having had the assistance of others in the act of signing his own name. The general conclusion to which these signatures point is that William Shakspere was not an adept at handling a pen, and that he had the help of others in trying to conceal the fact.

An important omission.

As a last remark on the question of penmanship we must point out the absence of an important signature. The actual deed of purchase of the Blackfriars property: a document which was formerly in the possession of Halliwell-Phillipps but is now in America, although the most important of the three documents concerned in the transaction has only Shakspere's "seal," not his "hand." In other words his own part was just such as might have been performed by a completely illiterate man accustomed to place his "mark" on documents; just as his father and mother had done, and as his daughter Judith continued to do. It is upon what Halliwell-Phillipps calls a duplicate of this document, now in the Guildhall Library, that there appears the signature which Sir E. Maunde Thompson says might have been the work of an uneducated man: a signature which looks to the ordinary reader as if it had been finished by another hand. The "wilful perversity" signature is on the mortgage deed, now in the British Museum, and is to anyone but a Stratfordian quite evidently a connived forgery.

The Stratford impossibility.

Viewing then the three periods of William Shakspere's career in their relation to one another we have an opening and a closing period which are perfectly homogeneous in the completely negative aspect they present to all literary considerations. Between them we have an intermediate period by which there is attributed to him the greatest works in English literature. The two extreme and homogeneous periods belong to his residence in one place, quite in keeping with his own non-literary records whilst residing there. The intermediate period, with which we shall presently deal specially, stands in marked and unprecedented contrast to its extremes, and was lived in quite another part of the country. With our present-day conveniences, news agencies and means of communication, it is perhaps impossible for us to realize how remote Stratford was from London in the days of Queen Elizabeth. We are quite entitled to claim, however, that their separateness, so far as intercourse is concerned, was in keeping with the role that William Shakspere was called upon to play.

So far as the transition from stage to stage is concerned, few would deny that if the William Shakspere who had been brought up at Stratford, who was forced into a marriage at the age of eighteen with a woman eight years his senior, and who on the birth of twins deserted his wife, produced at the age of twenty-nine a lengthy and elaborate poem in the most polished English of the period, evincing a large and accurate knowledge of the classics, and later the superb Shakespearean dramas, he accomplished one of the greatest if not actually the greatest work of self-development and self-realization that genius has ever enabled any man to perform. On the other hand, if, after having performed so miraculous a work, this same genius retired to Stratford to devote himself to houses, lands, orchards, money and malt, leaving no traces of a single intellectual or literary interest, he achieved without a doubt the greatest work of self-stultification in the annals of mankind. It is *difficult* to believe that with such a beginning he could have attained to such heights as he is supposed to have done, it is *more difficult* to believe that with such glorious achievements in his middle period he could have fallen to the level of his closing period; and in time it will be fully recognized that it is *impossible* to believe that the same man could have accomplished two such stupendous and mutually nullifying feats. Briefly, the first and last periods at Stratford are too much in harmony with one another, and too antagonistic to the supposed middle period for all three to be credible. The situation represented by the whole stands altogether outside general human experience. The perfect unity of the two extremes justifies the conclusion that the middle period is an illusion: in other words William Shakspere did not write the plays attributed to him. To parody the dictum of Hume in another connection, it is contrary to experience that such things should happen, but not contrary to experience that testimony, even the testimony of rare and honest Ben Jonson, should be false. The question of culpability we leave to ethical absolutists.

Obituary silence.

The circumstances attending the death of Shakspere are quite in keeping with all that is known and unknown of his closing period. The supposed poet-actor, the greatest of his race, passed away *in affluence but without any contemporary notice.* Spenser, his great poet contemporary, "a ruined and broken-hearted man," dying, as Jonson said, "for lack of bread," was nevertheless "buried in Westminster Abbey near the grave of Chaucer, and his funeral was at the charge of the Earl of Essex."[28] Burbage, his great actor contemporary, died about the same time as the Queen (wife of James I), March 1618-19, and "sorrow for his loss seems to have made men forget to show the sorrow due to a Queen's death. The city and the stage were clothed in gloom. . . . Men poured forth their mourning . . . [and] a touching tribute to his charm came from the pen of the great Lord Pembroke himself."[29] The death of William Shakspere passed quite unnoticed by the nation. No fellow poet poured forth mourning. The Earl of Southampton whom he is supposed to have immortalized showed no interest. For seven years, except for his mysterious "Stratford monument," he remained "unwept, unhonoured and unsung."[30] Mrs. Stopes attributes this neglect to his retirement: which supports the view we are now urging, that his retirement involved a severance of such literary and dramatic ties as he might have had.

---

[28] Richard William Church, *Spenser*, p. 178.
[29] Charlotte C. Stopes, *Burbage and Shakespeare's Stage*, p. 116.
[30] This is a line from Sir Walter Scott's poem "The Lay of the Last Minstrel," Canto VI, "Breathes there the Man?"

Jonson's first tribute.

At last the silence is broken. The first tribute to his memory comes from the pen of Ben Jonson, who many years later writes of having "loved the man, on this side idolatry as much as any." For seven years, we must suppose, had grief for the loss of so matchless a friend been hidden in his soul. Then a great occasion presents itself. The collected works of his idol are to be published and Ben is invited to furnish the opening words of the historic volume. Now must his long pent-up grief find its fitting expression. Yet these are his words:

> This figure that thou here seest put
> It was for gentle Shakespeare cut;
> Wherein the graver had a strife
> With Nature, to out-do the life:
> O could he but have drawn his wit
> As well in brass, as he hath hit
> His face; the print would then surpass
> All, that was ever writ in brass,
> But, since he cannot, Reader, look
> Not on his picture, but his book.

These words are addressed "To the Reader"; and the reader who can discover a trace of genuine affection, grief, or "idolatry" in these lines possesses a faculty to which the present writer lays no claim. From such obituary idolatry who would not wish to be preserved? Sir George Greenwood's view that Jonson had two different people in his mind when he spoke of "Shakespeare" seems the most feasible. We shall not plunge into the discussion of what Ben may or may not have meant by the above lines; but as the first printed reference to a departed genius who was also the object of intense personal affection the words are a palpable mockery. Yet the later and much belated references of Jonson to "Shakespeare" forms the last ditch of Stratfordianism.

V

William Shakspere's middle period.

We come now to William Shakspere's middle period. Sandwiched in between two inglorious Stratford periods, what are the actual facts of his London career in reference to the works which have made him famous? It is not as an actor, nor as a stage or theatre manager—the latter being a purely hypothetical vocation—nor even as a writer of plays for the contemporary stage, but as the author of literary works that he has won renown. As such, Sir Sidney Lee assures us that he had no hand in the publication of any of the plays attributed to him, but "uncomplainingly submitted to the wholesale piracy of his plays and the ascription to him of books by other hands."[31] The absence of all participation in the publication of plays which, as literature, have immortalized his name, is certainly a huge gap in his literary records to begin with.

Indefinite duration of the period.

Again, although it has been found necessary to ascribe the first composition of plays to the years 1590-1592—otherwise time could not have been found for their production—the first of the series was not published until 1597, nor any with "Shakespeare's" name attached until 1598. Before that time, however, New Place, Stratford, had become William Shakspere's established residence.

> There is no doubt that New Place [Stratford] was henceforward [from 1597] to be accepted as his established residence. Early in the following year, on February the 4th, 1598, he is returned as the holder of ten quarters of corn in the Chapel Street ward, that in which the newly-acquired property was situated, and in future indentures he is never described as a Londoner, but always as William Shakespeare of Stratford-on-Avon.[32]

---

[31] Lee, *Life*, p. 94.
[32] Halliwell-Phillipps, *Outlines*, p. 118.

Thenceforward his land, property and tithes purchases, along with the fact that in 1604 he takes legal action to enforce payment of a debt for malt which he had been supplying for some months past, are circumstances much more suggestive of permanent residence in Stratford, with an occasional visit maybe to London, than of permanent residence in London, with occasional trips to Stratford. The duration of this middle period is therefore most uncertain. Even on the assumption that he was the author of the plays, authorities differ by at least eight years respecting the date at which it closed (1604-1612); and when the date furnished by that assumption is rejected, as it must be in an enquiry like the present, the margin of uncertainty becomes considerably enlarged. The absence of definite information respecting the limits of this London period is certainly another serious omission from the records.

Absence of incidents.

"Of the incidents of his life in London," Professor Sir Walter Raleigh tells us, "nothing is known."[33] He lodged at one time in Bishopsgate and, later on, in Southwark. We know this, not because lords and ladies in their coaches drove up to the door of the famous man, nor because of anything else which could be called a personal "incident," but because he was a defaultant taxpayer (for two amounts of 5s. and 13s. 4d. respectively) for whom the authorities were searching in 1598, ignorant of the fact that he had moved, some years before, from Bishopsgate to Southwark. Evidently, then, he was not at that time living in the public eye and mixing freely in dramatic and literary circles. Sir Sidney Lee tells us that Shakspere "with great magnanimity, ultimately paid"[34] the money. If the claimant had been a private individual there might have been generosity in paying an account which could not legally be enforced; but it is not easy to associate "magnanimity" with the paying of taxes. We must suppose then that either the money was due or was paid to save trouble. If the money were due then William Shakspere had been trying to

---

[33] Raleigh, *Shakespeare*, p. 56.
[34] Lee, *Life*, p. x.

defraud: if the money were not due one is a little curious to know what special inconveniences could have arisen from his contesting the claim. Every record we have of him proves that he was not the kind of man to submit to an illegal exaction without very substantial reasons. The point is a small one by itself: in connection with the general mysteriousness of his London movements, however, it has its proper significance.

The absence of precise information respecting the actual location, period and form of his established residence in London is yet another of the great gaps in the record.

Chronological confusion.

From the time when he was described as William Shakspere of Stratford-upon-Avon (1597) there is no proof that he was anywhere domiciled in London, whilst the proofs of his domiciliation in Stratford from this time forward are irrefutable and continuous. Clearly our conceptions of his residency in London are in need of complete revision. It would appear that an attempt has been made to construct a London career for him out of materials furnished by the meagre particulars known of his actual life combined with the necessities of the assumed authorship, and from this material it has not been possible to form a consistent picture. In order to bring out this fact more clearly we shall place together two sentences from Halliwell-Phillipps's *Outlines.*

> It was not till the year 1597 that Shakespeare's public reputation as a dramatist was sufficiently established for the booksellers to be anxious to secure the copyright of his plays.[35]
> In the spring of this year [1597] the poet made his first investment in realty by the purchase of New Place . . . [which] was henceforward to be accepted as his residence.[36]

Uncertain habitation after 1596.

We are consequently faced with this peculiar situation that what has been regarded as the period of his highest fame in London, began at the same as his formal retirement to Stratford;

---

[35] Halliwell-Phillipps, *Outlines*, p. 127.
[36] Halliwell-Phillipps, *Outlines*, p. 116.

and whilst there is undoubted mystery connected with his place or places of abode in London, there is none connected with his residence in Stratford. A curious fact in this connection is that the only letter that is known to have been addressed to him in the whole course of his life was one from a native of Stratford addressed to him in London, which appears amongst the records of the Stratford Corporation, and which "was no doubt forwarded by hand [to Shakspere whilst in London] otherwise the *locality of residence would have been added*" (Halliwell-Phillipps).[37] Evidently his fellow townsmen who wished to communicate with him in London were unaware of his residence there; and the fact that this letter was discovered amongst the archives of the Stratford Corporation suggests that it had never reached the addressee. It also permits of the alternative supposition, already mentioned, that having received it he was nevertheless unable to read it (notwithstanding the superior quality of its penmanship) and was obliged to forward it to his lawyer in Stratford, who resided in Shakspere's house there. At all events the only letter known to have been addressed to him in the whole course of his life adds to the mysteriousness of his lodging in London.

Shrinkage of middle period.

Altogether our efforts to come to close grips with the period of his greatest fame, on the solid ground of authenticated fact, have yielded most unsatisfactory results. We have no positive knowledge of his being in London before 1592: the year of Greene's attack, in which he is accused of beautifying himself in the feathers of others, along with an innuendo suggesting that he was an uncultivated man, a "rude groome" and a "usurer." And we have *no record of actual residence in London after* 1596, when "according to a memorandum by Alleyn he lodged near the Bear Garden in Southwark."[38] This is precisely the time at which his

---

[37] I have been unable to locate this quotation in Halliwell-Phillipps's *Outlines* or in Lee's *Life*, or in any other source. It appears to be Looney's text mistakenly put in quotation marks.

[38] Halliwell-Phillipps, *Outlines*, p. 115, notes that "At this time, 1596, he appears to have been residing, when in town, in lodgings near the Bear Garden in Southwark." But there is no mention of a memorandum by Alleyn.

father, who resided at Stratford, acting, it is generally agreed, upon William Shakspere's initiative, made his first attempt to obtain a coat of arms on false pretences. The following year saw his purchase of New Place, Stratford, and as, in the next year, he is returned as one of the largest holders of corn in Stratford, everything points to this being the actual time at which he established himself in his native town—if we may so dignify the Stratford of that day. The definitely assured London period appears then to be shrinking from twenty to a mere matter of four years (1592-1596), during which there is not a single record of his *personal* activities beyond the appearance of his name in a list of actors, but evidently much mystery as to his actual whereabouts. The *literary* references to the poems we shall treat separately. It was in this period that *Venus* and *Lucrece* appeared (1593 and 1594 respectively), and it was in this period that the great man who was supposed to have produced these famous poems eluded the vigilance of the tax gatherer.

> The Bishopsgate levy of October, 1596, as well as that of 1598 is now shown to have been based on an assessment made as early as 1593 or 1594. Payment was obviously sought at the later dates *in ignorance of the fact that Shakespeare [i.e. Shakspere] had by that time left St. Helens* [Bishopsgate] long since for South London.[39]

According to modern Stratfordians he lived in London as a famous man for sixteen years after this (1596-1612) without betraying his settled place of residence.

William Shakspere's alibi.

In 1597 the publication of the plays begins in real earnest. In 1598 they begin to appear with "Shakespeare's" name attached. From then till 1604 was the period of full flood of publication during William Shakspere's lifetime: and this great period of "Shakespearean" publication (1597-1604) corresponds exactly with William Shakspere's busiest period in Stratford. In 1597 he began the business connected with the purchase of New Place. Complications ensued, and the purchase was not completed till 1602. "In 1598 he procured stone for the repair of the house,

---

[39] Lee, *Life*, p. x.

and before 1602 had planted a fruit orchard."[40] In 1597 his father and mother, "doubtless under their son's guidance" began a lawsuit "for the recovery of the mortgaged estate of Asbies in Wilmcote . . . [which] dragged on for some years."[41] "Between 1597 and 1599 [he was] rebuilding the house, stocking the barns with grain, and conducting various legal proceedings."[42] In 1601 his father died and he took over his father's property. On May 11 1602, he purchased 107 acres of arable land. In September, 1602, "and Walter Getley transferred to the poet a cottage and garden which were situated at Chapel Lane opposite the lower grounds of New Place."[43] "As early as 1598 Abraham Sturley had suggested that Shakespeare [William Shakspere] should purchase the tithes of Stratford."[44] In 1605 he completed the purchase of "an unexpired term of these tithes."[45] "In July, 1604, in the local court at Stratford he sued Philip Rogers whom he had supplied since the preceding March malt to the value of £1 19s. 10d. and on June 25 lent 2s. in cash."[46]

In a personal record from which so much is missing we may justly assume that what we know of his dealings in Stratford forms only a small part of his activities there. Consequently, to the contention that this man was the author and directing genius of the magnificent stream of dramatic literature which in those very years was bursting upon London, the business record we have just presented would in almost any court in the land he deemed to have proved an *alibi*. The general character of these business transactions, even to such touches as lending the trifling sum of 2s. to a person to whom he was selling malt, is all suggestive of his own continuous day to day contact with the details of his Stratford business affairs: whilst the single money transaction which connects him with London during these years, the recovery of a debt of £7 from John Clayton in 1600, might easily be the

---

[40] Lee, *Life*, p. 201.
[41] Lee, *Life*, p. 202.
[42] Lee, *Life*, p. 207.
[43] Lee, *Life*, p. 212.
[44] Lee, *Life*, p. 212.
[45] Lee, *Life*, p. 212.
[46] Lee, *Life*, p. 213.

result of a short visit to the metropolis, or merely the work of an agent.

The actors' licenses.

The licenses granted in 1603 to the company of actors in which "Shakespeare's" name appears would not necessitate his presence; and the fact that his name as it appears in these documents is spelt "S-h-a-k-e-s-p-e-a-r-e, (i.e. the same as in the printed editions of the plays), whilst this spelling is not that of his own signatures, nor of some of the important Stratford documents, bears out the suggestion that these matters were arranged by the same person as was responsible for the publication of the plays; although, as we have already pointed out, William Shakspere had no hand in that publication. Moreover, these licenses were not for immediate use, but for "when the plague shall decrease."[47] As, further, his name occurs second, it is clear that he was not the directing head of the company of players.

Whilst, then, everything about William Shakspere's records suggests that he was settled permanently at Stratford during the important years of the publication of the plays, everything about the plays themselves betokens an author living at the time in intimate touch with the theatrical and literary life of London. So strong is the presumption in favour of this latter fact that no writer of any school has yet ventured to suggest the contrary. In attributing the authorship to William Shakspere it has been imperative to assume a settled residence in London during these fateful years. The utmost that could be allowed was an occasional journey to Stratford; and this notwithstanding the mysteriousness of his whereabouts and doings in London, the fact of his always being described as "of Stratford," never "of London," and the large amount and special character of his Stratford business affairs.

If, then, William Shakspere, the reputed author of the works, was not sent off to Stratford to be out of the way at the time when the literary public was being interested in the plays, he has certainly contrived matters so as to make it appear that such was the case, and thus to justify the strongest suspicion, on this

---

[47] Halliwell-Phillipps, *Outlines*, p. 586.

ground alone, that the famous dramas were not of his composing.

It is from a consideration of the manner of publication that Sir Sidney Lee concludes that William Shakespeare had no part in the work. On the other hand we arrive at precisely the same conclusion from a consideration of the circumstances of his life: in the present instance on the grounds of what we are entitled to claim as an *alibi*. It is certainly interesting that two totally different sets of considerations should lead to precisely the same conclusion, although approached from two different standpoints and with different intentions; leaving but little room for doubt as to the soundness of the common conclusion. Whilst then we agree that William Shakspere had no hand in the publication of this literature, to maintain that its actual author, if living, in no way shared in any part of the work, is the kind of belief which practical men in touch with life would hardly acknowledge without serious misgiving.

VI

Anti-Stratfordian difficulties: motives.

We do not say that the alternative belief, the belief, that is to say in a hidden author, is without difficulties. We may justly wonder why the author of such works should, prefer to remain unknown, just as we may wonder why "Ignoto," "Shepherd Tony" and "A. W.", the writers of some of the best Elizabethan poetry, have elected to remain unknown. The facts are, however, incontestable realities of literary history. Moreover, the motives for mysterious and secret courses are, no doubt, frequently as mysterious and secret as the courses themselves, so that inability to fathom motives cannot be put in as an argument against the evidence of a fact: though knowledge of a motive may he accepted as corroborative of other evidence. Difficult as it is to penetrate and appreciate the private motives even of people circumstanced like ourselves, the difficulty is immeasurably creased when the entire social circumstances are different, as in the case before us. The man who thinks that anyone living in the reigns of Queen

Elizabeth and James I would he be as proud to acknowledge himself the author of "Shakespeare's" plays as anyone living in the nineteenth and twentieth centuries would be, has not understood the Shakespeare problem in its relationship to the age to which it belongs. He is, moreover, judging the question largely from the point of view of the professional littérateur as author, and over-looking the numerous considerations which may arise when an author of a vastly different type is supposed.

"It is difficult to realize," says Halliwell-Phillipps,

> a period when . . . the great poet, notwithstanding the immense popularity of some of his works, was held in no general reverence. It must be borne in mind that actors then occupied an inferior position in society, and that *even the vocation of a dramatic writer was considered scarcely respectable.* The intelligent appreciation of genius by individuals was not sufficient to neutralize in these matters the effect of public opinion and the animosity of the religious world; all circumstances thus uniting to banish general interest in the history of persons connected in any way with the stage.[48]

To have laid claim to the authorship of even "Shakespeare's" plays would therefore have been of no assistance to any man seeking to obtain, preserve, or recover the social dignity and eminence of himself and his family.

Preservation of the incognito.

We may wonder that the secret should have been so well kept, and be quite unable to offer a satisfactory explanation of the complete success of the "blind," just as we may stand puzzled before the other mysteries of history. This again is a difficulty which is greatly magnified by giving it a modern setting. In "Shakespeare's" day, however, according to Halliwell-Phillipps, "no interest was taken in the events of the lives of authors . . . non-political correspondence was rarely preserved, [and] elaborate diaries were not the fashion."[49]

---

[48] Halliwell-Phillipps, *Outlines*, pp. v-vi.
[49] Halliwell-Phillipps, *Outlines*, p. vi.

The lack of interest in the personality of authors is bourne out by some contemporary records of the performance of "Shakespeare's" plays without any suggestion of an author's name. The educated readers of the printed works, interested mainly in these works as literature, might well be content to know an author merely by name, especially when that author was supposed to be living in what would then be a remote village. The contemporary records of the "Shakespeare" literature are moreover just such as belong to an author whose name is known but whose personality is not; and Shakspere would escape personal attention by taking up permanent residence in Stratford just at the time when this literature began to appear.

Mystery and concerted secrecy were moreover characteristic not only of the literary life of the times, but even more so of the general social and political life. Plots and counterplots, extreme caution and reservation in writing letters—men habitually writing to friends as if suspicious that their letters would be shown to their enemies—every here and there some cryptic remark which only the addressee would be able to understand, such are the things that stand out from the mass of contemporary documents preserved in the State Papers and the various private collections. We can be quite sure that in those times no important secret would be imparted to anyone without first of all receiving the most solemn assurances that no risk of disclosure should be run. Certainly the writer of *Hamlet* was not the man to neglect any precaution. The carefully framed oaths by which Hamlet binds Horatio and Marcellus to secrecy, and the final caution he administers, is clearly the work of a man who knew how to ensure secrecy so far as it was humanly possible to do so. And we do know, as a matter of actual human experience, that when a superior intelligence is combined with what may be called a faculty for secrecy and a sound instinct in judging and choosing agents, secret purposes are carried through successfully in a way that is amazing and mystifying to simpler minds.

Difficulties versus Incredibilities.

These, then, are certain difficulties of the anti-Stratfordian position which it would be folly to ignore. Most truths, however, have had to win their way in spite of difficulties. Whilst, then, difficulties do not kill truth, incredibilities are fatal to error; and it is the incredible that Stratfordianism has to face. The same general human experience that compels us to accept facts for which we cannot adequately account, compels us also to reject, on pain of irrationality, what is inherently self-contradictory, or at complete variance with the otherwise invariable course of events. It is thus that the commonsense of mankind instinctively repudiates a moral contradiction as incredible. Such we hold is the belief in the Stratford man: the belief that the author of the finest literature lets others do just as they please during his own lifetime in the matter of publishing his works but does nothing himself. "It is questionable," says Sir Sidney Lee, "whether any were published under his supervision."[50] He is thus represented as creating and casting forth his immortal works with all the indifference of a mere spawning process, and turning his attention to houses, land, malt and money at the very moment when the printed issue of these great triumphs of his own creative spirit begins. This is the fundamental incredibility which along with the incredible reversion represented by Shakespeare's second Stratford period, and a succession of other incredibilities ought to dissolve completely the Stratfordian hypothesis, once it has become possible to put a more reasonable hypothesis in its place.

VII

Contemporary notices.

The only thing that can be described as a reliable personal reference to William Shakspere in the whole course of his life was made in 1592 when Greene attacked him as an "upstart crow," beautiful in the feathers of others. Chettle the publisher's

---

[50] Lee, *Life*, p. 49.

subsequent apology is couched in terms which indicate the intervention of highly placed and powerful patrons. Clearly Shakspere had behind him some friend that writers and publishers could not afford to ignore. At that time nothing had been published under his name, his London career was just opening, and this, we repeat, is the only thing that can be called a personal incident in the whole of his London record, which according to modern Stratfordians continued for twenty years after this affair. As a matter of fact his own attitude in this so-called incident was purely passive, Chettle's apology making no reference to any protest or resentment on the part of the man attacked, but solely to the "divers of worship" who had made representations on his behalf. After this it would appear that no one ventured upon personal references, good, bad, or indifferent. The experience of Chettle was evidently a warning to others.

Only as poet till 1598.

Subsequently, *Venus* and *Lucrece* were published with "Shakespeare's" name as author, and we then get a few references to the poems, such as any reader of the works might have penned.

> Yet Tarquyne pluckt his glistering grape,
> And Shake-speare paints poore Lucrece rape.

(1594. The year of the publication of *Lucrece*.)

> All praise worthy Lucrecia: Sweet Shak-speare.

(1595.)

> And Shakespeare, thou whose hony flowing vaine
>
> .   .   .   .
>
> Whose Venus, and whose Lucrecc sweet and chaste,
> Thy name in fames immortall booke have plac't.

(1598.)

This is all that we have in the period prior to the actual publication of the dramas. They are self-evidently inspired by the poems, make no reference to the plays, and have nothing more to do with the man than could be learnt from the works: a fact to which the spelling and splitting up of the name "Shake-speare" bears witness. Nor have they anything to do with him as an actor.

As dramatist: only after 1598.

Not till we reach the year 1598, the year in which the first of the dramas with "Shakespeare's" name were published, do we meet with any contemporary reference to "Shakespeare" as a writer of plays; by this time we are justified in supposing that William Shakspere was duly established at Stratford. Here, again, there is no personal reference: the name merely appearing in long lists of ancient and contemporary writers with an occasional remark upon the quality or contents of the work published under their names. This work of Francis Meres—his *Palladis Tamia*—at the same time bears testimony to what may be called the high classic quality of "Shakespeare's" English in the eyes of contemporary scholars, and also to "Shakespeare's" familiarity with the ancient classics.

In 1599 we meet with another literary reference in which, in addition to *Venus* and *Lucrece*, the plays of *Romeo* and *Richard* (II or III) are referred to. These plays had already been published.

In 1600 the name again occurs in a list of over twenty *poets* of Elizabeth's reign.

In 1604 his name appears along with Jonson's and Greene's in couplets calling for verses in honour of Elizabeth.

Again in 1604, the year of the revised edition of *Hamlet*, the name occurs in a literary reference to this play: and in 1603 or 5 in another list of contemporary poets. In the *Returne from Pernassus* (written 1602, printed 1606) he is first and most particularly mentioned as the author of *Venus* and *Lucrece*, and afterwards as one of those that "pen plaies."

Such is the character of all the contemporary references which the industry of Halliwell-Phillipps has brought together: references, that is to say, of people who knew "Shakespeare" in print, but who have nothing to tell us about William Shakspere in the flesh. The single instance of a contemporary reference to the man, after the 1591 affair ("The sole anecdote of Shakespeare that is positively known to have been recorded in his lifetime,"[51]) is a wretched immoral story; evidently the invention of some would-be wit: a story which is rightly discarded, as apocryphal, by most authorities on both sides of the question. The magnitude of this omission of real contemporary reference to the personality of the man can only be appreciated by those who, for any special purpose, have had to search into the collections of Elizabethan documents that have been published, or who know anything of the immense amount of personal details, concerning the most unimportant of people, preserved in our various local histories. Such a silence seems only explicable on the assumption that the utmost care was taken to keep the man out of sight.

The silence of William Shakspere.

It has already been pointed out that none of his activities in Stratford has left the slightest trace of a letter from his pen. The same strange feature marks his middle period in London. Again, it is not merely preserved autograph letters which are conspicuously absent, but there is a total absence of evidence, or even rumour, that he ever corresponded with a single soul. At the same time literary men of recognized inferiority to "Shakespeare" were the regular correspondents of the aristocratic patrons of literature; and even when the actual letters are missing traces of such correspondence can be found in the literary history of the times. In William Shakspere's case there is not the faintest trace. Even Ben Jonson, separated by many miles and for many years from his idol, makes no suggestion of letters having passed between them at any time. Nor during these years is there the slightest record of any of those things by which a genius impresses his personality upon his contemporaries. Outside the printed works nothing but blank negation meets us whenever we seek to

---

[51] Lee, *Life*, p. 274.

connect this man with any of those things by which eminent literary men have left incidental impressions of themselves upon contemporary life. As then we have the best authority for saying that he had nothing to do with the publication of the dramas—and even the poems which contained "Shakespeare's" dedication to the Earl of Southampton had no author's name on their title-pages—if William Shakspere were not a mere mask for another writer, perhaps some Stratfordian will tell us what else he could have done, or left undone, to make it appear that such was the part he was playing.

Spenser's silence.

In addition to William Shakspere's own silence we must not overlook the complete silence of "Shakespeare's" great contemporary Edmund Spenser in respect to everything Shakespearean. His reference to "Willie" in his poem, the *Tears of the Muses*, it is very commonly agreed nowadays, could not, on account of its date, have any reference to William Shakspere. The only possible allusion to Shakespeare which he makes is in 1595, in his poem *Colin Clout's Come Home Again*. That his "Aetion" has anything to do with Shakespeare is pure conjecture, based upon the assumption that only "Shakespeare" could deserve the high praise which Spenser bestows upon the poet so designated When, however, in the following lines he places Sir Philip Sidney first amongst the poets to whom he is alluding, we cannot accept "Aetion" as Shakespeare—that is to say, as a *poet* inferior, in Spenser's judgment, to Sidney—without discrediting Spenser's judgment. In other words, we destroy the very grounds upon which we originally suppose that "Aetion" is Shakespeare. In any case, the allusion is only to "Shakespeare" the *poet*, whose poems might have reached Spenser ("Colin Clout") in Ireland prior to his coming home. If, however, we accept the date which Spenser himself attaches to the dedication of the poem to Sir Walter Raleigh, namely 1591, it is evident that "Aetion" could not be "William Shakspere," and could have no connection with the great "Shakespeare" poems, which were not published until 1593 and 1594.

VIII

William Shakspere, actor.

So much for William Shakspere the business man and the reputed author: we come now to the question of William Shakspere the famous actor and theatre shareholder, whose wealth has been partly accounted for by reference to the revenues of prominent contemporary actors and actor-shareholders. In this connection we shall place together passages from his two leading biographers.

Sir Sidney Lee:

> It was as an actor that at an early date he acquired a genuinely substantial and secure income. . . . [Meanwhile he] was gaining great personal esteem outside the circles of actors and men of letters. His genius and 'civil demeanour' of which Chettle wrote arrested the notice not only of Southampton, but of other noble patrons of literature and the drama. His summons to act at Court with the most famous actors of the day at the Christmas of 1594 *was possibly due in part to personal interest in himself. Elizabeth quickly showed him special favour, etc.*[52]

Here, then, was fame of a most exceptional character, hardly to be excelled by those who endure the "fierce light that beats upon a throne." The tax gatherers who could not lay their hands readily upon this man were guilty, at best, of culpable incapacity; and should have been summarily dismissed for deliberate connivance. Nevertheless, we shall see what Halliwell-Phillipps says:

> There was not a single company of actors in Shakespeare's time which did not make professional visits through nearly all the English counties, and in the hope of discovering traces of his footsteps during his provincial tours I have personally examined the records of the following cities and towns—Warwick, Bewdley, Dover, Shrewsbury, Oxford, Worcester, Hereford, Gloucester,

---

[52] Lee, *Life*, p. 205, 85. Italics added by Looney.

etc.[53]

The Lord Chamberlain's company in the provinces.

And so he proceeds to enumerate no less than forty-six important towns and cities in all parts of the country, as far north as Newcastle-upon-Tyne, and including, in addition to both the great university cities, Stratford-upon-Avon itself, whose fame throughout the world it owes to the lustre which "Shakespeare's" name has given it, and he concludes:

> *In no single instance have I at present found in any municipal record a notice of the poet himself,* but curious material of an unsuspected nature respecting his company and theatrical surroundings has been discovered.[54]

Thus do the generous surmises of one biographer suffer at the hands of the unkindly facts presented by another. In the interval between the writing of the two biographies the number of "extant archives" examined is increased to "some seventy," and although Sir Sidney Lee passes over the salient fact that the later investigations were equally without result, so far as discovering traces of Shakespeare's footsteps are concerned, his faith in the Stratford man gives rise to the poetic supposition that "Shakespeare may be credited with faithfully fulfilling all his professional functions, and some of the references to travel in his sonnets were doubtless reminiscences of early acting tours."[55] The workers who have continued the enquiries begun by Halliwell-Phillipps, in their anxiety to find such traces of Shakspere as must exist if he were in reality what is claimed for him, have pushed their investigations as far north as Edinburgh, where the names of Lawrence Fletcher and one Martin are found in the records for 1599. Fletcher's name appears first, evidently as manager, of a company of actors who were "welcomed with enthusiasm by the King,"[56] and this Fletcher also heads the list of the company of actors licensed in London as the King's Players

---

[53] Halliwell-Phillipps, *Outlines*, p. 281.
[54] Halliwell-Phillipps, *Outlines*, p. 282. Italics added by Looney.
[55] Lee, *Life*, p. 41.
[56] Lee, *Life*, p. 42.

by James on his accession to the English throne—the list in which the name Shakespeare is inserted second. But there is no Shakspere in the Edinburgh records, nor in any of the other municipal archives that have been examined. The name Martin seems otherwise quite unknown.

The point that concerns us at present, however, is the fact that whilst the names of other actors of no great repute occur in these municipal records, the name of the man who is represented as enjoying almost unparalleled fame in his vocation—poet, dramatic author, actor and actor-shareholder—never appears once, although a most painstaking and laborious search has been made. The inevitable conclusion to which we are forced is that either he was not there or he was not a famous actor. In short, he was not a prominent active member of the Lord Chamberlain's Company, but rather a kind of "sleeping partner" whose functions were quite consistent with his settled residence at Stratford: a situation much more in accord with the idea of a man whose name was being used as a cloak, but whose personality was being carefully kept in the background, than of one enjoying in his own person the attentions and social intercourse which come to a distinguished man whom even royalty delighted to honour.

IX

Shakspere as London actor.

It remains now only to examine the data upon which rests the theory of William Shakspere being an eminent London actor. Neither as a writer of plays for the stage nor as an author of works for the press is it possible to account for his wealth. In the former capacity his income would not be a handsome one; and in the latter capacity, seeing that he took no part and held no rights, he would depend upon good-will gratuities from publishers. As an actor, we have seen, no single record of his appearance in the provinces has been discovered. It is as a London actor, therefore, that he must have made his wealth, if that wealth had nothing mysterious about it. Here, then, are the records of his career.

Treasurer's accounts.

Halliwell-Phillipps "had the pleasure of discovering some years ago in the accounts of the Treasurer of the Chamber" the following entry: "To William Kempe, *William Shakespeare* and Richard Burbage, servants to the Lord Chamberlaine, upon the councelles warrant dated at Whitehall xv. to Marcij, 1594, for twoe several comedies or enterludes showed by them before her Majestie in Christmas tyme laste paste viz. upon St. Stephens daye and innocentes daye . . . in all £20."[57] Mrs. Stopes, however, in her work on *Burbage and Shakespeare*, furnishes the interesting information that this "account [was] *drawn up after date* by Mary Countess of Southampton, after the decease of her second husband Sir Thomas Henneage, who had left his accounts rather in a muddle."[58] And Sir Sidney Lee points out that "neither plays nor parts are named."[59] We may also point out that whereas according to the last named authority Kemp was "the chief comedian of the day and Richard Burbage the greatest tragic actor," no record exists to tell us and no one has yet ventured to guess what William Shakspere was as an actor. Since, then, no part is assigned to him in this record, it is possible, even accepting it as being in proper order as an official document, that he received the money as the supposed author of the "comedies or enterludes." And this, although occurring three years before the opening of the period of his fame [1597] *is the only thing that can be called an official record of active participation in the performances of the Lord Chamberlain's Company,* afterwards called the King's Players, and erroneously spoken of as Shakespeare's company: the company of which he is supposed to have been one of the leading lights.

The "orthodoxy" of Mrs. Stopes, like that of Halliwell-Phillipps, is beyond suspicion, and she has performed in respect to William Shakspere's London career something analogous

---

[57] Halliwell-Phillipps, *Outlines*, p. 300.
[58] Stopes, *Burbage*, p. 251.
[59] Lee, *Life*, p. 45.

to what Halliwell-Phillipps has done for his work in the provinces, and with a not altogether dissimilar result. In note xxviii of the book just mentioned she records "The performances of the Burbage Company at Court for 80 years";[60] the record consisting mainly of a catalogue of brief items of payments made by the Treasurer of the Chamber for actual performances of plays, and occupying seventeen pages of her work. Over four pages are taken up with entries referring to performances of the company from 1597 to the death of William Shakspere in 1616. Separate entries occur for the years 1597, 1598, 1599, 1600, 1601, 1603, 1604, 1605, 1606, 1607, 1608, 1609, 1610, 1611, 1612, 1613, 1614, 1615, and 1616. It will thus be seen that only the year 1602 is missing from these records. The names of the actors mentioned are Heminge, Burbage, Cowley, Bryan and Pope; elsewhere these official accounts mention the actor Augustine Phillipps, but *not once does the name of William Shakspere occur in all these accounts.*

There is a danger that in multiplying evidences and opening up discussions on side issues the full force of some particular facts may be lost. We would urge, therefore, that the reader allow his mind to dwell at length on one fact, namely, that the whole of the municipal records of the acting companies are silent with regard to William Shakspere, and the whole of the Treasurer of the Chamber's records, with the one irregular exception of an account made up *by a strange hand after date*, are equally silent respecting him: even the irregular entry referring to a date (1594) several years before the period of his fame; so that both are absolutely silent respecting him during his great period. If the reader still persists in believing that William Shakspere was a well-known figure on the stage, or a prominent member of the Lord Chamberlain's company of actors, or in any way much in evidence in connection with the doings of that company, we would respectfully suggest that his time could be more profitably spent than in reading the remainder of these pages.

---

[60] Stopes, *Burbage*, p. 246.

The Lord Chamberlain's books.

Following up the investigations by means of the same work, we find that the Lord Chamberlain's books "supply much information concerning plays and players. *Unfortunately they are missing for the most important years of Shakespearean history.*"[61] Twice in the course of her work does Mrs. Stopes refer to the unfortunate disappearance of the Lord Chamberlain's books. In the light of all the other mysterious silences regarding William Shakspere, and the total disappearance of the "Shakespeare" manuscripts, so carefully guarded during the years preceding the publication of the First Folio, the disappearance of the Lord Chamberlain's books, recording the transactions of his department for the greatest period in its history, hardly looks like pure accident. More than one contemporary forgery in respect to Shakespeare records is admitted by most authorities, a well-known one being the 1611 reference to *The Tempest*, so that suspicion is quite justifiable. The one volume of these records that has been preserved records nothing of any acting engagement of William Shakspere's, but merely his receiving, along with others, a grant of cloth in preparation for the coronation procession. Whilst stating that "many believe . . . that the players did not go on that procession," Mrs. Stopes argues in favour of their being there; but adds: "it is true the grant of cloth was not in itself an invitation to the coronation."[62] It is therefore no evidence that he was present. Similarly the appearance of his name in the list of members of the company licensed in 1603 for prospective activity as the King's players furnishes no proof of his recognition as a prominent actor, and leaves us ignorant of the plays in which he may have participated, the roles which he performed, or the manner of his acting. All that we have of an official nature during this period are therefore two appearances of his name in general non-informative lists quite consistent with the theory that during the most important years of what is supposed to have been the

---

[61] Stopes, *Burbage*, p. 257. Italics added by Looney.
[62] Stopes, *Burbage*, p. 100.

great London period he was not in constant personal touch with the business of the company.

Shakspere and Jonson's plays.

Of non-official acting records—we again give the facts in the words of Sir Sidney Lee—"Shakespeare's name stands first on the list of those who took part in the original performance of Ben Jonson's plays. *Every Man in his Humour*"[63] (1598—the year in which Jonson, having been imprisoned for killing Gabriel Spenser, was liberated, apparently as a result of influential intervention). "In the original edition of Jonson's *Sejanus* [1605] the actors' names are arranged in two columns, and Shakespeare's name heads the second column. . . . But here again the part allotted to each actor is not stated."[64] Nor is it mentioned that this list was only published two years after the performance (1603).

These two appearances of his name are the only things that might be called records of his acting during the whole period of his fame; the first at its beginning, and the second, according to several authorities, at its close. ("There is no doubt he never meant to return to London except for business visits after 1604."[65]) We know neither what parts he played nor how he played them; but *the one thing we do know is that they had nothing to do with the great "Shakespeare" plays.* There is not a single record during the whole of his life of his ever appearing in a play of "Shakespeare's"; whilst the writer responsible for the appearance of his name in these instances is the same as lent the sanction of his name to the deliberate inaccuracies of the First Folio. It is worthwhile noticing that although Jonson gives a foremost place to the name of "Shakespeare" in these lists, when Jonson's *Every Man Out of His Humour* was played by the Lord Chamberlain's company, the whole of the company, with one notable exception, had parts assigned to them. That one

---

[63] Lee, *Life*, p. 45.
[64] Lee, *Life*, p. 45.
[65] "Shakspeare, William," in *National Encyclopaedia*. [Quote is unverified; pages 615-618 are missing in the only copy available for examination.]

exception was Shakspere, who does not appear at all in the cast. (See the collected works of Jonson.)

Missing references.

Other striking absences of William Shakspere's name in connection with this particular company remain to be noticed. The company became implicated in the "Essex Rebellion," and Augustine Phillips, one of the members, had to present himself for examination in connection with it. His statement, made on oath and formally attested with his signature, involves a play of "Shakespeare's" *Richard* (II). William Shakspere himself was, however, quite out of the business. He was not called upon, and his name was not even mentioned in connection with the play, which is spoken of as "so old and so long out of use."

Again in August, 1604 the company was appointed to attend on the Spanish Ambassador at Somerset House and were paid for their services; "Augustine Phillipps and John Hemynges for th' allowance of themselves and tenne of their fellows . . . for the space of 18 dayes [receiving] £21 12s."[66] We again notice the absence of the name of one whom we have been taught to regard as the chief personality in the company.

The modern Stratfordian postpones Shakspere's retirement to Stratford to the year 1612 or 1613. In 1612 the company was engaged in litigation, and the names of "John Hemings, Richard Burbage and Henry Condall"[67] appear in connection with it, but there is no mention of Shakspere.

On the installation of Prince Henry as Prince of Wales the services of the company were enlisted and the names of Anthony Munday, Richard Burbage, and John Rice occur in the official records, the first as writer and the last two as actors; but no mention is made of the great writer-actor William Shakspere.

In 1613 the Globe Theatre, the supposed scene of William Shakspere's great triumphs, was burnt to the ground, and a contemporary poet sang of the event in verses that commemorate

---

[66] Stopes, *Burbage*, p. 101.
[67] Lee, *Life*, p. 285.

Anthony Munday, Richard Burbage, Henry Condell, and the father of John Heminge, but without ever a backward glance at the retiring or retired William Shakspere whose name has immortalized the name of the building.

Doubtful claims.

After such a contemporary record the appearance of his name, in the 1623 folio edition, seven years after his death, at the *head* of the list of "the *principall* actors in all these plays,"[68] confirms the bogus character of the whole of the editorial pretensions of that work. With such a send-off, it is remarkable that subsequent tradition has done so little for him. More than eighty years later Rowe in his *Life of Shakspere* (1709) assigns but one role to the "principall actor in all these plays": namely the Ghost in Hamlet. This tradition, though quite unreliable—seeing that the whole body of Shakespearean tradition is mixed with much that is now known to be untrue—is nevertheless interesting: for the role of the Ghost in *Hamlet* is just such as a third-rate man about the theatre might have been trained to perform upon occasion. The discussion of the shifting sands of Shakespearean tradition hardly comes within the province of this work. It is interesting to note, however, that Mrs. Stopes flatly refuses to believe the body of Shakespeare traditions, for the very substantial reason that they arose at too late a period after the events. How little of solid biographical fact remains when mere tradition is discounted, the general reader, who simply interests himself in the plays, is seldom aware.

It is possible that we may have omitted the discussion of some contemporary reference which others might consider important. Enough, however, has been said to show that William Shakspere's connection with the Lord Chamberlain's company was of a distinctly anomalous character. On the one hand there are distinct traces of an effort to give him a marked prominence in respect to the constitution and operations of the company, and on the other hand a total absence of the inevitable concomitants of such a

---

[68] Lee, *Life*, p. 45.

prominence. What others, using him as an instrument of their purposes, were able to do with his name, is done; what could only be brought about by the force of his own genius is lacking. Outside the formal lists of names no single contemporary that we know of records an event or impression of him as an actor during all the years of his literary fame. It may safely be said, therefore, that neither in the provinces nor in London did the public who were buying and reading "Shakespeare's" plays know much about William Shakspere the actor. Even the objectionable anecdote which represents Burbage in the dramatic role of Richard the Third does not imply dramatic functions of any kind for Shakspere, but represents him as a silent listener, not necessarily one living in the public eye: a person whom someone in the outside public might have thought of as implicated in the inner workings of the company. In the face of so pronounced a silence in respect to him, why should there have been these two efforts of Jonson's to thrust his name forward as an actor in a way which neither the records of the Lord Chamberlain's company nor the constitution of the cast for his own play *Every Man Out of His Humour* warranted? And how does it happen, in view of the total silence of the records of the Lord Chamberlain's company during all the years, both before and after, that his name was inserted twice in one year (1603) in the business formalities of the company? In a word, how does it happen that we have the name occupying an artificial eminence in two connections and nothing else to correspond? The most natural answer is, of course, that false claims were being made for him fitting in exactly with the admitted false pretensions of the First Folio in which the same party, Ben Jonson, was implicated. In the matter of motives, however, we again put in a plea for Jonson that he is entitled to the same indulgence as has been freely accorded to Heminge and Condell, although he probably was deeper in the secret than they were.

X

We may now summarize the results of our examination of the middle or London period of William Shakspere's career.

1. He was purely passive in respect to all the publication which took place under his name.

2. There is the greatest uncertainty respecting the duration of his sojourn in London and the strongest probability that he was actually resident at Stratford whilst the plays were being published.

3. Nothing is known of his doings in London, and there is much mystery concerning his place of residence there.

4. After Greene's attack and Chettle's apology the "man" and the "actor" was ignored by contemporaries.

5. Before the printing of the dramas began in 1598 contemporary references were always to the poet—the author of *Venus* and *Lucrece*—never to the dramatist.

6. Only after 1598, the date when plays were first printed with "Shakespeare's" name, are there any contemporary references to him as a dramatist.

7. The public knew "Shakespeare" in print, but knew nothing of the personality of William Shakspere.

8. The sole anecdote recorded of him is rejected by the general consensus of authorities, and even the contemporary currency of this anecdote is consistent with the idea of his being personally unknown.

9. He has left no letter or trace of personal intercourse with any London contemporary or public man. He received no letter from any patron or literary man. The only letter known to have been sent to him was concerned solely with the borrowing of money.

10. Edmund Spenser quite ignores him.

11. Although the company with which his name is associated toured frequently and widely in the provinces, and much has been recorded of their doings, no municipal archive, so far as is known, contains a single reference to him.

12. There is no contemporary record of his ever appearing in a "Shakespeare" play.

13. The only plays with which as an actor his name was associated during his lifetime are two of Ben Jonson's plays.

14. The accounts of the Treasurer of the Chamber show only one irregular reference to him three years before the period of his greatest fame, and none at all during or after that period.

15. The Lord Chamberlain's Books, which would have furnished the fullest records of his doings during these years, are, like the "Shakespeare" manuscripts, missing.

16. His name is missing from the following records of the Lord Chamberlain's company in which other actors' names appear:

    (1) The cast of Jonson's *Every Man Out of His Humour* in which all the other members of the company appear.

    (2) The record of proceedings respecting the Essex Rebellion in 1604.

    (3) The company's attendance on the Spanish Ambassador in 1604.

    (4) The company's litigation in 1612.

    (5) The company's participation in the installation of the Prince of Wales.

    (6) References to the burning of the Globe Theatre.

17. Even rumour assigns him only an insignificant role as an actor.

Shakspere and contemporaries.

We must now ask the reader to bring all these various considerations carefully into focus, and see them in their natural relationship to one another. He ought to have no difficulty in realizing that so completely negative a record is altogether inconsistent with the career William Shakspere is supposed to have enjoyed. We place him above Edmund Spenser as a poet, yet Spenser's biography is no mere tissue of learned fancies and generous conjectures. We place him above Jonson as a writer of plays, yet Jonson's literary life and social relationships make up a very real and tangible biography. We attempt to class him with Burbage as an actor, yet Burbage is a very living and substantial figure in the history of the English stage. But he, the one man who is supposed to have combined in a remarkable way the powers and vocations of all three; the contemporary of Spenser: the protégé of the Burbages—for we are now told it was they who discovered and brought out Shakspere—the idol of Jonson, and the greatest genius that has appeared in English literature, leaves behind in all literary and dramatic concerns but the elusive and impalpable record we have been considering.

The genial spirit of Spenser kept pouring itself out in verse until crushing disaster came upon him, and death approached: his last verses indeed seem to have been written with death before his eyes. To the end Ben Jonson kept writing and publishing: his last and posthumous work being the expression of his latest thoughts. The central figure on the English stage at the time when Richard Burbage died was Burbage himself. But William Shakspere, possessed of a genius so compelling as to have raised him from a level quite below his literary contemporaries to a height far above them, abandons his vocation at the age of forty, retires to the uncultured atmosphere of Stratford, devotes his powers to land, houses, malt and money, leaving unfinished literary masterpieces in the hands of actors and theatre managers to be finished by the pens of strangers; ultimately dying in affluence but in total dissociation from everything that has made his name famous.

Had the work attributed to him been merely average literature, his record, once grasped in its *ensemble*, would have justified the strongest doubts as to the genuineness of his claims. Being what it is, however, the unique character of the work, and the record, equally unique but opposite in character, justifies the complete rejection of his pretensions. To borrow Emerson's metaphor on the subject, we "cannot marry" the life record to the literature. We are compelled, therefore, to make a very clear separation between the writer "Shakespeare" and the man William Shakspere. As soon as this is done we are able to coordinate this middle period of the life of William Shakspere with the two extremes we have previously considered. We thus arrive at the conception of a man of very ordinary powers and humble purposes, the three parts of whose career become perfectly homogeneous. In the place of the tremendous mass of Stratfordian incongruities and impossibilities we get a sane and consistent idea of a man in natural relationship with human experience and normal probabilities—a man who played a part and had his reward. His motives were no doubt like those of the average amongst us, a mixture of high and low; and, seeing that no one else was being injured by the subterfuge, he might, if he were capable of apprizing the work justly, have felt honoured in being trusted by "Shakespeare" in furthering his literary purposes. But that he was himself the author of the great poems and dramas stands altogether outside the region of natural probabilities, and he must now yield for the adornment of a worthier brow the laurels he has worn so long.

CHAPTER II*

I

CHARACTER OF THE PROBLEM

Recognized mystery.

THE three greatest names in the world's literature are those of Homer, Dante, and Shakespeare. The first belongs to the ancient world and the personality behind the name is lost beyond recall in the perished records of a remote antiquity. The two last belong to the modern world. The former of these belongs to Italy; and Italy is quite certain of the personality and cherishes every ascertained detail in the records of her most illustrious son. The last of the three—and who will venture to say it is not the greatest of all?—belongs to England, and although nearer to us than Dante by three hundred years, the personality behind the name is today as problematic as that of Homer; his identity being a matter of dispute amongst men whose capacity and calmness of judgment are unquestionable.

The inquiry into the authorship of the Shakespeare plays has therefore long since earned a clear title to be regarded as something more than a crank problem to be classed with such vagaries as the "flat-earth theory" or surmises respecting the "inhabitants of Mars." It is common in serious works on Elizabethan literature to take cognisance of the problem, thus making the authorship an open question still awaiting a decisive answer; and every theory advanced in regard to it either implies

---

* Looney's Note: The work as originally written begins here. Only a few slight verbal adjustments to the preceding pages have been possible.

or affirms the mysteriousness of the whole business. Those who maintain the orthodox view, that the plays and poems were written by the Stratford citizen, William Shakspere, are obliged to recognize the fact that a writer, the whole of whose circumstances and antecedents rendered the production of such a work as the Shakespeare plays one of the most extraordinary feats recorded in history, and who with the intelligence attributed to him must have seen that this would eventually raise doubts as to the genuineness of his claims, deliberately reduced to a minimum all that kind of evidence which might have placed his title beyond question. For, as we have seen, neither that part of his life prior to his appearance in the London theatre, nor that subsequent to his retirement from the stage, nor a single word in his will, shows any mark of those dominating literary interests to which the writings bear witness. In a word, though willing to enjoy the honour, and, maybe, the pecuniary advantages of authorship, he must have actually gone out of his way to remove the normal traces of his literary pursuits; in this way casting about the production of his plays that kind of obscurity which belongs to anonymous rather than to acknowledged authorship.

Probably one of the most significant facts connected with this paucity of personal literary details, upon which we have so much insisted, has been the issue in modern times of literary series without volumes on Shakespeare. The original issue of *English Men of Letters*, including Elizabethan writers, like Spenser and Sidney, appeared without a volume on the greatest of all. The omission continued through later editions, and was only made good at the extreme end of the series with the apparent purpose of removing an anomaly; adding to the series thereby, however, a most valuable work upon the Shakespeare literature, which yet admits frankly the meagreness of the material available for a real literary biography. In addition to this the long list of the "Great Writer" series is still without its volume on England's greatest writer. The explanation of all this seems to lie in the uncertainty of everything connecting the Shakespeare literature with the personality behind it; thus exposing such scholarly works as Sir

Sidney Lee's *Life of William Shakespeare* to criticism on the grounds of the supposititious character of much of the biographical details.

Whilst then the view of authorship hitherto current implies its mysteriousness, those who oppose that view postulate thereby an uncertain authorship. All therefore must agree that the whole business is a profound mystery. Only the Shakespeare tyro believes nowadays that William Shakspere's credentials stand on the same plane with those of Dante and Milton; and only the too old or too young are disposed to represent the sceptics as cranks and fanatics. Our last chapter has but outlined the arguments by which we claim the incredibility of the old belief has been established; other points will arise in the course of our discussion. What we do now is to assume an undecided authorship and attempt to lift the veil from this, the most stupendous mystery in the history of the world's literature.

A solution required.

The objection, though not so frequently raised as formerly, is still occasionally met with, that the enquiry is unnecessary; that the great dramatic masterpieces stand there, that we cannot be deprived of them, and that such being the case all we need to do is to say that the name "Shakespeare" stands for their writer, whoever he may have been, and that there the matter may be allowed to rest. Such indifference to the personality of the author is usually, however, but the counterpart to an indifference to the writings themselves. Those who appreciate some great good that they have received cannot remain indifferent to the personality of the one to whose labours they owe it. Such an attitude, moreover, would be unjust and ungrateful to the memory of our benefactors. And if it be urged that "Shakespeare" in leaving things as he did, showed that he wished to remain unknown, there is still the possibility that arrangements were made for ultimately disclosing his identity to posterity, and that these arrangements have miscarried. Again, it is one thing for a benefactor of mankind to wish to remain unknown, it is quite another matter for others to acquiesce in this self-effacement. Then there is the possibility that the writer's effort to obliterate the memory of himself may not have succeeded, and that there may be current an incomplete, distorted and unjust conception of him, which can only be rectified by establishing his position as the author of the world's greatest dramas.

The discovery of the author and the establishing of his just claims to honour is therefore a duty which mankind owes to one of the most illustrious of men; a duty from which Englishmen, at any rate, can never be absolved, if by any means the task can be accomplished. He is the one Englishman of whom it can be most truly said that he belongs to the world; and in any Pantheon of Humanity that may one day be set up he is *the* one of our countrymen who is already assured of an eternal place. England's negligence to put his identity beyond question would therefore be a grave dereliction of national duty if by any means his identity could be fully established.

Problem defined.

Accepting the duty thus laid upon us, our first task must be to define precisely the character of the problem that confronts us. Briefly it is this. We have before us a piece of human work of the most exceptional character, and the problem is to find the man who did it. Thus defined, it is not, as we have already remarked, strictly speaking a literary problem. Those who enter upon the search must obtain much of their data from literary men; they must rest a substantial part of their case upon the authority of literary men; and they must, in the long run, submit the result of their labours very largely to the judgment of literary men. But the most expert in literature may be unfitted for prosecuting such an investigation, whilst a mind constituted for this kind of enquiry may have had only an inferior preparation so far as purely literary matters are concerned.

It is the kind of enquiry with which lawyers and juries are faced every day. They are called upon to examine questions involving highly technical matters with which they are not themselves conversant. Their method is naturally to separate what belongs to the specialist from what is matter of common sense and simple judgment; to rely upon the expert in purely technical matters, and to use their own discrimination in the sifting of evidence, at the same time allowing its full weight to any particular knowledge they may chance to possess in those things that pertain specially to the expert's domain. This is the course proper to the investigation before us. The question, for example, of what is, or is not Shakespearean; what are the distinguishing characteristics of Shakespeare's work; what were its relationships to contemporary literature; between what dates the plays appeared; when the various editions were published, are matters which may be left, in a general way, to the experts. As, however, there is a considerable amount of disagreement amongst the specialists (and even a consensus of expert opinion may sometimes be at fault): where it is necessary to differ from the experts—a thing which is more or less inevitable in the breaking of entirely new ground, and especially in presenting a new and potent factor—such differences ought to be clearly indicated and adequately discussed. Nevertheless the cumulative effect of all the evidence gathered together ought to be of such convincing weight as to be in a measure independent of such personal differences, and indeed strong enough to sustain an unavoidable admixture of errors and slips in matters of detail.

"Shakespeare's" self-effacement.

Our task being to discover the author of what is acknowledged generally to be Shakespeare's work, the exceptional character of that work ought, under normal conditions, to facilitate the enquiry. The more commonplace a piece of work may be the greater must be the proportion of men capable of doing it, and the greater the difficulty under ordinary circumstances of placing one's hand on the man who did it. The more distinctive the work the more limited becomes the number of men capable of performing it, and the easier ought it, therefore, to be to discover its author. In this case, however, the work is of so unusual a character that every competent judge would say that the man who actually did it was the only man living at the time who was capable of doing it.

Notwithstanding this fact, after three hundred years the authorship seems more uncertain today than at any previous time. The natural inference is that special obstacles have intentionally and most carefully been laid in the way of the discovery. There is no mere accident in the obscurity which hangs round the authorship, and the very greatness of the work itself is a testimony to the thoroughness of the steps taken to avoid disclosure. This fact must be borne in mind throughout the enquiry. It is not merely a question of finding out the man who did a piece of work, but of circumventing a scheme of self-concealment devised by one of the most capable of intellects. We must not expect, therefore, to find that such a man, taking such a course, has somewhere or other gone back childishly upon his intentions, and purposely placed in his works some indications of his identity, in the form of a cryptogram or other device. If the concealment were intended to be temporary it would hardly be within the works themselves or in any document published at the same time that the disclosure would be made.

Genius and the problem.

As it is not from intentional self-disclosure that we should expect to discover the author, but from more or less unconscious indications of himself in the writings, it is necessary to guard at the outset against certain theories as to the possibilities of genius which tend to vitiate all reasoning upon the subject. Upon hardly any other literary topic has so much that is misleading been written. There is a frequent assumption that the possession of what we call genius renders its owner capable of doing almost anything. Now William Shakspere is the one stock illustration of this contention. In all other cases, where the whole of the circumstances are well known, we may connect the achievements of a genius with what may be called the external accidents of his life. Though social environment is not the source of genius, it certainly has always determined the forms in which the faculty has clothed itself, and even the particular direction which its energies have taken: and in no other class of work are the products of genius so moulded by social pressure, and even by class relationships, as in works involving the artistic use of the mother tongue. To what extent the possession of abnormal powers may enable a man to triumph over circumstances no one can say; and if a given mind working under specified conditions is actually proved to have produced something totally unexpected and at variance with the conditions, we can only accept the phenomenon, however inexplicable it may appear. It is not thus, however, that genius usually manifests itself; and, failing conclusive proof, a vast disparity or incompatibility between the man and the work must always justify a measure of doubt as to the genuineness of his pretensions and make us cast about for a more likely agent.

Now no one is likely ever to question the reality or the vastness of "Shakespeare's" genius. If he had enjoyed every advantage of education, travel, leisure, social position and wealth, his plays would still remain for all time the testimony to his marvellous powers: though naturally not such stupendous powers as would have been required to produce the same results without the advantages. Consequently, if we regard the authorship as an open question we shall be much more disposed to look for the author amongst those who possessed some or all of those advantages than amongst those who possessed none of them. That is to say, we must go about the task of searching for the author in precisely the same way as we should seek for a man who had done some ordinary piece of work, and not complicate the problem by the introduction of such incommensurables as are implied in current theories of genius.

Maturity and masterpieces.

If we find that a man knows a thing we must assume that he had it to learn. If he handles his knowledge readily and appropriately we must assume an intimacy born of an habitual interest, woven into the texture of his mind. If he shows himself skillful in doing something we must assume that he attained his skill by practice. And therefore, if he first comes before the world with a masterpiece in any art, exhibiting an easy familiarity with the technique of the craft and a large fund of precise information in any department, we may conclude that preceding all this there must have lain years of secret preparation, during which he was accumulating knowledge, and by practice in his art, gaining skill and strength for the decisive plunge; storing up, elaborating and perfecting his productions so as to make them in some degree worthy of that ideal which ever haunts the imagination of the supreme artist.

Most of the other poets differ from Shakespeare in that they furnish us with collections of their juvenile productions in which, though often enough poor stuff, we may trace the promise of their maturer genius. Apart from this value, much of it is hardly entitled to immortality. Amongst the work of Shakespeare the authorities, however, ascribe priority in time to *Love's Labour's Lost*; and what Englishman that knows his Shakespeare would care to part with this work? We could easily mention quite a number of Shakespearean plays of even high rank that would more willingly be parted with than this one. It would, however, be perfectly gratuitous to argue that this work is a masterpiece.

Masterpieces, however, are the fruits of matured powers. Dante was over fifty years of age before he finished his immortal work; Milton about fifty-five when he completed *Paradise Lost*. Quite a long line might be made out of illustrating this principle in works of even the second order; Cervantes at sixty producing *Don Quixote*, Scott at forty-three giving us the first of the Waverley Novels, Defoe at fifty-eight publishing *Robinson Crusoe*; Fielding at forty-two giving *Tom Jones*, and Manzoni at forty *I Promessi Sposi*. Or, if we turn to Shakespeare's own domain, the drama, we find that Molière, after a lifetime of dramatic enthusiasm and production, gave forth his masterpieces between the ages of forty and fifty, his greatest work *Tartuffe* appearing just at the middle of that period (age forty-five), whilst Goethe's *Faust* was the outcome of a long literary lifetime, its final touches being given only a few months before his death at the age of eighty-two.

Drama, in its supreme manifestation, that is to say as a capable and artistic exposition of our many-sided human nature and not mere "inexplicable dumb-shows and noise," is an art in which, more than in others, mere precocity of talent will not suffice for the creation of masterpieces. In this case genius must be supplemented by a wide and intense experience of life and much practice in the technical work of staging plays. Poetic geniuses who have not had this experience, and have cast their work in dramatic form, may have produced great literature, but not great dramas. Yet, with such a general experience as these few facts illustrate, we are asked to believe that a young man—William Shakspere was but twenty-six in the year 1590, which marks roughly the beginning of the Shakespearean period—began his career with the composition of masterpieces without any apparent preparation, and kept pouring out plays spontaneously at a most amazing rate. He appears before us at the age of twenty-nine as the author of a superb poem of no less than twelve hundred lines, and leaves no trace of those slight youthful effusions by means of which a poet learns his art and develops his powers. If, however, we can disabuse our minds of fantastic notions of genius, regard the Shakespearean dramas as anonymous, and look at them with the eyes of common sense, we shall be inclined rather to view the outpouring of dramas from the year 1590 onwards as the work of a more matured man, who had had the requisite intellectual and dramatic preparation, and who was elaborating, finishing off and letting loose a flood of dramas that he had been accumulating and working at during many preceding years.

When in 1855 Walt Whitman gave to the world his *Leaves of Grass*, Emerson greeted the work and its writer in these words: "I find it the most extraordinary piece of wit and wisdom that America has yet contributed . . . I greet you at the beginning of a great career, *which yet must have had a long foreground somewhere.*"[69] This concluding surmise was merely common sense, and, as the world now knows, perfectly true. What is wanted is to apply the same principle and the same common sense to work of a higher order, and to recognize that if by the year 1592, by which time we are assured that the stream of Shakespearean drama was in full flood, Shakespeare was manifesting an exceptional facility in the production of works that were at once great literature and great stage plays, there had been "a long foreground somewhere."

A modern problem.

The considerations we have been urging in this chapter are necessary for getting the problem into its right perspective and on the same plane of vision as the other problems and interests of life. We must free the problem from illogical entanglements and miraculous assumptions, and look for scientific relationship between cause and effect. This must be the first step towards its solution. It may appear, however, that if it is simply a question of searching for a particular man, according to the same methods which we would employ in any other case, that the man should have been discovered long before now, if the material for his discovery were really available; and that as he has not been discovered after three hundred years the necessary data do not exist, and his identity must remain for ever a mystery. It must not

---

[69] Ralph Waldo Emerson, July 21, 1855 letter to Walt Whitman.

be forgotten, however, that "Shakespeare" had to wait until the Nineteenth Century for his full literary appreciation; and this was essential to the mere raising of the problem. "Not until two centuries had passed after his death," says Emerson, "did any criticism which we think adequate begin to appear."[70] Recognition he had, no doubt, in abundance before that time. But that exact and critical appreciation which made it possible to distinguish the characteristics of his work; and begin to separate true Shakespearean work from spurious; that enabled a Shakespearean authority to condemn *Titus Andronicus* as "repulsive balderdash"; which has enabled us to say of *Timon of Athens* that it contains but "a fragment from the master hand"; that *Pericles* is "mainly from other hands" than Shakespeare's; that *Henry VIII* was completed by Fletcher; all this belongs to the last hundred years, and has only been preparing the way for raising the question of Shakespeare's identity.

Even up to the present day the problem has hardly passed definitely beyond the negative or sceptical stage of doubting what is called the Stratfordian view, the work of Sir George Greenwood being the first milestone in the process of scientific research. The Baconian view, though it has helped to popularize the negative side, and to bring into prominence certain contents of Shakespeare's works, has done little for the positive aspect except to institute a misleading method of enquiry: a kind of pick-and-try process, leading to quite a number of rival candidates for Shakespeare honours, and setting up an inferior form of Shakespearean investigation, the "cryptogram." Amongst all the literature on the subject, we have so far been able to discover no attempt, starting from an assumed anonymity of the plays, to institute a systematic search for the author. Yet surely this is the point towards which the modern movement of Shakespearean study has been tending; and once instituted it must continue until either the author is discovered or the attempt abandoned as

---

[70] Ralph Waldo Emerson, *Representative Men*.

hopeless.

II

METHOD OF SOLUTION

Failing the discovery of some new and sensational documentary evidence, if any headway is to be made towards the solution of the problem it must result very largely from the inauguration of new methods of investigation. Even when these lead to conclusions which have ultimately to be abandoned they give cohesion and definite direction to the efforts that are made, and thus assist in clearing up the situation, suggesting new methods, and preparing the way for more reliable conclusions.

The writings in question not having been produced in some distant country or in a remote age, but here, in England, in an age so near as to have transmitted to us masses of details relating to most unimportant individuals, and yet so little advance having, as yet, been made in the direction of either solving the Shakespeare problem or of pronouncing it insoluble, confirms the impression that, in addition to the mystery purposely thrown over the authorship, the investigation has not yet been prosecuted on right lines. Prepossessions of one kind or another have stood in the way of sounder methods; for people who spend themselves in glorifying every new detail discovered about the Stratford man, or who lose themselves in the labyrinths of Baconian cryptograms, can hardly be expected to assume the impartiality necessary for the invention of new and reliable instruments of enquiry. The clearing out of all this impediments is therefore the first essential condition of any real progress.

Ridding the mind of all such personal prepossessions, we must now make a beginning from some hitherto untried standpoint. The standpoint adopted at the outset of these researches, and already indicated, was to assume the complete anonymity of the writings, and to apply to the search for the author just those ordinary methods which we should have had to apply if it had been some practical question involving important issues of life and conduct.

What then is the usual common-sense method of searching for an unknown man who has performed some particular piece of work? It is simply to examine closely the work itself, to draw from the examination as definite a conception as possible of the man who did it, to form some idea of where he would be likely to be found, and then to go and look for a man who answers to the supposed description. When some such man has been found we next proceed to gather together all the particulars that might in any way connect him with the work in question. We rely, in such cases, very largely upon what is called circumstantial evidence; mistakenly supposed by some to be evidence of an inferior order, but in practice the most reliable form of proof we have. Such evidence may at first be of the most shadowy description; but as we proceed in the work of gathering together facts and reducing them to order, as we hazard our guesses and weigh probabilities, as we subject our theories to all available tests, we find that the case at last either breaks down or becomes confirmed by such an accumulation of support that doubt is no longer possible. The predominating element in what we call circumstantial evidence is that of coincidences. A few coincidences we may treat as simply interesting; a number of coincidences we regard as remarkable; a vast accumulation of extraordinary coincidences we accept as conclusive proof. And when the case has reached this stage we look upon the matter as finally settled, until, as may happen, something of a most unusual character appears to upset all our reasoning. If nothing of this kind ever appears, whilst every newly discovered fact adds but confirmation to the conclusion, that conclusion is accepted as a permanently established truth.

The above is an epitome of the method of research and the line of argument we have followed. In reviewing the work done the critic may disagree with one or other of the points on which we have insisted; he may regard this or that argument as trifling or insufficient in itself, and it is possible we should agree with many of the several objections he might raise. It may even transpire that, notwithstanding all our efforts to ensure accuracy, we have fallen into serious mistakes not only in minor details but even upon important points: a danger to which the wanderer into unwonted fields is specially liable. It is not, however, upon any point separately, but upon the manner in which all fit in with one another, and form a coherent whole, that the case rests; and it is this that we desire should be kept in mind. We proceed, therefore, to present a short statement of the details of the method of enquiry, outlining its several stages as determined prior to entering on the search.

1. As a first step it would be necessary to examine the works of Shakespeare, almost as though they had appeared for the first time, unassociated with the name or personality of any writer; and from such an examination draw what inferences we could as to his character and circumstances. The various features of these would have to be duly tabulated, the statement so arrived at forming the groundwork of all subsequent investigation.

2. The second step would be to select from amongst the various characteristics some one outstanding feature which might serve best as a guide in proceeding to search for the author, by furnishing some paramount criterion, and at the same time indicating in some measure where the author was to be looked for.

3. With this instrument in our hands the third step would be to proceed to the great task of searching for the man.

4. In the event of discovering any man who should adequately fulfil the prime condition, the fourth step would be to test the selection by reference to the various features in the original characterization; and, in the event of his failing in a marked degree to meet essential conditions, it would be necessary to reject this first selection and resume the search.

5. Supposing the discovery of some man who should in a

general way have passed successfully through this crucial test, the next step would be to reverse the whole process. Having worked from Shakespeare's writings to the man, we should then begin with the man; taking new and outstanding facts about his performances and personality, we should have to enquire to what extent these were reflected in Shakespeare's works.

6. Then, in the event of the enquiry yielding satisfactory results up to this point we should next have to accumulate corroborative evidence and apply tests arising out of the course of the investigation.

7. The final step would be to develop as far as possible any traces of a personal connection between the newly accredited and the formerly reputed authors of the works.

This, then, was the method outlined at the start, and, in the main, adhered to throughout the investigations we are about to describe: one which might be justly styled a coldly analytical process, quite at variance with literary traditions and the synthetic soul of poetry but which, it appeared, was the method proper to the case. The danger of the plan was, not that we might have too many claimants for the honour, but that its severity might cause us to pass over the very man for whom we were looking, supposing his name and personality were really accessible to us. At any rate, it avoided the random picking first of one man and then of another in the hope of alighting eventually on the right one: after the manner of certain other investigations.

Supposing, and it is a perfectly reasonable possibility, that every other trace of the writer has been effectually destroyed beyond what we have in Shakespeare's work, then, of course, the enquiry must in the end prove futile; for any false selection would almost certain break down under the various tests, leaving an altogether negative result for our efforts. In the event of anything like a really good case being made out for any man there seemed a chance that other investigators with more leisure, greater resources, and a readier access to necessary documents than the present writer possesses, might be led to more important discoveries.

Opinions may differ as to the soundness or appropriateness of the course outlined; but, as it is the result of researches pursued in accordance with it that we are about to describe, it was necessary to lay bare the method at the outset, however crude or commonplace it may appear for so lofty a theme.

CHAPTER III

THE AUTHOR—SOME GENERAL FEATURES

THE first task—following the course just outlined—must be to form, from a general survey of the position as a whole, and from a review of the contents of the writings, some conception of the outstanding characteristics of the author. This should include some legitimate surmises as to what we might expect to be the conditions of his life, and the relationship of his contemporaries towards him.

Of recognized genius, and mysterious.

Although we are obliged, from the nature of our problem, to assume that his contemporaries generally were not aware of his producing the great works, it is hardly probable that one endowed with so commanding a genius should have been able to conceal the greatness of his powers wholly from those with whom he habitually associated; and therefore we may reasonably expect to find him a man of recognized and recorded genius. At the same time the mysteriousness in which he has chosen to involve the production of his works ought not to have escaped the observation of others. Consequently we may suppose that he would appear to many of the people about him something of the enigma he has proved to posterity. We must not look, however, for an exact representation of actual facts in any recorded impressions of the personality and actions of the man. Between what contemporary records represent him as being, and what he really was, we ought, indeed, to be prepared to find some striking discrepencies: the important thing is that there must be some notable agreement in essentials. Certain discordances may, however, become important evidence in his favour. For example, a man who has produced so large an amount of work of the highest quality, and was not seen doing it, must have passed a considerable part of his life in what would appear to others like doing nothing of any consequence. The record of a wasted genius is, therefore, what we might reasonably look for in any contemporary account of him.

Apparent eccentricity.

Again, unless some special reasons should appear to account for his self-effacement we are bound to recognize that the whole manner of his anonymity marks the writer as being, in a manner, something of an eccentric: his nature, or his circumstances, or probably both, were not normal. And, when the indications of his intense impressionability are considered, along with his peculiar power of entering into and reflecting vividly the varied moods, fierce passions and subtle movements of man's mind and heart, when the magnitude of his creative efforts is weighed, and account taken of the mental exhaustion which frequently follows from such efforts, we may even suppose that he was not altogether immune from the penalties that have sometimes accompanied such powers and performances. Altogether we may say his poetic temperament and the exuberance of his poetic fancy mark him as a man much more akin mentally to Byron or Shelley than to the placid Shakespeare suggested by the Stratford tradition. Add to this his marvelous insight into human nature, revealing to him, as it must have done, such springs and motives of human actions as would be hidden from his associates, and we may naturally expect to find him giving vent to himself in acts and words which must have seemed extraordinary and inexplicable to other men: for the man who sees most deeply into the inner workings of the human mind must often act upon knowledge of which he may not speak. It ought not, therefore, to surprise us if his contemporaries found him, not merely eccentric in his bearing, as they have frequently found the genius whom they could not understand, but even on occasion, guilty of what seemed to them vagaries of a pronounced type.

A man apart, and unconventional.

The possession of abnormal powers, and a highly strung temperament like that of Byron or of Shelley, interposes a barrier between a man and his social environment. The mediocrity, and what seems like the insensibility of the average people about him, place him in an irritating milieu, against which he tends to protect himself by a mannerism, sometimes merely cold and aloof, at times even repellent or defiant. To be a general social favourite a man needs to combine with personal graces a certain average of intellect and sensibility, which assimilates him to the generality of the people about him. The poetic genius has always, therefore, been more or less a man apart, whose very aloofness is provocative of hostility in smaller men. Towards these he tries to assume a mask, often most difficult to penetrate but which, once pierced, may necessitate a complete reversal of former judgments—one of the most difficult things to accomplish once such judgment has passed beyond mere individual opinion, and has taken firm root in the social mind.

Apparent inferiority.

We venture to say that, whatever course the discussion may take, either now or in a distant future, one of the most serious hindrances to the formation of correct views will be the necessity of reversing judgments that have had a long standing social sanction. We shall first have to dissociate from the writings the conception of such an author as the steady, complacent, business-like man-of-the-world, suggested by the Stratford Shakspere. Then there will be the more arduous task of raising to a most exalted position the name and personality possibly of some obscure man hitherto regarded as quite unequal to the work with which he is at last to be credited. And this will forth compel us to re-read our greatest national classics from a totally new personal standpoint. The work in question being the highest literary product of the age, it cannot be otherwise than that the author, whoever he may have been, when he is discovered must seem in some measure below the requirements of the situation; unequal, that is, to the production of such work. We shall therefore be called upon in his case radically to modify and correct a judgment of three hundred years' standing.

An Englishman of literary tastes.

Although apparently unequal to the full measure of Shakespeare's capacity, there is a natural limit to such allowable inferiority in appearance. It might, in a given instance, be so great as to make it absurd to entertain the thought of connecting the man with the work. His writings being masterpieces of English literature, and all the world's literary masterpieces having been produced by men who wrote in their mother-tongue of matters in which they were keenly interested, and to whom writing, or more properly speaking the mental occupation of composing, has been a master passion, we are entitled to require in the person put forward as the author a body of credentials corresponding to the character of the work. That is to say, we are bound to assume that the writer was an Englishman with dominating literary tastes, to whom the classical literature of the world, the history of England during the period of the Lancastrians and Yorkists, and Italian literature, which form the staple materials of his work, were matters of absorbing interest, furnishing the milieu in which his mind habitually worked. To think of him as one who made an excursion into literature in order to win a competency for himself, and who retired from literary pursuits when that purpose had been served, is to contradict everything that is known of the production of such masterpieces. Other interests he may have had, just as men who were chiefly occupied with social and political affairs, dabbled also in literature, poetry, or the drama; but what to them was a mere hobby or pastime would be to him a central and consuming purpose. Unless, then, we are to recast all our ideas of how the great things of literature have beenachieved, we cannot think of him otherwise than as one who had been swept by the irresistible force of his own genius into the strong literary current of his times. The fact that he was himself busy producing such works, he may have hidden from the men of his day, but it is inconceivable that he should have hidden from them where his chief interest lay.

Enthusiasm for drama.

Again, the great mass of the literature he has given to the world being in the form of dramas, we may repeat in relation to this particular class of work what has already been said of literature generally: namely, that an intense, even passionate devotion to the special form of art in which his masterpieces are produced is invariably characteristic of a genius. And although, again, this writer's absorption may have been partially concealed, it is hardly possible that it could have been wholly so. We are entitled, therefore, to expect that "Shakespeare" appeared to his contemporaries as a man over whom the theatre and all that pertained to play-acting exercised an irresistible fascination.

Carlyle treats of this matter as though play-writing were but an incidental element in "Shakespeare's" work: almost an accident of circumstances, arising out of the material necessities of life. He "had to write for the Globe Playhouse: his great soul had to crush itself, as it could, into that and no other mould"[71]—the particular mould in which he worked having evidently no necessary connection with his distinctive genius. For what perversions of fundamental truths has not the orthodox view of the authorship been responsible! The world's greatest productions in a given art coming from a man to whom the art and its essential accessories furnished but an uncongenial medium of expression! His special domain chosen for him, not by the force of his peculiar genius, but by the need for money! If this proved true, the plays of Shakespeare would, from that point of view alone, probably remain for all time unique amongst the masterpieces of art. It is much more reasonable, however, to suppose that the dramatist was one who was prepared to give both himself and his substance to the drama, rather than one who was engaged in extorting a subsistence from it.

---

[71] Thomas Carlyle, *On Heroes, Hero-worship and the Heroic in History*, p. 102.

That he was one over whom the theatre exercised a strong attraction is, moreover, borne out by the contents of the plays themselves. There is no better key to the interests that stir the enthusiasm of poets than, on the one hand the imagery they employ, and on the other the passages in their works which arrest the attention of their readers and fix themselves in the popular memory. It hardly needs pointing out how frequently in Shakespeare's works, the simile of the "stage" recurs, and how commonly the passages are quoted. We must expect, therefore, to find the author of the writings well known as a literary and dramatic enthusiast.

Contrast to the orthodox Shakespeare.

To represent him as a man who, having made a snug competency for himself, left dramatic pursuits behind him voluntarily whilst still in the full enjoyment of his marvellous powers, abandoning some of his unfinished manuscripts to be finished by strangers and given to the world as his, in order that he might be at liberty to devote himself more exclusively to houses, lands and business generally, is to suggest a miracle of self-stultification in himself and an equal miracle of credulity in us. Yet this is the exact position into which the orthodox view forces so eminent a scholar and literary authority as Sir Sidney Lee. "Shakespeare," he says, "in middle life brought to practical affairs a singularly sane and sober temperament,"[72] acting on the following advice, "'when thou feelest thy purse well lined buy thou some piece of lordship in the country, that growing weary of playing, thy money may bring thee to dignity and reputation.' It was this prosaic course that Shakespeare followed."[73] "If in 1611 Shakespeare finally abandoned dramatic composition, there seems little doubt that he left with the manager of the company more than one play that others were summoned at a later date to

---

[72] Lee, *Life*, p. 192.
[73] Lee, *Life*, p. 192.

complete."[74] Thus must incongruities be piled increasingly upon one another if we are to make the man who has got himself credited with the authorship adjusted to the role that Fate has called upon him to play. Once, however, the old theory is repudiated we are bound to look for an author who believed with his whole soul in the greatness of drama and the high humanizing possibilities of the actor's vocation.

Known as a lyric poet.

Whether attention be directed to the contents of the dramas or to his other writings, no one will question his title to a foremost place amongst the lyric poets of his time. It is questionable whether any other dramatist has enriched his plays with an equal quantity—to say nothing of the superior quality—of lyrical verse; whilst his sonnets, *Venus and Adonis,* and other lyric poems, place him easily amongst the best of the craftsmen in that art. Now, although his contemporaries may not have known that he was producing masterpieces of drama, it is extremely improbable that his production of lyric verse was as completely concealed. He may have hidden lengthy poems like *Venus and Adonis* or *Lucrece,* or brought them out under a nom-de-plume. But that no fugitive pieces of lyric verse should ever have gained currency under his own name is hardly possible. The writer with the facile pen for lyric, is only too prone to throw out his spontaneous products lavishly, sometimes in a cruder form than his better judgment would approve. Whilst, therefore, he may have concealed the actual authorship in the case of works involving prolonged and arduous application, we may be sure that some of those short lyrics, which are the spontaneous expression of passing moods, would be known and appreciated. We may expect, therefore, that he was actually known as a writer of lyric verse.

At the same time it would be unreasonable to look for anything like a large volume of such poem in addition to the Shakespearean writings. This would have necessitated his living

---

[74] Lee, *Life,* p. 267.

an additional lifetime. A few scattered fragments of lyric verse, under his own name, is all that we should expect to find. Elizabethan poetry is, however, characterized by the mass of its lyric pieces of unknown or doubtful authorship. The mere fact that a person's name or initials are attached to a fragment is never a sufficient guarantee that he actually wrote it. Tradition alone, or the mere fact that it was found among his papers, may be the only ground upon which he is credited with the authorship. Nevertheless, after full allowance has been made for the peculiar conditions under which the writing and issuing of poetry was at that time conducted, it remains highly probable that the writer of Shakespeare's works has left something authentic published under his own name amongst the lyric poetry of the days of Queen Elizabeth.

Classical education.

In no matter has the hitherto accepted view of the authorship of the Shakespearean writings played such sad havoc with common sense as in the matter of the relationship of genius to learning. Place the documents before any mixed jury of educated, semi-educated, and ignorant men, men of practical common sense, and stupid men, and, unless for some prepossession, they would unanimously declare, without hesitation, that the writer was one whose education had been of the very best that the times could offer. And even a moderately educated set of men would assure us that it was not the mere bookish learning of the poor, plodding student who in loneliness had wrested from an adverse fate an education beyond what was enjoyed by his class. There is nothing in Shakespeare suggestive of the close poring over books by which a man of scanty educational advantages might have embellished his pages with learned allusions. Everything indicates a man in contact at every point with life itself, and to whom books were but the adjunct to an habitual intercourse with men of intellectual interests similar to his own. His is the learning which belonged to a man who added to the advantages of a first-class education at the start, a continued association with the best educated people of his day. No ordinary theory of genius would account for the production of the plays otherwise; the intervention of some preternatural agency would be required.

In respect of the leading feature of his learning one would judge it to have lain in the direction of classic poetry. There is "law" in his works, but it is open to question whether it is the law of a professional lawyer, or that of an intelligent man who had had a fair amount of important business to transact with lawyers, and was himself interested in the study of law as many laymen have been. It may be claimed that there is "medicine" in his writings, but it is more suggestive of the man accustomed to treat his own common ailments, than that of a medical man accustomed to handle patients. There are indications of the dawning movement of modern science in his works, but they are such as suggest a man alive to the intellectual currents of his time, but no enthusiast for a merely materialistic science. But over all these there presides constantly a dominant interest in classic poetry.

Summing up the general inferences treated in this chapter, supplemented by conclusions drawn from the preceding one, we may say of Shakespeare that he was:

1. A matured man of recognized genius.
2. Apparently eccentric and mysterious.
3. Of intense sensibility—a man apart.
4. Unconventional.
5. Not adequately appreciated.
6. Of pronounced and known literary tastes.
7. An enthusiast in the world of drama.
8. A lyric poet of recognized talent.
9. Of superior education—classical—the habitual associate of educated people.

CHAPTER IV

THE AUTHOR—SPECIAL CHARACTERISTICS

OUR object in the last chapter being to form a conception of some of the broader features of the life and character of Shakespeare, our present object must be to view the writings at closer quarters and with greater attention to details so as to deduce, if possible, some of his more distinctive characteristics.

Feudalism.

It is hardly necessary to insist at the present day that Shakespeare has preserved for all time, in living human characters, much of what was best worth remembering and retaining in the social relationship of the Feudal order of the Middle Ages. Whatever conclusion we may have to come to about his religion, it is undeniable that, from the social and political point of view, Shakespeare is essentially a medievalist. The following sentence from Carlyle may be taken as representative of much that might be quoted from several writers bearing in the same direction: "As Dante the Italian man was sent into our world to embody musically the Religion of the Middle Ages, the Religion of our Modern Europe, its Inner Life; so Shakespeare we may say embodies for us the Outer Life of our Europe as developed then, its chivalries, courtesies, humours, ambitions, what practical way of thinking, acting, looking at the world, men then had."[75]

When, therefore, we find that the great Shakespearean plays were written at a time when men were revelling in what they considered to be a newly-found liberation from Medievalism, it is evident that Shakespeare was one whose sympathies, and

---

[75] Carlyle, *On Heroes*, p. 94.

probably his antecedents, linked him on more closely to the old order than to the new: not the kind of man we should expect to rise from the lower middle-class population of the towns. Whether as a lord or a dependent we should expect to find him one who saw life habitually from the standpoint of Feudal relationships in which he had been born and bred: and in view of what has been said of his education it would, of course, be as lord rather than as a dependent that we should expect to meet him.

Shakespeare an aristocrat.

It might be, however, that he was only linked to Feudalism by cherished family traditions; a surviving representative, maybe, of some decayed family. A close inspection of his work, however, reveals a more intimate personal connection with aristocracy than would be furnished by mere family tradition. Kings and queens, earls and countesses, knights and ladies move on and off his stage "as to the manner born." They are no mere tinselled models representing mechanically the class to which they belong, but living men and women. It is rather his ordinary "citizens" that are the automata walking woodenly on to the stage to speak for their class. His "lower-orders" never display that virile dignity and largeness of character which poets like Burns, who know the class from within, portray in their writings. Even Scott comes much nearer to truth in this matter than does Shakespeare. It is, therefore, not merely his power of representing royalty and the nobility in vital, passionate characters, but his failure to do the same in respect to other classes that marks Shakespeare as a member of the higher aristocracy. The defects of the playwriter become in this instance more illuminating and instructive than do his qualities. Genius may undoubtedly enable a man to represent with some fidelity classes to which he does not belong; it will hardly at the same time weaken his power of representing truly his own class. In a great dramatic artist we demand universality of power within his province; but he shows that catholicity, not by representing human society in all its forms and phases, but by depicting our common nature in the entire range of its multiple and complex forces; and he does this best when he shows us that human nature at work in the classes with which he is most intimate. The suggestion of an aristocratic author for the plays is, therefore, the simple common sense of the situation, and is no more in opposition to modern democratic tendencies, as one writer loosely hints, than the belief that William Shakspere was indebted to aristocratic patrons and participated in the enclosure of common lands.

An aristocratic outlook upon life marks the plays of other dramatists of the time besides Shakespeare. These were known, however, in most cases to have been university men, with a pronounced contempt for the particular class to which William Shakspere of Stratford belonged. It is a curious fact, however, that a writer like Creizenach, who seems never to doubt the Stratfordian view, nevertheless recognizes that "Shakespeare" was more purely and truly aristocratic in his outlook than were the others. In a word, the plays which are recognized as having the most distinct marks of aristocracy about them, are supposed to have been produced by the playwright furthest removed from aristocracy in his origin and antecedents.

We feel entitled, therefore, to claim for Shakespeare high social rank, and even a close proximity to royalty itself.

Lancastrian Sympathies.

Assuming him to have been an Englishman of the higher aristocracy, we turn now to these parts of his writings that may be said to deal with his own phase of life, namely, his English historical plays, to seek for distinctive traces of position and personality. Putting aside the greater part of the plays *Henry VI*, parts 1 and 2 as not being from Shakespeare's pen, and also the first acts of *Henry VI*, part 3, for the same reason, we may say that he deals mainly with the troubled period between the upheaval in the reign of Richard II and the ending of the Wars of the Roses by the downfall of Richard III at the Battle of Bosworth. The outstanding feature of this work is his pronounced sympathy with the Lancastrian cause. Even the play of *Richard II*, which shows a measure of sympathy with the king whom the Lancastrians ousted, is full of Lancastrian partialities. "Shakespeare" had no sympathy with revolutionary movements and the overturning of established governments.

Usurpation of sovereignty would, therefore, be repugnant to him, and his aversion is forcibly expressed in the play; but Henry of Lancaster is represented as merely concerned with claiming his rights, desiring to uphold the authority of the crown, but driven by the injustice and perversity of Richard into an antagonism he strove to avoid. Finally, it is the erratic wilfulness of the king, coupled with Henry's belief that the king had voluntarily abdicated, that induces Bolingbroke to accept the throne. In a word, the play of *Richard II* is a kind of dramatic *apologia* for the Lancastrians. Then comes the glorification of Prince Hal, "Shakespeare's" historic hero. Henry VI is the victim of misfortunes and machinations, and is handled with great tenderness and respect. The play of *Richard III* lays bare the internal discord of the Yorkist faction, the downfall and destruction of the Yorkist arch-villain, and the triumph of Henry Richmond, the representative of the House of Lancaster, who had received the nomination and benediction of Henry VI. We might naturally expect, therefore, to find Shakespeare a member of some family with distinct Lancastrian leanings.

Italian enthusiasm.

Having turned our attention to the different classes of plays, we arc again faced with the question of his Italianism. Not only are we impressed by the large number of plays with an Italian setting or derived from Italian sources, but we feel that these plays carry us to Italy in a way that *Hamlet* never succeeds in carrying us to Denmark, nor his French plays in carrying us to France. Even in *Hamlet* he seems almost to go out of his way to drag in a reference to Italy. Those who know Italy and are familiar with the *Merchant of Venice* tell us that there are clear indications that Shakespeare knew Venice and Milan personally. However that may be, it is impossible for those who have had, at any time, an interest in nothing more than the language and literature of Italy, to resist the feeling that there is thrown about these plays an Italian atmosphere suggestive of one who knew and felt attracted towards the country. Everything bespeaks an Italian enthusiast.

Sport.

Going still more closely into detail, it has often been observed that Shakespeare's interest in animals is seldom that of the naturalist, almost invariably that of the sportsman; and some of the supporters of the Stratfordian tradition have sought to establish a connection between this fact and the poaching of William Shakspere. When, however, we look closely into the references we are struck with his easy familiarity with all the terms relating to the chase. Take Shakespeare's entire sportsman's vocabulary, find out the precise significance of each unusual term, and the reader will probably get a more distinct vision of the sporting pastimes of the aristocracy of that day than he would get in any other way. Add to this all the varied vocabulary relating to hawks and falconry, observe the insistence with which similes, metaphors and illustrations drawn from the chase and hawking appear throughout his work, and it becomes impossible to resist the belief that he was a man who had at one time found his recreation and delight in these aristocratic pastimes.

Music.

His keen susceptibility to the influence of music is another characteristic that frequently meets us; and most people will agree that the whole range of English literature may be searched in vain for passages that more accurately or more fittingly describe the charm and power of music than do certain lines in the pages of Shakespeare. The entire passage on music in the final act of *The Merchant of Venice*, beginning "Look how the floor of heaven," right on to the closing words, "Let no such man be trusted," is itself music, and is probably as grand a paean in honour of music as can be found in any language.

Money matters.

Nothing could well be clearer in itself, nor more at variance with what is known of the man William Shakspere than the dramatist's attitude towards money. It is the man who lends money gratis, and so "pulls down the rate of usuance" in Venice, that is the hero of the play just mentioned. His friend is the incorrigible spendthrift and borrower Bassanio, who has "disabled his estate by showing a more swelling port than his faint means would grant continuance," and who at last repairs his broken fortunes by marriage. Almost every reference to money and purses is of the loosest description, and, by implication, teach an improvidence that would soon involve any man's financial affairs in complete chaos. It is the arch-villain, Iago, who urges "put money in thy purse," and the contemptible politician, Polonius, who gives the careful advice "neither a borrower nor a lender be"; whilst the money-grubbing Shylock, hoist with his own petard, is the villain whose circumvention seems to fill the writer with an absolute joy.

It ought not to surprise us if the author himself turned out to be one who had felt the grip of the money-lender, rather than a man like the Stratford Shakspere, who, after he had himself become prosperous, prosecuted others for the recovery of petty sums.

Of the Stratford man, Pope asserts that "Gain not glory winged his roving flight." And Sir Sidney Lee amplifies this by saying that "his literary attainments and successes were chiefly valued as serving the prosaic end of providing permanently for himself and his daughters."[76] Yet in one of his early plays (*Henry IV*, part 2) "Shakespeare" expresses himself thus:

> How quickly nature falls into revolt
> When gold becomes her object.
> For this the foolish over-careful fathers

---

[76] Lee, *Life*, p. 288.

> Have broke their sleep with thoughts, their brains with care,
> Their bones with industry;
> For this they have engrossed and piled up
> The canker'd heaps of strange achieved gold.

From its setting the passage is evidently the expression of the writer's own thought rather than an element of the dramatization.

Finally we have, again in an early play, his great hero of tragic love, Romeo, exclaiming:

> There is thy gold, worse poison to men's souls,
> Doing more murders in this loathsome world
> Than these poor compounds.

In a word, the Stratfordian view requires us to write our great dramatist down as a hypocrite. The attitude of William Shakspere to money matters may have had about it all the "sobriety of personal aims and sanity of mental attitude."[77] claimed for it. In which case, the more clearly he had represented his own attitude in his works the greater would have been their fidelity to objective fact. Money is a social institution, created by the genius of the human race to facilitate the conduct of life; and, under normal conditions, it is entitled to proper attention and respect. Under given conditions, however, it may so imperil the highest human interests, as to justify an intense reaction against it, and even to call for repudiation and contempt from those moral guides, amongst whom we include the great poets, who are concerned with the higher creations of man's intellectual and moral nature. Such, we judge, was the dramatist's attitude to money.

Woman.

The points treated so far have been somewhat on the surface; and most, if not all, might be found adequately supported by other writers. There are, however, two other matters on which it would be well to have Shakespeare's attitude defined, if such were possible, before proceeding to the next stage of the enquiry. These are his mental attitude towards Woman, and his relation to Catholicism.

---

[77] Lee, *Life*, p. 288.

Ruskin's treatment of the former point in *Sesame and Lilies*[78] is well known, but not altogether convincing. He, and others who adopt the same line of thought, seem not sufficiently to discriminate between what comes as a kind of aura from the medieval chivalries and what is distinctly personal. Moreover, the business of a dramatist being to represent every variety of human character, it must be doubtful whether any characterization represents his views as a whole, or whether, indeed, it may not only represent a kind of utopian idealism. Some deference, too, must be paid by a playwriter to the mind and requirements of his contemporary public; and the literature of the days of Queen Elizabeth does certainly attest a respectful treatment of Woman at that period. In quotations from Shakespeare on this theme, however, one is more frequently met with suggestions of Woman's frailty and changeableness. In his greatest play, *Hamlet*, there are but two women; one weak in character, the other weak in intellect, and Hamlet trusts neither.

Shakespeare, however, is a writer of other things besides dramas. He has left us a large number of sonnets, and the sonnet, possibly more than any other form of composition, has been the vehicle for the expression of the most intimate thoughts and feelings of poets. Almost infallibly, one might say, do a man's sonnets directly reveal his soul. The sonnets of "Shakespeare," especially, have a ring of reality about them quite inconsistent with the fanciful non-biographical interpretation which Stratfordianism would attach to them.

Mistrust and affection.

Examining, then, these sonnets, we find that there are, in fact, two sets of them. By far the larger and more important set embracing no less than one hundred and twenty-six out of a total of one hundred and fifty-four, is addressed to a young man, and express a tenderness, which is probably without parallel in the recorded expressions of emotional attachment of one man to another. At the same time there occurs in this very set the

---

[78] John Ruskin, *Sesame and Lilies*, Lecture II: "Of Queens' Gardens."

following reference to woman:

> A woman's face with Nature's own hand painted,
> Hast thou, the master mistress of my passion;
> A woman's gentle heart, but not acquainted
> With shifting change, as is false woman's fashion;
> An eye more bright than theirs, less false in rolling.

The second set of sonnets, comprising only twenty-eight, as against one hundred and twenty-six in the first set, is probably the most painful for Shakespeare admirers to read, of all that "Shakespeare" has written. It is the expression of an intensely passionate love for some woman; but love of a kind which cannot be accurately described otherwise than as morbid emotion; a combination of affection and bitterness; tenderness, without a touch of faith or of true admiration.

> Two loves I have of comfort and despair,
> Which, like two spirits, do suggest me still.
> The better angel is a man right fair.
> The worser spirit, a woman, coloured ill.
>
> In loving thee [the woman] thou knowest I am forsworn,
>
>   *   *   *   *   *
>
> And all my honest faith in thee is lost.
>
> I have sworn thee fair and thought thee bright,
> Who art as black as hell and dark as night.

Whether this mistrust was constitutional or the outcome of unfortunate experiences is irrelevant to our present purpose. The fact of its existence is what matters. Whilst, then, we have comparatively so little bearing on the subject, and that little of such a nature, we shall not be guilty of over-statement if we say that though he was capable of great affection, and had a high sense of the ideal in womanhood, his faith in the women with whom he was directly associated was weak, and his relationship towards them far from perfect.

Catholicism.

To deduce the dramatist's religious point of view from his plays is perhaps the most difficult task of all. Taking the general religious conditions of his time into consideration, there are only two broad currents to be reckoned with. Puritanism had no doubt already assumed appreciable proportions as a further development of the Protestant idea; but, for our present purposes, the broader currents of Catholicism and Protestantism are all that need be considered. In view of the fact that Protestantism was at that time in the ascendant, whilst Catholicism was under a cloud, a writer of plays intended for immediate representation whose leanings were Protestant would be quite at liberty to expose his personal leanings, whilst a pronounced Roman Catholic would need to exercise greater personal restraint. Now it is impossible to detect in "Shakespeare" any Protestant bias or any support of those principles of individualism in which Protestantism has its roots. On the other hand, he seems as catholic as the circumstances of his times and the conditions under which he worked would allow him to be. Macaulay has the following interesting passage on the point:

> The partiality of Shakespeare for Friars is well known. In *Hamlet* the ghost complains that he died without extreme unction, and, in defiance of the article which condemns the doctrine of purgatory, declares that he is
>
> Confined to fast in fires,
> Till the foul crimes, done in his days of nature,
> Are burnt and purged away.
>
> These lines, we suspect, would have raised a tremendous storm in the theatre at any time during the reign of Charles the Second. They were clearly not written by a zealous Protestant for zealous Protestants.[79]

We may leave his attitude towards Catholicism at that; except to add that, if he was really a Catholic, the higher calls of his religion to devotion and to disciple probably met with only an indifferent response. It is necessary, moreover, to point out that Auguste Comte in his *Positive Polity* refers to "Shakespeare" as a sceptic.

---

[79] Macaulay, "Lord Burghley and His Times," p. 248.

Summary.

To the nine points enumerated at the end of the last chapter we may therefore add the following:

1. A man with Feudal connections.
2. A member of the higher aristocracy.
3. Connected with Lancastrian supporters.
4. An enthusiast for Italy.
5. A follower of sport (including falconry).
6. A lover of music.
7. Loose and improvident in money matters.
8. Doubtful and somewhat conflicting in his attitude to woman.
9. Of probable Catholic leanings, but touched with scepticism.

Such a characterization of Shakespeare as we have here presented was, of course, impossible so long as the Stratford tradition dominated the question; for there is scarcely a single point that is not more or less in contradiction to that tradition. Since, however, people have begun to throw off the dominance of the old theory in respect to the authorship of the plays, most, if not all, of the points we have been urging have been pointed out at one time or other by different writers; as well, no doubt, as other important points of difference which we have overlooked. If, then, it be urged that there is not a single original observation in the whole of these two chapters, then so much the better for the argument; for such a criticism would but add authority to the delineation and we should, moreover, feel that the statement had been kept freer from the influence of subsequent discoveries than we can hope to be the case.

Although these subsequent discoveries have doubtless affected in some degree the manner in which the present statement is made, the several points, along with other minor and more hypothetical matters, were roughly outlined before the search was begun; whilst the statement as here presented was written, substantially as it stands now, in the first days of the investigations: as soon, that is to say, as it seemed that the researches were going to prove fruitful. There are some of the above points which we should now be disposed to modify and others which we should like to develop. The appearance of others of them in the interpolated anti-Stratfordian chapter would under ordinary conditions have required their omission here. As, however, one of our objects is to represent something of the way in which the argument has developed almost spontaneously—in some respects one of the strongest evidences of its truth—we leave the statement, with what vulnerable points it contains, to remain as it is.

The various points are, indeed, the outcome of the labours and criticisms of many minds spread over a number of years, and it may be that the only thing original about the statement is the gathering together and tabulating of the various old points. So collected, these seem to demand such an aggregate and unusual combination of conditions that it is hardly probable that any man other than the actual author of the plays himself could possibly fulfil them all. When to this we add the further condition that the man answering to the description must also be situated, both in time and external circumstances, as to be consistent with the production of the work, we get the feeling that if such a man can be discovered it must be none other than the author himself.

With this we complete the first stage of our task which was to characterize the author from a consideration of the work.

CHAPTER V

The Search and Discovery

Time's glory is to calm contending Kings,
To unmask falsehood and bring truth to light.
(*Lucrece* 135)

AT this point I must ask for the reader's indulgence for a change in the method of exposition. What must be now stated is so purely a personal experience, that it will facilitate matters if, even at the risk of apparent egotism, I adopt frankly the First Person Singular. Perhaps, in view of certain admissions it will be necessary to make, it may become evident that there could be little ground for any egotism. At all events, the mode of presentation seems essential to the argument, and that, it appears to me, is all the justification it requires.

Choice of a guide.

In accordance with the plan upon which the investigation had been instituted, the author had been characterized from an examination of his works. The next step was to proceed to search for him. The method of search was to select from the various features some one which, by furnishing a crucial test and standard of measurement, would afford the surest guidance. Now, if there had been any likelihood of his having left other dramas under his own name, this would certainly have been the best line to follow. A little reflection, however, soon convinced me that not much was to be hoped for in this direction; for already the experts have been able to discriminate to a very large extent between what is really his and what is not his, in writings that, for centuries, had been regarded as pure Shakespearean work; and this process is going on progressively as the distinctive qualities of his work are being more clearly perceived. Consequently, had whole plays of his existed elsewhere it is natural to suppose that they would have been recognized before now.

The point which promised to be most fruitful in results, supposing he had left other traces of himself, was his lyric poetry. The reasons for this choice have already been indicated in the chapter in which the lyric powers of Shakespeare are discussed. It was, therefore, to the Elizabethan lyric poets that I must go.

This decision marked the second stage in the enquiry; I must now proceed to the third and most important, namely, the actual work of searching for the author.

Narrowing the operations.

Whether the scantiness of my own knowledge of this department of literature at the time was a hindrance or a help it is impossible now to say positively. Certainly, it was the very imperfection of my knowledge that decided the method of search, and this, along with a fortunate chance, was the immediate cause of whatever success has been achieved. In addition to "Shakespeare's" works, parts of Edmund Spenser's and Philip Sidney's poems were all that I could claim to know of Elizabethan poetry at the time. Beyond this I had only a dim sense of a vast, rich literary region that I had not explored, but in which a number of names were indiscriminately scattered.

To plunge headlong into this unexplored domain in search of a man, who, on poetic grounds alone—for that I deemed to be essential—might be selected as the possible author of the world's greatest dramas, seemed, at first, a well-nigh hopeless task. The only way was to compensate, if possible, my lack of knowledge by the adoption of some definite system. What was possibly a faulty piece of reasoning served at this point in good stead. I argued that when he entered upon the path of anonymity, wherein he had done his real life's work, he had probably ceased altogether to publish in his own name; and that, dividing his work into two parts, we should find the natural point of contact between the two, the point, therefore, at which discovery was most likely to take place, just where his anonymous work begins. Now the poet himself comes to our aid at this juncture. He calls his *Venus and Adonis*, published in 1593, under the name of William Shakespeare, "the first heir of my invention" (see the dedication to the Earl of Southampton). I must, therefore, try to work from this poem, to the work of some lyric writer of the same period.

The point of contact.

Turning to this "first heir" I read a number of stanzas with a vague idea that the reading might suggest some line of action. As I read, with the thought uppermost m my mind of it being an early work, kept in manuscript for some years and now published for the first time, I soon came to feel that the expression "first heir" was to be interpreted somewhat relatively; being possibly the first work of any considerable size: whereas the writer had as a matter of fact already become a practised hand in the particular form of stanza he employed. Except for the fact that "Shakespeare" has proved too blinding a light for most men's eyes we should long ago have rejected the idea that he actually "led off" on his literary career with so lengthy and finished a work as *Venus and Adonis*. At any rate the facility with which he uses the particular form of stanza employed in this poem pointed to his having probably used it freely in shorter lyrics. I decided, therefore, to work, first of all, on the mere form of the stanza. This may appear a crude and mechanical way of setting about an enquiry of this kind. It was, at any rate, a simple instrument and needed little skill in handling. All that was necessary was to observe the number and length of the lines—six lines, each of ten syllables—and the order of the rhymes: alternate rhymes for the first four lines, the whole finishing with a rhymed couplet.

The actual quest.

With this in mind I turned to an anthology of sixteenth-century poetry, and went through it, marking off each piece written in the form of stanza identical with that employed by Shakespeare in his *Venus and Adonis*. They turned out to be much fewer than I had anticipated. These I read through several times, familiarizing myself with their style and matter, rejecting first one and then another as being unsuitable, until at last only two remained.

An important poem.

One of these was anonymous; consequently I was left ultimately with only one: the following poem on "Women," by Edward de Vere, Earl of Oxford—the only poem by this author given in the anthology and also the only poem of his, as I afterwards noticed, that Palgrave gives in his *Golden Treasury*.

> If women could be fair and yet not fond,
>   Or that their love were firm not fickle, still,
> I would not marvel that they make men bond,
>   By service long to purchase their good will,
> But when I see how frail those creatures are,
> I muse that men forget themselves so far.
>
> To mark the choice they make, and how they change,
>   How oft from Phoebus do they flee to Pan,
> Unsettled still like haggards wild they range,
>   These gentle birds that fly from man to man,
> Who would not scorn and shake them from the fist
> And let them fly, fair fools, which way they list?
>
> Yet for disport we fawn and flatter both,
>   To pass the time when nothing else can please,
> And train them to our lure with subtle oath,
>   Till, weary of their wiles, ourselves we ease;
> And then we say, when we their fancy try,
> To play with fools, Oh what a fool was I.

I give this poem in full because of its importance to the history of English literature if the chief contention of this treatise can be established. Had I read it singly or with no such special aim as I then had, its distinctive qualities might not have impressed me as they did. But, reading it in conjunction with a large amount of contemporary verse whilst the cadences of the *Venus* stanzas were still running in my mind, its distinctive qualities were, on the one hand, enhanced by the force of contrast with other work of the same period, and on the other hand emphasized by a sense of its harmony with Shakespeare's work. Having, therefore, fixed provisionally on this poem I must first of all follow up the enquiry along the line it indicated until that line should prove untenable.

Seeking expert support.

Although the selection had been in a measure a personal exercise of literary judgment, it was part of the original plan that I should not, at any critical part of the investigation, rest upon my own private judgment where the issue was purely literary; and as this was a matter for the expert I must first of all seek some kind of an endorsement of my selection from literary authorities. Meanwhile the choice must be considered tentative. To those who are specialists in the literature of that age it may appear like the confession of colossal ignorance when I say that, far from having prepossessions in favour of Edward de Vere, although I must have come across his name before, it had never arrested my attention; and, so far as any knowledge of his personality and history is concerned, I had either never possessed it, or had quite forgotten everything I had ever known. Nor was I wishful to know more until the choice had been duly tested on purely poetic grounds. The name De Vere I knew to be that of an ancient house; the Earls of Oxford I remembered had appeared in English history in certain secondary connections; and the dates of the poet's birth and death (1550 and 1604), the only piece of information vouchsafed in the anthology, accorded sufficiently well, for the time being, with the general theory I had formed of the production and the issuing of the plays. He would be about forty years of age at the time when the plays began to appear, and, according to the generally accepted dating of them, the most and best of the work would be given to the world before his death.

Still these considerations might apply with equal force to others whose poems appeared in the collection, and therefore must not be allowed to exercise undue weight at this stage.

Turning to the literary section of several text books, and standard works of English history with varying amounts of reference to literature, I found all as silent as the grave in reference to the Earl of Oxford. Creighton's *Age of Elizabeth* has a special chapter on Elizabethan literature, but not a single word on this particular poet. Beesly's *Queen Elizabeth* barely mentions his name in a footnote of quite insignificant import that has nothing to do with poetry or literature. Altogether, I got the impression at first that he was almost an unknown man. So far the result was discouraging and I turned again to the anthology to try some of the other poems. None of them seemed to have the same Shakespearean grip as this one. In addition to the identity in the form of the stanza with that of *Venus and Adonis*, there was the same succinctness of expression, the same compactness and cohesion of ideas, the same smoothness of diction, the same idiomatic wording which we associate with "Shakespeare"; there was the characteristic simile of the hawks, and finally that peculiar touch in relation to women that I had noted in the sonnets.

First indications.

Again I consulted my books. Although Green, in the part of the *Short History* dealing with Elizabethan literature, makes no mention of the poet, I found in another part of his work the following sentence. Speaking of the Jesuit mission to England under Campion and Parsons, he says, "The list of nobles reconciled to the old faith by these wandering apostles was headed by Lord Oxford, Cecil's own son-in-law and the proudest among English peers."[80] It was impossible to avoid a touch of excitement in reading these words; for the first indications of the man justified the selection on two of the points of my characterization. Still it was not what I was immediately in search

---

[80] John Richard Green, *Short History*, vol. 2, p. 819.

of; and until the vital question of his acknowledged lyrical eminence was settled it was important not to be led away by what might turn out to be only a specious coincidence. All the other points were to be so many tests held in reserve as it were, to be applied only when his lyric credentials had been duly presented. For the time being then all available resources had been exhausted. The next step must be to consult such larger works as might be found in a reference library.

Dictionary of National Biography

On consulting the *Dictionary of National Biography* and turning to the Veres, or more properly the De Veres, I found myself confronted with quite a formidable number of them. By means of the Christian name and the dates, the one for whom I was seeking was speedily recognized: Edward de Vere, Seventeenth Earl of Oxford; the article being contributed by the Editor of the work, Sir Sidney Lee. This is perhaps as fitting a point as any at which to remark that, both by his biography of Edward de Vere in the article from which I am about to quote, as well as by his invaluable work, *A Life of William Shakespeare*, Sir Sidney Lee, convinced Stratfordian though he is, has furnished more material in support of my constructive argument than any other single modern writer. Although differing widely from his general conclusions I do not wish therefore in any way to stint my acknowledgment of indebtedness to his researches and opinions upon important questions of Shakespearean literature.

Selection justified.

Skimming lightly over the article at first, with the attention directed towards the one thing for which I was searching, I nevertheless felt some elation as I ran up against new facts bearing upon other aspects of the enquiry. Then came the following sentences, every word of which, in view of the conception I had formed of "Shakespeare," read like a complete justification of the selection I had made.

Oxford, despite his violent and perverse temper, his eccentric taste in dress, and his reckless waste of substance, *evinced a genuine taste in music and wrote verses of much lyric beauty.* . . .

Puttenham and Meres reckon him *among the best for comedy* in his day; but though he was a patron of players *no specimens of his dramatic productions survive.*

A sufficient number of his poems is extant *to corroborate Webbe's comment,* that he was the *best of the courtier poets* of the early days of Queen Elizabeth, and that 'in the rare devices of poetry he may challenge to himself the title of the most excellent amongst the rest.'[81]

I venture to say that if only such of those terms as are here used to describe the character and quality of his work were submitted without name or leading epithet to people, who only understood them to apply to some Elizabethan poet, it would be assumed immediately that Shakespeare was meant. We have in these words a contemporary opinion that he was the *best* of these poets, and we have a modern authority of no less weight than Sir Sidney Lee corroborating this judgment from a consideration of the poems themselves.

All that I wanted, for the time being, on the first issue, I had found; and so I was at liberty to go over the whole of the article, to see to what extent the Earl of Oxford fulfilled the other conditions belonging, as I had judged, to the authorship of Shakespeare's works. In making the selection the enquiry had passed its third stage. The fourth was the testing of the selection by reference to the characterization outlined in the first stage.

Competing solutions.

Although, in the course of subsequent enquiries, difficulties have presented themselves, as was inevitable, none of these has ever raised any insurmountable objections to the theory of Edward de Vere being the author of Shakespeare's works; whilst, as we shall see, the evidence in favour of the theory has steadily accumulated. Other names, too, have presented themselves or have been suggested by other writers as possible alternatives, and

---

[81] Sir Sidney Lee, "Vere, Edward," *Dictionary of National Biography*, vol. 58, p. 228.

I have not hesitated to consider such cases most carefully. These, however, have always in my own view broken down readily and completely, and their very failure has only served to add weight to the claims of De Vere. Such cases I do not, as a rule, discuss in full, and thus an important element of negative evidence will be missed so far as the reader is concerned. It is of first importance, however, that he should realize the precise extent of the evidence upon which the choice was made; the great mass of the evidence we shall have presently to submit, coming as it did subsequently to the selection, forms such a sequence and accumulation of coincidences, that if the manner of its discovery is clearly apprehended, only one conclusion seems possible.

CHAPTER VI

THE CONDITIONS FULFILLED

As it will be necessary to discuss the life and character of Edward de Vere from a totally different standpoint from that of Sir Sidney Lee's article in the *Dictionary of National Biography*, and also to add particulars derived from other sources, we shall, at present, in order to avoid as much unnecessary repetition as possible, merely point out the numerous instances in which the portraiture answers to the description of the man for whom we have been seeking.

Personal traits.

Although we are not given much information as to what his "eccentricity" consisted in, beyond the squandering of his patrimony, the distinctiveness of his dress, and his preference for his Bohemian literary and play-acting associates, rather than the artificial and hypocritical atmosphere of a court frequented by ambitious self-seekers, it is clear that in those latter circles he had made for himself a reputation as an eccentric, and as a man apart. When, therefore, we are told that his eccentricities grew with his years, we may take it to imply that this preference became accentuated as he grew older, that he became less in touch with social conventionality, more deeply immersed in his special interests and in the companionship of those who were similarly occupied.

His impressionability is testified by his quickness to detect a slight and his readiness to resent it, whilst his evident susceptibility to perfumes and the elegancies of dress, involving, no doubt, colour sensitiveness, bespeak that keenness of the senses which contributes so largely to extreme general sensibility.

Connected with these traits is his undoubted fondness for,

and a superior taste in, music. The matter is twice referred to. The first instance is in connection with his education, and from this reference it appears as if music had not formed part of the scheme of education which others had mapped out for him, and that his musical training was therefore the outcome of his own natural bent and choice. The second reference is the passage quoted in the last chapter, from which it appears that his musical taste was of so pronounced a character as to secure special mention in the records of him that have been handed down, notwithstanding their extreme meagreness.

His looseness in money matters, and what appears like a complete indifference to material possessions, is undoubtedly one of the most marked features of his character. So long as he had money to spend or give away, or lands which he could sell to raise money, he seems to have squandered lavishly; much of it, evidently, on literary men and on dramatic enterprises. Consequently, from being one of the foremost and wealthiest of English noblemen he found himself ultimately in straitened circumstances.

Personal circumstances.

His connection with play-actors and the drama was not the superficial and evanescent interest of a wealthy patron. It was a matter in which he was actively engaged for many years. He had his own company, with which he both toured in the provinces, and established himself for some years in London. It was quite understood that his company was performing plays which he was himself producing. It is evident, too, that he made a name for himself in the production of comedies and that the celebrity he enjoyed in this respect came not merely from the masses, but from the literary men of the time. On the other hand, we are informed in the article that "*no specimens of his dramatic productions survive*"[82]—a most mysterious circumstance in view of the vast mass of drama of all kinds and qualities that the Elizabethan age has bequeathed to us.

---

[82] Lee, "Vere, Edward," p. 218.

Of his family, we learn from the first series of articles on the De Veres, that it traced its descent in a direct line from the Norman Conquest and that for five and a half centuries the direct line of male descent had never once been broken. As a boy, not only had he been a prominent figure about Elizabeth's court, but from the age of twelve he was a royal ward, and may be said to have been actually brought up at court near the person of the Queen herself. The irksomeness to him of court life seems to have manifested itself quite early in manhood and he made several efforts to escape from it.

His education was conducted first of all by private tutors among whom were celebrated classical scholars. He was a resident at Cambridge University and ultimately held degrees in both universities. We may add here, what is not mentioned in the article, that his poems are replete with classical allusions, which come to him as spontaneously as the figure of a field mouse, a daisy, or a haggis comes to Burns.

So keen was his desire for travel that when permission was refused him he set the authorities at defiance and ran away; only to be intercepted and brought back. When at last he obtained permission to go abroad he speedily made his way to Italy; and so permanent upon him was the effect of his stay there, that he was lampooned afterwards as an "Italianated Englishman."

Summary of points attested.

The article in the *Dictionary of National Biography* testifies therefore to the following points:

1. His high standing as a lyric poet.
2. His reputation for eccentricity.
3. His highly strung sensibility.
4. His being out of sympathetic relationship with conventional life.
5. His maturity (1590) and genius.
6. His literary tastes.
7. His practical enthusiasm for drama.

8. His classic education and association with the best
   educated men of his time.
9. His belonging to the higher aristocracy.
10. His feudal ancestry.
11. His interest in and direct personal knowledge of Italy.
12. His musical tastes.
13. His looseness in money matters.

Remaining points.

Four points insufficiently supported in the article are:
1. His interest in sport.
2. His Lancastrian sympathies.
3. His distinctive bearing towards woman.
4. His attitude towards Catholicism.

The eighteenth point—inadequate appreciation—needs no special treatment, being involved in the problem itself and in any proposed solution to it.

Before proceeding to the next step in the investigation we shall finish this section by adducing other evidence and authority for the four points mentioned above.

Sport.

1. In relation to sport we notice—and this is really the point that matters—that his poems, few as they are, bear decided witness to the same interest. The haggard hawk, the stricken deer, the greyhound, the mastiff, the fowling nets and bush-beating are all figures that appear in his lyric verses. In addition to this we notice that his father, John de Vere, 16th Earl of Oxford, who died when Edward was twelve years of age, had quite a reputation as a sportsman, and until his death Edward was, of course, living with him. The article from which we first quoted mentions his interest in learning to shoot and to ride, so that there is abundant evidence of his familiarity with those sporting pastimes which Shakespeare's works amply illustrate.

Lancastrianism.

2. Though no statement of his actual sympathies with the Lancastrian cause has been found, we are assured by several writers that he was proud of his ancient lineage, which, taken along with the following passage, on the relationship of the De Veres to the Lancastrian cause, may be accepted as conclusive on the subject:

> John the 11th Earl [of Oxford] was attainted and beheaded in 1461, suffering for his loyalty to the Lancastrian line. His son John was restored to the dignity in 1464, but was himself attainted in 1474 in consequence of the active part he had taken on the Lancastrian side during the temporary restoration of Henry VI in 1470. . . . [He] distinguished himself as the last of the supporters of the cause of the red rose, which he maintained in the castle of St. Michael's Mount in Cornwall for many months after the rest of the kingdom had submitted to Edward IV. . . . Having been mainly instrumental in bringing Henry [VII] to the throne he was immediately restored to the Earldom of Oxford, and also to the office of Lord Chamberlain which he enjoyed until his death in 1513.[83]

Woman.

3. So far as his attitude towards woman is concerned, the poem already quoted in full is sufficient evidence of that deficiency of faith which we have pointed out as marking the Shakespeare sonnets; the very terms employed being as nearly identical as Shakespeare ever allowed himself in two separate utterances on one topic. Then that capacity for intense affection combined with weakness of faith which is one of the peculiarities of Shakespeare's mind, has not, so far as we are aware, so close a parallel anywhere in literature as in the poems of Edward de Vere. It is not merely in an occasional line, but is the keynote of much of his poetry. Indeed we may say that it probably lies at the root of a great part of the misfortune and mystery in which his life was

---

[83] John Gough Nichols, "On the Descent of the Earldom of Oxford," *Archaeological Journal*, vol. 9, no. 1, 1852, p. 24.

involved, and may indeed afford an explanation for the very existence of the Shakespeare mystery.

Only when these poems shall have become as accessible as Shakespeare's sonnets will this mental correspondence be fully appreciated. Meanwhile we give a few lines each from a separate poem:

> For she thou [himself] lovest is sure thy mortal foe.

> O cruel hap and hard estate that forceth me to love my foe.

> The more I sought the less I found
> Yet mine she meant to be.

> That I do waste, with others, love
> That hath myself in hate

> Love is worse than hate and eke more harm hath done.

With these lines in mind all that is necessary is to read the last dozen of Shakespeare's sonnets, in order to appreciate the spiritual identity of the author or authors in this particular connection.

Religion.

So far as the last point, his attitude to Catholicism, is concerned, the quotation we have already given from Green's *Short History* is all that is really necessary.[84] The fact that his name appears at the head of a list of noblemen who professed to be reconciled to the old faith shows his leanings sufficiently well for us to say of him, as Macaulay says of Shakespeare, that he was not a zealous Protestant writing for zealous Protestants. When, further, we find that his father had professed Catholicism, it is not unlikely that on certain sentimental grounds his leaning was that way. Roman Catholicism would, moreover, be the openly professed religion of his home life during his first eight years. There is also evidence in the State Papers of the time that the English Catholics abroad were at one crisis looking to him and to

---

[84] See footnote 80, p. 110.

the Earl of Southampton for support. At the same time it is not improbable that intellectually he was touched with the scepticism which appears to have been current in dramatic circles at that time, for amongst the charges made against him by one adversary was that of irreligion: the name "atheist" being given him by another (State papers). Classic paganism, medievalism and scepticism, in spite of the contradiction the combination seems to imply, can certainly all be more easily traced in him than can Protestantism; and in this there is a general correspondence between his mind and that of "Shakespeare."

On all the points then which we set before ourselves in entering upon the search, we find that Edward de Vere fulfils the conditions, and the general feeling with which we finish this stage of our enquiry is this, that if we have not actually discovered the author of Shakespeare's works we have at any rate alighted upon a most exceptional set of resemblances.

We have thus, in a general way, carried the enquiry successfully through four of its stages, and completed the *a posteriori* section of our argument.

Note.

In the contemporary State Papers of Rome there is a list of English nobility, classified as (i) Catholics, (ii) of Catholic leanings, (iii) Protestants. Oxford's name appears in the second group.

CHAPTER VII

EDWARD DE VERE AS LYRIC POET

IN proceeding from an examination of Shakespeare's work to search for the man himself we made lyric poetry the starting point, and the crucial consideration in attempting to establish his identity. Similarly, in reversing the process, that is to say in proceeding *a priori* from Edward de Vere to the work of Shakespeare, which must be the longest and most decisive section of the argument, we again begin with lyric poetry. We take the lyric poetry of Edward de Vere and see how far it justifies the theory of his being the real "Shakespeare."

Expert testimony.

Up to the present we have had before us the single poem and a few odd lines of Oxford's supported by the testimony of the *Dictionary of National Biography.* It becomes necessary first of all to obtain further testimony as to his poetic powers and characteristics, and then to see to what extent others of his poems warrant his being chosen as the writer of Shakespeare's work.

In the *Cambridge History of English Literature*—the section being written by Harold H. Child, sometime scholar of Brasenose, Oxford—there occurs the following reference to a collection of poems called *The Phoenix' Nest.* "The Earl of Oxford has a *charming* lyric."[85] Most of the other contributors are simply enumerated. Oxford, however, it will be noticed, is singled out for a special compliment.

Professor Courthope

Again, we would draw special attention to the following excerpts from the *History of English Poetry* by W. J. Courthope,

---

[85] Harold H. Child, "The Song-Books and Miscellanies," *Cambridge History of English Literature*, vol. 4, p. 135.

C.B., M.A., D.Litt. (Professor of Poetry at the University of Oxford):

> Edward de Vere, Seventeenth Earl of Oxford, . . . a great patron of literature . . . His own verses are distinguished for their wit . . . and terse ingenuity. . . . His studied concinnity of style is remarkable. . . . He was not only witty himself but the cause of wit in others. . . . Doubtless he was proud of his illustrious ancestry. . . . . He was careful in verse at any rate to conform to the external requirements of chivalry, but in later years his turn for epigram seems to have prevailed over his chivalrous sentiments.[86]

It is interesting to notice in passing that he is described in words that Shakespeare puts into the mouth of Falstaff, "I am not only witty in myself but the cause that wit is in others" (*II Henry IV*, I.2).

In another passage in the same work we are told that the court littérateurs were divided into two parties, one headed by Philip Sidney, and the other by the Earl of Oxford, "a great favourer of the Euphuists and himself a poet of some merit in the courtly Italian vein."[87] This rivalry between Philip Sidney and the Earl of Oxford touches our problem somewhat closely and will have to be referred to later. It is important at present as affording testimony to Oxford's recognized poetic eminence and to his Italian affinities. It also comes as a reminder that it was to Oxford that Lyly dedicated his *Euphues and his England*, and affords a sufficient explanation of that familiarity with Euphuism which is noticed in Shakespeare, if we credit Oxford with being Shakespeare, but is very difficult to account for in William Shakspere of Stratford.

There remains one other striking fact connected with these references to the Earl of Oxford in Professor Courthope's work. It will be remembered that we took the form of the stanza in *Venus and Adonis* as our first guide in the search. Now Professor Courthope quotes three separate stanzas of Oxford's work and all

---

[86] W. J. Courthope, *History of English Poetry*, vol. II, pp. 311-312.
[87] Courthope, *History of English Poetry*, vol. II, p. 211.

these are identical with that of Shakespeare's *Venus* and Oxford's on "Women," which gave us our first point of contact. The poem on which we had alighted was therefore no isolated effort in that particular form of versification. It was a familiar and practised form in which he evidently excelled, just as had been noticed in the case of Shakespeare.

Edmund Spenser.

In collecting corroboration of De Vere's poetic eminence it is specially fitting that the testimony of so eminent a poet as Edmund Spenser, second only to Shakespeare in that poetic age, should be added. In the series of sonnets with which he prefaces the *Fairie Queen*, there is one addressed to the Earl of Oxford, wherein occurs the following passage:

> The antique glory of thine ancestry,
>   *   *   *   *
> And eke thine own long living memory
> Succeeding them in true nobility,
> And also for the love which thou dost bear,
> To the 'Heliconion imps'*, and they to thee.
> They unto thee, and thou to them most dear.

Dr. Grosart's collection.

Valuable as is the testimony which we have adduced it cannot absolve us from the necessity of knowing the poems themselves and of subjecting them to a very careful examination, for this must form the crux of a very great deal of future investigation. It is greatly to be regretted, therefore, that these poems have not been readily accessible to everyone. For the most part they have been scattered amongst various anthologies; a mode of publishing poetry characteristic of the Elizabethan age. Dr. Grosart, however, in 1871 gathered together all the extant recognized poems of the Earl of Oxford and published them in the *Fuller Worthies' Library*. Some of these poems had appeared in old anthologies, others had only existed in manuscript, and were

---

* Looney's note: The Muses.

published for the first time by Dr. Gorsart. It is desirable, therefore, that all who are interested in English literature may before long be in possession of the entire collection.

There are, in all, only twenty-two short poems (Dr. Grosart numbers them up to twenty-three, but number eight is omitted) and the biographical introduction is possibly the shortest with which any similar collection was ever presented to the world. It explains its own brevity, however, and is of great significance from the point of view of this enquiry. "An unlifted shadow," he remarks, "lies across his memory. Park in his edition of *Royal and Noble Authors* has done his utmost, but that utmost is meagre."[88] "Our collection of his poems," he concludes, "will prove a pleasant surprise, it is believed, to most of our readers. They are not without touches of the true Singer and there is an atmosphere of graciousness and culture about them that is grateful."[89]

We have already, in the chapter in which we described the search, had to mention the contemporary testimonies of Meres, Puttenham, and Webbe, and also a modern authority—Sir Sidney Lee. Meres and Puttenham deal specially with his dramatic preeminence, mentioning him as amongst the "best for comedy." Therefore, leaving this on one side and confining ourselves to his lyric credentials, we may sum up the matter thus:

Summary

   Contemporary:

      1. Edmund Spenser.

         One most dear to the Muses.

      2. Webbe.

         Best of the courtier poets. In the rare devices of poetry the most excellent amongst the rest.

   Modern:

      1. Sir Sidney Lee.

         Corroborates Webbe's statement—much lyric beauty.

      2. Professor W. J. Courthope, C.B., M.A., D.Litt.

---

[88] Alexander B. Grosart, *Fuller Worthies' Library*, vol. 4, p. 359.
[89] Grosart, *Fuller Worthies'*, vol. 4, p. 359.

Concinnous, terse, ingenious, epigrammatic—leader
of a party of poets.
3. *Cambridge History of English Literature*
(Harold H. Child)
Charming.
4. Dr. Grosart.
Gracious, cultured, true singer.

Oxford's early poetry.

Looking over the notes appended to the separate poems of
Dr. Grosart's collection we find that these poems fulfil one very
important condition which, at the outset, we imagined would
belong to the lyric work which Shakespeare might have published
in his own name. Notwithstanding the rare ability they show, and
several true Shakespearean characteristics, they are for the most
part early poems. Many of them are proved to have been in
existence when the writer was about twenty-six years of age. How
long before that time they were in existence, or how many others
which are not so attested may also have existed then, we cannot
say. Most of these others, and it is only a small collection to begin
with, bear unmistakable internal evidence of belonging to the
same early period. Moreover, De Vere is spoken of as "the best
of the courtier poets of *the early part* of Queen Elizabeth's
reign."[90] As, however, he lived right on to the end of the reign,
and into the reign of James I, it is evident that the poetry for
which he is celebrated is regarded as belonging to his early life.
Direct corroboration of this theory is found in the following
passage from Arthur Collins's *Historical Collections of Noble
Families*, published in 1752. "He [Edward de Vere] was *in his
younger days* an excellent poet and comedian, as several of his
compositions, which were made public, showed; which I presume
are now lost or worn out."[91]

---

[90] Lee, "Vere, Edward," p. 228.
[91] Arthur Collins, *Historical Collections of Noble Families*. The original reads, "He
was, in his younger days, an excellent poet and comedian, as several of his
compositions that were made public showed, which I presume are now lost and
worn out."

Hidden productions.

Now the assumption with which we set out was that if we found writings under the true name of the author of Shakespeare's works, it would be mainly his early works, issued prior to his assuming a disguise. As we examine this early poetry of De Vere it becomes impossible to believe that a writer possessed of the genius that these verses manifest could possibly have stopped producing early in his manhood, unless, of course, he had suddenly dropped his literary interests and directed his energies into another channel. With De Vere, however, the continuance, or rather the intensification of his literary interests in later years is amply proved. He was sharing the Bohemian life of literary men, he was running his own company of play-actors; some of the plays which they were staging were quite understood to be from his own pen; and although he is spoken of as "the best in comedy" we are also told that "none of his plays have survived": that they have become "lost or worn out."

The actual amount of poetry which is recognized as his is such as one with such a faculty might have written within a single twelvemonth, although his contemporary says that "in the rare devices of poetry he may be considered the most excellent amongst the rest." It is evident, therefore, that in Edward de Vere we have a writer of both drama and lyric poetry who published under his own name only a small part of what he produced, however he may have disposed of the remainder. This point will receive further corroboration when we come to deal with the relationship of the poet Spenser to our problem.

Two counterparts of one career.

Everything points to his having, after the first period of poetic output, deliberately thrown a veil over his subsequent work, whilst in "Shakespeare" we have a writer who we are justified in supposing assumed anonymity in his maturity, leading off with an elaborate and highly finished poem of about two hundred stanzas. These two facts alone, in work of such exceptional character, if not simply the counterparts one of the other, constitutes alone one of the most remarkable coincidences in the history of literature. When to this we add the fact that the dates in the respective cases are such as to fit in exactly with the theory of one work being but the continuation of the other, Oxford being, as has been remarked, about forty when the Shakespearean dramas began to appear, and having filled in the interim with just the kind of experiences necessary to enable him to produce the dramas, it is difficult to resist the conviction, on this ground alone, that it is indeed but one writer with whom we are dealing.

And, so far as that mysteriousness is concerned which we attributed to Shakespeare, it must be admitted that the sudden nonappearance of work from such a pen as that of De Vere's is as mysterious as the subsequent appearance of the "Shakespeare" poems and dramas.

Literary development.

Now although the authority we have quoted for Edward de Vere's poetic eminence may appear ample there is nevertheless a special caution to be observed in regard to it. Assuming that he is the author of Shakespeare's plays it will still be necessary to distinguish between his work as Edward de Vere and his work as "Shakespeare." The former belonging mainly to his early manhood, and the latter to his maturity, we must expect to find a corresponding difference in the work. How vast may be the difference between a man's early and his later literary style can be seen by contrasting Carlyle's first literary essays with *Sartor* or his *French Revolution*. We must not, therefore, expect to find Oxford ranked spontaneously with Shakespeare; especially as the Shakespearean work is primarily dramatic, whereas we have not a scrap of dramatic work published under the name of Oxford. All that we are entitled to expect is some marked correspondence in the domain of lyric poetry, and a reasonable promise of the Shakespearean work in general. Of these we have at least some evidence, in the verses already quoted, and in the testimony that experts have offered as to the distinctive qualities of his poetry.

Great literary transition.

There is, however, another very important fact to be taken into consideration. Between the time when Edward de Vere produced his earliest poems and the period of the production of the Shakespearean dramas (roughly the interval between 1580 and 1590), a very marked change had come over the character of English literature as a whole. The nature of this change can best be gathered from the following passage from Dean Church's *Life of Spenser*: "The ten years from 1580 to 1590 present . . . a picture of English poetry of which, though there are gleams of a better hope . . . the general character is feebleness, fantastic absurdity, affectation and bad taste. Who could suppose what was preparing under it all? But the dawn was at hand."[92] During the next ten years, 1590-1600, "there burst forth suddenly a new poetry, which with its reality, depth, sweetness, and nobleness took the world captive. The poetical aspirations of the Englishmen of the time had found at last adequate interpreters, and their own national and unrivalled expression."[93]

This vital change, then, was preparing in England between the time when Edward de Vere produced his early poetry and the time when the Shakespearean dramas appeared. Such a change in the national literature we must naturally expect to find reflected in some degree in his writings. The roots of the matter may, however, be even deeper than this. In making the contrast between the two periods Dean Church cites Philip Sidney's *Defense of Poesie* as representing the earlier and feebler period, and the "rude play houses with their troops of actors, most of them profligate and disreputable"[94] as being the source of the later and more virile movement.

---

[92] Church, *Spenser*, p. 34.
[93] Church, *Spenser,* p. 35.
[94] Church, *Spenser*, p. 35.

Transition embodied in De Vere.

Now the ten years mentioned by Dean Church corresponds generally to what we shall speak of as the middle period of the life of Edward de Vere as a writer. It is the period immediately following upon his first poetic output, and it was during these years that he was in active and habitual association with these very troupes of play-actors, whilst the third period of his life synchronizes exactly with the sudden outburst of the great Shakespearean dramas. In his first literary period he is the recognized chief of a party of court poets, and the rival of Philip Sidney. As to who his fellows were, there is very little information to be had. If, however, we compare his poetry with the work of Sidney we can only account for Sidney's being considered in any sense a rival by the fact that the feeble affected style of Sidney was in vogue at the time. What distinguishes Oxford's work from contemporary verse is its strength, reality, and true refinement. When Philip Sidney learnt to "look into his heart and write," he only showed that he had at last learnt a lesson that his rival had been teaching him.

The reader may or may not be able to agree with the ideas and sentiments expressed by Oxford, but he will be unable to deny that every line written by the poet is a direct and real expression of himself in terms at once forceful and choice and no mere reflection of some fashionable pose. Even in these early years he was the pioneer of realism in English poetry. In his middle period he was a leading force in those dramatic circles from which was to emerge that realist literature so aptly characterized by Dean Church; so that, whoever the real author of Shakespeare's work may have been, that work represents the triumph of the De Vere spirit in poetry over the movement which claimed Sidney as its head. It will also be the triumph of his matured conceptions over his youthful compliance with conventional standards, in so far as he may have complied with them; some measure of such compliance being almost inevitable in youth.

We have already had to remark his restiveness under all kinds of restraints imposed by the artificiality of court life and his strong bent towards that Bohemian society within which were stirring the energetic forces making for reality, mingled with much evil in life and literature. Having been pre-eminent amongst the lyric poets in his early years, and prominent in the dramatic movement of his middle period, he is the natural representative and probably even the personal embodiment and original source of the transition by which the lyric poetry of the early days of Queen Elizabeth was merged in the drama of Elizabeth's, and his own later years; and before he died he witnessed the beginning of the decline of that great dramatic and literary efflorescence. These matters we believe to have a profound significance in relation to the problem before us.

Oxford's style and Shakespeare's.

When the necessary matter is readily accessible to the public it ought to be possible to read these verses of De Vere's alongside such contemporary poems as appear in Dr. Grosart's volumes. Then their distinctive qualities will be more than ever apparent. Poems by Sir Edward Dyer, Lord Vaux, The Earl of Essex and others, such as may be found in the *Fuller Worthies' Library*, though by no means mediocre or negligible, lack the distinctiveness of De Vere's poetry and fail to grip and hold the mind in the same way as do these early productions of the Earl of Oxford. That terse epigrammatic style, on which all readers comment, is the index of a mind that sees things in sharply defined outline and fastens itself firmly on to realities, this being further assisted by a complete mastery over the resources of the language employed, so that ideas do not have to force themselves through clouds of words.

If to these qualities we add an intense sensibility to all kinds of external impressions, and a faculty of passionate response, brought to the service of clear, intellectual perceptions we shall have seized hold of the outstanding features of De Vere's mentality. The result is the production of poems which impress the mind with a sense of their unity. The ideas cohere, following one another in a natural sequence, and leave in the reader's mind a sense of completeness and artistic finish.

That this concinnity is characteristic of Shakespeare's mind and work needs no insisting on at the present day. It is one of the distinctive marks of the individual sonnets of Shakespeare and we fear a much rarer feature of reflective poems than it ought to be; the lack of it being responsible for that distressing feeling of "jumpiness" so frequently experienced in reading works of this order. In this matter of cohesion and unity we have certainly met with no similar correspondence between Shakespeare and any other of the many Elizabethan poets whose work we have been constrained to read in the course of this enquiry, nor any other poet with the same vast range of sentiment between charming love lyric and violently passionate verses.

Richness of imagery.

Again, as there are no hazy atmospheres about the images which such a mind employs and no words are wasted in struggling to define, we get quite a wealth of images presented to the mind in rapid succession. In reading the poems of De Vere, as in reading the works of Shakespeare, one lives in a world of similes and metaphors. In both cases there is a wealth of appropriate classical allusions; but this is mingled harmoniously with an equal wealth of illustration drawn from the common experiences and what appear like the personal pursuits of life.

Allied possibly to these mental qualities is the colour consciousness which is observable in both groups of writings. There is also the attendant sensibility to flowers, the favourite flowers in both cases being the lily, the rose, and the violet.

Oxford's character in his writings.

Turning from these mental indications to the matter of moral dispositions, we find in the poems the impress of a character quite above what one would gather either from the biography in the *Dictionary of National Biography*, or from the scattered references to him in other works. There is, moreover, in addition to the

poems in Dr. Grosart's collection, a letter written by the Earl of
Oxford and attached to one of the poems, which gives us a
glimpse into the nature of the man himself as he was in these early
years. Whatever may have been the pose he thought fit to adopt
in dealing with some of the men about Elizabeth's court, this
letter bears ample testimony to the generosity and largeness of his
disposition, the clearness and sobriety of his judgment, and the
essential manliness of his actions and bearing towards literary men
whom he considered worthy of encouragement. His poems may
in a measure reflect the mannerisms of his day, but in the letter
we get a glimpse of the man himself; and if he comes to be
acclaimed as Shakespeare this letter will be an invaluable treasure
as the first, and it may prove the only, Shakespearean letter
bearing upon literary matters and cast in literary form, if we except
the dedications of his poems to Southampton. The fragments we
get of Oxford's letters in the Calendered State Papers and other
contemporary manuscripts are generally in a formal business cast
with only occasional poetic or literary flashes.

Oxford's prose.

As a letter it is, of course, prose; but it is the prose of a genuine
poet: its "terse ingenuity," wealth of figurative speech, and even
its musical quality being almost as marked as they are in his verse.
We subjoin a few passages, asking the reader to consider that the
writer was but twenty-six years old when the letter was published.
It has reference to a translation that had been submitted to him,
though apparently not intended for publication, but which was
published by his orders—presumably, therefore, at his expense.

The Bedingfield letter.

After I had perused your letters, good Master Bedingfield,
finding in them your request far differing from the desert of your
labour, I could not choose but greatly doubt, whether it were
better for me to yield to your desire or execute mine own intention
towards the publishing of your book. . . .

At length I determined it were better to deny your unlawful
request, than to grant or condescend to the concealment of so
worthy a work. Whereby, as you have been profited in the

translating, so many may reap knowledge by the reading of the same. . . . What doth it avail a mass of gold to be continually imprisoned in your bags and never to be employed to your use: I do not doubt even you so think of your studies and delightful Muses. What do they avail if you do not participate them to others? . . . What doth avail the vine unless another delighteth in the grape? What doth avail the rose unless another took pleasure in the smell? . . .

Why should this man be esteemed more than another but for his virtue, through which every man desireth to be accounted of? . . .

And in mine opinion as it beautifyeth a fair woman to be decked with pearls and precious stones, so much more it ornifyeth a gentleman to be furnished in mind with glittering virtues.

Wherefore considering the small harm I do to you, the great good I do to others I prefer mine own intention to discover your volume before your request to secret the same. Wherein I may seem to you to play the part of the cunning and expert mediciner. . . . So you being sick of so much doubt in your own proceedings, through which infirmity you are desirous to bury your work in the grave of oblivion, yet I am nothing dainty to deny your request. . . . I shall erect you such a monument that in your lifetime you shall see how noble a shadow of your virtuous life shall remain when you are dead and gone. . . . Thus earnestly desiring you not to repugn the setting forth of your own proper studies.

From your loving and assured friend,
E. OXENFORDE.[95]

We ask our readers to familiarize themselves thoroughly with the diction of this letter, and then to read the dedication of *Venus and Adonis.* So similar is the style that it is hardly necessary to make any allowance for the seventeen intervening years.

Whilst, then, we find him paying high compliments to a literary man, from whom he could expect no return, at the time when others were penning extravagant eulogies to the Queen, we have not a single line of poetry from the pen of Oxford, ministering to the royal vanity, and this notwithstanding the high place he undoubtedly held in the queen's regards and her indulgence of what seemed to others like a provocative willfulness

---

[95] Grosart, *Fuller Worthies',* pp. 424-426.

in him. This absence of compliments to royalty is also characteristic of the Shakespeare work, and has been the occasion for much surprised comment.

General results.

Reviewing the present chapter as a whole it will be recognized that to the remarkable set of resemblances with which we dealt in the last chapter, must now be added an equally remarkable set of correspondences in the general literary situation and in the leading characteristics of Shakespeare's and De Vere's writings. And when the value of the authorities cited is duly weighed it will be readily conceded that, whatever may be said for the rest of the argument, it cannot be urged that in dealing with the question of Shakespearean honours, we are inviting the public to consider the claims of one who can be lightly brushed aside, as in any way "out of the running."

CHAPTER VIII

THE LYRIC POETRY OF EDWARD DE VERE

UP to this point we have sought to rest our case upon the judgment of men of some authority in Elizabethan literature. Another step, however, requires to be taken in which there is distinctly new ground to be broken, and where, therefore, such external support can hardly be looked for. This decisive step is to bring the writings of Edward de Vere alongside the Shakespearean writings, in order to judge whether or not the former contain the natural seeds and clear promise of the latter. As this has never been done before, being indeed the special outcome of the particular researches upon which we are at present engaged, no outside authority is available; and, therefore, all we can hope to do is to submit such points for consideration as may give a lead in this new line of investigation, by which eventually, we believe, our case will either stand or fall.

Six-lined stanza.

So far as forms of versification are concerned De Vere presents just that rich variety which is so noticeable in Shakespeare; and almost all the forms he employs we find reproduced in the Shakespeare work. When his contemporary spoke of his excellence in "the rare devices of poetry" we recognize at once his affinity with the master poet, and the distinction between him and his rival Sidney, who headed a party that brought ridicule upon themselves by attempts to set up artificial rules that would have fettered the development of our national poetry. Towards such tongue-tying of art by authority Oxford was instinctively antagonistic, and the rich variety of poetic forms, even in this small collection, is the natural result of the free play he allowed to his genius. At the same time Oxford had his partialities, and the six-lined pentameter stanza, with rhymes as in *Venus and Adonis*, was undoubtedly a favourite with him; since it appears in seven out of the twenty-two pieces that have been preserved. How great a favourite it was with "Shakespeare," has perhaps not been pointed out before. In addition to its employment for the first of the two long poems we find it frequently used in his plays. *Romeo and Juliet* has two such stanzas: the play, in fact, ending with one of them. We find it also in *Love's Labour's Lost*, *A Midsummer Night's Dream*, *The Taming of the Shrew*, and *The Comedy of Errors*. In *Richard II* it occurs worked into the text in such a way as easily to escape detection; the six lines beginning:

> But now the blood of twenty thousand men.
>
> (III.2)

As it is not the only case of this kind it is probable that it may be found in other plays not mentioned above. These plays, it will be observed, belong mainly to what is regarded as Shakespeare's early work.

The poems of Lord Vaux.

This particular form of stanza we were tempted at one time to call the De Vere stanza; for although Chaucer has a six-lined stanza it is quite different from this. Spenser uses it in the first part of the *Shepherd's Calendar*; but De Vere's work in this form had been before the public for some years before the *Shepherd's Calendar* appeared. There is, however, one possible competitor for the honour; and the mention of his name will introduce an interesting little point which may have a bearing upon our argument. In Dr. Grosart's collection, the poet whose work immediately precedes that of De Vere is Thomas Lord Vaux, the representative of another old family whose ancestor, like De Vere's, had "come over with the Conqueror"; a family interesting to people in the North of England as having been lords of Gilsland. Some doubt seems to exist as to whether the poet was really Thomas Lord Vaux, who was a generation older than Edward De Vere and who died in 1562, or his son William, who was De Vere's contemporary. It is possible that both father's and son's work appear mingled together in Dr. Grosart's collection, but the collector himself pronounces emphatically and exclusively in favour of the elder man. In this case the honour of inventing this particular stanza must belong to Thomas Lord Vaux unless an earlier poet should subsequently be found using it.

Shakespeare and Lord Vaux.

What is of special interest is that this particular form of verse is not the only thing that De Vere appropriates from Lord Vaux. Although his own poetry is of quite a superior order to that of his aristocratic forerunner in verse making, a close comparison of the two sets of verses as they stand together in this important collection leaves little room for doubt that, when as a young man De Vere began to write poetry he was strongly under the influence of Lord Vaux' work, if he did not actually, as is natural to youth, take Lord Vaux as his model. Now, by a curious chance, the last poem in the "Vaux" collection, the poem therefore that immediately precedes the De Vere collection, is the identical song of Lord Vaux' which "Shakespeare" adapts for the use of the gravedigger in *Hamlet*. This may not have much weight as evidence. Nevertheless, if it can be maintained, as it reasonably may, that Edward de Vere in his earliest poetic efforts built upon foundations that Lord Vaux had laid, then the reappearance of an old song of Lord Vaux', in Shakespeare's supreme masterpiece, forty years after the death of the writer of the song, is certainly not without significance as part of our general argument.

Before leaving this question of the six-lined stanza we would point out that one feature common to the De Vere and the Shakespeare work is the appearance of single isolated stanzas. For example, the only stanza in *The Taming of the Shrew* is in this form; and no less than three of the poems in De Vere's small collection are single stanzas of this kind. A fondness for other six-lined stanzas differing in small details from this one is also characteristic of both sets of work. It is curious, too, how often "Shakespeare," even in his blank verse, casts a speech or a thought into a set of six lines.

Central theme.

Turning now to the question of the theme or subject matter of De Vere's poetry, we find that whatever its surface appearance, its underlying interest is always, as in Shakespeare, human nature. In handling this theme figures of speech borrowed from the classics and taken for the most part from Ovid are as copious and are introduced as naturally as the ordinary words of his mother-tongue, illuminating his thought as aptly as any homely simile. At the same time we find the same Shakespearean wealth of illustration drawn from the common objects about him: ordinary flowers; common materials like glass, crystal, amber, wax, sugar, gall and wine, and a host of other things; the deer, hawks, hounds, the mastiff, birds, worms, the bee, drone, honey, the stars, streams, hill, tower, cannon, and so on. All these images crowd his lines, not as themes in themselves, but as similes and metaphors for handling his central theme of human life and human nature.

Personality.

So far as the natural disposition of the writer is concerned, it is fortunate for the name of Edward de Vere that we have these poems collected by Dr. Grosart and the letter included in the collection. The personality they reflect is perfectly in harmony with that which seems to peer through the writings of Shakespeare, though in many ways out of agreement with what Oxford is represented as being in several of the references to him with which we have met. There are traces undoubtedly of those defects which the sonnets disclose in "Shakespeare," but through it all there shines the spirit of an intensely affectionate nature, highly sensitive, and craving for tenderness and sympathy. He is a man with faults, but stamped with reality and truth; honest even in his errors, making no pretense of being better than he was, and recalling frequently to our minds the lines in one of Shakespeare's sonnets:

> I am that I am, and they that level
> At my abuses reckon up their own.

As one reads the poems and then recalls particular references to him one feels that injustice has somehow been done, and that a great work of rectification is urgently needed, quite apart from the question of Shakespearean authorship.

We shall now proceed to place side by side some passages from Edward de Vere's poetry and others from "Shakespeare's" writings which illustrate their correspondence either in mentality or literary style.

Haggard hawk.

Beginning with the poem on "Women" already given in full, we note first of all its similarity to Shakespeare's work in the general characteristics of diction, succinctness, cohesion and unity; and also in the similes employed. The word "haggard," a wild or imperfectly trained hawk, is the word which naturally arrests the attention of the modern reader. Now "Shakespeare" uses it five times, and out of these no less than four are when he uses the word as a figure of speech in referring to fickleness or indiscipline in women. In *Othello* it is used identically as in the poem by De Vere, meaning a woman who "flies from man to man."

> If I do find her haggard,
> Though that her jesses were my dear heart strings,
> I'd whistle her off, and let her down the wind
> To play at fortune. (III.3)

Even the sentiment and idea are exactly the same as in De Vere's poem:

> Like haggards wild they range,
> These gentle birds that fly from man to man
> Who would not scorn and shake them from the fist

And let them fly, fair fools, which way they list?

In the same poem he speaks of making a "disport" of "training them to our lure," which is quite suggestive of this from *The Taming of the Shrew* (IV.1):

> For then she never looks upon her lure.
> Another way I have to man my haggard,
> To make her come and know her keeper's call.

Again De Vere speaks of the subtle oaths, the fawning and flattering by which men "train them to their lure" in exactly the same vein as that in which Hero in *Much Ado* says (III.1):

> Then go we near her, that her ear lose nothing
> Of the false sweet bait that we lay for it.
> I know her spirits are as coy and wild
> As haggards of the rock.

In making this comparison we have not had before us a large number of instances out of which it was possible to select a few that happened to be similar. What we have in this instance is, as a matter of fact, a complete accordance at all points in the use of an unusual word and figure of speech. Indeed if we make a piece of patchwork of all the passages in Shakespeare in which the word "haggard" occurs we can virtually reconstruct De Vere's single poem on "Women." Such an agreement not only supports us in seeking to establish the general harmony of De Vere's work with Shakespeare's, but carries us beyond the immediate needs of our argument; for it constrains us to claim that either both sets of expressions are actually from the same pen, or "Shakespeare" pressed that license to borrow, which was prevalent in his day, far beyond its legitimate limits. In our days we should not hesitate to describe such passages as glaring plagiarism, unless they happen to come from the same pen.

Lily and damask rose.

We shall take next some verses from a poem already referred to in a passage quoted from the *Cambridge History of Literature*. This is the "charming lyric" there mentioned, entitled "What

Cunning can express?" and which appeared in *England's Helicon* in 1600 as "What Shepherd can express?" How these and others of Oxford's verses have escaped for so long the attention of the compilers of anthologies is one of the mysteries of literature.

> The Lily in the field
>   That glories in his white,
> For pureness now must yield
>   And render up his right.
> Heaven pictured in her face
> Doth promise joy and grace.
>
> Fair Cynthia's silver light,
>   That beats on running streams,
> Compares not with her white,
>   Whose hairs are all sunbeams.
> So bright my Nymph doth shine,
> As day unto my eyne.
>
> With this there is a red
>   Exceeds the Damask-Rose,
> Which in her cheeks is spread;
>   Whence every favour grows.
> In sky there is no star
> But she surmounts it far.
>
> When Phoebus from his bed
>   Of Thetia doth arise,
> The morning blushing red
>   In fair Carnation wise,
> He shows in my Nymph's face
> As Queen of every grace.
>
> This pleasant Lily white,
>   This taint of roseate red,
> This Cynthia's silver light,
>   This sweet fair Dea spred,
> These sunbeams in mine eye,
> These beauties make me die.

This is the only poem in the De Vere collection in which the writer lingers tenderly and seriously on the beauty of a woman's face; and in it, it will be observed, his whole treatment turns upon the contrast of white and red, the lily and the damask rose. *The beauty of Lucrece.*

It is a striking fact then that the only poem of "Shakespeare's" in which he dwells at length in the same spirit upon the same theme is dominated by the identical contrast. This is the set of stanzas in which he deals with the beauty of *Lucrece* (Stanzas 2, 4, 8, 9, 10, 11). Indeed, there is hardly a term used by De Vere in the poem quoted above which is not reproduced in these stanzas. Whilst drawing special attention to the red and white contrast, and to the general similarity in tone and delicacy of touch, we also put in italics a number of the subordinate outstanding words that appear in both poems.

Stanza 2.
To *praise that clear unmatched red and white*
Which triumph'd in the *sky* of his delight,
Where mortal *stars*, aa bright as *heaven's beauties*,
With *pure* aspects did him peculiar duties.

Stanza 4.
The *morning's silver* melting dew
Against the *golden splendour of the sun.*

Stanza 6.
So rich a thing *braving compare.*

Stanza 8.
When beauty boasted *blushes*, in despite
Virtue would stain, that o'er with *silver white.*

Stanza 10.
This heraldry in Lucrece's face was seen,
Argued by beauty's red and virtue's white
Of either colour was the other *queen.*

Stanza 11.
This silent war of lilies and of roses,
Which Tarquin view'd in her fair face's field.

Stanza 11 brings to a close this poem on the beauty of *Lucrece*; but the conception which dominates it is maintained throughout the work to which it belongs. It occurs in stanza 37:

> First red as roses that on lawn we lay,
> Then white as lawn the roses took away.

Stanza 56.
> Her lily hand her rosy cheek lies under.

Stanza 69.
> The colour of thy face,
> That even for anger makes the lily pale,
> And the red rose blush at her own disgrace.

Shakespeare on the lily and the rose.

That all this belongs to the personality of "Shakespeare" himself will be seen from the following quotations from the *Sonnets*:

> Nor did I wonder at the lily's white,
> Nor praise the deep vermillion of the rose.
> > (sonnet 98.)
> The lily I condemned for thy hand,
> And buds of marjoram had stol'n thy hair.
> The roses fearfully on thorns did stand,
> One blushing shame, another white despair,
> A third, nor red nor white had stol'n of both.
> > (sonnet 99.)
> I have seen roses damask'd red and white.
> > (sonnet 130.)

It also appears in the play of *Coriolanus* (II.1):

> Our veiled dames commit the war of white and damask.

And in *Love's Labour's Lost* (I.2):

> If she be made of white and red
> Her faults will ne'er be known, etc.

> A dangerous rhyme, my masters, against the reason of white and red.

In *Venus* this red and white contrast is mentioned no less than three times in the first thirteen stanzas.

The Passionate Pilgrim

Finally we have this from *The Passionate Pilgrim*, which bears more than one mark of Shakespearean or De Vere influence, if not of actual origin:

> Fair is my love but not so fair as fickle,
> Mild as a dove, but neither true nor trusty,
> Bright as a glass and yet as glass is, brittle.
> Softer than wax, and yet as iron rusty;
> A lily pale with damask dye to grace her,
> None fairer nor none falser to deface her.

This is not the place to discuss the mystery of Jaggard's piratical publication. We insert this particular stanza because, if it was not "Shakespeare's," it at any rate shows what was considered at that time to be characteristic of Shakespeare's work. It will be noticed that it is in the familiar *Venus* stanza; it turns upon the idea of feminine fickleness; it brings in the lily and damask contrast; at the same time the similes of glass and wax are distinctive of De Vere's work. Though the stanza contains figures and phrases suggestive of De Vere or Shakespeare, as a piece of versification it is quite inferior in several points. It looks rather like a piece of patchwork from De Vere's poems; and if this is what it really is, to have it put forward as Shakespeare's work suggests that Jaggard either knew or suspected that De Vere was "Shakespeare." In this connection it is interesting to note that the folio edition of Shakespeare, which was published just a generation later, was printed by someone with a different Christian name but with the same unusual surname of Jaggard. Sir Sidney Lee ascribes the printing to the same man, who had associated his son with the issue of the later work.

The damask rose.

Returning to De Vere's verses the outstanding word is "damask," associated with the "damask rose." In the small collection of his poems this word occurs twice, and in Shakespeare the word occurs six times, one of which is of doubtful Shakespearean origin. On both of the occasions on which De Vere uses the word it has reference to a woman's complexion, and in four out of the five times when "Shakespeare" uses the word it is used in precisely the same connection.

Poetic unity.

Before leaving this matter it will be well at this point to emphasize a principle which is vital to the argument contained in this chapter: namely, that we are not here primarily concerned with the mere piling up of parallel passages. What matters most of all is mental correspondence and the general unity of treatment which follows from it. Of this, the poem by De Vere, and the set of stanzas from *Lucrece*, form an excellent example to begin with. Here we have what are virtually two complete poems upon one theme, dominated by an identical conception, permeated by precisely the same spirit, illustrated by the same imagery and clothed in a remarkably similar vocabulary. Such a comparison, it hardly needs pointing out, stands on a totally different plane from the Baconian collations of words and phrases. The kind of criticisms which have quite justly been levelled at these mere text-gathering labours do not, we believe, apply to the main body of the comparisons treated in this chapter.

Love's difficulties and troubles.

Turning now from such details of workmanship as have governed the above comparison we may now consider a more general matter: his treatment of the subject of Love. We find first of all in these early poems of De Vere's something very far removed from the conventional or weakly sentimental expressions of affection then in vogue. In some of Philip Sidney's early poetry this kind of thing becomes positively silly. In De Vere's work on the other hand we have a firmly knit personified treatment of Love in the abstract, the dominant notes of which are as unaffected as they are Shakespearean. There is, in particular, a set of lyrics highly praised by more than one writer, which are in the form of a dialogue with "Desire." The prominence of this word and idea in the work of "Shakespeare" and of De Vere will receive special attention later; for the present we shall simply take a few lines from the latter as bearing upon the theme of love:

Is he god of peace or war?
What be his arms? What is his might?
His war is peace, his peace is war,
Each grief of his is but delight;
His bitter ball is sugared bliss.
What be his gifts? How doth he pay?
Sweet dreams in sleep, new thoughts in day.
Beholding eyes, in mind received.

          *   *   *

What labours doth this god allow?
Sit still and muse to make a vow.
Their ladies if they true remain.

          *   *   *

Why is he naked painted? Blind?

          *   *   *

Though living long he is yet a *child*,
A god begot *beguiled*.

          *   *   *

When wert thou born, Desire?
In pride and pomp of May.

          *   *   *

What was thy meat and daily food?
Sad sighs and great annoy.

          *   *   *

What had'st thou then to drink?
Unfeigned lovers' tears.

A Midsummer Night's Dream.

As part of our work is to represent the process of investigation, it may be worthwhile to indicate its operation in this instance. When the contents of De Vere's poem had become quite familiar as a result of repeated reading, the next step was to select the plays of "Shakespeare" in which we were most likely to find the substance of this poem deposited. Amongst these, *A Midsummer Night's Dream* naturally occupied a foremost place. After then, the reader has, in his turn, thoroughly familiarized himself with these lines let him refer to *A Midsummer Night's Dream* (I.i) and begin reading from, "The course of true love never did run smooth," continuing to the end of the scene and noticing specially such expressions as the following:

True lovers have been ever cross'd.

      *   *   *

It is a customary cross
As due to love as thoughts and dreams and sighs,
Wishes and tears.

      *   *   *

By all the vows that ever men have broke
In number more than women ever spoke.

      *   *   *

We must starve our sight from lover's food.

      *   *   *

Love looks not with the eyes but with the mind.

      *   *   *

Therefore is winged Cupid painted blind.

      *   *   *

Therefore is Love said to be a *child*
Because in choice he is so oft *beguiled*.

As De Vere's lines are from lyrics on Desire it is interesting to note that the word "desire" occurs no less than three times in the part of the scene that precedes the lines we quote from "Shakespeare," whilst the idea of Desire presides over the whole scene. In both cases we have passing allusions to the skylark and the month of May, revealing not only a similar concatenation of ideas, but also of their associated words and figures of speech. Had the lines been culled from different parts of De Vere 's work on the one hand, or from different parts of Shakespeare's on the other, their force would not have been the same. It is the unity of treatment in each case and a similarity extending to identical words and even rhymes ("child" with "beguiled") which is so suggestive of a single mind at work in both cases: a theory strengthened by the absence of anything analogous in the work of contemporary poets.

Love's contrariness.

This is further supported by the appearance of similar rhetorical forms in dealing with the same theme. In *A Midsummer Night's Dream* we have the following:

> *Hernia.* The more I hate the more he follows me.
> *Helena.* The more I love the more be hateth me.

In another poem of De Vere's we have the following:

> The more I followed one the more she fled away
> As Daphne did, full long ago, Apollo's wishful prey.
> The more my plaints I do resound the less she pities me.

This idea of Love's contrariness runs right through the poem of De Vere's from which the last lines are quoted; and we might almost describe *A Midsummer Night's Dream* as a burlesque on the same idea. With the two passages just quoted in mind turn to Act II, scene 1, in the play, and read the encounter between Demetrius and Helena, where the former enters with the latter following him.

> *D.* Get thee gone and follow me no more. Do I not in plainest truth tell you I do not nor I cannot love you.
> *H.* And even for that do I love you the more. The more you beat me, I will fawn on you: only give me leave, unworthy as I am to follow you. Run when you will, the story shall be changed: Apollo runs and Daphne holds the chase.

Here again it will be noticed we have an exact correspondence in conception, heightened by the introduction of Apollo and Daphne in both cases; and Demetrius's treatment of Helena's "plaints" is exactly described in De Vere's line:

> The more my plaints I do resound the less she pities me.

Desire.

A most signal instance of the essential unity of the two sets of work we are now comparing, is presented in connection with this idea of "Desire." By far the longest of De Vere's poems, containing no less than nineteen stanzas, and representing nearly a quarter of the entire collection of his poetry, is on this theme: a theme which frequently reappears in the other three quarters.

As to its position in Shakespeare's works it will suffice to quote the following passage from Mr. Frank Harris's work on *The Man Shakespeare*:

> Shakespeare gave immortal expression to desire and its offspring, love, jealousy, etc. . . . . Desire, in especial, has inspired him with phrases more magically expressive even than those gasped out by panting Sappho.[96]

---

[96] Frank Harris, *The Man Shakespeare*, p. 233.

In De Vere's work, again, Desire is personified just as we find it in stanzas 101 and 102 of Shakespeare's *Lucrece*; and the word "desire" ranks, for importance, in the vocabulary of the great dramas, with the word "will," to which, as Sir Sidney Lee points out, it was closely allied in Shakespeare's day. This single word, then, forms an important bridge between the two sets of writings; and, by itself, makes quite a significant addition to the evidence in support of a common authorship.

Love's penalties.

In a somewhat different strain is "Shakespeare's" treatment of Love in the dialogue between Valentine and Proteus in *The Two Gentlemen of Verona* (I.1):

> To be in love where scorn is bought with groans,
> Coy looks with heart-sore sighs, one fading moment's mirth
> With twenty watchful weary tedious nights.
> If haply won perhaps a hapless gain;
> If lost why then a grievous labour won:
> However, but *a folly bought with wit*
> *Or else a wit by folly vanquished.*
> .   .   .   .   As in the sweetest bud
> The eating canker dwells, so eating love
> Inhabits in the finest wits of all.
> .   .   .   .   By love the young and tender wit
> Is turn'd to folly
> *Losing all the fair effects of future hopes.*
>
> *   *   *   *
>
> But wherefore waste I time to counsel thee
> That art *a votary to Fond Desire?*
>
> *   *   *   *
>
> Made me neglect my studies, *lose my time*,
> War with good counsel, set the world at *nought*;
> Made wit with musing weak, heart sick with *thought*.

Again we must ask the reader first of all to make himself thoroughly familiar with these lines, noting the wit and folly paradoxes, wasted time, defeated hopes, and though last not least the concluding rhyme. Now compare this with the following from two of De Vere's poems:

My meaning is to work
What wonders love hath wrought;
Wherewith I muse why men of wit
Have love so dearly bought.

It's now a peace and then a sudden war,
A hope consumed before it is conceived.
At hand it fears; it menaceth afar;
And he that gains is most of all deceived.
Love whets the dullest wits, his plagues be such,
But makes the wise by pleasing dote as much.

Love's a desire, which, for to wait a time,
Doth *lose an age of years,* and so doth pass
As doth a shadow sever'd from his prime,
Seeming as though it were, yet never was.
Leaving behind nought but repentent *thought*
Of days ill spent on that which profits *nought.*

Here again we have an exact correspondence short of mere transcription, even to the extent of an identical rhyme; whilst Valentine's raillery of his friend, "that he had become "a votary to Fond Desire," is redolent of De Vere's verses on this theme, which finish with the words:

Then Fond Desire farewell,
   Thou art no mate for me,
I should be loath, methinks, to dwell,
   With such a one as thee.

As a final remark on the question of love, we shall merely point out, that, if the reader wishes to have a summary of Edward de Vere's treatment of the subject, let him turn to Shakespeare's *Venus and Adonis* and read the first five of the last ten stanzas of the poem, in which Venus is prophesying the fate of love.

Love poems reviewed.

When the passages we have quoted are weighed carefully side by side, phrase by phrase and word by word, hardly anyone will question the similarity of mind behind them, and most people, we believe, will agree that these are striking resemblances of expression. Exact repetition, of course, is not to be looked for; for one of the astonishing features of "Shakespeare's" work is the freshness and constant variety maintained throughout so great a mass of writing. But, to the modest contention that one contains the possible germs of the other, few readers will have any difficulty in acceding. An intensified interest in De Vere's work will doubtless cause everything he has written to be subjected to a most careful scrutiny, and its comparison specially with the lyric work of Shakespeare with appropriate allowances for the differences between early and matured work will probably settle conclusively the claims we are now making on his behalf.

Oxford's mental distraction.

As reflecting the correspondence, alike in mental constitution and general literary style in another vein, take first of all the following three verses, each of which forms the opening stanza of a separate poem of De Vere's:

> Fain would I sing but fury makes me mad,
> And rage hath sworn to seek revenge on wrong.
> My mazèd mind in malice is so set
> As death shall daunt my deadly dolours long.
> Patience perforce is such a pinching pain,
> As die I will or suffer wrong again.

> If care or skill could conquer vain desire,
> Or reason's reins my strong affections stay,
> There should my sighs to quiet breast retire,
> And shun such sights as secret thoughts betray;
> Uncomely love, which now lurks in my breast
> Should cease, my grief by wisdom's power oppress'd.

> Love is a discord and a strange divorce
> Betwixt our sense and rest; by whose power,
> As mad with reason we admit that force
> Which wit or reason never may . . . . . . (word lost through an obvious misprint in Dr. Grosart's collection).[97]

We would draw attention first to the "double-barrelled alliterations" contained especially in the first of these stanzas—an artifice of Shakespeare's upon which writers have commented.

---

[97] "Divorce" is the word given in the 1872-76 edition cited in the bibliography, vol. 4, p. 416. Because the word at the end of the line must rhyme with "power," "devour" would fit. The final two lines of the stanza are: "It is a will that brooketh no consent; / It would refuse yet never may repent."

"Shakespeare's" mental distraction.

We have quoted stanzas from three separate poems in order to show that the frame of mind they express—a restlessness of the emotional nature—was characteristic of the poet. Now take the sentiment and manner of expression represented by the three stanzas as a whole and compare them with the following passages from two of Shakespeare's sonnets (140 and 147):

1. For if I should despair I should grow mad,
    And in my madness might speak ill of thee,
    Now this ill-wresting world is grown so bad
    Mad slanderers by mad ears believed be.

2. My reason, the physician to my love,
    Hath left me, and I desperate now approve;
    Desire is death, which, physic did except.
    Past cure I am now reason is past care,
    And frantic mad with evermore unrest.
    My thoughts and my discourse as madmen's are
    At random from the truth, vainly expressed;
    For I have sworn thee fair and thought thee bright
    Who are as black as hell and dark as night.

We might safely challenge anyone to find in the whole range of Elizabethan literature another instance of a poet expressing the same kind of thought and feeling in lines of the same distinctive quality as is represented by the two sets here presented for comparison. Unsupported by any other evidence they would justify a very strong ground of suspicion that Edward de Vere and "Shakespeare" were one and the same man. It is of first importance to keep in mind that the lines here quoted from "Shakespeare" are not extracted from a drama, but are from the most realistic of personal poetry. Even those who would deny an autobiographical significance to many of the sonnets admit the intensely realistic character of the particular group from which the above are taken. We have therefore, in each case, the simple and direct expression of the private mind of the poet in a vein so distinctive as to leave hardly any room for doubt that both are from one pen.

Interrogatives.

Of rhetorical forms common to the two sets of writings, a minor point is a fondness for stanzas formed of a succession of interrogatives for the expression of strong emotion. Indeed, in the De Vere work, we have an entire sonnet formed of a series of questions. It is the only sonnet in the collection; and the most important point about it is that it is in the form which we now call the Shakespearean sonnet. This is an important matter and must receive attention in another connection. We shall, therefore, give a stanza in the interrogative form from another poem.

> And shall I live on earth to be her thrall?
> And shall I live and serve her all in vain?
> And shall I kiss the steps that she lets fall?
> And shall I pray the gods to keep the pain
> From her that is so cruel still?
> No, no, on her work all your will.

Similar series of interrogations occur here and there throughout the most impassioned parts of *Lucrece*; and in the Shakespearean part of *Henry VI*, part 3 (III.3), we have the following:

> Did I forget that by the house of York
> My father came untimely to his death?
> Did I let pass the abuse done to my niece?
> Did I impale him with the regal crown?
> Did I put Henry from his native right?
> And am I guerdon'd at the last with shame?

(A six-lined fragment of blank verse.)

It is difficult to read these two sets of lines side by side without a feeling that both are from the same pen, and when, in the same play, we find Queen Margaret answering her own question with a repeated negative, resembling the last line of Oxford's stanza, the resemblance is most striking.

> What's worse than murderer that I may name it?
> No, no, my heart will burst an if I speak.
> (3 Henry VI, V.5)

Stanzas formed of similar lines.

Continuing these comparisons of style we would ask the reader to turn to *Lucrece*, and commence reading from stanza 122, which begins:

Why should the worm intrude the maiden bud?

and read on to stanza 141, which begins:

Let him have time to tear his curled hair.

In addition to the two stanzas which illustrate the succession of questions just dealt with, he will notice quite a number of stanzas in which each line, in its opening phrase, is but the repetition of a single form. Stanza 127, for example, has lines beginning:

"Thou makest," "Thou blow'st," "Thou smother'st," "Thou foul abettor," "Thou plantest," "Thou ravisher."

Stanza 128:

"Thy secret pleasure," "Thy private feasting," etc.

Stanza 135:

"To unmask falsehood," "To stamp the seal," etc.

Similar stanzas are also found in other parts of the poem.

Stanza 82:

"By knighthood," "By her untimely fears," etc.

Stanza 95:

"Thou nobly base," "Thou their fair life," etc.

Or, in stanzas 106 and 107, where it takes the form of alternate lines:

"He like a thievish dog," "She like a wearied lamb," etc.

Now De Vere's poem from which we last quoted is composed of six six-lined stanzas almost entirely built up in this way: the stanza already given and also:

Stanza 1:

"The trickling tears," "The secret sighs," etc.

Stanza 3:

"The stricken deer," "The haggard hawk," etc.

Stanza 4:

"She is my joy," "She is my pain," etc.

A closing malediction.

Then, as a final comparison of verses so constructed, we shall place side by side the last stanza in the series from *Lucrece* (141), with the last stanza in this poem of De Vere's: the stanza in which the poet, or respective poets, wind up with a closing malediction:

Shakespeare's Lucrece; stanza 141:

> Let him have time to tear his curled hair.
> Let him have time against himself to rave,
> Let him have time of Time's help to despair,
> Let him have time to live a loathed slave,
> Let him have time a beggar's orts to crave,
> And time to see one that by alms doth live,
> Disdain to him, disdained scraps to give.

De Vere's "Rejected Lover":

> And let her feel the power of all your might,
> And let her have her most desire with speed,
> And let her pine away both day and night,
> And let her moan and none lament her need,
> And let all those that shall her see
> Despise her state and pity me.

Again we repeat, if these are not both from the same pen, never were there two poets living at the same time whose mentality and workmanship bore so striking a resemblance. Traces of this kind of work may, no doubt, be found in Chaucer, and there can be little doubt that De Vere was under the influence of Chaucer's poetry; it is also one of the literary forms he seems to have learnt from Lord Vaux, to which reference has already been made, but in De Vere, and in Shakespeare's *Lucrece*, it assumes a marked development, and in the verses just cited, produces a startling correspondence quite unparalleled, so far as we know, in the poetry of the time.

So striking is the similarity of the two stanzas quoted above that it hardly seems possible to further strengthen the case they represent; and yet, in the stanza immediately preceding that quoted from *Lucrece* the following line occurs:

> To make him moan, but pity not his moans.

This is almost identical with De Vere's line:

> And let her moan and none lament her need.

The former is hardly entitled to be called even a paraphrase of the latter, so nearly a copy is it. Again we point out that we have not had to search the pages of "Shakespeare" to find the selected line, but that it stands in immediate juxtaposition to the particular stanza under consideration. A comparison of these two verses, taken along with the particular line, entitles us to say that "Shakespeare" was either a kind of literary understudy of De Vere's, guilty of a most unseemly plagiarism from his chief, or he was none other than the Earl of Oxford himself.

A peculiar literary form.

As an example of a very unusual literary form of De Vere's, reproduced in Shakespeare, we give the following:

De Vere:
> What plague is greater than the grief of mind?
> The grief of mind that eats in every vein,
> In every vein that leaves such clots behind,
> Such clots behind as breed such bitter pain.
> So bitter pain that none shall ever find
> What plague is greater than the grief of mind?

This repetition of the last phrase of each line in the succeeding line occurs in *The Comedy of Errors* (I.2):

Shakespeare:
> She is so hot because the meat is cold;
> The meat is cold because you come not home;
> You come not home because you have no stomach;
> You have no stomach having broke your fast;
> But we that know what 'tis to watch and pray
> Are penitent for your default to-day.

(The reader will notice that this is again one of the six-lined passages in which Shakespeare frequently indulges, even when he does not work them into finished stanzas.)

Grief of mind.

No one will deny that each line in the above stanza of De Vere's is eminently Shakespearean in diction, whilst the idea and sentiment are quite familiar to Shakespeare readers. "The grief of mind," or as we would say, the distress that has its roots in mental constitution, temperament, or mood, rather than in external misfortune, is a thoroughly Shakespearean idea. We have it in the opening words of the *Merchant of Venice*:

> In sooth I know not why I am so sad,
> It wearies me, you say it wearies you,
> But how I caught it, found it, or came by it,
> What stuff 'tis made of, whereof it is born
> I am to learn.
> And such a want-wit sadness makes of me
> That I have much ado to know myself.

We have it again in *Richard II* in the dialogue between the Queen and Bushy (II.2):

> I know no cause
> Why I should welcome such a guest as grief.
> My inward soul with nothing trembles.
> Each substance of a grief hath twenty shadows
> Which shows like grief itself but is not so.
> Howe'er it be
> I cannot be but sad; so heavy said
> As, though on thinking on no thought I think,
> Makes me with heavy nothing faint and shrink.
> For nothing hath begot my something grief,
> Or something hath the nothing that I grieve.

All this is eminently suggestive of that undercurrent of constitutional melancholy which has been remarked in "Shakespeare," and is quite a noticeable feature of the Earl of Oxford's poetry.

Loss of good name.

In Shakespeare's sonnets there occur several references to the disrepute into which the writer had fallen, along with an expressed desire that his name should be buried with his body—a fact quite inconsistent with either the Stratfordian or the Baconian theory of authorship, but a strong confirmation of the theory that William Shakspere was but a mask for someone who desired personal effacement. From those expressions we need only quote one:

> When in *disgrace* with Fortune and *men's eyes*,
> I, *all alone, beweep my outcast state*,
> And *trouble deaf heaven, with my bootless cries*,
> And look upon myself and curse my fate, . . .
>   (sonnet 29)

When the reader has made himself familiar with the numerous passages in the sonnets dealing with the same theme (sonnets 71, 72, 81, 110, 111, 112, 121), let him compare them, and especially the words italicized above, with the following from De Vere's poem on the loss of his good name, published between 1576 and 1578:

> Fram'd in the front of forlorn hope past all recovery,
> *I stayless stand* to abide the shock of shame and infamy.
>   *   *   *
> My spirtes, my heart, my wit and force in deep distress are
>   drown'd,
> The only loss of my good name is of those griefs the ground.
>   *   *   *
> *Help crave I must, and crave I will, with tears* upon my face,
> Of *all that may in heaven or hell*, in earth or air be found,
> To wail with me this loss of mine, as of those griefs the ground.

Personally I find it utterly impossible to read this poem of Edward De Vere's and the sonnets in which "Shakespeare" harps upon the same theme, without an overwhelming sense of there being but one mind behind the two utterances. Indeed this fact of "Shakespeare" being a man who had lost his good name ought to have appeared in our original characterization. Inattention, and some remnants of the influence of the Stratfordian tradition, which has treated this insistent idea as a mere poetic pose, probably accounts for its not appearing there.

Edward de Vere's poem on the loss of his good name, and Shakespeare's sonnets on the same theme, are the only poems of their kind with which we have met in our reading of Elizabethan poetry—the only poems of their kind, we believe, to be found in English literature. The former, written at the age of twenty-six, and whilst still smarting under the sense of immediate loss, is more intense and passionate in its expression, and is full of the unrestrained impetuosity of early manhood. The latter is more the restrained expression of a matured man who had in some measure become accustomed to the loss; and would as a matter of fact, whoever the writer, be written when Oxford was forty years of age or over. Even then Oxford's words, "I stayless stand" are almost repeated in Shakespeare's "I all alone"; Oxford's "Tears upon my face" seems referred to in Shakespeare's "Beweep my outcast state"; and Shakespeare's "Troubling deaf heaven with bootless cries" is exactly descriptive of what Oxford did in his early poem. Is this all mere chance coincidence?

Othello and weeping.

A significant detail in the two poems under review is the proneness to floods of tears which both illustrate. This involuntary manifestation of a supersensitive nature and a highly strung temperament is quite a marked feature of De Vere's poetry and is repeated more than once in the "Shakespeare" sonnets. It is curious, also, that "Shakespeare's" two heroes of tragic love, Romeo and Othello, though differing in many particulars, are both subject to the same weakness. The play of *Othello*, we shall have to show later, deals with events which, as we believe, occurred about the time when Oxford's poem was written; and it is a remarkable circumstance that it is this play which contains Shakespeare's well-worn lines on the loss of good name:

> Good name in man or woman, dear my lord,
> Is the immediate jewel of their souls.
> Who steals my purse steals trash, ...
> But be who filches from me my good name,
> Robs me of that which not enriches him,
> And makes me poor indeed.

And so, first one thing and then another fits into its place with all the unity of an elaborate mosaic the moment we introduce Edward de Vere as the author of the Shakespeare writings. Is this too the merest coincidence?

Fortune and Nature.

Of works in a totally different vein take now this from a poem of De Vere's:

> Faction that ever dwells
> In court where wit excels
>   Hath set defiance.
> Fortune and love have sworn
> That they were never born
>   Of one alliance.
>
>   *   *   *
>
>   Nature thought good,
> Fortune should ever dwell
> In court where wits excel,
>   Love keep the wood.
>
>   *   *   *
>
> So to the wood went I,
> With Love to live and die,
>   Fortune's forlorn.

Shakespeare's play, *As You Like It*, it will be recognized, is but a dramatic expansion of this idea, and contains such significant touches as the following:

This from the dialogue between Rosalind and Celia (I.ii):

> Let us mock the good housewife Fortune.
>
>   *   *   *
>
> Nay now thou goest from Fortune's office to Nature's: Fortune reigns in gifts of the world, not in the lineaments of Nature.
>
>   *   *   *
>
> Nature hath given us wit to flout at Fortune.
>
>   *   *   *

Peradventure this is not Fortune's work, but Nature's, who perceiveth our natural wits too dull.

Later we have the Duke's remark and the reply of Amiens (II.1):

Are not these woods more free from peril than the envious court?

*   *   *

Happy is your grace
That can translate the stubborness of Fortune
Into so quiet and so sweet a style?

It is not merely that there appear together the ideas of Nature, Fortune, Love, court-life and life in the woods, in the two sets of writings under review—ideas which may possibly be as recurrent in other writings of the times as they are in Shakespeare's. It is rather the similarity in the peculiar colligation of ideas, and also the correspondence of such chance expressions as De Vere's "Fortune's Forlorn" and Shakespeare's "Out of suits with Fortune," which give a stamp of fundamental unity to the two works.

Desire for pity.

There are minor points of similarity, which though insignificant in themselves, help to make up that general impression of common authorship which comes only with a close familiarity with the poems as a whole. Of these we may specify the recurrence of what seems to us a curious appeal for pity. From two separate poems of De Vere's we have the following:

And let all those that shall her see
Despise her state and pity me.

The more my plaints I do resound
The less she pities me.

And from Shakespeare's sonnets we take these:

Pity me and wish I were renewed (111).
The manner of my pity-wanting pain (140).
Thine eyes I love and they as pitying me (132).
But if thou catch my hope, turn back to me,
And play the mother's part, kiss me, be kind (143).

Shakespeare's Echo poem.

In making this parallel between the work of Edward de Vere
and Shakespeare we shall turn now to an example which carries
us back to the beginning of our enquiry. Starting with
Shakespeare's lyric poetry, we fastened upon *Venus and Adonis* as
furnishing the connecting link between the two sections of work.
Reverting now to this poem we find, in the first place, it contains
all the imagery of these early works of De Vere's and then one of
the most striking parallels we have noticed so far.

In *Venus and Adonis* we have the following verses on the
"Echo." Venus is bemoaning her troubles and the echo is
answering her (Stanzas 139-142):

> And now she beats her heart whereat it groans,
> That all the *neighbour caves, as seeming troubled,*
> Make verbal repetition of her moans;
> Passion on passion deeply is redoubled:
> 'Ay me!' she cries, and twenty times "Woe, woe!"
> And twenty echoes twenty times cry so.
>
> She marking them begins a wailing note,
> And *sings extemporally a woeful ditty;*
> How love makes young men thrall and old men dote,
> How love is wise in folly, foolish witty:
> Her heavy anthem still concludes in "Woe."
> And still the choir of echoes answers "So."
>
> *   *   *
>
> For who hath she to spend the night withal,
> But idle sounds resembling parasites,
> Like shrill-tongued tapsters answering every call,
> Soothing the humour of fantastic wights?
> She says "'Tis so"; they answer all, "'Tis so";
> And would say after her if she said "No!"

(We observe in passing in the second stanza a repetition of the
wit and folly paradox.)

Oxford's Echo poem.

We shall now give Edward de Vere's echo poem in full. It is
one of the most quaintly conceived and most skillfully executed
pieces of versification, and hardly admits of curtailment. To enjoy
it fully the reader must remember that "Vere," retaining its

French sound, is pronounced somewhat like the word "bare," and the last syllable in words like "fe*ver*" and "qui*ver*" must, in this instance, be given the same full sound. Oxford's name, we may remark, frequently appears in old records as "Ver."

VISION OF A FAIR MAID, WITH ECHO VERSES.

Sitting alone upon my thoughts in melancholy mood.
In sight of sea, and at my back an ancient hoary wood.
I saw a fair young lady come her secret fears to wail.
Clad all in colour of a nun, and covered with a veil.
Yet (for the day was calm and clear) I might discern her face,
As one might see a damask rose hid under crystal glass.
Three times with her soft hand full hard on her left side she knocks,
And sighed so sore as *might have made some pity in the rocks.*
From sighs and shedding amber tears *into sweet song she brake,*
When thus the Echo answer'd her to every word she spake.

Oh heavens. who was the first that bred in me this fe*ver?*—Vere.
Who was the first that gave the wound. whose fear I wear for e*ver?*—
    Vere.
What tyrant, Cupid, to my harm, usurps thy golden qui*ver?*—Vere.
What wight first caught this heart, and can from bondage it deli*ver?*—
    Vere.

Yet who doth most adore this wight, oh *hollow caves* tell true?—You.
What nymph deserves his liking best yet doth in sorrow rue?—You.
What makes him not reward good will with some reward or ruth?—
    Youth.
What makes him show besides his birth such pride and such untruth?—
    Youth.

May I his favour match with love if he my love will try?—Ay.
May I requite his birth with faith? Then faithful will I die?—Ay.

And I that knew this lady well, said, Lord, how great a miracle.
To her how Echo told the truth as true as Phoebus oracle.

Romeo and Juliet.

After studying these two poems carefully and comparing specially the words in italics, then recalling De Vere's poem on "Women" turning upon the simile of the haggard hawk and keeping in mind that in De Vere's Echo poem we have a young woman making the caves re-echo with her lover's name, considering now the speech that "Shakespeare" puts into the mouth of Juliet:

> Hist! Romeo hist! Oh for a falconer's voice
> To lure this tassel-gentle back again.
> Bondage is hoarse and may not speak aloud,
> Else would I tear *the cave where Echo lies*
> And make her airy tongue more hoarse than mine
> *With repetition of my Romeo's name.* (II.2)

(A six-lined fragment of blank verse.)

In presence of such a correspondence in the work as these verses present, it seems almost like a waste of effort to add further comparisons; and yet, so redolent of De Vere's work is this particular play of Shakespeare's that we feel compelled to draw attention to parallel passages like the following:

De Vere:
> (I) that with the careful culver, climbs the worn and withered
>   tree,
> To entertain my thoughts, and there may hap to moan,
> *That never am less idle, lo! than when I am alone.*

Shakespeare (*Romeo and Juliet*, I.1):
> He stole into the covert of the wood
> I, measuring his affection by my own,
> *That most art busied when they're most alone.*

De Vere:
> Patience perforce is such a pinching pain.

Shakespeare (*Romeo and Juliet*, I.5):
> Patience perforce . . . makes my flesh tremble.

De Vere:
> His bitter ball is sugared bliss.

Shakespeare (*Romeo and Juliet*, I.I):
> A choking gall and a preserving sweet
> Now seeming sweet convert to bitter gall. (I.5)

De Vere:
> O cruel hap and hard estate,
> That forceth me to love my foe.

Shakespeare (*Romeo and Juliet*, I.2):
> Prodigious birth of love it is to me
> That I must love a loathed enemy.

The morning lark.

Returning now to the *Venus* echo verses we find that they are immediately followed by this:

> Lo! here the lark, weary of nest,
> From his moist cabinet mounts up on high,
> And wakes the morning from whose silver breast
> The sun ariseth in his majesty;
> Who doth the world so gloriously behold,
> That cedar tops and hills seem burnished gold (stanza 143).

To this add the following line from *Romeo and Juliet*:

> It was the lark *the herald of the morn*. (III.5).

Now compare this Shakespearean work with the following from De Vere:

> The lively lark stretched forth her wings
> The *messenger of morning bright*;
> And with her *cheerful voice* did sing
> The Day's approach discharging Night.
> When that *Aurora* blushing red
> Descried the guilt of *Thetis' bed*.

This again suggests the following from *Romeo and Juliet*:

> Many a morning hath he there been seen
>
>   *   *   *   *
>
> But all too soon as the *all-cheering sun*
> Should in the furthest east begin to draw
> The shady curtains from *Aurora's bed*, etc. (I.1.)

Romeo and Juliet also contains two separate six-lined stanzas (on the Lord Vaux model), and also what are probably the first of the Shakespearean sonnets—which are, as already mentioned, identical in form with the only sonnet that appears in De Vere's early poems.

Oxford's child-wife.

Another matter, which is not poetical, deserves to be mentioned here. It must have struck many people as strange that Juliet at the time of her marriage should be represented as a mere child of fourteen. There is no special point in the play to necessitate having one so young for the tragical part she had to play. Extraordinarily young as she was, however, she was the actual age of De Vere's wife at the time of their marriage: the ceremony being merely postponed until her fifteenth birthday was reached.

The poems and the enquiry.

We must now recall the fact that when we selected De Vere as the possible author of Shakespeare's plays and poems, and found that he satisfied the essential conditions of our original characterization, we had no knowledge whatever of these poems of his, almost every line of which we now find paralleled in Shakespeare. To discover such a correspondence in the poems under such circumstances furnishes, to the discoverer at any rate, a much greater weight of evidence than if he had been acquainted with the writings at the outset. It will be observed that, in making these comparisons, the passages quoted from Shakespeare which are suggestive of Oxford's early poetry belong mainly to what is accepted as Shakespeare's early work, such as *Venus, Lucrece, The Two Gentlemen of Verona,* and *Romeo and Juliet.* On the other hand the traces of the De Vere poetry in the later Shakespearean work are very slight. This, it will also be remembered, is in precise accordance with the principle which guided us in the first stages of our search, namely, that it would be the poet's early work which would appear under his own name, and that it would be found to link itself on to the earliest Shakespearean work. Again, as the De Vere collection is only a small one, it will be seen, from the number of poems quoted, that practically the whole of the De Vere work is deposited, as it were, in Shakespeare. The evidence furnished by such parallelism must not, however, be viewed alone; it must be connected specially with the testimony which literary authorities have given us as to the specific qualities of De Vere's poetry adduced in the preceding chapter. It must also be connected with these important considerations of chronology which allow the early career of Oxford to fit in exactly with later production of the "Shakespeare" dramas, and to all this must also be added the fact of his presenting in his person so many of the conditions and attributes which recent Shakespearean study has assigned to the great dramatist. The reader should then ask himself whether it would be common sense to keep on believing that all this is mere accident.

Tragedy and comedy.

If from reading the echo poem of De Vere with its quaint and delicate humour, the reader will turn to such verses as those beginning,

> Fain would I sing, but fury makes me mad,

or,

> Fram'd in the front of forlorn hope,

and then again recall the fact that Edward de Vere, in his work for the stage, is reported as being "the best in comedy" in his day, he will get an idea of the striking combination of humour and tragedy in the nature and work of this remarkable man. All the startling contrast of high comedy and profound tragedy which stands out from the pages of Shakespeare finds its counterpart in the work of De Vere, as we shall also find it does in his actual life. With this in mind, let it be recalled that, at the very moment when Shakespeare was writing the sonnets, with all their tragic depth, and with hardly a trace of lightheartedness, revealing a soul darkened by disappointment, disillusionment and self-condemnation, he was also preparing for the stage plays which for three hundred years have, by their exquisite fun, supplied the world with inexhaustible laughter. We read some of the sonnets and we feel that the writer must have been the most despairing of pessimists.

> Give notice to the world that I am gone
> From this vile world with vilest worms to dwell.

We turn to the comedies he wrote for the stage, and we think of him as the merriest of men. Which was the real Shakespeare? The Shakespeare revealed in the sonnets or the Shakespeare revealed in the comedies? Probably neither by itself. The sonnets are, however, direct personal poetry; the comedies are literature and stage plays. The natural assumption, therefore, is that in his inmost life he was more the Shakespeare of the sonnets than of the comedies. If, therefore, we suppose that "Shakespeare" is Edward de Vere, we find him expressing himself directly on the point in the following lines:

> I am not as I seem to be,
> For when I smile I am not glad,
> A thrall, although you count me free,
> *I, most in mirth, most pensive sad.*
> I smile to bide my bitter spite,
> As Hannibal that saw in sight,
> His country's soil with Carthage town,
> By Roman force defaced down.

A possible pun.

We give the entire stanza in order that, in passing, its structure may be noted. It will be seen that it is identical in metre and rhyme with Shakespeare's poem "When daisies pied and violets blue," with which *Love's Labour's Lost* finishes (leaving out, of course, the interjected word "cuckoo"). The observant reader may notice, too, that the latter poem is preceded by the words, "*Ver*, begin"; and remembering that Oxford's name was very frequently spelt "Ver," he will be able to imagine the elation which would have appeared in certain quarters, if, in this the first Shakespearean play, for such it is considered, there had occurred the words, "Bacon, begin."

Hidden suffering.

Another stanza in the same poem of De Vere's runs thus:

> I Hannibal that smile for grief

> And let you Ceasar's tears suffice,
> The one that laughs at his mischief
> The other all for joy that cries.
> I smile to see me scorned so,
> You weep for joy to see me woe.

This is at once suggestive of the lines in *Lear* (I.4):

> Then they for sudden joy did weep
> And I for sorrow sung.

Returning to our theme, one of the most penetrating of observers amongst writers on Shakespeare, Richard Bagehot, although believing in the essential gaiety of the poet's nature, remarks that "all through his works there is a certain tinge of *musing sadness* pervading, and as it were *softening their gaiety*,"[98] exactly as Edward de Vere described himself in the former of the above stanzas. This is just what we might expect to find in a writer whose life had been saddened, but who preserved by a deliberate effort his appreciation of fun; whose self-command enabled him to throw aside the burden of melancholy and revel for a while in the enjoyment of his own lighter faculties, but who, throughout it all, never quite forgot the sadness that lay at the bottom of his soul, and who, when the special effort was over, would swing back upon himself with an intensified sense of his own inner sufferings. These are just the conditions to yield that remarkable combination of tragedy and comedy which distinguishes Shakespeare, and they are the conditions, too, most likely to be furnished by the nature and circumstances of Edward de Vere.

Viewing the lyric work of Edward de Vere as a whole we feel justified in claiming that it contains much more than a possible promise of the work of Shakespeare. What is wanting to it is the vast and varied knowledge of human nature depicted in the Shakespearean dramas. This demands a wide and intense experience of life; a life involving loss as well as gain; and the years intervening between the two sets of works, years in which he was

---

[98] Walter Bagehot, "*Shakespeare—The Man*," p. 67.

busy with his troupes of play-actors, the "Oxford Boys," would certainly be full of such experience to him. And if we assume the identity of Oxford with "Shakespeare" it must be conceded that one misses from the personal poems of Shakespeare, the sonnets, certain sweet and "gracious" touches contained in the early personal poems of De Vere, whilst one meets also with some harsher and more defiant notes. The iron had evidently entered more deeply into his soul, his nature had become in a measure "subdued to what it worked in, like the dyer's hand," but out of the tragedy of his own life were born the imperishable masterpieces in tragic drama that will probably remain for all time the supreme glory of English literature.

General review.

In working out our investigations we found, first of all, a remarkable set of coincidences between the circumstances of Edward de Vere and the conditions which we supposed to pertain to the writer of Shakespeare's dramas. Our last chapter showed us an equally remarkable set of coincidences connected with the general literary position and the dominant qualities of Oxford's poetry. The chapter we are now finishing, the most critical in the piecing together of the case, reveals what we claim to be a most extraordinary correspondence in the details of the work.

When, therefore, the poems of De Vere shall have become familiar to English readers, it will not be surprising if those who are thoroughly intimate with Shakespeare's work are able to detect much more striking points of similarity than any that are here indicated. It must, however, be kept in mind that the value of these correspondences depends not so much upon the striking character of a few of them, which might conceivably be matched elsewhere, but upon the cumulative effect of them all. Taken in their mass then, we believe that sufficient has already been made out, which, supported as it is by the other lines of our argument, leaves little room for doubt that the problem of the authorship of Shakespeare's works has at last been solved. Valuable as is the other evidence which we have been able to collect, we might have hesitated for a very long while before venturing, on the strength of that alone, to assume the responsibility of claiming publicly that we had succeeded in identifying Shakespeare. Now, however, that we have been able to examine the early poetry of De Vere, and subject it to a careful comparison with the early Shakespearean work, it has become impossible to hesitate any longer in proclaiming Edward de Vere, Seventeenth Earl of Oxford, as the real author of "Shakespeare's" works.

CHAPTER IX

THE RECORDS AND EARLY LIFE OF EDWARD DE VERE

> Horatio, I am dead;
> Thou livest; report me and my cause aright
> To the unsatisfied.
>
> *   *   *
>
> If ever thou didst hold me in thy heart
> Absent thee from felicity awhile,
> And in this harsh world draw thy breath in pain
> To tell my story.
>
> *Hamlet* (V.2)
>
> An unlifted shadow somehow lies across his memory.
> Dr. Grosart

Authorities. The biographical records in the succeeding chapters are taken chiefly from the *Dictionary of National Biography*, *Historical Recollections of Noble Families*, by Arthur Collins; *The Great Lord Burleigh*, by Martin Hume; *The House of Cecil*, by G. Ravenscroft Dennis; *Histories of Essex*, by Morant and Wright; *The Hatfield Manuscripts*, and *Calendars of State Papers.*[99]

I

THE REPUTATION OF THE EARL OF OXFORD

FOLLOWING the general scheme of the investigation as outlined at the beginning of this work, it will be well to recall at this point the nature of the phase with which we are at present occupied, and the exact stage of it now reached. The fifth step

---

[99] The word "Recollections" in the title of Collins's book should be "Collections." A more complete title is *The Historical Collections of the Noble Families of Cavendishe, Holles, Vere, Harley, and Ogle.*

By Morant and Wright, Looney is referring to two different books, one by each author: *History and Antiquities of the County of Essex* by Philip Morant, and *History and Topography of the County of Essex* by Thomas Wright.

being to proceed from the man chosen to the works of Shakespeare, in order to see to what extent the man is reflected in the works, the comparison of the two sets of writings just concluded forms the natural introduction to this phase of the enquiry. Continuing this step our next business must be to examine, in whatever detail possible, the life and circumstances of the man in order to ascertain how far they, too, relate themselves to the contents of, and the task of producing, the Shakespearean plays and poems.

In entering upon this series of biographical chapters we must remind the reader that the object of this work is twofold: to prove our case, and to help towards a fuller and more accurate view of the life and personality of the Earl of Oxford. Here our task is one of special difficulty, for our theory presupposes a man who had deliberately planned his self-concealment. Our material is bound, therefore, to be as scanty as he could make it, and, at the outset, probably misleading. We shall, therefore, be under the necessity of reconstructing a personality from the most meagre of data, with the added disadvantage of a large amount of contemporary misrepresentation, which it will be necessary to correct.

Motives for concealment.

One naturally asks why the author of the great dramas should have wished to throw a veil over his identity as he did; and the strange thing about the matter before us, is this, that, with the Shakespeare sonnets before us, we should have been so slow in framing this question and answering it satisfactorily. For, not merely in an odd sentence, but as the burden of some of his most powerful sonnets, he tells us in the plainest of terms, that he was one whose name had fallen into disrepute and who wished that it should perish with him.

> No longer mourn for me when 1 am dead,
> Than you shall hear the surly sullen bell
> Give warning to the world that I am fled
> From this vile world, with vilest worms to dwell;
> Nay, if you read this line, remember not
> The hand that writ it

> My name be buried where my body is,
> And live no more to shame nor me nor you.

> Or I shall live your epitaph to make,
> Or you survive when I in earth am rotten,
> From hence your memory death cannot take,
> Although in me each part will be forgotten.
> Your name from hence immortal life shall have,
> Though I, once gone, to all the world must die.

> Alas, 'tis true, I have gone here and there,
> And made myself a motley to the view.

> Thence comes it that my name receives a brand.

> Your love and pity doth the impression fill,
> Which vulgar scandal stamp'd upon my brow.

Disrepute.
   When to all this we find him adding the fear

> That every word doth almost tell my name,

it is made as clear as anything can be that he was one who had elected his own self-effacement, and that disrepute was one, if not the principal, motive. We may, if we wish, question the sufficiency or reasonableness of the motive. That, however, is his business, not ours. The important point for us is that he has by his sonnets disclosed the fact that he, "Shakespeare," was one who was concealing his real name, and that the motive he gives, adequate or not, is one which unmistakably would apply to the Earl of Oxford; and would not apply in the same literal manner to anyone else to whom it has been sought to attribute the Shakespeare dramas. If the Earl of Oxford had filled an exalted place in general estimation, it ought to have worked against the theory of authorship we are advancing. That he was one "in disgrace with Fortune and men's eyes" is what we should have expected, and is therefore an element of evidence in confirmation of our theory.

   Under the Stratfordian and Baconian views mystifying interpretations have had to be read into the utterances just quoted. In spite of their intense reality and genuine autobiographical ring, they have been treated as cryptic poetry or mere dramatic pose; and one of our greatest difficulties will be to combat the non-literal constructions forced upon these poems. In the proper place we shall have to show that their contents are as real and literal as the spirit and temper of the works suggest. Puzzling, Shakespeare could undoubtedly be, as in the "Will" sonnets (135 and 136) where he is obviously dealing in enigmas. The curious thing is that he has been read seriously and literally when in a playful mood, by the same people who have treated passionate, heart-wrung utterances as mere freaks of fancy.

Autobiography in the Sonnets.

When moving on the plane of experience his conceptions attain a definiteness unequalled in poetry, whilst there has probably never been a writer capable of securing a more precise correspondence between a thought and its expression. When, therefore, he tells us, in so many words, that "vulgar scandal" had robbed him of his good name, and that, although he believed his work would be immortal he wished his name to be forgotten, we are quite entitled to take his own word for it, and to demand no further motive for the adoption of a disguise. No mere *nom de plume* could have been so successful as his adoption of a mask: its success for over three hundred years will probably be a matter of astonishment for many generations to come.

Had these sonnets been published by their author during his own lifetime they would have been absurd from the point of view of the particular contents we have just been considering. Imagine any man publishing, or allowing the publication under his own name, of documents in which he specifically states that he wished his name to be buried with his body! It is equally absurd to suppose that their author permitted the issue of documents implying that William Shakspere was but a mask. They were, however, published during the lifetime of all the men to whom it has been sought to attribute their authorship: William Shakspere, Francis Bacon, William Stanley and Roger Manners: but *after* the death of Edward de Vere. The particular sonnets seem to belong to a date at which Oxford's fortunes were at about their lowest and when the motive assigned for hiding his name would be most applicable; the works being published under the mask would then be the two long poems published in 1593 and 1594.

Social considerations.

We do not maintain that the motive assigned in the sonnets was the only one that operated. By the time that the mask was employed again, after an interval of four years during which some of the plays had appeared anonymously, there are evidences that Oxford was making efforts to retrieve his position socially as well as financially. When plays were being published under Shakespeare's name, Oxford was seeking to regain favour with the Queen and setting family influences to work to obtain for himself the position of governor of Wales. Needless to say to have appeared at the time in the role of dramatic author would have been completely fatal to any chances he may have had: for in those days "dramatic authorship was considered hardly respectable." And Oxford especially, having incurred his disgrace in the first instance by deserting the court for a Bohemian association with actors and play-writers, could only hope to recover his social position and secure an appropriate official appointment, by being seen as little as possible in such connections.

Family motives.

After Oxford's death his widow, a lady of private means, assisted by her brother, continued the struggle to recover for her son Henry, the eighteenth Earl of Oxford, the prestige which had been lost to the family by the extraordinary career of his father. A legal case that arose out of this is a recognized landmark in the history of the law, and shows clearly that the recovery of what had been lost had become a settled object of family policy. Even supposing, then, that they may not have considered themselves under a moral or contracted obligation to continue the secrecy, it would hardly have been in harmony with their general policy to have discontinued it.

Although we have put forward these considerations with regard to motives, we must make it clear that no obligation to furnish motives rests upon an investigator in such a case as this. Motives are sometimes altogether impenetrable. Objective facts, and the evidence for the truth of such facts, form the proper material for enquiries like the present.

The shadow lifting.

From the biographer's point of view, however, all these considerations constitute a double difficulty. We have first to surmount the obstacles which an able intellect, bent on secrecy, would himself interpose between himself and the public; and then we must penetrate the mists of disrepute which he assures us had gathered round his name. Before this can be properly done many years must elapse, and many minds must be interested in it: the correction of an erroneous estimate of an historic personality being one of the slowest of human processes. We make here only a first simple effort in that direction.

No one who is able to appreciate humanity's debt to "Shakespeare" can, under any circumstances, regard him as a man who has merited abiding dishonour. The world has taken to its heart men like Robert Burns and Molière, whose lives have fallen far short of the pattern we could have wished for them. And if Edward de Vere is, as we have every reason to believe, the real "Shakespeare," the world will not be slow to allow the great benefits he has conferred upon mankind to atone for any shortcomings that may be found in him. Our task at the present, however, is to see him as he was, in so far as his character and the events of his life have a bearing upon our problem. Everything that comes before us in the form of mere traditional view, inference, or impression must be rigidly separated from ascertained facts; and even these will need to be accepted cautiously and reinterpreted from the point of view of one great dominating possibility—that of his being endowed with the heart and genius of Shakespeare and of having produced the Shakespeare literature.

Need for reinterpretation.

If, for example, the Earl of Oxford was only a son-in-law of Lord Burleigh's, who had achieved nothing more noteworthy than the writing of a few short lyrics, and had spent the best years of his life in fruitless amusement with a company of play-actors, then we must judge him mainly by the part he played in the life of Burleigh. If, however, the Earl of Oxford was Shakespeare, then he towers high above Lord Burleigh, and we shall have to judge Burleigh very largely by the part he played in the life of Oxford. Or if, in the domain of poetry, he is chiefly to be remembered as the man who called his rival, Philip Sidney, a "puppy," we shall have to judge him by his bearing towards Sidney. If, however, Oxford was "Shakespeare," gifted with all Shakespeare's penetration into human nature, our interest will lie in discovering how far Sidney may have merited the epithet.

Unjust treatment.

Again, if, as we shall see was the case, we find that, as a young man, he begged to join the army; when that was refused him he begged to be allowed to join the navy; when that in turn was refused he begged to travel abroad; and when, though by this time he was twenty-four years of age and married, that was also refused, so that he seemed condemned to spend his life hanging about the court, and finding the court life irksome, ran away to the continent, only to be brought back before he had had a chance of seeing anything of life, we may be able to agree with those who speak of him as being wayward, if we suppose him to have been incapable and an intellectual mediocrity. But if we suppose him possessed of the genius of Shakespeare, with Shakespeare's capacity for experiencing life, and all that capacity as so much driving force within him, urging him to seek experience of life; indeed, if we take into account nothing more than what is positively known of his powers as revealed in his poems and dramatic record, we shall be much more inclined to consider him a badly used man, the victim of most unfavourable circumstances and manifest injustice, with a very genuine grievance against the guardian and father-in-law, Burleigh, who had so persistently thwarted him.

Secret occupations.

Finally, if, remembering the character borne by the play-actors of the time, as described in the passage we have quoted from Dean Church, we believe him to have wasted the best years of his life in intimate, useless association with them, we shall be inclined to see in his conduct a manifestation of dissoluteness and to acquiesce in Burleigh's statement that he had been "enticed away by lewd persons."[100] If, on the other hand, we believe that Oxford was Shakespeare, and that during these years he was hard at work, seriously, but in a measure secretly, engaged in the activities that have produced at once the greatest dramas and the finest literature that England boasts, then the facts have a totally new light thrown upon them, and admit of a vastly different interpretation. For, the secrecy in which his work as a whole is involved would surely be maintained towards those who were out of sympathy with him, amongst whom we can certainly place his father-in-law and probably his wife; all of which seems clearly alluded to in sonnet 48:

> How careful was I, when I took my way,
> Each trifle under truest bars to thrust,
> That to my use it might unused stay,
> From hands of falsehood, in sure wards of trust.

False stories.

We shall avoid, therefore, all unauthenticated stories which seem to have had their roots in personal animosity. Such particulars as are narrated in the *Dictionary of National Biography*, that a certain man's "story that the Earl" did so-and-so, but that it "is not confirmed, and was warmly denied by"[101] the very man whom he was reported to have injured, is not biography. It serves to show, however, that he was the victim of

---

[100] Lee, "Vere, Edward," p. 226.
[101] Lee, "Vere, Edward," p. 227.

false and unscrupulous calumny. When, therefore, we find great admirers of Philip Sidney, like Fulke Greville, Sidney's biographer, promulgating impossible stories about projected assassinations, and another antagonist making, almost in so many words, the same false charges that Oliver makes against Orlando in *As You Like It*, we begin to realize the type of men with whom we are dealing; what freedoms the group of court adventurers, to whom Oxford was clearly hostile, had taken with his name and reputation; and how little reliance is to be placed generally upon their records either of their friends or of their enemies.

It is unfortunate, then, that the names which predominate in the article upon which we are dependent for so many of the facts of Oxford's life are those of people antagonistic to him, and most of the facts bear evidence of having come to us through these unfriendly channels. Anything which bears the mark of Burleigh, Fulke Greville, or Raleigh, the true type of the picturesque but unscrupulous adventurer of those days, must be suspect in so far as it touches Edward de Vere; and anything which research may be able to recover, that shall furnish us with the names and the opinions of his friends about the court, and, more important still, his dealings with men of letters, and with playwrights and actors, will be invaluable as tending to furnish us with a truer view of the man. So far as we can make out up to the present, however, his friends seem to have respected loyally his desire for personal oblivion, and have remained silent about him; thus, of course, allowing free currency to all that his enemies have been able to circulate to his discredit.

As this is not intended to be a complete biography, facts which do not appear relevant to the argument, either for or against it, and which, from some other consideration, might necessitate lengthy discussion, will, for the most part, be omitted.

Note.

To illustrate again the curious way in which evidence has fallen into our hands, we would draw attention to the above reference to Oliver in *As You Like It*. When we came across the murderous charges made against Oxford by Charles Arundel, the first thing that seemed to stand out was the name "Charles," and an evident vulgarity in the man, which brought Charles the wrestler, of *As You Like It*, to the mind. Being somewhat "rusty" at the moment in reference to subordinate details in the play, the next thing was to look up the parts dealing with Charles the wrestler; only, of course, to find the same charges that Charles Arundel made against Oxford being insinuated by Oliver into the mind of Charles the wrestler. And so the parts of the mosaic keep fitting in. The jesting threats of Touchstone in the same play may therefore furnish the explanation of the charges made against Oxford: for practical joking could hardly be above the dignity of the writer of some of "Shakespeare's" comedies, who, according to his own confession, had made himself "a motley to the view."

II

THE ANCESTRY OF EDWARD DE VERE

It is waste labour usually to trace the ancestral connections of literary men. It is themselves and what they accomplished that really matter, and literary biographies which go beyond this generally succeed in being tedious. In the case before us, however, these ancestral connections and the writer's attitude towards them are vital; so that some brief notice of the family of the De Veres is essential to the argument.

Family origins.

The founder of the family was one Aubrey de Vere (derived, it is supposed, from Ver near Bayeux) who came to England with the Conqueror, and was rewarded for his support with extensive estates in Essex, Suffolk, Cambridge, Huntingdonshire and Middlesex; and "the continuance of his family in the male line, and its possession of an earldom for more than five and a half centuries have made its name a household word."[102] During these

---

[102] Lee, "Vere, Family of," p. 219.

centuries the vast estates of the family, as well as its titles and dignities, were further augmented by marriage or by royal favour.

In the time of the anarchy which marked the reign of the Conqueror's grandson Stephen, the title of Earl of Oxford was bestowed by Matilda upon the representative of the family, another Aubrey (1142), whilst nine years prior to this a son or grandson of the founder, also of the same name, had been created Great Chamberlain. On the accession of Henry II the title conferred by Matilda was confirmed by the new monarch. Amongst the hereditary dignities obtained through marriage was that of Chamberlain to the Queen, and the titles of Viscount Bolebec, Lord Sandford, and Lord Badlemere. Lyly in dedicating his *Euphues and his England* to Oxford, whom he addresses as his master, takes occasion to string all these various titles together.

"Shakespeare" and Richard II.

All through the long period of the Plantagenet kings, the lands, titles and dignities of the family were transmitted through a succession of Aubreys, Johns, and Roberts, like so many representatives of a royal dynasty; and, in the reign of the last of the Plantagenets, Richard II, the Earl of Oxford, who was the royal favourite, was created a Marquis, being thus raised above all the rest of the nobility and ranked next to the King himself. This is the Robert, Earl of Oxford, mentioned in ordinary history text books as the favourite responsible partly for the troubles that befell the King, and who earned for himself a reputation of extreme dissoluteness.

Earl Robert.

The personal relationship of Richard II to the Earl of Oxford of his day, and the honour he conferred upon the family, might account for "Shakespeare's" slight partiality to Richard, if we suppose the former to have been a later earl of the same family; whilst the unfortunate character borne by Richard's favourite would explain the curious fact of his non-appearance in a play written by a member of the same house, one in whom family pride was a pronounced trait. For the character of this Robert, Earl of Oxford, of Richard II's reign, made it impossible to introduce him without either immortalizing his infamy or of so altering the facts as to have betrayed the authorship. The silence of the author at this point is therefore even more significant than his utterances in the case with which we shall presently deal. For be it observed that Shakespeare deals with this very question of the pernicious influence of evil associates upon Richard and leaves out all mention in this connection of the one particular evil counsellor that history has clearly recorded for us. Shakespeare, whoever he was, had evidently some special reason for screening the Earl of Oxford. He had not overlooked him, for at the end of the play the Earl is mentioned as having been executed for supporting the King;* possibly the only thing in his favour that could be recorded.

Shakespeare and high birth.

Edward de Vere's pride in his ancient ancestry is commented on by more than one writer; and so marked a feature of Shakespeare's is this regard for high and honoured birth, that one writer, believing it to be written by the Stratford man, does not hesitate to speak of it as "snobbery." By whatever name we may choose to call it, it is at any rate an outstanding mental trait which Edward de Vere and "Shakespeare" have in common. To have found it in one situated like the Stratford man would, however, have bespoken a measure of "snobbery" inconsistent with the intellectual largeness of "Shakespeare." In the case of Edward de Vere it is merely the spontaneous fruit of centuries of family tradition and the social atmosphere into which he was born, and shows us that even the broadest minds remain more or less at the mercy of their social milieu.

---

* Looney's note: In the First Folio edition "Spenser" is substituted for "Oxford." Such a substitution (not noticed until the above was in print) is very striking.

We have had occasion already to point out that Shakespeare did not understand the "lower orders." What is even more striking is the fact that he did not understand the middle-classes. Mr. Frank Harris, who, if our own theory of authorship be accepted, has, in many particulars, shown great sureness of psychological analysis, but who never expresses a single doubt as to the truth of the Stratfordian position, asserts, in his work on *The Man Shakespeare*, that Shakespeare did not even know the middle classes. "He utterly missed," he says, "what a knowledge of the middle classes would have given him," whilst "in all his writings he praises lords and gentlemen." And again, "Shakespeare, one fancies, was a gentleman by nature, *and a good deal more.*"[103] That one, like Shakespeare, whose studies of human nature rest so obviously upon observation, could both remain ignorant of his own class and also assimilate rapidly the characteristics and courtesies of another class is neither more nor less than a contradiction in terms. The logical conclusion is that "Shakespeare" was himself an aristocrat: a point on which anti-Stratfordians of all schools agree, and on which some Stratfordians, in return, most weakly try to make merry.

It would unnecessarily overload these pages with quotations to give all that Shakespeare says on the question of high birth, whilst a few selected passages would not accurately represent the position. Some measure of its importance to him may, however, be gathered from the fact that he does honour to the idea in more than twenty separate plays. Now, a person may happen to be of high birth and yet be able to take a true measure of its value. In the case of Edward de Vere, however, it would seem that he had the same exaggerated idea of its importance that we meet with in Shakespeare. And as we have chosen the play of *All's Well that Ends Well* to preside in great measure over the first part of our biographical argument, we would ask the reader to notice as an

---

[103] Harris, *The Man*, p. 386. Italics added by Looney.

illustration of Shakespeare's attitude to this question how the idea of high birth dominates the whole of the play.

III

THE EARL OF OXFORD IN THE WARS OF THE ROSES

When the Wars of the Roses broke out, John de Vere, Twelfth Earl of Oxford, became, as we have already seen, a staunch supporter of the Lancastrian cause. In the early part of Edward IV's reign, whilst matters were still unsettled between the two parties, he was executed along with his eldest son, Aubrey de Vere, for corresponding with the defeated Queen Margaret. The title then passed to his second son, John, the Thirteenth Earl, who took part in the temporary restoration of Henry VI. For this he was attainted in 1474, but restored to his family honours on the defeat of the Yorkists and the accession of Henry Tudor.

In relating these particulars to the plays of Shakespeare a strictly chronological parallel between the historical events and the plays is not possible. If, however, we take the four plays which deal specially with these wars, the three parts of *Henry VI*, and the play of *Richard III*, we may say that *Henry VI*, part 1, deals mainly with the years prior to the outbreak of civil war, during which England was losing power in France through the heroism of Joan d'Arc, whilst the first rumblings of the coming storm in England were distinctly heard. In *Henry VI*, part 2, the tension becomes acute, and the opening phase of the conflict, that in which the Twelfth Earl of Oxford was prominent, forms the subject matter of part of the play. *Henry VI*, part 3, is concerned mainly with the short period of Henry's temporary restoration during the reign of Edward IV, ending in the overthrow of the Lancastrians and the murder of Henry VI. The play of *Richard III* is presented as the final triumph of the red rose over the white.

Shakespeare and the Earls of Oxford.

Now of these plays, *Henry VI*, part 1, we are assured, is probably not from Shakespeare's hand at all. The same remark applies to *Henry VI*, part 2, and to a considerable portion even of *Henry VI*, part 3. The most Shakespearean work in this trilogy is to be found, however, in the latter half of *Henry VI*, part 3. *Richard III* is wholly Shakespearean. Turning then to *Henry VI*, parts 1 and 2, the non-Shakespearean plays, we find there is no mention made whatever of the 12th Earl of Oxford; whilst, on coming to *Henry VI*, part 3, we find a very prominent and honoured place given to John, the 13th Earl of Oxford, along with the striking fact that he does not make his appearance on the stage until Act III, Scene 3. That is to say, he is not brought into these plays at all until he is brought in by "Shakespeare"; and then, which makes it still more striking, we have very particular mention made of the father and brother who had laid down their lives in the Lancastrian cause, but who are completely ignored in the other two plays. In a word, the non-Shakespearean work ignores the Earls of Oxford, whilst the Shakespearean work gives them a leading and distinguished position.

Oxford speaks:

> Call him my King, by whose injurious doom
> My elder brother, the Lord Aubrey de Vere,
> Was done to death? And more than so, my father,
> Even in the downfall of his mellow'd years,
> When nature brought him to the door of death?
> No, Warwick, no, while life upholds this arm,
> This arm upholds the house of Lancaster.

Having been thus introduced into the play he is hardly mentioned except to be praised:

> And thou, brave Oxford, wondrous well beloved.
> Sweet Oxford.
> Where is the post that came from valiant Oxford?
> O cheerful colours! see where Oxford comes.
> Oxford, Oxford, for Lancaster.

> O! welcome Oxford, for we want thy help.
> Why, is not Oxford here another anchor?

Then towards the close of the play, when King Henry VI blesses Henry of Richmond and names him as successor to the throne, it is Oxford who, along with Somerset, arranges to send him to Brittany for safety, until "the storms be passed of civil enmity." And, in the last act, even such a detail as his place of imprisonment is remembered and named:

> Away with Oxford to Hames Castle straight.

Richard III.

Finally, we have the concentration of Shakespeare's matured powers in the great tragic drama of *Richard III*, which sets forth the overthrow of the house of York, and the triumph of Henry of Richmond, as representative of the House of Lancaster. In this play King Edward remembers, in his distress over the death of Clarence, that it was he who saved him "in the field of Tewkesbury, when Oxford had me down." In the last act of all, when the Yorkists are overthrown and Henry Tudor appears, it is with Oxford by his side; and it is Oxford who, as premier nobleman, replies first to the king's address to his followers. Whether, therefore, Shakespeare was an actual representative of the family of the De Veres or not, we are quite entitled to claim that he shows a marked partiality for the family, a careful regard for its honour, and a precise acquaintance with details pertaining to its several members.

A significant silence.

Such a fact would not have given a justification for the selection of Edward de Vere in the first instance; for the family might have had intense admirers outside the circle of its own members. When, however, the selection has been made on quite other grounds, and supported by other lines of argument, the discovery that "Shakespeare" displays this special partiality has immense value, and hardly leaves room for doubt as to the soundness of the choice. The poet and dramatist who wrote the passages we have quoted from *Henry VI*, part 3, could hardly fail to have been interested also in the particular representative of the family who at that time bore the title, and who happened, moreover, to be a poet and dramatist quite in "Shakespeare's" line. Yet this particular nobleman's name is never once met with in connection with the "Shakespeare" dramas, although he was living at the time in Hackney, then a London suburb immediately adjacent to Shoreditch, where Burbage had his theatre, and the Shakespeare dramas were being staged. All this is more than suggestive of a wish not to be seen in it.

It is worth remarking, too, that Shakespeare's expression of partiality is more guarded in *Richard III* than in *Henry VI*, part 3. The former play is a later and more matured work, belonging to the time when the Shakespeare mask had been adopted. Great publicity was given to it, and it passed through several editions in the lifetime of Edward de Vere. The play of *Henry VI*, part 3, evidently an earlier work, in which he betrays his Oxford partialities more freely, was not printed in its present form until it appeared in the Folio edition of 1623. That is to say, it is really a posthumous publication of a youthful production, never having been published with Shakespeare's imprimatur, and may, indeed, never have been staged during the later years of "Shakespeare's" fame.

Of the earls who succeeded to the domains and titles between John the 13th Earl, who stood by the side of Henry VII, and Edward the 17th Earl, little need be said. After the death of the 14th Earl the direct male line came to an end, and the 15th Earl, the grandfather of the poet, succeeded by right of descent from Richard de Vere, the 11th Earl of Oxford.

The Great Chamberlain.

Before leaving the matter of Edward de Vere's ancestry, it is necessary to offer a few observations on the office of Lord Great Chamberlain, which had been hereditary in his family for centuries, and to which he succeeded, along with the other dignities, on the death of his father. This office must not be confused with that of Lord Chamberlain, rendered familiar to

Shakespeare students by its association with the performance and publication of many of Shakespeare's plays. *The Merchant of Venice*, for example, was published "as it hath beene diverse times acted by the Lord Chamberlain, his servants." Amongst the functions of the Lord Chamberlain are the arrangements relating to royal patronage of the drama and the licensing of plays and theatres. It was the company of actors under the special patronage of the Lord Chamberlain which in Queen Elizabeth's day performed many of "Shakespeare's" plays, and has in consequence been erroneously styled "Shakespeare's Company." The disappearance of the Lord Chamberlain's books for the "Shakespeare" period is dealt with in another chapter.

The position of the Lord Great Chamberlain, though of higher social dignity, appears to have been less onerous and its functions more intermittent. These had more to do with state functions and the royal person, near whom this official was placed on such great occasions as coronations and royal funerals.

It is necessary to point out the distinction, otherwise the unwary might be misled into supposing that Edward de Vere, by virtue of his office, had something to do with the direct management of the company with which William Shakspere was connected. The Lord Chamberlain during part of the "Shakespeare" period was Lord Hunsdon; and though Edward de Vere might possibly have something to do with the matter indirectly, through his fellow official, directly as Lord Great Chamberlain, it would not come within his province.

Queen Elizabeth's funeral.

As Lord Great Chamberlain he officiated near the person of James I at his coronation, just as, doubtless, when a boy, he had witnessed his father officiating at the coronation of Queen Elizabeth. Although his officiating at Elizabeth's funeral is not mentioned so explicitly as the part he took at the coronation of James, it is natural to assume that he would be there. It is just possible that this ceremony is directly referred to in sonnet 125:

Were't aught to me I bore the canopy,
With my extern the outward honouring,
Or laid great bases for eternity,
Which prove more abort than waste or ruining?

     *   *   *   *

No, let me be obsequious in thy heart,
And take thou my oblation, poor but free.

If this can be shown to have any direct connection with the functions of Lord Great Chamberlain, it will be a very valuable direct proof of our thesis. The particular sonnet from which we have quoted comes at the extreme end of the series to which it belongs; and, as we are assured that the whole series was brought to a close shortly after the death of Queen Elizabeth, sonnet 125 must have been written about the time of that event. It is difficult to imagine in what impressive ceremony William Shakspere of Stratford could have participated about the same time, necessitating his bearing the canopy and laying great bases for eternity. On the other hand, the reference to "dwellers on form and favour losing all by paying too much rent" is strongly suggestive of an allusion to royalty, and is exactly descriptive of what Oxford represents Elizabeth's treatment of himself to have been: that she had encouraged his lavish expenditure with promises of favour that had not been fulfilled. His application, in her later years, for the presidency of Wales had met with fair words and disappointment. Altogether the suggestion of an allusion in the sonnet to the hereditary office of the Lord Great Chamberlain seems very strong.

IV

FATHER OF EDWARD DE VERE

Edward de Vere, Seventeenth Earl of Oxford, was born at Earl's Colne in Essex, in the year 1550, being the only son of John de Vere, Sixteenth Earl of Oxford. His mother was Margaret, daughter of John Golding and sister of Arthur Golding, the translator of Ovid. His father died at Earl's Colne in the year 1562 and was buried at Castle Hedingham, in Essex, and the future poet became a royal ward at the age of twelve. As this fact of his being a royal ward furnished the starting point of an argument with a remarkable culmination, we ask for the reader's special attention to it now. Earl's Colne and Castle Hedingham in Essex we may suppose are probably destined to attain an unexpected notoriety when the purpose of this work has been achieved.

Father-worship.

As we have every reason to believe that the influence and memory of De Vere's father were important factors in the poet's life, and add an element to our evidences of identification, it is necessary to point out certain facts concerning him. The article in the *Dictionary of National Biography* dealing with John de Vere, Sixteenth Earl of Oxford, mentions him as a man greatly honoured in his county and highly respected, especially by his tenantry; from which we may infer a habit of direct personal intercourse with them and a kindly attention to their interests. He was also a keen sportsman, being evidently noted as such. To a lad of twelve a father of this kind is an ideal. His qualities appeal much more powerfully to the lad's admiration than more distinguished or exceptional powers would do; and, especially in the case of an intensely affectionate nature like that of Edward de Vere's, to which his poetry bears unquestionable testimony, one can easily conceive of them forming the basis of a genuine comradeship between the two. When, therefore, we find that the father, who left large estates, nominated the boy in his will as one of his executors, it is impossible to doubt that the relationship between them was warm and intimate. The loss of such a father, with the complete upsetting of his young life that it immediately involved, must have been a great grief to one so sensitively constituted. We may naturally suppose, then, that the figure of a hero-father would live in his imagination; and the reader of "Shakespeare" who has missed this note of father-worship in the great dramas has been found wanting in serious attention to their finer contents.

The greatest play of Shakespeare's, *Hamlet*, has father-worship as its prime motive:

> He was a man, take him for all in all,
> I shall not look upon his like again.

The All's Well argument.

Or, what could be more striking than the opening passages of *All's Well that Ends Well*:

> *Countess*: In delivering my son from me I bury a second husband.
>
> *Bertram*: And I in going, madam, weep o'er my father's death anew; but I must attend his majesty's command, *to whom I am now in ward* evermore in subjection.
>
>   *   *   *   *
>
> *Countess*: Be thou blest, Bertram, and succeed thy father
> In manner as in shape! Thy blood and virtue
> Contend for empire in thee; and thy goodness
> Share with thy birthright.

Then in the second scene when Bertram is brought before the king, he is addressed thus:

> *King:*
>   Thy father . . . did look far
> Into the service of the time and was
> Discipled of the bravest.
>   It much repairs me
> To talk of your good father.
> So like a courtier, contempt nor bitterness
> Were in his pride, or, if they were,
> His equal had awaked them: who were below him
> He used as creatures of another place,
> And bowed his eminent top to their low ranks,
> Making them proud of his humility.
> In their poor praise be humbled. Such a man
> Might be a copy to these younger times.

In addition to the special point we are now emphasizing, and the startling correspondence in so many details, to the actual circumstances of Edward de Vere, especially that of the royal wardship, is it possible to conceive of these lines being penned by anyone but an aristocrat, in close connection with royalty, and dominated by the feudal ideals of *noblesse oblige*? The latter part of the quotation, so suggestive of the reputation borne by Edward de Vere's father, following upon a passage descriptive of the actual position of the son, affords a strong presumption that if the writer was not Edward de Vere he, at any rate, had that nobleman in his mind as the prototype of Bertram. The last sentence bespeaks not only the aristocrat but also a man who felt out of touch with the new and less chivalrous order then emerging from the protestant middle classes, where individualism and personal ambition were less under the discipline of social principles than in the best manifestations of the departing feudal ideals.

"Shakespeare" and Boccaccio.

As in dealing with the early life of Oxford we shall have to notice throughout the remarkable parallelism between him and Bertram in *All's Well*, it is important to bear in mind that very many of the personal details are original to "Shakespeare's" play, and do not form part of Boccaccio's story upon which the central episode is based. *All's Well* might indeed be compendiously described as Boccaccio's story *plus* the early life of Edward de Vere.

V

A ROYAL WARD

Owing to his being in his minority at the time of his father's death, the latter's nomination of him as one of the executors of his will was inoperative, and he became, as we have seen, a royal ward. Just at this point the records are not so precise as we could wish. We learn that, as royal ward, he was brought from his home to the court, and as Cecil (not yet Lord Burleigh) was master of the court of royal wards, he became an inmate of Cecil's house in the Strand.

Oxford's mother.

His mother, we also learn, remarried. We have tried in vain to discover the exact dates at which he was brought to court, and when his mother remarried, not as matters of mere curiosity, but because we believe these points may have their bearing both on our problem and upon questions of Shakespearean interpretation. The date of his mother's second marriage might prove of especial interest. It is to be regretted, therefore, that although references to the event appear in histories of Essex, no date is given; thus strengthening our suspicion that not much prominence was given to the marriage at the time: the date especially being kept in the background. It is a curious fact, too, that with the exception of her once interesting herself in his financial affairs, of which mention is made in the State Papers, we have not been able to discover a single reference to his mother in connection with any act in his life.

Countess of Southampton.

In this connection his circumstances contrast in a marked way with those of Henry Wriothesley, Third Earl of Southampton, to whom "Shakespeare" dedicated his great poems and probably addressed many of his sonnets. He, too, just a generation later, became a royal ward at an early age and passed under the guardianship of Burleigh. In his case, however, his mother remained near him, looking after his interests and not remarrying until he had reached his majority: when she married Sir Thomas Henneage, Treasurer of the Chamber, and was herself responsible, as we have seen, for the single "official" mention of "Shakespeare" in the records of her husband's department. We thus get glimpses of her in everything relating to her son, either directly or indirectly, in those early years. We may remark here that as Oxford's own mother was dead at the time of his later domestic troubles, in dealing with the domestic troubles of Bertram in *All's Well* he may have taken the Dowager Countess of Southampton as the prototype of Bertram's mother: and certainly the representation seems to fit.

Oxford at Court.

In Oxford's own case everything is different from Southampton's. His mother does not appear, and one gets a sense of there being a complete severance between his early childhood with its home associations and father's influence, and the remainder of his boyhood and youth. Henceforth it is "by public means which public manners breeds," that his bringing-up is provided for. From the age of twelve true domestic influences were lost to him; he becomes a prominent figure about Elizabeth's court, subjected to corrupting influences, in which it must be admitted the Queen herself was a potent factor. At the same time it is quite evident that he was only uncomfortably domiciled in Cecil's house. Between the Earl of Oxford and the Earl of Southampton there was therefore a striking parallel with an important difference.

Arthur Golding's Ovid.

The only family connection of which there are any traces is that of his uncle, Arthur Golding, the translator of Ovid, who entered Cecil's house as Oxford's tutor and as receiver of his property. The vital significance of the relationship of Arthur Golding to the man we are putting forward as the author of Shakespeare's plays will be fully appreciated by those Shakespearean students who are also students of the Latin classics, and who are able to trace in Shakespeare passages borrowed from Ovid, which follow the original more closely than do the standard translations.

We shall again quote from Sir Sidney Lee's *Life of Shakespeare* on this point: "Although Ovid's Latin text was certainly familiar to him [Shakespeare] his closest adaptations of Ovid's *Metamorphoses* often *reflect the phraseology of the popular English version by Arthur Golding* of which some seven editions were issued between 1565 and 1597."[104] That is to say, these editions of Ovid were being issued by Arthur Golding in the very years in which he was Latin tutor to the Earl of Oxford, so that special point is given by the theory we are now putting forward to the biographer's later remark that "Golding's rendering of Ovid had been one of Shakespeare's best-loved books in youth."[105]

To this we may add the testimony of Professor Sir Walter

---

[104] Lee, *Life*, p. 16.
[105] Lee, *Life,* p. 262.

Raleigh that: "He certainly knew Ovid, for he quotes him in the original more than once, and chooses a motto for *Venus and Adonis* from the Elegies. But his more elaborate borrowings from Ovid come, for the most part, by way of Arthur Golding's translations."[106]

"Shakespeare" and Ovid.

To find "Shakespeare" more exact in some instances than the translator raises an acknowledged difficulty in connection with the Stratfordian view. It has for a long while been one of the vexed questions of Shakespearean authorship, and is discussed at some length in Sir George Greenwood's work on the "Shakespearean Problem." What is a difficulty with the accepted authorship becomes transformed into a substantial corroboration of the theory of authorship we are now advancing; and all mystery immediately vanishes when we assume that Arthur Golding, the Ovid enthusiast and translator, was himself a relative as well as a private tutor and Latin teacher to "Shakespeare," engaged in the latter capacity in the very years in which he was translating and publishing the works of this particular poet.

The importance of this little piece of evidence can hardly be over-estimated. By itself it proves nothing, but in view of the prominent position which the Ovid controversy has taken in the question of Shakespearean authorship, and in conjunction with the other lines of evidence we are now offering, its value is unquestionable. Ovid is the one Latin poet who has been specially singled out as having directly left deep traces in Shakespeare's work, at the same time that the dramatist shows an equal intimacy with the translation. This is precisely the result we should expect from the Earl of Oxford's relationship to Arthur Golding. An intimate acquaintance with one particular translation of a classic, and also such an acquaintance with the original as to make his own rendering more complete and exact in some respects is not a usual combination in a student of the classics, and needs some such relationship as existed between Edward de Vere and Arthur

---

[106] Lee, *Life*, p. 39.

Golding to explain it. The connection of Edward de Vere, Arthur Golding, and "Shakespeare" with Ovid thus constitutes an important link in our chain of evidence.

De Vere and Golding.

In this connection we would, in conclusion, offer a suggestion. Arthur Golding was the author of other works besides the translation of Ovid. From references to these we gather that all are quite inferior to the Ovid work: itself only of second rate order. If, then, the translation of Ovid formed part of Oxford's Latin studies—as it most assuredly would do under the circumstances—it may be that what is taken to be the influence of Golding's work in "Shakespeare" is in reality due to the influence of the young Earl of Oxford upon the work of Arthur Golding.

Oxford and Law.

Considering the place occupied by the translator of Ovid in the early life and education of the Earl of Oxford, we would draw particular attention to the fact that, in the Inner Temple Records, there appears an entry indicating that after finishing his work as tutor to his nephew, Arthur Golding was admitted to the Bar. Evidently then, *pari passu* with the work of translating classics and instructing the Earl of Oxford, there had been proceeding the study of law. Oxford's course of reading had been mapped out for him by Cecil, and it goes without saying that a plan of studies drawn up by Cecil would most certainly embrace legal procedure. Oxford's letters of a much later date, preserved in the Hatfield Manuscripts, certainly appeal to a layman as the work of a man conversant with legal forms and terminology, and one passage of special interest we shall presently submit. The question of whether his legal knowledge was on the same plane with that of "Shakespeare" the experts must decide: meanwhile we shall give one or two examples:

Earl of Oxford to Sir Robert Cecil:

It is now a year since Her Majesty granted her interest in Danver's escheat. I find that the lands will be carried without deed. I have twice moved Her Majesty to grant me that ordinary course, whereof there are more than one hundred examples. Mine answer was that I should receive her pleasure from you. But I understand by Cauley that she hath never spoken thereof. The matter hath been heard twice before the judges but their report hath never been made. I challenge that something be done whereby I may, upon ground, seek and try Her Majesty's right, which cannot be done without this deed aforesaid. I desire to know Her Majesty's pleasure touching her patent (de bene esse) whether she will perform it or no.[107]

Hackney, 22ⁿᵈ March, 1601.

If Her Majesty's affections be forfeits of men's estates we must endure it.[108]

What the lawyers tell us of Shakespeare's use of the word "forfeit," coupled with the reference to endurance, makes this sentence eminently Shakespearean.

More than once we get evidence of his chafing under "the law's delays," and of royal promises unsupported by performance.

I was promised favour that I should have assistance of Her Majesty's counsel in law, that I should have expedition. Her Majesty's counsel hath been against me. Her Majesty used me very graciously . . . I have written Her Majesty and received a most gracious answer to do me good in all that she can.[109]

December, 1601.

Her Majesty's promises and gracious answers, however, came to nothing in these cases.

---

[107] Oxford's March 22, 1602 letter to Robert Cecil. Hatfield MSS, Vol. XII (CP 85/103). Although in quotation marks, this excerpt is only a paraphrase. It is also incorrectly dated in the 1920 editions as 22 March 1601. The verbatim wording is too long to reproduce here, but can be seen in William P. Fowler, *Shakespeare Revealed in Oxford's Letters*, p. 707.

[108] Hatfield MSS, Vol. V.

[109] Oxford's December 4, 1601 letter to Robert Cecil. Hatfield MSS, Vol. XI. In quotation marks, but only a paraphrase. For the original text, see Fowler, *Shakespeare Revealed*, p. 623.

The significance of the following passage (in one of Oxford's letters) either from the legal or Shakespearean point of view we do not profess to understand. Its chief interest lies in the two names it introduces together. We shall therefore preface it with two passages from Mrs. Stopes's *Burbage and Shakespeare's Stage*:

Sergeant Harris and Bacon.

"On 13th November, 1590 Mr. Sergeant Harrys for Burbage prayed consideration of a former order made in his behalf in the suit of Burbage v. Braynes."[110] Sergeant Harris was evidently then engaged in legal business connected with Burbage's theatre. On 17th June, '44, Eliz. (1602),

> The Court referred [another legal case involving theatrical connections] to the consideration of the right worshipful Francis Bacon, Esq. . . . Here at last I have found a real association of Francis Bacon with the Theatre. . . . in his legal capacity, not a poetic one at all. . . . This case was running concurrently with [another theatrical legal case brought in in 1601].[111]

The Earl of Oxford to Sir Robert Cecil (1601):

> I am advised that I may pass my book from Her Majesty to my cousin Bacon and to Sergeant Harris to perfect it.[112] From Hackney.

Bacon was a cousin of Robert Cecil's and therefore a cousin of Oxford's by marriage; and the evidence here presented of the cooperation of the two men in legal matters may go far to explain the many interesting similarities of expression brought together by the Baconians. These matters take us far beyond the period of his history with which we are immediately concerned: the object of introducing them now is to show that both in the education of Oxford, and in his subsequent career, there is much to account for the prominence of legal terms in any writing which might be attributed to him.

---

[110] Stopes, *Burbage*, p. 50.
[111] Stopes, *Burbage*, p. 84.
[112] Oxford's October 7, 1601 letter to Robert Cecil. Hatfield MSS (CP 88/101). Only a paraphrase; original text can be seen in Fowler, p. 593.

Book-learning and life.

Resuming now the account of his education generally, we are told that Cecil had drawn up some scheme of instruction; that he was "thoroughly grounded in French and Latin"; that he "learnt to dance, ride and shoot"; and that he manifested a natural taste for music and a marked interest in literature. On the other hand, every word of the records we have of him, taken along with what he has himself written, represents him as one combining with his interest in books a more intense interest in life itself. Or, rather, we should say he was one in whom life and literature, especially classic poetry, seem to have worked themselves into some kind of unity: one who interpreted life in terms of classic poetry, carrying into life the conceptions of classic poetry, and reading classic poetry as but the reflection of ordinary practical life. To say that all this is characteristic of Shakespeare is as banal a remark as could well be made; and the words which the dramatist puts into the mouth of Berowne in *Love's Labour's Lost* might quite easily be taken as Edward de Vere's expression of personal opinions:

> Learning is but an adjunct to ourself.

And this:

> *Berowne:*
>   That (delight is) most vain
> Which with pain purchased doth inherit pain:
> As painfully to pore upon a book,
> To seek the light of truth; while truth the while
> Doth falsely blind the eyesight of his look:
> Small have continual plodders ever won
> Save base authority from others' books.
> These earthly godfathers of heaven's light
> That give a name to every fixed star,
> Have no more profit of their shining nights
> Than those that walk and wot not what they are.
> Too much to know is to know nought but fame,
> And every godfather can give a name.

> *King:*
> How well he's read to reason against reading.

The Shakespeare revealed in the dramas was no mere

bookworm "falsely blinding the eyesight" of his mind in close plodding at academic studies. On the other hand it is almost impossible to conceive of a man in the position of the Stratford Shakspere rising to such a literary level otherwise than by the most assiduous and constant application of his mind to books. The man "self-educated" in this way has invariably to pay a penalty in those sides of his nature which relate him to practical life: a penalty which "Shakespeare" had not paid, and need not be paid by a man living in contact with educated people to whom "book-learning" is an "adjunct" to life rather than its chief concern.

Latin and French.

It is interesting to notice, however, that the outstanding subjects of De Vere's book-learning are French and Latin; and in this connection we are again able to adduce the testimony of Shakespeare's leading modern biographer as to the dramatist's linguistic attainments:

> With the Latin and French languages indeed, and with many Latin poets of the school curriculum, Shakespeare in his writings openly acknowledged his acquaintance. In *Henry V* the dialogue in many scenes is carried on in French, which is grammatically accurate if not idiomatic.[113]

In other words, Shakespeare's French was not mere school-book French, but the living speech of a man acquainted with the language in direct relationship with thought processes: and this nearly three hundred years before the oral method of teaching languages was introduced into school curricula. Similarly Edward de Vere's facility in the use of French was such that one of the few duties with which he was officially entrusted was to meet and conduct an important emissary from France. Again, by itself, the point might seem unimportant. The reason, however, why we dwell upon it, and why we quote Shakespearean authorities in the matter, is to show that there is probably not a single outstanding fact recorded of Edward de Vere, but we have some Shakespearean scholar who has asserted it to be also true of the

---

[113] Lee, *Life*, p. 15.

writer of the plays.

The Universities.

In addition to the advantages of the best private tuition he had also a university education; first at Queens' College, Cambridge, then at St. John's College. Subsequently he received degrees from both universities. The references to this matter are, however, peculiarly slight, and leave the impression of his having been one who had merely trifled for a short time with university life, and to whom it did not count for much. Even the dates of his residence are not given, and the degrees we judge to have been honorary degrees in both cases, given in after years. It is claimed by some writers that Shakespeare shows a knowledge of the universities. Such contact as Edward de Vere had with them would be sufficient to account for that knowledge, whilst the apparently small part it played in his life would quite agree with the almost negligible part that college and university matters occupy in the plays. There are only two occasions on which Shakespeare mentions the word "university." Hamlet, in poking fun at Polonius, draws him out by exciting his vanity about what he had done "at the university." The other occasion is when another old man, with a slight suggestion of Polonius about him, Vincentio, in the *Taming of the Shrew*, bewails "I am undone! While I play the good husband at home my son and my servant spend all at the university." It may be that the dramatist had the same personality in his mind's eye in both cases.

Relationship with the Cecils.

Oxford's life in the Cecil household seems to have been far from happy. For it was during these years, between the death of his father and his coming of age, that he first of all sought relief from it by begging for some military occupation. There was probably in him, too, some idea of winning military glory quite in keeping with the family traditions and the later achievements of his cousins the "Fighting Veres." It is clear, however, that his relationships with the Cecil family were not harmonious. At any rate, the record of him, which is evidently originally from Cecilian sources, is to the effect that he quarrelled with the other members of the household. In view of the fact that when Oxford entered the house Anne Cecil was a child five years old, Robert Cecil was still unborn and Thomas Cecil had already left home, it is not easy to see who there would be to quarrel with except the irascible Lady Burleigh. The quarrels are mentioned with the evident object of proving him quarrelsome. What is not mentioned, probably because the modern recorder had not observed it, is that three of the noblemen most hostile to the Cecils and the Cecil faction in Elizabeth's court, had all been royal wards, having had the great Lord Burleigh as their guardian—Edward de Vere, Earl of Oxford; Henry Wriothesley, Earl of Southampton; and Robert Devereux, Earl of Essex. These noblemen apparently considered it no great blessing to have had the paternal attentions of the great minister, and cherished no particular affection for the family. So far as the Earl of Oxford is concerned, whatever disaster may have come into his life, we are confident, had its beginning in the death of his father, the severance of his home ties, and the combined influences of Elizabeth's court and Burleigh's household, from which he was anxious to escape. The expression of it all is heard in sonnet 111:

> O! for my sake do you with Fortune chide
> The guilty goddess of my harmful deeds;
> That did not better for my life provide
> Than public means that public manners breeds.
> Thence comes it that my name receives a brand,
> And almost thence my nature is subdued
> To what it works in, like the dyer's hand.

The attempt to explain this passage as William Shakspere's lament over a public career that was raising him, in early manhood, from poverty and obscurity to wealth and fame, after he had left—on the Stratfordian theory—a wholesome home-life enlightened by a superior education, is as grotesque a piece of explanatory comment as that theory has been responsible for.

Oxford and Queen Elizabeth.

The part which Burleigh took actively in Oxford's troubles belongs to a later stage of our story. Our present concern is with the nine years during which he was a royal ward (age 12 to 21), the period of his education proper. In these years we find him having just those experiences which, taken along with his own and his family's antecedents, and the evident bent of his genius, were supplying the precise kind of training needed for the production of the plays of Shakespeare, in several of their prime essentials. Without being actually a prince of royal blood he was so near to it, in all the points material to our argument, as to be regarded in that light. He enjoyed an easy familiarity with the Queen; he accompanied her on her journeys; he seems in his early life to have had a real affection for her and she for him; and, later on, as he developed into manhood, received attentions of such a nature from the Queen, now middle-aged, as to cause his irate mother-in-law to take her royal mistress to task about it. An entry appears in the Calendered State Papers stating that it was affirmed by one party that "the Queen wooed the Earl of Oxford but he would not fall in."[114] Elizabeth indeed showed a marked indulgence to what seemed like waywardness in him; and when, again at a later time, the quarrel between him and Sidney occurred she took his side and demanded an apology from Sidney—basing her demand, it is asserted, on the grounds of Oxford's superior rank. We have already had to draw attention to the startling character of the analogy between Oxford and the central character in *All's Well*, the royal ward, Bertram Count of Roussilon, to which must now be added this proximity in social rank and intimate intercourse with royalty, to which Helena refers in her conversation with the King. It will be interesting to notice, too, the emphasis given both in this play and in *Hamlet* to the idea that by virtue of their birth the chief characters had no personal liberty of choice in the matter of marriage.

---

[114] Calendar of State Papers, Domestic, 1601-03, p. 56.

Dancing.

Before leaving the consideration of these formative influences in the early life of Oxford, we return to its being specially recorded of him that he learnt to "dance, ride and shoot." Oxford's skill in dancing and its influence over the Queen is emphasized by one contemporary English writer, whilst an interesting illustration of it appears in the Spanish Calendered State Papers. When the Duke of Anjou visited England, Elizabeth sent for Oxford to come and dance before the Duke: but this he refused to do though repeatedly sent for. So far as dancing is concerned, "Shakespeare" was evidently well acquainted with it, as shown by the number of references to it and his knowledge of the names of different kinds of dances and steps. These references do not, however, seem to express any enthusiasm for it, or suggest that it occupied at all a prominent position amongst Shakespeare's interests. Indeed Bertram, in *All's Well*, seems rather to be expressing the author's own attitude when he complains about having to

> Stay here,
> Creaking my shoes on the plain masonry,
> Till honour be bought up, and no sword worn
> But one to dance with.

It is the attitude of a man who danced because he was denied a more manly outlet for his energies: secretly ashamed possibly of his own accomplishment and unwilling to put himself on exhibition.

Shooting.

Again, in the matter of shooting, if it is shooting with firearms that is meant, this is less than anything in Shakespeare's line; but if it be archery to which allusion is made, then it is in every way typical of "Shakespeare." Shakespeare has, of course, references to firearms; in one or two instances he even uses out-of-the-way terms; but, in the matter of archery his vocabulary is almost as rich, and his illustrations drawn from it almost as copious, as in the case of falconry; so that, in examining the matter now one wonders how it chanced to be overlooked at the beginning of our enquiry, when specifying his leading characteristics.

Horsemanship.

Most important of all, however, is this point of De Vere's horsemanship. Not only did Oxford learn to ride, but, in those days when horsemanship was much more in vogue than it will probably ever be again, and when great skill was attained in horse-management, he was amongst those who excelled, particularly in tilts and tourneys, receiving special marks of royal appreciation of his skill. Horsemanship was, therefore, a very pronounced interest of his. His father, too, had been the owner of valuable horses, special mention of them being made in his will, which Arthur Collins quotes in his *Historical Recollections of Noble Families.*

Turning now to Shakespeare's works we feel again that it was another grave omission from our original statement of Shakespearean interests not to have mentioned horses. We find there is more in Shakespeare about horses than upon almost any subject outside human nature. Indeed we feel tempted to say that Shakespeare brings them within the sphere of human nature. There is, of course, his intimate knowledge of different kinds of horses, their physical peculiarities, all the details which go to form a good or a bad specimen of a given variety, almost a veterinary's knowledge of their diseases and their treatment. But over and above all this there is a peculiar handling of the theme which raises a horse almost to the level of a being with a moral nature.

In *Venus and Adonis,* for example, we have what is in reality a poem within the poem, amounting to over seventy lines, in which a mere animal instinct is raised in horses to the dignity of a complex and exalted human passion.

Or, take the following dialogue from *Richard II:*

Groom:
> O! how it yearn'd my heart when I beheld
> In London streets that coronation day,
> When Bolingbroke rode on roan Barbary.
> That horse that thou so oft hast bestrid,
> That horse that I so carefully have dress'd.

King Richard:
>Rode he on Barbary? Tell me, gentle friend,
>How went he under him?

Groom:
>So proudly as if he disdain'd the ground.

King Richard:
>So proud that Bolingbroke was on his back!
>That jade hath eat bread from my royal hand,
>This hand hath made him proud with clapping him.
>Would he not stumble? Would he not fall down,
>Since pride must have a fall, and break the neck
>Of that proud man that did usurp his back?
>Forgiveness, horse! Why do I rail on thee?

It reads like a real personal experience; as if the man who wrote it knew what it was to own valuable horses and to suffer the mortification of seeing the animals he loved passing, as a result of his misfortunes, into the possession of others: an experience which, without any surmising, must have been endured by Edward de Vere.

Early poetry.

In thus working from the early life of De Vere to the works of Shakespeare little remains to be said. With the scanty materials before us it is impossible to visualise the poet's life during those very early years. Whether or not he had begun to write poetry we cannot say. The poems before us seem from their contents to belong mainly to the early part of the next ten years, when he was between the ages of twenty and thirty. We wish to throw out a suggestion, however, which it may be worthwhile for literary men to examine. In *England's Helicon* there is a set of poems of superior merit, which, nevertheless, seem to us inferior to the poetry of Edward de Vere already examined. They appear over the signature of Shepherd Tony and constitute another of the mysteries of Elizabethan literature. They do, however, contain certain marks of Edward de Vere's work, and it is not impossible that they may include his earliest juvenile efforts. For notwithstanding the evidence that his known work belongs mainly to his early years, it seems much too skillfully done to have been his first production. Even *it* seems to demand a "foreground somewhere"; and Shepherd Tony may represent that foreground. These particular poems seem to contain rather more of the affectation of the early Elizabethan poetry than do De Vere's recognized work, and have not always the same smoothness of diction. At the same time they mark a distinct advance in the direction of realism; and one poem of Shepherd Tony's, "Beauty sat bathing by a spring," which has been erroneously attributed to Anthony Munday, is a very decided break from the weaker work of earlier Elizabethan times.

Oxford and Italy.

Before leaving this early stage of his career we may add a somewhat inexplicable memorandum of Cecil's which concerns his affairs, dated July 10th, 1570, and preserved in the Hatfield manuscripts. Rumour was evidently rife that Cecil was managing Oxford's affairs in the matter of lands, to his own advantage and to Oxford's detriment: a matter on which the latter attacked him some six or seven years later. Cecil emphatically contradicts the allegation, and continues:

> Whosoever saith that I did stay my Lord of Oxford's money here so as he had no money in Italy by the space of six months they say also untruly.

We cannot find any other indication of Oxford's visiting Italy before his tour in 1575 and 1576.

Summary.

This chapter as a whole may be said to be concerned with biographical foundations; all the particulars of which relate themselves directly to the "Shakespeare" literature. The reputation which "vulgar scandal" had fixed upon him is represented in the sonnets. His pride of birth displays itself throughout the dramas, and is reflected specially in Shakespeare's partiality to the Earls of Oxford. The hereditary office of his family is possibly alluded to in the sonnets. His orphanhood, royal wardship, and particulars of his early life are represented in *All's Well*. Details of his education, particularly the part taken oy his uncle, Arthur Golding, reproduce themselves in the outstanding features of "Shakespeare's" education, as given by eminent Stratfordians. The prominence of law in "Shakespeare" for the first time finds an explanation consistent with all the other requirements of the work. We therefore ask again, is all this mere accidental coincidence?

CHAPTER X

EARLY MANHOOD OF EDWARD DE VERE

As Burleigh's papers are the chief original source of biographical matter relating to the Earl of Oxford's private life, and the writers upon whom we depend for most of our details are marked by Cecilian partialities, it is necessary to point out that, though we accept many of the facts upon their authority, they share in no degree the responsibility for the interpretation of them. This is entirely our own.

Marriage.

On coming of age, in April, 1571, Oxford took his seat in the House of Lords, and in the same year distinguished himself at a solemn joust which took place in the Queen's presence at Westminster. In December of the same year he married, with the Queen's consent, Anne, daughter of Lord Burleigh. The Queen "attended the ceremony which was celebrated with great pomp."[115]

As we have already had occasion to point out the remarkable parallelism between the case of the Earl of Oxford and Bertram in *All's Well*, we must now add to it this fact of his marriage with a young woman with whom he had been brought up. In Bertram's case, however, they had lived together at his own home, whereas in Oxford's case they had lived together in the home of the lady. If we are to believe contemporary report on the matter the resemblance between the two cases extends to even more interesting particulars. Helena was socially inferior to Bertram. In the early part of the play he shows no inclination towards this young woman who is in love with him, and it is she who pursues the young man until she succeeds in winning him as her husband.

---

[115] Lee, "Vere, Edward," p. 226. The exact wording is "The queen attended the ceremony, which was celebrated with much pomp."

WILLIAM CECIL, FIRST BARON BURGHLEY

FROM THE PORTRAIT BY AN UNKNOWN ARTIST BUT ATTRIBUTED TO M. GHEERAEDTS, AFTER 1587. REPRODUCED BY PERMISSION OF THE NATIONAL PORTRAIT GALLERY.

Helena:

> I am from humble, he from honour'd name;
> No note upon my parents, his all noble;
> My master, my dear lord he is; and I
> His servant live, and will his vassal die.

We may remark in passing that it is difficult to believe that these words could have been written by anyone but an aristocrat in whom pride of birth was a pronounced feeling. We may also compare the last lines of this passage with the concluding part of De Vere's Echo poem:

> May I his favour match with love if he my love will try?
> May I requite his birth with faith then faithful will I die?

Most people will agree that the similarity of these two passages is startling.

Lady Oxford.

Now, not only did Anne Cecil belong to the newly emerging middle class, so much held in contempt by the few remaining representatives of the ancient aristocracy, but we have it reported by a contemporary, Lord St. John, that, "the Erle of Oxenforde hath gotten himself a wyffe, or, at *leste a wyffe hath caught him.* This is the mistress Anne Cycille, whereunto the Queen hath given her consent."[116] One may conclude, therefore, that the Earl of Oxford was not supposed to have been very active himself in bringing about the marriage. Rightly or wrongly others regarded Oxford's marriage with Burleigh's daughter in much the same light as is represented by the marriage of Bertram with Helena.

Juliet.

All this reads very strangely in view of the age of the bride: for Anne was born on December 5, 1556. Like Juliet she was, therefore, but fourteen years of age at the time when the courting alluded to took place, and when all the wedding arrangements were made. The marriage itself seems merely to have been delayed until the moment when she could be spoken of as being fifteen.

---

[116] July 28, 1571 letter from Lord St. John, Baron Bletsoe, to the Earl of Rutland. Cal. Rutland MSS.

This combination of extreme youthfulness and the bearing and conduct of a matured woman, common to Juliet and Anne Cecil, we shall find in a later dramatic representation of Lady Oxford. The resemblance to Juliet, however, must be viewed in the light of the remarkable correspondence in literary particulars between the work of De Vere and Shakespeare's play of *Romeo and Juliet*. This play is recognized as one of the early productions of Shakespeare, and it is also interesting to notice that Mr. Frank Harris selects Romeo as a personal self-representation of Shakespeare in his early years.

Helena.

The resemblance between Lady Oxford and Helena with which we are particularly concerned at this stage is further supported by letters in the Hatfield manuscripts, in which her smallness of stature and sweetness of manner are indicated. She is spoken of, on two occasions, by different writers, as the "sweet little Countess of Oxford," precisely as Helena, in *All's Well*, is spoken of as "little Helena" (I.1) and "sweet Helena" (V.3): the latter epithet being specially emphasized by repetition.

What the actual inward relationships of Oxford and his wife may have been, is one of the secrets over which the grave has closed for ever. We have impressions recorded, however, which are derived evidently from hostile Cecil sources. Oxford himself, on the other hand, preserves an almost complete silence, proof against all provocation; his enemies call it sulkiness. The one thing clear about it is that the union was unhappy, and had a marked influence upon his career. This being so, the matter concerns our present enquiry.

Sordid considerations.

The antagonism between Oxford and Philip Sidney has already been referred to. Now we find that Sidney had first of all been proposed as a husband for Anne Cecil, and her father's conduct of the negotiations, however it may strike an aristocrat, appears to an ordinary Englishman as sordid a piece of bargaining over the disposal of a daughter as could well be. Sidney, notwithstanding his family connections and personal prospects, which had evidently been quite enough to satisfy the demands of a prospective aristocratic father-in-law like Lord Devereux, was nevertheless too poor a man to satisfy the cupidity of Sir William Cecil, as he then was. He must needs procure for his daughter, he says, another husband than Master Philip Sidney. The difficulty was overcome, however, and arrangements were made for the marriage of Anne Cecil to Sidney, though both were hardly more than children at the time; for Sidney was Oxford's junior by four and a half years, whilst Anne was only 12 years old in 1569 when the marriage arrangement was made.

A broken engagement.

At the time when the marriage between Anne and Sidney was arranged the Earl of Oxford was, socially, "out of Anne's star." Now Cecil's care for the social and material advancement of his own family is one of the outstanding features of his policy. From this point of view the marriage of his daughter to one of the foremost of the ancient nobility, and a man of vast possessions, would be a great acquisition and the gratification of a high personal ambition. These social connections evidently meant much to him, for he had tried to make out an aristocratic ancestry for himself and had failed. Whether or not Elizabeth would sanction such an alliance might, however, be considered extremely doubtful; and if she were to consent, such consent would be almost as great a concession to Cecil as was that of Denmark's King and Queen to the marriage of Hamlet with the daughter of Polonius.

What may have transpired "behind the scenes" we shall probably never know; but we find that early in 1571 Cecil was raised to the peerage with the title of Lord Burleigh, the marriage arrangement with Sidney was cancelled, the Queen gave her consent to Oxford's marriage with Burleigh's daughter Anne, and in the latter part of the same year the marriage took place in the Queen's presence, being "celebrated with great pomp!" It is not improbable, then, that Burleigh owed his own peerage to the proposed marriage.

Castle Hedingham.

A most curious circumstance, suggestive of more sordid bargaining, is what is recorded of Burleigh and Oxford's estates. Amongst the extensive estates of the De Veres, the two most directly associated with the family appear to have been those of Earls Colne and Hedingham in Essex. Now we find that, shortly after his marriage, the Earl of Oxford made over the important ancestral domain of Castle Hedingham to his father-in-law. What influences may have been at work to get him to part with Castle Hedingham to Burleigh it is impossible to surmise; but when we find that his father-in-law had been complaining of his poverty only a few years before, that he had managed to get himself made master of the court of royal wards, and that when he died he left three hundred landed estates, it needs no stretch of imagination to suppose that he had been able to exercise over the affairs of other royal wards something of the same kind of undue influence which he had evidently been able to exert over his youthful son-in-law.

Burleigh and Jephtha.

If, therefore, there is any character in Shakespeare's work whom we may be able to identify with Burleigh, to have had him likened to Jephtha, as Hamlet does Polonius, would have been something of a slander upon Jephtha. For the conduct of this Old Testament character towards his daughter seems quite respectable compared with the sordid dealings of the great Lord Burleigh; and the tears which the latter seems ostentatiously to have shed at the death of her whom he called his "filia carissima" ought to have sprung from the grief of shame and repentance rather than the grief of bereavement. In the subsequent troubles Burleigh made much of the faultiness of Oxford's bearing whilst an inmate of the former's house, and if his accusations were found to be well grounded they would only render more contemptible the sacrifice he made of his "filia carissima" for personal and family ambition. He cannot have it both ways.

Domestic tutelage.

Notwithstanding, therefore, the royal consent, the pomp of the ceremony, and the elaborate festivities, it is evident that the marriage had not taken place under the happiest of auspices for those most immediately concerned. To all these initial drawbacks must be added the fact that the young couple seem to have remained under the eye and direction of the lady's father who, we shall presently show, was about as incompatible with her husband in disposition, interests and circumstances as one man could possibly be with another. Oxford's mother-in-law was also an important factor to be reckoned with. The stern and vigilant Lady Burleigh apparently considered it part of her duty to keep a strict watch upon her young son-in-law, and was not afraid of rebuking the great Queen Elizabeth herself, then forty years of age, for attempting to flirt with the young man. The Queen's angry retort that "his lordship [Burleigh] winketh at these love affairs,"[117] is illuminating on more points than one, and helps us to envisage the whole moral situation. Finally, whatever the actual facts behind Burleigh's general accusations against Oxford whilst he was an inmate of the Cecil home, it is quite evident that Oxford's relationships with the family had not been harmonious, and only the best of luck and the utmost circumspection all round could have averted disaster.

Oxford and Burleigh.

As the personality of Elizabeth's great minister looms large in the life of the poet during the years immediately following the marriage, and probably exercised an influence over the whole of his career, it is necessary that the character of their relationship should be duly weighed. It is not part of our business to estimate Burleigh's value as a statesman or politician, nor even to take his moral measure as a whole. It is his dealings with one man that concern us, and how these dealings would be likely to impress the man in question. In brief, we are concerned principally with Bur-

---

[117] Sir Harris Nicolas, *Memoirs of the Life and Times of Sir Christopher Hatton*, p. 23.

leigh's dealings with Oxford, from Oxford's point of view.

On the one hand we have a man who for many years had maintained a supreme position in the political world at a time when such eminence could only be secured and retained by the most shifty opportunism. On the other hand we have a very young man, hardly more than a boy, with the sensitive and idealist temperament of the poet, keenly alive to the literary and intellectual movements of his time, and with a fervent attachment to the departing feudal order, the social and moral principles of which were at direct variance with the political opportunism of the age in which he lived. To the young man, politics, in their contemporary sense, would be as great an abomination, as they would be a ruling interest in the mind of the elder man. It is difficult, therefore, to conceive of two men more thoroughly antipathetical or less likely to understand each other. If, then, we recollect that the younger one had been subjected to the elder one's dominance from childhood, it speaks well for the former's strength of character and the decided bent of his genius, that his literary and poetic inclinations were not crushed by the weight of the influences working against them.

Burleigh and literary men.

As some of the admirers of Burleigh have tried to make out that his influence was favourable to the literary movement of the times, we can, perhaps, best judge him in this respect by indicating his relationship to the second genius of that age, the poet Spenser. One or two expressions from Church's life of the poet will suffice:

> Burleigh's dislike to Spenser.[118]

> Burleigh hated him and his verses.[119]

> Under what was popularly thought the crabbed and parsimonious administration of Burleigh . . . . it seemed as if the poetry of the time was passing away in chill discouragement.[120]

---

[118] Church, *Spenser*, p. 47.
[119] Church, *Spenser*, p. 87.
[120] Church, *Spenser*, p. 107.

Burleigh's espionage.

No treatment of the question of Burleigh's dealings with other men would be adequate which omitted to mention the system of espionage which he practiced. Even his eulogists are compelled to admit the far-reaching and intricate ramifications of the system he set up, the application of it to even those servants of the state who had every reason to believe themselves most trusted, and the low, unscrupulous character of the agents he employed to watch men of high station and approved honour. The article on Burleigh in the *Dictionary of National Biography*, which is very partial towards its subject, nevertheless admits all this, and it appears occasionally in the *Life of Spenser*,[121] of which we have made frequent use. Of course his admirers find a justification for this in the dangers to which his life was exposed. Other men in exalted positions have, however, been exposed to similar dangers and some of them have had to protect themselves by similar means, but have been able to do it without outraging the sense of decency to the same extent as was done by Burleigh. It is quite evident, moreover, from G. Ravenscroft Dennis's work on *The House of Cecil*, that when his eldest son, Thomas, afterwards Earl of Exeter, was in Paris, Burleigh had him watched and secretly reported on, quite in the manner of Polonius's employment of the spy Reynaldo. In this case no such excuse as that proffered would apply. It seems more like the insensibility of a vulgar nature to the requirements of ordinary decency. The man who, having risen to eminence through his patron, the Duke of Somerset, saved himself when his patron fell by drawing up the articles of impeachment against his benefactor, was perhaps unable to believe that others could act from higher motives than his own, and was prepared to trust nobody. Certainly, no one could feel himself free from the attentions of Burleigh's spies, and least of all the son-in-law who knew that, beneath any external show of amicability, there lay between them a natural and rooted antipathy.

---

[121] The title of Richard W. Church's book is, simply, *Spenser.*

An early tragedy.

In these spying methods of Burleigh's we may possibly find an explanation of a mysterious incident recorded as happening prior to Oxford's marriage, especially if we suppose Oxford to be "Shakespeare." Oxford had inflicted a wound on an under-cook in Burleigh's employ, and this wound unfortunately proved fatal. None of the circumstances are told, possibly because they are unknown, but, like everything else, the event must needs be set down to Oxford's discredit. Now, remembering Burleigh's spying methods and the peculiar circumstances under which Polonius received his death wound at the hands of Hamlet, we may possibly find in the drama a suggestion of something that had actually happened in the experience of its author; especially in view of Hamlet's exclamation:

> Thou wretched, rash, intruding fool, farewell!
> *I took thee for thy better.*

Hostility.

If, then, in Shakespeare there is any character whom we might identify with Burleigh we should expect to find a spying craftiness amongst his characteristics. This, of course, is the case with Polonius. In the thinly-veiled conflict between the two men it is evident that Burleigh had not all his own way. Accustomed as he had been to the thought of others yielding to his domination—a domination possibly less real than he imagined, as he appears to have been more of an instrument in the hands of his capable mistress and less a ruling power than he supposed—treated as he undoubtedly had been with extreme deference by one of the most autocratic of a despotic dynasty, he nevertheless found himself contradicted, remonstrated with, and embarrassed by a son-in-law who was little more than a boy, and who undoubtedly regarded the great minister as belonging to an inferior order.

Burleigh's charge of "ingratitude."

It is difficult to appreciate the point of view of writers who speak of Oxford's "ingratitude" to Burleigh, and of his having added to his own eminence by marriage. The fact is they merely repeat Burleigh's own account as it appears in the documents he has left. As master of the court of royal wards, Burleigh had had charge of Oxford and had used his position both to elevate the social prestige of his own family and to add to his own estates. So far as De Vere is concerned it is difficult to see that he owed any substantial advantage to his connection with Burleigh; whilst the latter was undoubtedly the source of a very great deal that acted as a drag upon the life of his son-in-law, interfering with the natural expansion of his powers, intensifying the chagrins of domestic trouble, and fastening a stigma on his reputation. We have already referred to Burleigh's repeated thwarting of Oxford's desire for a more useful career and a more extended experience of life; and whatever reason he may have offered, it is quite clear that behind it all there was no real friendliness towards the younger man. The pretence of a good motive behind the repeated refusal—that he hoped the Queen might find something better for him—is so evidently a subterfuge as to make the real hostility all the more evident.

Raleigh and Hatton.

Nor is it the only instance in which we find Burleigh trying to give a gloss of friendliness to his attempts to injure his son-in-law. Some years later, when Oxford was in trouble with the authorities, we find Burleigh appealing to Raleigh and Hatton to use their influence with Queen Elizabeth on Oxford's behalf. This reads at first like a friendly act. When, however, we remember that Raleigh was possibly the one man about court whom his royal mistress most delighted in teasing; whose real influence with the Queen was practically negligible; and between whom and Oxford there was a long-standing antagonism; if to all this we add the fact that Burleigh, in making the appeal to Hatton, uses the occasion to gather together all the charges he can formulate against the very man for whom he is supposed to be interceding, and pours them into unfriendly ears—for Hatton also was of the hostile party and wrote a letter of complaint to Queen Elizabeth speaking of himself as the "sheep" and Oxford as the "boar"— we can only wonder at the clumsiness of a manoeuvre, hardly entitled to rank even as low cunning.

As we have had occasion thus to mention the unfriendly relationship of Oxford to Raleigh we may see a reflection of it in Shakespeare's allusion to "the sanctimonious pirate that went to sea with the Ten Commandments, but scraped one out of the table, 'Thou shalt not steal.'" (*Measure for Measure.*) For it is not easy to reconcile the religious pietism of Raleigh's poetry with certain of his well-known sea-faring episodes. The moral standards of the time are sometimes urged in extenuation of Raleigh's doings; but Burleigh himself, to his credit, disapproved of the great sailor's buccaneering, although on the other hand he saw that the Queen secured some share of the spoil.

Desire for travel.

We cannot yet piece together with a sense of true sequence the recorded details of the early life of Oxford. It is evident, however, that such efforts to obtain a relief from court life in a life of wider experience and greater usefulness as he had made before his marriage, were repeated after his marriage, and still without success: presenting a shameful contrast to the treatment extended to his rival Sidney. Oxford was one of the foremost and wealthiest of the nobility; Sidney at the time was simply Master Philip Sidney; for he only rose to the inferior honour of knighthood three years before his death. He was considered too poor to marry a daughter of Burleigh's, and he was more than four and a half years younger than Oxford. Yet, at the age of seventeen, Sidney began his travels on the Continent, visiting Paris, Frankfort, Vienna, Hungary and Venice, and having every facility afforded him for meeting prominent men. On the other hand, Oxford with his superior social position, wealth, culture and genius, at the age of twenty-four was still to be kept at home in the leading strings of an uncongenial father-in-law. It is difficult, even for those who are in no way involved, and after a lapse of nearly three hundred and fifty years, to contemplate such treatment without a feeling of indignation. Certainly the man who was responsible for it was no friend to the Earl of Oxford.

Bertram's unauthorized travel.

At length, finding his entreaties useless, he resolved to take the law into his own hands, and, in 1574, without the consent of the authorities, left the country in order to fulfil his purpose of travelling on the continent. He had got no further than the Low Countries when he was overtaken by Burleigh's emissaries and brought back. Again we find the extraordinary parallel between the Earl of Oxford and Bertram, in *All's Well*, maintained. Bertram had begged in vain to be allowed to undertake military service just as Oxford had done. He had begged to travel only to be put off with specious excuses, "'too young' and 'the next year' and ''tis too early,' "until, yielding to the suggestion of some friend" (II.1) he exclaims, in a passage already quoted:

> I shall stay here the forehorse to a smock,
> Creaking my shoes on the plain masonry,
> Till honour be bought up and no sword wom
> But one to dance with. By heavens! I'll steal away.

This he did forthwith.

We venture to say that it would be difficult to find in English literature a closer analogy anywhere between the particulars narrated of a fictitious personage and the detailed records of a living contemporary than we have here between Bertram and the Earl of Oxford. Shakespeare's partiality for the Earls of Oxford has already been pointed out (*Henry VI*, part 3). His interest in the particular Earl who was then living, and who was a poet and dramatist, is the most natural assumption. Whether, therefore, the Earl of Oxford was the writer of the play, *All's Well*, or not, one cannot doubt, in the face of such a continued parallelism, that the man who wrote the play had the Earl of Oxford in his mind as the prototype of Bertram. Amongst the records of royal wards of the time we can find no other instance which touches Bertram at so many points. Reiterating a principle, therefore, upon which we have insisted from the first, we would urge that to discover such a parallelism in Shakespeare's works at an advanced stage of the investigation strengthens our convictions immeasurably more than if the case of Bertram and its analogy with Oxford had been known before the selection was made.

Shakespeare and travel. Hamlet.

The special point with which we are now dealing— the obstacles thrown in the way of a young man's wish to travel— appears again in *Hamlet*. Laertes applies for the king's permission to go abroad, and the king asks, "Have you your father's leave? What says Polonius?" To which Polonius replies:

> He hath, my lord, wrung from me my slow leave
> By laboursome petition, and at last
> Upon his will I seal'd my hard consent:
> I do beseech you, give him leave to go.

Then there is the king and queen's opposition to Hamlet's wish to go to Wittenberg, and the false reasons assigned:

> *King:*
> It is most retrograde to our desire;
> And we beseech you, bend you to remain
> Here in the cheer and comfort of our eye,
> Our chiefest courtier, cousin, and our son.

Again, we notice that it is Polonius who is chiefly opposed to his son's travelling, exactly as Burleigh raised his own opposition into a settled maxim of policy:

> Suffer not thy sons to cross the Alps . . . . and if by travel they
> get a few broken languages they shall profit them nothing more

than to have one meat served up in divers dishes.[122]

Resuming the story of De Vere's early manhood, we find that in the year following his abortive attempt to travel he was at last granted permission to go abroad. How important a matter this was to him may be judged by the fact that it is spoken of as "the ambition of his life"; yet by this time he was twenty-five and a half years old, and inferior men had enjoyed the privilege whilst in their teens. Even at this age he had only been able to wring the concession from Elizabeth by means of entreaties; and, considering the favour and indulgence that the Queen showed to him both before and after this, it appears as if the concession had at last been gained in spite of the covert opposition of his father-in-law. In view of all this the speech of Polonius's just quoted is of extraordinary significance. In October, 1575, then, he reached Venice, having travelled by way of Milan.

Shakespeare and travel. Two Gentlemen.

Our present business being to trace in the works of Shakespeare indications of the life and circumstances of the Earl of Oxford we ought not to leave this question of foreign travel without drawing attention to the play of Shakespeare's in which this subject comes in for special treatment, namely, *The Two Gentlemen of Verona*. The date usually assigned to this work is 1590-92; that is to say it is recognized as being amongst the first of Shakespeare's dramas, although it was not published until it appeared in the Folio edition of 1623. Now we find that a play whose title is suggestive of this one was being acted by the company of Anthony Munday, who more than ten years before the date assigned to this drama acknowledged himself the servant of the Earl of Oxford. As Munday's play, *The Two Italian Gentlemen*, may have formed the basis for Shakespeare's work, it is not improbable that the latter was, in fact, the first play of Shakespeare's and may, if we assume the De Vere authorship, have been begun shortly after his return from Italy. It is worth

---

[122] Martin A. S. Hume, *The Great Lord Burghley*, p. 25.

remarking, too, that in it the scene moves from Verona to Milan, a town specially mentioned in the slight record of Oxford's travels. We have had occasion, moreover, to point out already a very striking parallel between the early work of De Vere and the discussion on love with which this particular play opens.

On the subject of travel we have first of all Valentine's statement that "Home-keeping youth have ever homely wits," followed by his urging Proteus,

> rather
> To see the wonders of the world abroad,
> Than, living dully sluggardised at home,
> Wear out thy youth with shapeless idleness.

This is followed in Act III by Panthino's taxing the father of Proteus with having suffered him,

> to spend his youth at home,
> While other men of slender reputation
> Put forth their sons to seek preferment out.

He therefore proceeds to "importune" him,

> To let him spend his time no more at home,
> Which would be great impeachment to his age,
> In having known no travel in his youth.

To this the father of Proteus replies:

> I have considered well his loss of time,
> And how he cannot be a perfect man,
> Not being tried and tutor'd in the world.

On the one hand we cannot ascribe these lines to a man indifferent to foreign travel, and on the other hand it is difficult to think of them as being written by one who had found the way to foreign travel readily open to him. Everything points to the writer being one who had chafed at "living dully, sluggardised at home," and who had had to fight to get himself "tried and tutor'd in the world"; whilst "men of slender reputation" had been freely accorded the advantages which had been denied to himself.

Occupations.

Before leaving the play of *The Two Gentlemen of Verona*, we notice that the passage just quoted is followed by another which touches a point already mentioned elsewhere:

> 'Twere good, I think, your lordship sent him thither:
>   (to the royal court)
> There shall be practise tilts and tournaments,
> Hear sweet discourse, converse with noblemen,
> And be in eye of every exercise
> Worthy his youth and nobleness of birth.

Associate this with Edward de Vere and again we have a case in which comment is superfluous. To think of the passage coming from a writer of lower or middle-class origin demands considerable credulity. Every word bespeaks the special interests of De Vere, and pulsates with that excessive respect for high birth which is common to De Vere and "Shakespeare."

Oxford in Italy.

The records give no indication as to how his time was spent in Italy. This could only be learnt accurately from himself, and as a large reserve and secretiveness in respect to his doings seem to have been characteristic of him throughout, we can only surmise what his occupation would be during the six months of his stay. Considering, however, the literary and dramatic movement in Italy at the time, his own particular bent, and the course his life took after his return to England, there can be little doubt as to his chief interest whilst in that country. He would be much more likely to be found cultivating the acquaintance of those literary and play-acting people of whom his father-in-law would disapprove, than mixing in the political and diplomatic circles that the great minister would consider proper to an eminent English nobleman.

Baptista Minola's crowns.

As an illustration of a principle and method upon which much stress has been laid throughout these researches we would draw attention to a detail in connection with Oxford's Italian tour which though slight in itself, adds much to that sense of verisimilitude that has followed the investigations at each step. Whilst looking up references to Oxford in the published Hatfield manuscripts we noticed the record of a letter he had addressed to Burleigh from Italy. It is but a brief note concerned solely with the fact that he had borrowed five hundred crowns from someone named Baptista Nigrone; and requesting Burleigh to raise the money by the sale of some of his lands—a method of raising money which appears more than once in the pages of "Shakespeare."

As some discussion has taken place over Shakespeare's use of the name "Baptista," its presence in this note of Oxford's naturally arrested attention, and the thought immediately presented itself that if Oxford were actually the writer of the play in which Baptista, the rich gentleman of Padua, appears (*The Taming of the Shrew*) we should expect to find "crowns" introduced into the drama in some marked way, and probably in association with Baptista Minola himself. And this is so. As a matter of fact these particular coins are much more to the front here than in any other of Shakespeare's Italian plays. They are mentioned no less than six times whilst "ducats" are only twice mentioned. On the other hand, in *The Comedy of Errors*, for example, "ducats" are mentioned ten times and "crowns" not at all. *The Merchant of Venice*, which also contains no mention of "crowns" but abundant references to "ducats" is, for special reasons, unsuitable for purposes of comparison. What is more to the point than the actual number of references in *The Taming of the Shrew*, is the fact that the crowns of the wealthy Baptista are specially in evidence, and enter as an important element into the plot. Oxford, it appears from a letter sent home by an attendant, spent some time in Padua itself, and seems to have been involved in riotous proceedings there: not at all unlikely in the creator of the character "Petruchio."

It may be worthwhile adding that we even find a suggestion of Baptista's surname, "Minola," in another Italian, Benedict

Spinola, whose name also appears in connection with this tour. Burleigh, it seems, received from him a notification of Oxford's arrival in Italy. Benedick in *Much Ado* is a nobleman, also of Padua, and these are the only two gentlemen of Padua to be found in Shakespeare's plays. It must further be pointed out that the names "Baptista Nigrone" and "Benedict Spinola" are not selected from amongst a number of others, but are two out of the three Italian names with which we have met in connection with the Italian tour; and to find that, in combination, they almost furnish the identical name of Shakespeare's "Baptista Minola," will be admitted by the most sceptical as at any rate interesting. Certainly such discoveries as that of the place occupied by Baptista's "crowns," agreeing with the conclusions of mere *a priori* reasoning, have added, as can be easily imagined, no small spice of excitement to our researches.

Oxford and Othello.

After spending about six months in Italy Oxford, travelled back as far as Paris, and from a letter which he wrote there, addressed to Burleigh, it appears that he purposed making an extended tour embracing Spain on the one hand, and south-eastern Europe, Greece and Constantinople, on the other. At this point we approach a great crisis in his life which, when his biography comes to be written, will require much patient research, and the most careful weighing of facts, before a straight story can be made of it or the events placed in a clear light. From the documents preserved in the Hatfield manuscripts, however, certain facts specially relevant to our argument already stand out boldly and distinctly. The first is that he expresses a warm regard for his wife. The second is that a responsible servant of his, his receiver, had succeeded in insinuating into his mind suspicions of some kind respecting Lady Oxford. The third is that her father, for some reason or other, recalled Oxford to England, thus upsetting his project of extended travel. The fourth is that on his return he treated his wife in a way quite inexplicable to her, refusing to see her; whilst she, for her part, showed an earnest desire to appease him. The fifth is that reports unfavourable to Lady Oxford's reputation gained currency. And the sixth is that there seems to have been no shadow of justification for these reports.

It hardly needs pointing out that we have here a great many of the outstanding external conditions of Shakespeare's celebrated tragedy of jealousy in connubial life: *Othello*. Brabantio, the father-in-law of Othello, was, like Oxford's father-in-law, the chief minister of state and a great potentate, having "in his effect a voice potential as double as the duke's." Othello himself, like Oxford, was one who took his stand firmly and somewhat ostentatiously upon the rights and privileges of high birth:

> I fetch my life and being
> From men of royal siege, and my demerits
> May speak unbonneted to as proud a fortune
> As this that I have reached.

Desdemona is represented as one who, in the words of her father, "was half the wooer," just as Anne Cecil is represented in the contemporary letter already quoted; whilst a similar youthfulness combined with a premature development along certain lines is expressed in the lines:

> She that so young could give out such a seeming,
> To seal her father's eyes.

Iago, the arch-insinuator of suspicion, is Othello's own "ancient," and occupies a position analogous to Oxford's "receiver," who had dropped the poison of suspicion into his master's mind. Iago's reiterated advice, "Put money in thy purse," is redolent of the special functions of Oxford's receiver: a suggestion repeated in Iago's well-known speech "Who steals my purse steals trash." So the four central figures in this connubial tragedy of real life, Burleigh, Oxford, Lady Oxford, and Oxford's receiver, are exactly represented in Shakespeare's great domestic tragedy by Brabantio, Othello, Desdemona, and Iago.

Othello's recall.

To this correspondence in personnel must be added an even more remarkable correspondence in the two-fold character of the cause of rupture. Before alighting upon this letter of Oxford's and the memoranda of Burleigh's dealing with the crisis, we had supposed that the whole ground of the trouble between him and his wife was his being recalled to England by her father; she having been a party to the recall. The perception that there was yet another cause, suggestive of Othello's principal motive, altered the entire aspect of things; and this, along with the presence in both cases of the subordinate motive—the recall by the lady's father—brought the two cases immediately into line with one another; the whole complex situation finding its expression in Desdemona's pathetic and puzzled appeal to Othello:

> Why do you weep?
> Am I the motives of these tears, my lord?
> If haply *you my father do suspect,*
> *An instrument of this your calling back,*
> Lay not the blame on me.

It is worthwhile remarking that Othello was called back from Cyprus: the very part of the world which Oxford was prevented from visiting by his recall; and that he was called back to Venice, the city which Oxford had just left.

A striking parallel.

In the light of what we now know of the trouble between Lord and Lady Oxford, let the reader go carefully over the first two scenes of Act IV in *Othello*, noticing the intermingling of the two elements of mistrust insinuated by a subordinate, and the "commanding home" of Othello. A sense of identity—with due allowance for the difference between actualities and the poet's dramatization—will, we believe, be irresistible. We shall, therefore, finish off this particular argument by placing together a sentence taken from a letter written by Oxford to Burleigh in which he virtually closes the discussion of the subject and a sentence which "Shakespeare" introduces by the mouth of a subordinate character into the closing part of this particular episode:

> *Oxford:*
>   Neither will he [Oxford] trouble his life any more with such troubles and molestations as he has endured, nor to please his lordship [Burleigh] discontent himself.[123]

> *"Shakespeare" (in Othello):*
>   I will indeed no longer endure it, nor am I yet persuaded to
>   Put up in peace what already I have foolishly suffered.

Parallel passages in published writings may only be instances of plagiarism or unconscious memory. In this case, however, the passage published reproduces a sentence of a private letter not made public until centuries had elapsed. This is all that seems necessary from the point of view of this particular argument; and so conclusive does it appear that we are almost inclined to question the utility of accumulating further evidence. The letter from which we have quoted, we remark, contains also a familiar Shakespearean innuendo respecting parentage. It also expresses a continued regard for his wife; resenting Burleigh's so handling the matter as to have made her "the fable of the world and raising open suspicions to her disgrace."[124]

Domestic rupture.

What Burleigh's ubiquitous informers may have reported leading to Oxford's recall does not appear to be known. Certain it is that even from Italy Burleigh's agents had been forwarding reports the truth of which was denied by an Italian attendant on Oxford. At any rate Oxford himself on his return refused, in a most decided manner, to meet his wife. "Until he can better

---

[123] This is a paraphrase of Oxford's April 27, 1576 letter to Lord Burghley. (Hatfield MSS (CP 9/1). The exact text, from Folwer, p. 248, is "I mean not to weary my life any more with such troubles and molestations as I have endured; nor will I, to please your Lordship only, discontent myself."

[124] From the same letter, again only a paraphrase. The exact text is, "This might have been done through private conference before, and had not needed to have been the fable of the world . . . which made her so disgraced to the world."

satisfy himself concerning certain mislikings," he says, "he is not determined to accompany her."[125] Whether he suspected her of being a party to espionage practised upon him or to attempts at domination over him, or whether there were indeed other hidden matters of a graver nature we cannot say. It may not be without significance, however, that later on we find one of those spying agents of Burleigh's, Geoffrey Fenton, a continental traveller and a linguist, dedicating to Lady Oxford a translation he had made.

The cryptic explanation of his conduct which we have just quoted seems to have been the only one which Oxford would vouchsafe—to Burleigh at any rate. Burleigh complains of Oxford's taciturnity in the matter: that he would only reply, *"I have answered you"*[126]—which is strikingly suggestive of Shylock's laconic expression *"Are you answered?"* One account suggests that the attitude he assumed on his arrival was a sudden and erratic change. If this be correct it is certainly suggestive of that lightning-like change one notices in Hamlet's bearing towards Ophelia, when he detects that she is allowing herself to be made the tool of her father in spying upon Hamlet himself (III.1).

As usual the matter is reported as reflecting discredit upon Oxford. It was an instance merely of bad behaviour towards his wife. One writer, however, states that Oxford had at least offered the explanation that his wife was allowing herself to be influenced by her parents against himself. And this is a reasonable explanation of the only charge that Oxford makes against her, at a time when he makes other charges against Burleigh's administration of his affairs. Lady Oxford's father had undoubtedly treated her husband badly, and if she did not hotly resent and repudiate her father's actions she must be reckoned as being on his side. It was one of those simple cases in which there was no midway course possible, and in which it was impossible for her husband to mistake the side on which she stood.

---

[125] Same letter, again a paraphrase. The original reads, "Until I can better satisfy or advertise myself of some mislikes, I am not determined, as touching my wife, to accompany her."

[126] Apparently a letter from Oxford to Burghley.

Oxford's personality.

Oxford had at any rate come home with his mind fully made up to have done once and for all with Burleigh's domination. That he had borne with it at all seems to suggest that there had been about his personality something of that mildness of manner which dominating men are apt to mistake for weakness, a supposition to which the only portrait we have seen of him, taken at the age of twenty-five, seems to lend support. Certainly his poetry testifies to an affectionateness that might easily be so misconstrued. When such men are at last driven to strike, their blows have frequently a fierceness that comes as a surprise and a shock to their adversaries: and Oxford's poetry does indeed display a capacity for fierce outbursts. We suspect that something of this kind happened in the present instance. Burleigh had adopted a policy in relation to Oxford that the latter was not prepared to tolerate any longer. Anne, during the five years of married life, had passed from girlhood into womanhood. Her father had created a situation in which she must choose definitely between father and husband. The unravelling of the facts and their proper interpretation must, however, form matter for future investigations.

Most writers agree that much of Oxford's subsequent conduct was dictated by a determination to revenge himself on Burleigh for some reason or other; and that his plans of revenge included the squandering of his own estates, and separation from his wife. Castle Hedingham in Essex which Oxford had made over to Burleigh, we are told in local histories was almost razed completely, by Oxford's orders, as part of his plan of revenge. How he could have razed a castle which was no longer his own we do not pretend to explain: we merely repeat in this matter what is recorded. The following two stanzas from one of his early poems are, however, of special interest in this connection:

> I am no sot to suffer such abuse,
> *As doth bereave my heart of his delight;*
> Nor will I frame myself to such as use,
> With calm consent to suffer such despite.

No quiet sleep shall once possess mine eye,
   Till wit have wrought his will on injury.

My heart shall fail and hand shall lose his force,
   But some device shall pay Desire his due;
And fury shall consume my careful corse,
   Or raze the ground whereon my sorrow grew.
Lo, thus in rage of ruthful mind refus'd,
I rest revenged on whom I am abus'd.

The old records suggest a political motive—the imprisonment and execution of his kinsman the Duke of Norfolk—for Oxford's scheme of revenge. If, however, we may connect it with these verses, as we reasonably may, it is evident that the motive was much more directly personal to himself. If, moreover, we connect it with these political matters the time is carried back to the year 1572: the year immediately following his marriage. The disentangling of events and dates in these matters we do not feel to be sufficiently pressing to demand the arrest of our present argument.

A sensational discovery.

Without waiting, therefore, for these obscurities to be cleared up, we may introduce now what has been the most remarkable piece of evidence met with in the whole course of our investigations: a discovery made a considerable time after this work had been virtually completed and indeed after it had already passed into other hands. This evidence is concerned with the play, *All's Well*; the striking parallelism between the principal personage in the drama and the Earl of Oxford having led us to adopt it as the chief support of our argument at the particular stage with which we are now occupied. This argument was carried forward to its present stage at the time when our discovery was announced to the librarian of the British Museum. What we have now to state was not discovered until some months later.

The climax to All's Well.

In tracing the parallelism between Bertram and Oxford we confined our attention to the incidentals of the play, in the belief that the central idea of the plot—the entrapping of Bertram into marital relationships with his own wife, in order that she might bear him a child unknown to himself—was wholly derived from Boccaccio's story of Bertram. The discovery, therefore, of the following passage in Wright's *History of Essex* furnishes a piece of evidence so totally unexpected, and forms so sensational a climax to an already surprising resemblance that, on first noticing it, we had some difficulty in trusting our own eyes. We would willingly be spared the penning of such matter: its importance as evidence does not, however, permit of this. Speaking of the rupture between the Earl of Oxford and his wife, Wright tells us that, "He [Oxford] forsook his lady's bed, . . . [but] the father of Lady Anne by stratagem, contrived that her husband should unknowingly sleep with her, believing her to be another woman, and she bore a son to him in consequence of this meeting."[127] The only son of the Lady Anne, we may mention, died in infancy.

Thus even in the most extraordinary feature of this play; a feature which hardly one person in a million would for a moment have suspected of being anything else but an extravagant invention, the records of Oxford are at one with the representation of Bertram. It is not necessary that we should believe the story to be true, for no authority for it is vouchsafed. A memorandum in the Hatfield manuscripts to the effect that Burleigh laid before the Master of the Rolls and others some private matter respecting this domestic rupture may, however, have had reference to this. The point which matters is that this extraordinary story should be circulated in reference to the Earl of Oxford; making it quite clear that either Oxford was the actual prototype of Bertram, in which case false as well as true stories of the Earl might be worked into the play, or he was supposed to be the prototype and was saddled with the story in consequence. In any case, the connection between the two is now as complete as accumulated evidence can make it. We hesitate to make reflections upon prospective dissentients; but we feel entitled to assert that the man who does not now acknowledge a connection

---

[127] Wright, *History and Topography*, vol. I, pp. 516-17.

of some sort between Edward de Vere and Bertram in *All's Well*, has not the proper faculty for weighing evidence.

Angelo and Mariana.

Having thus raised the peculiar situation, represented in the play, in relation to our problem, we notice something analogous repeated in the relationship between Angelo and Mariana in *Measure for Measure* along with the fact that Angelo specifies a period of "five years" between the making of the marriage arrangement and the special episode (V.1): the exact period between the date of Oxford's marriage and the particular time with which we are now dealing (1571-1576). Angelo also remarks:

> I do perceive
> These poor informal women are no more
> But instruments of some more mightier member
> That sets them on. Let me have way, my lord,
> To find this practice out.

With such possibilities of discovery lying in the play of *All's Well*, it is not surprising that after having first of all appeared under the title of *Love's Labour's Won*, it should have disappeared for a full generation, and then, when the Earl of Oxford had been dead for nearly twenty years, reappeared under a new name, *Measure for Measure* is also one of the plays not published until 1623, although it had been played in 1604.

Burleigh and Oxford's reputation.

The one thing that stands out clearly from all these events is an unmistakable antagonism between Oxford and Burleigh, over which Burleigh especially tries to throw a cloak of benevolence. His next move is somewhat astute: he seems to have given it out that the Earl had been enticed away "by lewd persons." There is no suggestion, however, that Anne had left Oxford, or that Burleigh had sought to separate them because of dissoluteness on the Earl's part. The facts all point unquestionably in the opposite direction: for it was he who exerted all his influence to bring about a rapprochement when the mischief had been done. There was, therefore, no question of protecting a daughter against a profligate husband; and if his charges against Oxford were well founded it is upon the character of Burleigh himself that they react most disastrously. For it is hardly possible to conceive a more despicable character than that of a father exerting himself to throw back his daughter into the arms of her dissolute husband when she had been delivered from him by his own voluntary act. The probability is that Burleigh himself did not believe his own accusations, and that they were a mere *ruse de guerre* on the part of an unscrupulous and crafty fighter. Had he believed his own story he ought rather to have rejoiced at the turn things had taken.

Burleigh's interference.

The real root of much of the trouble, it is easy to see, was the control that Burleigh attempted to exercise over Oxford's movements; the purely negative and restrictive control of a man whose exercise of power, even in the greatest affairs of state, was always governed by considerations of himself, his family, his own policy and his instruments. To a man of Oxford's spirit the position must have been irksome in the extreme; and when we find the fact of his being held in leading strings pointedly alluded to in a poem of Edmund Spenser's, it must have been specially galling. If, then, Oxford succeeded in making himself a thorn in the flesh of his dominating relative, we shall probably agree that the astute minister had at last met his match and got hardly more than he deserved. Lady Oxford's fault was probably no worse than that of having weakly succumbed to a masterful father, or rather two masterful parents. Ophelia's weakness, then, in permitting herself to be made her father's tool in intruding upon Hamlet, certainly suggests her as a possible dramatic analogue to the unfortunate Lady Oxford.

Oxford's affections.

One is always upon uncertain ground in attempting to lay bare the facts which have lain behind the effusions of poets. A note recurs in more than one poem of De Vere's which seems to point to this trouble between himself and his wife. From the dates given we judge them to belong to this particular time of crisis in his life; and if the reference is actually to the breach between them, it would seem that, notwithstanding the course he had been obliged to take, there had been awakened in him an intense affection for his wife. This is certainly the peculiar situation represented in the poems: affection of the poet for one who had formerly sought him but who had become in some way at variance with him. We give two stanzas from separate poems on this theme:

> O cruel hap and hard estate
>   That forceth me to love my foe;
> Accursed be so foul a fate,
>   My choice for to prefix it so.
> So long to fight with secret sore,
> And find no secret salve therefor.

> Betray thy grief thy woeful heart with speed;
>   Resign thy voice to her that caused thee woe;
> With irksome cries bewail thy late done deed,
>   For she thou lov'st is sure thy mortal foe.
> And help for thee there is none sure,
> But still in pain thou must endure.

(As we shall have to refer to this stanza in dealing with the question of "Spenser's Willie" we ask the reader to keep it in mind.)

These two poems, both published when Oxford was but twenty-six years old, are certainly suggestive of Bertram's reference to Helena as one "whom since I have lost have loved." In the play of *All's Well*, everything works out to a satisfactory conclusion. In real life things do not always so work out, and though Oxford and his wife were ultimately, in some sort, reconciled, we are assured that henceforth the relationship between them was not altogether cordial.

Kicking over the traces.

Whatever view may be taken of Burleigh's character, and of the antagonism between him and Oxford, every record testifies unmistakably to the former's wish to exercise an unwarrantable ascendancy over the movements of the latter. Had Oxford been an adventurer and a needy supplicant for court favour like Raleigh, or one desirous of political and diplomatic advancement like Sidney, Burleigh's methods for holding him in subjection might have succeeded permanently. At this time, however, there was nothing in the shape of wealth or social eminence, which others sought that was not already his; and ambitions after military or naval glory, such as could only be realized through the cooperation of those in power, he seems definitely to have abandoned after his return from Italy. Henceforward his powers and interests seem to have been concentrated in literature and drama. Many of the poems from which we have quoted seem to have been published, and some of them evidently written, just about this time. His letter to Bedingfield, so completely free from any suggestion of personal unhappiness, was, in fact, written just at this time. In view of the whole of the circumstances, then, it seems quite safe to say that he returned from Italy, being then close on twenty-six years of age, with his mind finally determined on a literary and dramatic career. In this he was in no way dependent upon the authorities, and viewing the attitude of his powerful relative as a sheer impertinence he was at liberty to set him at defiance.

Oxford "takes his way."

The path he had chosen was one, however, in which he might expect to meet with still greater hostility from Burleigh; though now the hostility would be more or less baffled and impotent. His plans not being confided to those with whom he was in direct personal contact, would involve a good deal of reserve on his side, permit a similar amount of misconstruction on theirs, and afford free scope for efforts at working the situation to his discredit. This, it appears, is just what did happen.

The reference in Shakespeare's sonnets to a time of special crisis when "he took his way" has already been mentioned. Amongst the things which he kept "to his own use" "under truest bars" we may reckon the manuscripts at which he was working.[*] From a remark in one of Oxford's letters[128] it appears that he was accustomed to take with him, when going into the country, important papers secured in a small desk. His secret treasures would, no doubt, include also those Italian plays and other important documents which we now know were freely used by the great dramatist in the composition of his works. That De Vere would bring back such things from Italy it is impossible to doubt. The number and expensiveness of the articles he brought home from his Italian tour is dwelt upon at length, and in much detail, in the account from which many of our facts are taken. It is almost absurd to suppose that he brought back all these goods and omitted to bring with him just those things that touched his own keenest interest most directly. And it would he just such literary treasures that, as Shakespeare, he would guard:

> That to his use they might unused stay
> From bands of falsehood in sure wards of trust.

Burleigh's method of warfare.

The fulfilment of the purpose we suppose him to have set himself, involved his throwing himself into those literary and dramatic circles whose character has been already described. This is what we suppose Burleigh to refer to in speaking of his being enticed away by "lewd persons." It is remarkable, however, that, although we have an abundance of such general accusations against him, we have not been able to discover, up to the present, a single authoritative case in which his name appears in a discreditable personal connection; notwithstanding the fact that, through the records of those time, the evidence of such affairs in the lives of eminent people is only too frequent and unmistakable.

Of all the artifices by which an older man may seek to

---

[*] Looney's note: Amongst complaints formulated against his father-in-law and wife, Oxford states that he had been refused possession of some of his own writings. (Hat. MSS.)

[128] Hatfield MSS.

maintain an ascendancy over a younger one, there is hardly any more contemptible than that of playing upon his regard for reputation and good name; and Burleigh, in attempting to apply this method in bringing pressure to bear upon Oxford, was only employing one of his recognized stratagems. In this matter we are again able to present the testimony of no less a witness than the poet Edmund Spenser. The following passage taken from his poem, "Mother Hubbard's Tale," Dean Church assures us,[129] is generally accepted as referring to Burleigh:

> No practice sly
> No counterpoint of cunning policy,
> No reach, no breach, that might him profit bring
> But he the same did to his purpose wring.
>
>   *   *   *
>
> He no account made of nobility.
>
>   *   *   *
>
> All these through feigned crimes he thrust adown
> Or made them dwell in darkness of disgrace.

Burleigh's "cunning policy."

The last part of the quotation might almost be supposed to have direct reference to Burleigh's special treatment of the Earl of Oxford himself; whilst the character of trickster, which Spenser fixes upon Elizabeth's great minister, certainly meets us at more than one point in his dealings with his son-in-law. Indeed it appears almost as if it were a character in which he himself gloried, as the following story which we quote from Macaulay shows:

"When he [Burleigh] was studying the law at Gray's Inn he lost all his furniture and books at the gaming table to one of his friends. He accordingly bored a hole in the wall which separated his chambers from those of his associate, and at midnight bellowed through the passage threats of damnation and calls to repentance in the ears of the victorious gambler, who lay sweating with fear all night, and refunded his winnings on his knees next day. 'Many other the like merry jests,' says his old biographer, 'I have heard him tell.'"[130] "One who thus gloried almost childishly

---

[129] Church, *Spenser*, p. 110.
[130] G. Ravenscroft Dennis, *The House of Cecil*, p. 18-19.

in his own low cunning was not the kind of man to stick at any "practice sly, or counterpoint of cunning policy," that he could "to his own purpose wring."[131] Edward de Vere was certainly "made to dwell in darkness of disgrace"; and no sane reading of Shakespeare's sonnets can avoid the conclusion that "Shakespeare" was one who suffered in the same way, whilst no trace of contemporary disrepute has been pointed out respecting the Stratford Shakspere.

Freedom.

Even if Burleigh had good reasons for believing that what he was urging against Oxford was true, it seems clear that the opportunist minister who "winketh at these love affairs," was merely striking at his son-in-law's reputation as part of his usual cunning. That the attack upon De Vere's good name had not only succeeded in injuring him, but had cut him to the quick, is evident from the poem on the loss of his good name. That the plan did not succeed either in bringing him into subjection or in diverting him from his purpose is equally clear. Indeed, it looks as if, though at great cost to himself, Oxford had in a measure got the whip hand over Burleigh: possibly the only man who was ever able to do this. From this time forward his leading interests were literary and dramatic. He became "the best of the courtier poets of the early days of Queen Elizabeth," and in drama "amongst the best in comedy"; yet the only surviving poems known are a few fragments belonging mainly to his youth and early manhood, whilst of the fruits of the dramatic activity that filled the period of his life with which we are now to deal no single example is supposed to be extant—every line is supposed to have perished: "lost or worn out."

---

[131] Nicolas, *Memoirs*, p. 23.

CHAPTER XI

EDWARD DE VERE—MIDDLE PERIOD: DRAMATIC FOREGROUND

I

BEFORE entering upon a consideration of those dramatic enterprises which occupied an important part of the middle period of Oxford's life, which we place, in a general way, between 1576 and 1590, that is to say from the age of twenty-six to forty, we shall dispose first of all of some personal matters, which we are able to link on to the Italian tour and which furnish corroborative evidence of his identity with Shakespeare. His stay in Italy, it has already been pointed out, had so marked an influence over him as to affect his dress and manners and cause him to be lampooned as an "Italianated Englishman"; the same writer holding him up to ridicule as "a passing singular odd man."

Gabriel Harvey and Holofernes.

The writer in question was none other than Gabriel Harvey, the friend of Edmund Spenser, who, it has been affirmed, almost succeeded in leading Spenser's genius astray. *The Dictionary of National Biography* gives us a very careful study of this curious and learned pedant; and if we assume that the writer of Shakespeare's plays was acquainted with him personally, we can quite imagine from this account that the dramatist had him in mind in the writing of *Love's Labour's Lost*. We have first of all Berowne's speech on studious plodders (I.1) which is simply portraiture of Harvey, even to the touch about

These earthly godfathers of heaven's lights.

242

For Harvey was, amongst other things, a dabbler in astrology. Again in Act IV, 3, we have a return to the same antagonism to studious plodding in the remark that

> Universal plodding poisons up
> The nimble spirit in the arteries.

The whole spirit of the play is hostile to that merely bookish learnedness which is typified by scholars like Gabriel Harvey. A living specimen of the scholarly pedant is presented in the character of Holofernes, and so realistic is the representation that it has been very naturally supposed that Shakespeare had some contemporary in mind as the prototype of this eccentric pedant. Had the name and personality of Gabriel Harvey been previously associated in any way with Shakespeare, the problem of Holofernes' identification would not have remained unsolved for any length of time. William Shakspere of Stratford could hardly be expected to know much of Gabriel Harvey, and therefore the prototype of Holofernes has remained in doubt, notwithstanding the fact that the resemblance was recognized by Dean Church.[132] There is, of course, no correspondence between Holofernes in the play and the scriptural, or rather apocryphal character of the same name, who was decapitated by Judith. The name is therefore selected evidently for some other reason. That reason becomes apparent the moment we put side by side with the name of Holofernes that of Hobbinol, the name under which Gabriel Harvey appears in Spenser's works. For Hobbinol, the name used by Spenser, is generally recognized as a rough anagram made from the name of Gabriel Harvey, whilst Holofernes is but another anagram composed of Spenser's Hobbinol further strengthened by the characteristic letter "r," taken from both Gabriel and Harvey and an "f," suggestive of the "v" in Harvey. The choice of an out-of-the-way name as an anagram instead of the invention of a new one is characteristic of the more subtle genius of Shakespeare.

---

[132] Church, *Spenser*, p. 18.

Oxford and Harvey.

If, then, we are justified in connecting Holofernes with Gabriel Harvey it becomes impossible to avoid connecting the writer of the play with the Earl of Oxford. For this reason: Oxford, as Harvey admitted, had extended his customary munificence to this scholar when the latter was a poor student at the university; and Harvey, on an important occasion, had addressed complimentary verses to his benefactor. Then behind Oxford's back he had circulated privately satirical verses, supposed to be ridiculing the man whom he had complimented publicly. Now, turning to *Love's Labour's Lost*, we find, first of all, a speech of Holofernes' which bears some resemblance to the verses in which he had ridiculed Oxford (the speech introduced by the Latin phrase "Novi hominem," V.1). Then, in the by-play of the second scene in the same act—and this is really the important point—Holofernes is assigned the role of Judas Maccabeus, and by a turn that is given to the dialogue he is made to appear as "Judas Iscariot," the "kissing traitor." On being twitted on the point he shows resentment as though there was in it an allusion to himself. The ingenious way in which a part played by an actor is turned into a personal attack upon himself is suggestive of a covert personal application; and therefore, if it is not a direct confirmation of our theory, it certainly constitutes another of the series of surprising coincidences which have appeared at every stage of our investigation.

Oxford and Berowne.

Under the old hypothesis of the authorship of Shakespeare's works it has been frequently remarked that there is no character in the plays that can be identified with the author himself. If, however, we assume the De Vere authorship we may at once identify the author with the character of Berowne (Biron, in some editions). For it is he who mocks Holofernes as the "kissing traitor." The play as a whole is a satire upon the various affectations of the times: Holofernes representing learned affectation, Don Armado representing Euphuism, Boyet representing the affectations of courtesy. Now the satirist in the play is Berowne, so that he personates the spirit of the play as a whole, in other words he represents the writer, and is indeed the very life and soul of the drama, his biting mockery being something of a terror to his companions.

It is interesting to notice, therefore, that Sir Sidney Lee connects Rosaline who is loved by Berowne with the "dark lady" referred to in the sonnets as being loved by Shakespeare; and Mr. Frank Harris makes the same connection, thus identifying Berowne with the author of the play. The latter writer, though never swerving from the Stratfordian view, has done much to destroy the old notion that there is no character in the plays who can be identified with Shakespeare. He nevertheless asserts that Shakespeare usually represents himself as a lord or a king. If, then, we can accept Berowne as the dramatist's representation of himself under one aspect, we see at once how much more accurately he represents the Earl of Oxford than he does the Stratford man. "This mad-cap Lord Berowne," "a man replete with mocks, full of comparisons and wounding flouts which he on all estates will execute," is just what we have in a few of the glimpses we get of Oxford's dealings with the people about the court. All that merciless mockery, which Berowne does not hesitate to turn upon himself, mixed with depth of feeling and strong intelligence, and his irrepressible fun tinged with "musing sadness," marks him both as a dramatic representation of the Earl of Oxford, and, in part at any rate, a dramatic self-revelation of "Shakespeare."

Love's Labour's Lost.

We take this play to be largely representative of himself during the years in which, whilst still to be found at court, he was mainly occupied with literature and drama, and was earning for himself the title of "the best in comedy." Whether he succeeded at last, as Rosaline had urged Berowne "To weed this wormwood from his fruitful brain," we will not venture to say. Certain it is that amongst the courtiers of the time he appears to have had a reputation for stinging jibes, of which both Sidney and Raleigh seem to have come in for their share.

Philip Sidney and Boyet.

The quarrel with Sidney, in which he stung his adversary with the single word "puppy," is one of the few details recorded of his life about the court in the early years of this period. The story of the quarrel is variously told, differing in so much as this, that one account speaks of Sidney playing tennis when Oxford intruded, whilst another records that Oxford was playing when Sidney strolled in. In whichever way the story is told it must needs be so as to reflect discredit upon Oxford and credit upon his antagonist. The chief contemporary authority for the details, however, appears to be Fulke Greville, and when it is remembered that Greville was the life-long friend of Sidney, and that when he died, as Lord Brooke, he left instructions that this friendship should be recorded upon his tombstone, we can hardly regard him as an impartial authority.

"Were I a king."

One particular of this antagonism is, however, relevant to our present enquiry and must be narrated. Oxford had written some lines (again the familiar six-lined stanza) which are spoken of by two writers as specially "melancholy." They may be so, but they are certainly not more melancholy than many passages in "Shakespeare's" sonnets, and are quite in harmony with that substratum of melancholy which has been traced in the Shakespeare plays.

Oxford's stanza:

> Were I a king I might command content,
> Were I obscure unknown would be my cares,
> And were I dead no thoughts should me torment,
> Nor words, nor wrongs, nor love, nor hate, nor fears.
> A doubtful choice of three things one to crave,
> A kingdom or a cottage or a grave.

SIR PHILIP SIDNEY

FROM THE LINE ENGRAVING BY GEORGE VERTUE, 1745.
REPRODUCED BY PERMISSION OF
THE NATIONAL PORTRAIT GALLERY.

Melancholy or not, the Shakespeare student will have no difficulty in recognizing in this single stanza several marks of the master craftsman.

To this Sidney had replied in the following verse—which the same two writers, curiously enough, refer to in identical terms, as being a sensible reply:

> Wert thou a king, yet not command content,
> Since empire none thy mind could yet suffice,
> Wert thou obscure, still cares would thee torment;
> But wert thou dead all care and sorrow dies.
> An easy choice of three things one to crave,
> No kingdom nor a cottage but a grave.

These two stanzas form an important part of another argument, to be treated later, and, therefore, should be kept in mind.

The tennis-court quarrel.

It will be observed that the "sensible reply" contains no really inventive composition. It is a mere schoolboy parody, formed by twisting the words and phrases of the original stanza into an affront. Had it been an inventive composition it would have contained more matter than Sidney ever compressed into an equal space. Between two intimate friends it might have been tolerated as a harmless piece of banter. Between two antagonists it lacked even the justification of original wit. And if, as one writer suggests, this matter led up to the tennis-court quarrel, considering the whole of the circumstances, including age and personal relationships, Oxford's retort of "puppy" was possibly less outrageous, and certainly more original than Sidney's verse had been. Sidney's uncle, Leicester, upon whose influence at court the young man (then twenty-four years old) largely depended, admits having to "bear a hand over him as a forward young man," so that one less interested in him might be expected to express the same idea more emphatically. The personal attack, it must be observed, had, in this instance at any rate, come first from Sidney. As in other cases one gets the impression of Oxford not being a man given to initiating quarrels, but capable of being roused, and when attacked, striking back with unmistakable vigour. The story of the tennis-court quarrel is one of the few particulars about Oxford that have become current. Indeed, one very interesting history of English literature mentions the incident, and ignores the fact that the earl was at all concerned with literature. Now, concerning the prominence given to this story, it almost appears as if "Shakespeare," in *Hamlet*, had intended to furnish a clue to his identity when he represents Polonius dragging in a reference to young men "falling out at tennis."

Sidney's affectation.

If our identification of Oxford and Harvey with Berowne and Holofernes be accepted, an interesting point for future investigation will be the identification of other contemporaries with other characters in the play; and in view of Oxford's relationship with Sidney we shall probably be justified in regarding Boyet as a satirized representation of Philip Sidney; not, of course, the Philip Sidney that tradition has preserved, but Sidney as Oxford saw him. For, compared with the genius of Shakespeare, no competent judge would hesitate to pronounce Sidney a mediocrity. If to this we add Dean Church's admission that "Sidney was not without his full share of that affectation which was then thought refinement,"[133] it is not difficult to connect him with Boyet, the ladies' man, whom Berowne satirizes in Act V, Scene 2:

> Why this is he
> That kiss'd away his hand in courtesy;
> This is the ape of form, monsieur the nice,
> That, when he plays at tables, chides the dice
> In honourable terms; nay, he can sing
> A mean most meanly; and, in ushering,
> Mend him who can: the ladies call him sweet.
> The stairs as he treads on them kiss his feet.
> This is the flower that smiles on every one,
> To show his teeth as white as whale's bone;

---

[133] Church, *Spenser*, p. 24.

> And consciences that will not die in debt,
> Pay him the due of honey-tongued Boyet.

Sidney's debts.

The last two lines are somewhat puzzling apart from any special application. Applied to Sidney, however, they become very pointed from the fact that he died so deeply in debt as to delay his public funeral; his creditors being unwilling to accept the arrangements proposed to them. The difficulties were only overcome by his father-in-law Walsingham, who had a special political interest in the public funeral, advancing £6,000.

Sidney's plagiarism.

When, moreover, we find Sidney presenting at a pastoral show at Wilton a dialogue, which is obvious plagiarism from Spenser and De Vere, we can understand Berowne saying of Boyet, in the lines immediately preceding those quoted:

> This fellow pecks up wit as pigeons pease,
> And utters it again when God doth please.

We give a sentence or two by way of illustration:

Spenser (Shepherd's Calender-August).
> Will: Be thy bagpipes run far out of frame?
> Or lovest thou, or be thy younglings miswent?

Sidney (Dialogue between two shepherds).
> Will: What? Is thy bagpipe broke or are thy lambs miswent?

De Vere (Dialogue on Desire);
> What fruits have lovers for their pains?
> Their ladies, if they true remain,
> A good reward for true desire.
> What was thy meat and daily food?
> What hadst thou then to drink?
> Unfeigned lover's tears.

Sidney (Shepherd's Dialogue):
> What wages mayest thou have?
> Her heavenly looks which more and more
> Do give me cause to crave.
> What food is that she gives?
> Tear's drink, sorrow's meat.

Sidney's whole poem is, in fact, little more than the dishing-up of ideas and expressions from the two poems. If, in addition to this, the reader will turn back to the stanza of De Vere's beginning "I am not as I seem to be," noticing especially the reference in it to Hannibal, he will be able to detect more "pigeon's pease" in the following verse of Sidney's:

> As for my mirth, how could I be but glad,
> Whilst that methought I justly made my boast
> That only I the only mistress had?
> But now, if e'er my face with joy be clad
> Think Hannibal did laugh when Carthage lost.

A certain degree of rivalry between artists, in any department of art, may be quite consistent with mutual respect. But when one happens to be "a forward young man" guilty of petty pilfering from his rival, one can understand the rival's point of view when he protests:

> He is wit's pedlar, and retails his wares
> At wakes and wassails, meetings, markets, fairs,
> And we that sell by gross, the Lord doth know
> Have not the grace to grace it with such show.
>
> (*L. L. L.* V.2)

The second line of this quotation is especially interesting in view of the occasion of Sidney's plagiarism mentioned above (The Wilton Show). In support of our contention that plagiarism was characteristic of Sidney, we are able to offer the testimony of Sir Sidney Lee, who remarks that "Petrarch, Ronsard and Desportes inspired the majority of Sidney's efforts, and his addresses to abstractions like sleep, the moon, his muse, grief or lust are almost verbatim translations from the French."[134] Altogether, it is evident that Oxford was not without some justification for the use of the one word of his, "the comparison and wounding flout," which has passed into literary history. It would almost appear as though *Love's Labour's Lost* contained a direct allusion to the incident. For, after a passage of arms between Berowne and

---

[134] Lee, *Life*, p. 444.

Boyet we have the following:

> Margaret:
>   The last is Berowne, the merry mad-cap lord,
>   Not a word with him but a jest.
> Boyet:
>   And every jest but *a word*.
> Princess:
>   It was well done of you to take him at his word.

Sir Thomas Knyvet.

Before leaving this question of "Boyet" we wish to offer an interesting observation upon the name itself. We have been unable to discover any other use of the word. If, however, we replace "Boy" by its old equivalent "Knave" we get the name of one who was possibly the most pronounced foe of Edward de Vere, namely Sir Thomas *Knyvet*; the word is variously spelt, like most names in those days, but the etymological connection is obvious. The feud between the two men and their retainers was of the same bitter and persistent character that we have represented in *Romeo and Juliet* between the Montagues and the Capulets. Fighting took place between them in the open streets and lives were lost. A duel was fought between Oxford and Sir Thomas Knyvet and both were wounded: Oxford seriously. It is possible, therefore, that quite in keeping with dramatic and poetic work of the type of *Love's Labour's Lost*, Boyet is a composite character formed from Oxford's outstanding antagonists, Sir Philip Sidney and Sir Thomas Knyvet.

We have been trying to show that the plays of Shakespeare contain possible pen portraits of men with whom the Earl of Oxford had dealings, representing them, not as tradition has preserved them, but as they stood in relation to Oxford himself. It is no necessary part of our argument that these identifications should be fully accepted. They bear rather on a branch of Shakespearean study that must receive a special development once our main thesis is adopted. Meanwhile they assist in the work of giving to the plays those touches of personality which up to the present have been lacking, and which, in the mass, must go far to support or break down any attempt at identifying the author.

Eccentricity.

It was during the period of Oxford's life with which we are now dealing that he appears to have made for himself a reputation for eccentricity. Such eccentricity may have been partly natural. His reputation in this particular would, however, most certainly receive considerable addition from the mode of life he adopted as the necessary means of fulfilling his vocation. It is possible, too, that finding it served as a mask to have his way of living attributed to eccentricity, and that it protected him against annoyance and interference, he worked the matter systematically, as Hamlet did. The eccentricity and levity which he evidently showed in certain court circles, including doubtless the members of the Burleigh faction, was probably not only a disguise, but also an expression of contempt for those towards whom he adopted the manner. In those literary and dramatic relationships which mattered most to him his bearing was evidently of a different kind, for there he is spoken of as "a most noble and learned gentleman." It is possible, too, that he may not have succeeded altogether in throwing dust in the eyes of Burleigh; for we find the latter admitting that "his lordship hath more capacity than a stranger to him might think."[135]

Duality in "Shakespeare."

This dual attitude towards others is more than once illustrated in the works of Shakespeare. The most prominent illustration is, of course, that of Hamlet. We find something, too, of this double personality in the character of the "mad-cap Lord Berowne" and we have it exactly described in the case of Brutus in *Lucrece*:

> He with the Romans was esteemed so,
> As silly-jeering idiots are with kings,
> For sportive words and uttering foolish things.

---

[135] Lee, "Vere, Edward," p. 226. "Burghley wrote hopefully at the time that 'he found in the earl more understanding than any stranger to him would think' (Hist. MSS. Comm. 4th Rep. p. 95)."

> But now he throws that shallow habit by,
> Wherein deep policy did him disguise;
> And arm'd his long hid wits advisedly.

The same note appears again in his presentation of Prince Hal, or Henry V, whose

> vanities . . . .
> Were but the outside of the Roman Brutus
> Covering discretion with a coat of folly (II.4)

and who "obscured his contemplation under the veil of wildness."

In the case of Edgar in *King Lear* we have the most pronounced development of the idea. Here we have the carrying out of a definite purpose by means of a simulation of complete madness; a purpose which

> taught him to shift
> Into a madman's rags, to assume a semblance
> That very dogs disdained.

The conception was evidently quite a dominant one in the mind of the dramatist, and that it was characteristic of himself, whoever he may have been, is made quite clear in the oft quoted passage in the *Sonnets*:

> Alas 'tis true I have gone here and there
> And made myself a motley to the view,
> Gored mine own thoughts, sold cheap what is most dear.

There is nothing suggestive of enigma in these lines, and therefore only their obvious meaning should be attached to them. "Shakespeare," as the great leader of true realism—quite a different thing from the modern enormity which calls itself by that name—is entitled to be read literally when he speaks directly and seriously of himself; and therefore, when he tells us, in so many words, that he had acted the mountebank in some form, we may take it that he had actually done so. To think of him as a man who "brought to the practical affairs of life a wonderfully sane and sober judgment,"[136] meaning thereby that he was a practical steady-headed man of business with a keen eye for the "main chance," is to place his personality in direct contradiction to all that the sonnets reveal of him. Let anyone read these sonnets so full of personal pain, then turn to *Love's Labour's Lost*, much of which was evidently being penned at the very time when many of the sonnets were being written, and he will feel that he is in the presence of an extraordinary personality, capable of great extremes in thought and conduct, the very antithesis of the model citizen that "Shakespeare" is supposed to have been.

Duality in Oxford.

How suggestive is all this of De Vere's lines:

1. I most in mirth most pensive sad.

2. Thus contraries be used, I find,
   Of wise, to cloak the covert mind.

3. So I the pleasant grape have pulled from the vine,
   And yet I languish in great thirst while others drink the wine.

Every word of these sentences reveals a man hiding the soreness of his own nature under a mask of levity whilst adding to the world's store of joy and merriment.

We feel justified in assuming, therefore, that the impression of himself which he set up in official circles was largely such as he intended to establish, and that not the least part of the satisfaction he derived from his success in the matter was in the thought of fooling Burleigh and others about the court. It hardly needs pointing out how true all this is of Hamlet, and how Hamlet's attitude towards Polonius, Rosencrantz, Guilderstern and the other courtiers might be taken as a developed and idealized representation of Oxford's dealings with men like Burleigh, Raleigh, Greville and Hatton.

"Shakespeare" in his characters.

As a last remark upon this point we would draw attention to the fact that in his work *The Man Shakespeare* Mr. Frank Harris

---

[136] Lee, *Life*, p. 192. See footnote 72, p. 89.

rejects entirely the idea that Shakespeare cannot be identified with any of his characters; and, though approaching the question from a totally different standpoint and with other purposes, selects amongst the most outstanding examples of self-representation several of the cases we have just cited. From this work we quote the following passages:

> In *Hamlet* Shakespeare has discovered too much of himself. . . . [He makes] "Brutus an idealized portrait of himself. . . . Edgar is peculiarly Shakespeare's mouthpiece. . . . It can hardly be denied that Shakespeare identified himself as far as he could with Henry V.[137]

In every one of these cases, as has already been remarked, we have men hiding a superior nature under a veil of folly. There is probably an element of confusion between the two men named "Brutus," appearing with an interval of five hundred years in *Lucrece* and *Julius Caesar* respectively. But Shakespeare's linking of Prince Hal with the Brutus who pretended to be insane and swore to avenge the death of Lucrece furnishes all the connection needed.

"Vulgar scandal."

It is not our purpose to attempt to refute his reputed dissoluteness during those years of active association with dramatic companies. It has already been remarked, however, that, had his conduct been quite irreproachable in other respects, the absenting of himself from his normal social and domestic circles, which was partly a necessary condition of the enterprise he had in hand, and the known character of those with whom he had to associate, so frankly stated in the passage we have quoted from Dean Church, would have afforded ample foundations on which antagonists might build for him such a reputation. When we consider further the special character of Burleigh, so aptly described in the passage we have quoted from Spenser's *Mother Hubbard's Tale*, we may rest assured that the most would be made of these things to Oxford's discredit. Whatever his private

---

[137] Harris, *The Man*, p. 142.

character may have been, a reputation for dissoluteness was almost inevitable under the circumstances. It will be perfectly safe to say, therefore, that he was no worse, but probably very much better, than he has been portrayed. On the other hand, as the Shakespeare sonnets themselves clearly admit departures from recognized canons of rectitude, on the part of their writer, we are not concerned here to claim for De Vere a higher moral elevation than belongs to Shakespeare. At the same time, if we regard these sonnets as the product of Oxford's pen, we shall be able to clear his reputation of much of the slander that has hitherto been in undisputed possession.

II

Dramatic activities.

Our chief concern at this stage is with his dramatic activities. How soon after his return from Italy these were begun we cannot say; but the fact that he appears almost immediately to have adopted the practice of absenting himself from domestic and court life, and of sharing the Bohemian life of literary men and play-actors, suggests that he was not long in beginning his dramatic apprenticeship. Then, from this time up to about the year 1590, which we take as marking in a general way the beginning of the Shakespearean output, his life was largely of this Bohemian and dramatic character. Future research will probably furnish fuller details and dates of Edward de Vere's connection with the stage; sufficient has, however, already been established to show that by the year 1580 he was already deeply committed.

From the Calendar of State Papers we learn that in 1580 the heads of the Cambridge University wrote to Burleigh objecting to the Earl of Oxford's servants "showing their cunning" in certain plays which they had already performed before the Queen. By 1584 he had a company of players touring regularly in the provinces, and from this year until 1587 his company was established in London, occupying a foremost place in the dramatic world.

In connection with his tours in the province, it is worthwhile remarking that in 1584, that is to say just before settling in London, his company paid a visit to Stratford-on-Avon. William Shakspere was by this time twenty years of age and had been married for two years. There has been a great deal of guessing respecting the date at which William Shakspere left Stratford-on-Avon, and it is not improbable that it may have been connected with the visit of the "Oxford Boys." As it is the birth of twins, early in 1585, which furnishes the data from which the time of his leaving Stratford has been inferred, the latter half of 1584 may indeed have been the actual time.

Oxford as dramatist.

However these things may be, the fact is that, whether in the country or the metropolis, it appears to have been quite recognized that the Earl of Oxford had a hand in the composition of some of the plays that his company was staging, whilst others were substantially his own.

Anthony Munday.

The year 1580, which gives us the earliest evidence of his being directly implicated in dramatic work, connects him also with a writer of poetry and drama, and the manager of a theatrical company, called Anthony Munday; and as this connection is of a most important and interesting character it must be treated at some length.

One peculiar fact about Munday has been the attributing to him both of dramatic and poetic compositions of a superior order, which competent authorities now assert could not have been written by him. In order to establish this point we must first deal with matters which take us past the period of time with which we are now dealing. In the year 1600 there was published an important poetical anthology called *England's Helicon*, containing, amongst others, the poems of "Shepherd Tony," whose identity has been one of the much-discussed problems of Elizabethan literature. Some writers have inclined to the idea that Anthony Munday was "Shepherd Tony"; and in a modern anthology one of the best of the poems of Shepherd Tony, "Beauty sat bathing by a spring," is ascribed to Anthony Munday: as if no doubt existed on the point. Now Munday has, as a matter of fact, published a volume of his own poetry, *A Banquet of Dainty Conceits*; and of this the modern editor of *England's Helicon*, Mr. A. H. Bullen (1887), says:

> Intrinsically the poems have little interest; but the collection is on that account important, as affording excellent proof that Anthony Munday was not the Shepherd Tony of 'England's Helicon.' Munday was an inferior writer.[138]

He then gives a passage of ten lines from Munday's poems and adds: "Very thin gruel this, and there are eight more stanzas. After reading these *Dainty Conceits* I shall stubbornly refuse to believe that Munday could have written any of the poems attributed in *England's Helicon* to the Shepherd Tony."[139]

Munday credited with others' work.

We now revert to the period proper to this chapter, the years approaching 1580, in which De Vere was serving, as it were, the first term of his dramatic apprenticeship, and we ask for a very careful attention to the following passages taken from the *Cambridge History of English Literature*, vol. 5, chapter 10:

> Anthony Munday . . . a hewer and trimmer of plays.[140]

> Of the lesser Elizabethan dramatists Munday is the most considerable, interesting and typical.[141]

> These plays of Munday (have) no genius in them.[142]

> A translation from the Italian may be given as the beginning of Munday's work. . . . [It is] a comedy of *Two Italian Gentlemen* . . . Victoria's song at her window and Fedele's answer are of real

---

[138] A. H. Bullen (editor), *England's Helicon*, p. 0.
[139] Bullen, *England's Helicon*, p. 0.
[140] Rev. Ronald Bayne, "Lesser Elizabethan Dramatists," p. 312.
[141] Bayne, "Lesser," p. 312.
[142] Bayne, "Lesser," p. 320.

poetic charm, and Fedele's denunciation of woman's fickleness is exactly in the strain, as it is in the metre, of the rhyming rhetoric of *Love's Labour's Lost*. . . . Rhyming alexandrines and fourteen syllabled lines are generally employed; but in Fedele's speech . . . special seriousness and dignity of style are attained by the use of *rhyming ten-syllabled lines in stanzas of six lines* [The *Venus* and De Vere's 'Of Women' stanza] . . . What is unexpected is the idiomatic English . . . of the translation; . . . [for Munday's] prose translations do not display any special power in transforming the original into native English. . . .[143]

Munday and Oxford. Munday and Shakespeare.

Munday in 1580 and in his earliest published works is anxious to proclaim himself 'servant of the Earl of Oxford' . . . The Earl of Oxford's company of players acted in London between 1584 and 1587. . . . [In a certain play] 'as it hath been sundry times played by the right honourable Earle of Oxenford, the Lord Great Chamberlaine of England, his servant,' . . . the six-lined stanza occurs. . . . [Much of it] might be Munday's work . . . but he cannot have written the sonorous blank verse of the historic scenes . . . [One of] Munday's plays is a humble variation of the dramatic type of *A Midsummer Night's Dream*. . . . *and we find in* [another of Munday's plays] *phrases that may have rested in the mind of Shakespeare*.[144]

We feel entitled to say that the writer of these passages, the Rev. Ronald Bayne, M.A., was simply trembling on the brink of the discovery we claim to have made. The sentences quoted are not to be found in the close proximity to one another in which we have here placed them. They do, however, occur in the same chapter of the same work and are all from the same pen. A careful examination of the passages in these plays of Munday's, which "could not have been written by him," and containing passages which might have "rested in the mind of Shakespeare," would be necessary to make the present statement complete. They will need to be compared with Shakespeare's work on the one hand, and

---

[143] Bayne, "Lesser," p. 314, 315. Text in brackets was inserted by Looney.
[144] Bayne, "Lesser," pp. 315-316, 317, 318. Italics were added by Looney. Text in brackets was inserted by Looney.

with the De Vere work on the other. For the present we are
content to let it rest upon the authority quoted, and ask the
reader to observe the number and the important character of the
connecting links which Anthony Munday thus establishes for us
between Shakespeare and Edward de Vere. For, if the passages in
question fulfil the description given by Mr. Bayne, there seems
but one explanation possible, in view of the whole course our
investigations have so far taken, and that is that prior to 1580 the
Earl of Oxford was learning his business as dramatist, trying his
prentice hand, so to speak, upon inferior plays then current,
collaborating with inferior writers, interpolating passages of his
own into plays produced by his employee Anthony Munday—
such passages as "might have rested in the mind of Shakespeare."

Munday, Oxford and "Shakespeare."

As we are given one example of verse that appears in a play of
Munday's, we shall reproduce it, along with corresponding
passages from De Vere and Shakespeare, notwithstanding the
repetition it involves:

1. Munday's play:
> Lo! here the common fault of love, to follow her that flies,
> And fly from her that makes pursuit with loud lamenting cries.
> Fedele loves Victoria, and she hath him forgot;
> Virginia likes Fedele best, and he regards her not.

2. De Vere's poems:
> The more I followed one, the more she fled away,
> As Daphne did full long ago, Apollo's wishful prey.
> The more my plaints I do resound the less she pities me.
> The more I sought the less I found, yet mine she meant to be.

As the verse in Munday's play exactly reproduces the situation
of the lovers in *A Midsummer Night's Dream*, we quote the lines
of the latter play dealing with the situation:

3. Shakespeare, M.N.D., I.1 (Dialogue):
> I frown upon him, yet he loves me still.
> O! that your frowns would teach my smiles such skill.
> I give him curses, yet he gives me love.

O! that my prayers could such affection move.
The more I bate the more be follows me.
The more I love the more be hateth me.

We are content to leave these matters to the reflection of the reader; and, as a last reference to Anthony Munday, merely point out the interesting fact that the recently discovered manuscript, which forms the subject of Sir E. Maunde Thompson's work on the penmanship of William Shakspere, is an interpolation into a play by Anthony Munday.

III

Agamemnon and Ulysses.

It would be of inestimable value if some of Oxford's manuscripts or even the titles of his plays could be discovered. We should not, of course, expect to find an exact correspondence between these titles and those of the Shakespeare plays: but rather something furnishing connecting clues. Up to the present we have been able to discover only one such title, and the result has been by no means disappointing. In Mrs. Stopes's work on *Burbage and Shakespeare's Stage* we find the following from a contemporary record (1584).

> *The History of Agamemnon and Ulisses* presented and enacted before her maiestie by the Earle of Oxenford his boyes on St. John's daie at night at Greenwich.[145]

Troilus and Cressida.

There is, of course, no Shakespeare play entitled *Agamemnon and Ulysses*; but a careful examination of Shakespeare's play, *Troilus and Cressida*, from this point of view will, we think, yield very interesting results. Without actually counting words, we would be inclined to say, on a general inspection, that the speeches of Agamemnon and Ulysses account for as large, or maybe a larger, part of the drama, than do the words actually spoken by Troilus and Cressida themselves: This, however, is not

---

[145] Stopes, *Burbage*, p. 44.

the most interesting part of the case. Take the first act, for example, and compare carefully the three scenes of which it is composed. The first two scenes will be found to contain a large proportion of short sentences representing free and rapid dialogue, and also a fair admixture of prose. In this we have the work of the skilled playwriter. Scene three is totally different. Here each speaker steps forward in turn and utters a lengthy oration all in blank verse; prose being entirely absent. There is in it profound thought and skillful expression; but it is for the most part poetry pure and simple rather than drama: intellect and poetic skill, but not the proper technique of dialogue.

Evolution of drama.

This marked difference in point of technique between the third scene and the first two scenes is just the difference between the work of a poet making his early essays in drama and the work of the practised dramatist. And this apparently early Shakespeare drama is what might fittingly be called part of a play of *Agamemnon and Ulysses.* Agamemnon, as the king, holds precedence and leads off with his thirty lines of blank verse, and Ulysses has by far the lion share of orating throughout the scene. A careful study of the two kinds of work in *Troilus and Cressida* will perhaps bring home to the reader more clearly than anything else could a sense of what took place in the development of drama in Queen Elizabeth's reign. What we take to be the Earl of Oxford's play of *Agamemnon and Ulysses,* forming the original ground-work for the "Shakespeare" play of *Troilus and Cressida,* represents the Elizabethan drama in an early simple stage of its evolution, with few speakers and long speeches, and the finished play of *Troilus and Cressida* the work of the same pen when practice had matured his command over the resources of true dramatic dialogue and a multitude of dramatis personae. In the Agamemnon and Ulysses scene, Aeneas is introduced to establish a link with the Troilus and Cressida romance; and then for the first time the succession of long speeches is interrupted: and a little rapid dialogue takes place.

An examination of the play as a whole affords a very strong presumption that Shakespeare's play of *Troilus and Cressida* had for its foundation an earlier play of simple structure to which the name of *Agamemnon and Ulysses* might very fittingly be applied.

An aristocratic composition.

We would now ask for a careful reading of the whole of those speeches of Ulysses in Act 1, scene 3, of which we shall give but one short excerpt:

> O! when degree is staked,
> Which is the ladder to all high designs,
> The enterprise is sick. How could communities,
> Degrees in schools, and brotherhoods in cities,
> Peaceful commerce from dividable shores,
> *The primogenitive and due of birth,*
> *Prerogative of age, crowns, sceptres, laurels*
> But by degree, stand in authentic place?
>
>   *   *   *   *
>
>   Great Agamemnon,
> This chaos when degree is suffocate,
> Follows the choking.

The scene as a whole is a discussion of state policy, from the standpoint of one strongly imbued with aristocratic conceptions, and conscious of the decline of the feudal order upon which social life had hitherto rested. Make, then, the Earl of Oxford the writer, and Elizabeth's court the audience for "Shakespeare's" representation of *Agamemnon and Ulysses*, and the whole situation becomes much more intelligible than if we try to make the Stratford man the writer.

Dying lovers.

As illustrating the correspondence of the mind of Oxford, under other aspects, with the mind at work in *Troilus and Cressida*, we shall first of all recall two stanzas in the poem entitled, "What cunning can express?"

> . . . Each throws a dart
>   That *kindleth soft sweet fire:*
> Within my sighing heart
>   *Possessed by Desire.*
> *No sweeter life I try*
> *Than in her love to die.*
>
>   *   *   *
>
> This pleasant lily white,
>   This taint of roseate red;
> This Cynthia's silver light,
>   This sweet fair Dea spread;
> These sunbeams in mine eye,
> These *beauties make me die.*

The very extravagance of the terms arrests attention and almost provokes criticism. We would therefore draw attention to the following expression of sentiment on the part of Troilus whilst awaiting the entry of Cressida:

> I am giddy; *expectation whirls me round.*
> The *imaginary relish is so sweet*
> That *it enchants my sense:* what will it be
> When that the watery palate tastes indeed
> Love's thrice repured nectar? *death, I fear me*
> *Swooning destruction, or some joy too fine,*
> Too subtle-potent, tuned too sharp in sweetness,
> For the capacity of my ruder powers. (III.2)

Other links.

The previous speech of Troilus's in which occurs the line:

> Where I may wallow in the *lily-beds,*

reveals the working of the same imagery as in Oxford's poem; and the song in the immediately preceding scene, containing the couplet:

> These lovers cry,
> Oh! oh! they die,

shows the insistence of the central thought in a lighter vein.

A few lines further on appears that dominant note of high

birth, followed immediately by the expression: "Few words to fair faith," which almost reproduces an expression in a letter of Oxford's written at a later date and only published in modern times: "Words in faithful minds are tedious."[146]

We have by no means exhausted the connection of *Troilus and Cressida* with the plays, poems and life of Edward de Vere, the starting point for which is furnished by the *Agamemnon and Ulysses* play. Enough has been said, however, to establish a harmony and to add to the sum of these accordances which in their mass and convergence constitute the proof of our theory.

IV

Lyly and the Oxford boys.

Mention has been made of his association with and patronage of men of letters. One such instance of literary patronage carries us to the next landmark in tracing out his dramatic activities. The object of De Vere's benevolence in this case was Lyly, who dedicated the second part of his celebrated work to his patron. Shakespeare's intimacy with Euphuism is one of the much debated points in connection with the authorship problem, the difficulties of which disappear almost automatically under our present theory. Mr. W. Creizenach, in *English Drama in the Age of Elizabeth*, speaking of Lyly and his struggles against poverty, says,

> He found more effective patronage at the hands of the Earl of Oxford, who himself practised the dramatic art. By him Lyly was entrusted with the management of the troupe known as the 'Oxford Boys,' which was under his protection. It is probable that the players who had named their company after this nobleman publicly acted the plays written by their patron.[147]

In the same work occurs also the following passage:

> Side by side with the poets who earned their living by composing

---

[146] Letter to Robert Cecil around March, 1601. Cecil Papers 181/80.
[147] W. Creizenach, *English Drama in the Age of Elizabeth*, p. 42.

dramas we may observe a few members of the higher aristocracy engaged in the task of writing plays for the popular stage, just as they tried their hands at other forms of poetry for the pure love of writing. But the number of these high-born authors is very small and their appearance is evanescent. Edward Earl of Oxford, known chiefly as a lyric poet, is mentioned in Puttenham's *Art of English Poesie* as having earned, along with Edwards the choir-master, the highest commendation for comedy and interlude. Meres also praises him as being one of the best poets for comedy.[148]

The contemporary testimony to his dramatic pre-eminence mentioned in the passage quoted is of first importance, for, although we have fixed upon his lyric work as the key to the solution of the problem, it is his position as a writer of drama with which we are most directly concerned.

The "Oxford Boys."

Slight, then, as are the traces of his literary and dramatic activity during the fourteen years following his visit to Italy, they are of such a character as to prove that the greater part of the energy which he had sought at one time to devote to military or naval enterprises was largely directed to literature and the drama, and that he must have been expending his substance lavishly upon these interests. His position amongst the aristocratic patrons of drama was evidently quite distinctive. We do not find that any of the others were literary men of the same calibre, that they were associated so directly with the plays that were being staged by their companies, or that they shared in an equal degree the Bohemian life of the players as did the Earl of Oxford. Nor are any of the others singled out for the same kind of special notice in modern works on the Elizabethan drama. Although other companies of actors are referred to as "Boys," it is to Oxford's company that the name seems to have been most particularly attached. This frequent reference to his company as "The Oxford Boys" is suggestive, too, of a personal familiarity, and the kindly interest of an employer in the needs and welfare of the men he

---

[148] Creizenach, *English Drama*, p. 65.

employed. From every indication we have of his character he was not the man to keep his gold "continually imprisoned in his bags,"[149] to use his own phrase, whilst there were playwrights or actors about him whom he could benefit. Everything betokens a relationship similar to that which had existed between Hamlet and his players, and which he expresses in his welcome to them on renewing his intercourse with them:

> You are welcome, masters; welcome all. I am glad to
> see thee well. Welcome good friends. O! my old friend.

Hamlet as patron of drama.

Then there is Hamlet's admonition to Polonius:

> Good my lord, will you see the players well bestowed? Do
> You hear, let them be well used . . . Use them after your own
> honour and dignity: the less they deserve the more merit is in
> your bounty.

Seeing, moreover, that Oxford's company has passed into the history of English drama as the "Oxford Boys," what shall we make of Hamlet speaking of his company as "the boys"?

> Do the *boys* carry it away?

More important, however, are the instructions and criticism which Hamlet as a patron of playactors offers to his company. His whole attitude is just such as a patron of Oxford's social position, literary taste, and dramatic enthusiasm would naturally assume towards a company which he was not only patronising but directing. In this matter no quotation of passages would suffice for our purpose. We can only ask the reader, bearing in mind all we have been able to lay before him, of Oxford's poetic work, life and character, to read through the whole of that part of the play which treats of Hamlet's dealing with the players (Acts II and III. s. 2). If he does not feel that we have here an exact representation of what Oxford's handling of his own company would be, our own work in these pages must have been most im-

---

[149] From Oxford's letter to Thomas Bedingfield. See footnote 95, p. 133.

perfectly formed.

Lyly's and "Shakespeare's" dramas.

As the management of the Oxford Boys was entrusted to Lyly, it will be seen that the writer in most continuous association with the Earl of Oxford during those years in which he was producing the plays that are supposed to have perished, was the author of *Euphues*. Now, it was precisely in this period that Lyly was himself giving forth plays; so that some kind of correspondence between his own work and his master's was inevitable. It becomes, then, a question of some importance, whether these plays of Lyly's link themselves on in any distinctive way with the plays of "Shakespeare." We invite, therefore, some special attention first of all to what Sir Sidney Lee has to say on this point:

> It was only to two of his [Shakespeare's] fellow dramatists that his indebtedness as a writer of either comedy or tragedy was material or emphatically defined.[150] (Lyly and Marlowe)

Marlowe was a younger man, and the work from his pen (tragedy) which Sir Sidney Lee associates with Shakespeare's belongs to the later or "Shakespearean" period proper. Lyly is therefore the only dramatist of this earlier or preparatory period (1580-1592) whose work, in the opinion of Sir Sidney Lee, foreshadows the work of "Shakespeare."

Lyly's lyrics.

> Between 1580 and 1592 he [Lyly] produced eight trivial and insubstantial comedies, of which six were written in prose, one was in blank verse, and one in rhyme. Much of the dialogue in Shakespeare's comedies from *Love's Labour's Lost* to *Much Ado about Nothing* consists in thrusting and parrying fantastic conceits, puns and antitheses. This is the style of the intercourse in which most of Lyly's characters exclusively indulge. Three-fourths of Lyly's comedies lightly revolve about topics of classical and fairy mythology—in the very manner which Shakespeare first brought

---

[150] Lee, *Life*, p. 64.

to a triumphant issue in his *Midsummer Night's Dream*. Shakespeare's treatment of eccentric characters like Don Armado in *Love's Labour's Lost*, and his boy Moth reads like a reminiscence of Lyly's portrayal of Sir Topas, a fat, vainglorious knight, and his boy Epiton in the comedy of *Endymion*, while the watchmen in the same play clearly adumbrate Shakespeare's Dogberry and Verges. The device of masculine disguise for love-sick maidens was characteristic of Lyly's method before Shakespeare ventured on it for the first of many times in *Two Gentlemen of Verona*, and the dispersal through Lyly's comedies *of songs possessing every lyrical charm* is not the least interesting of the many striking features which Shakespeare's achievements in comedy seem to borrow from Lyly's comparatively insignificant experiments.[151]

In the article on Lyly which the same writer contributes to the *Dictionary of National Biography*[152] he raises doubts as to Lyly's authorship of certain lyrics which appear in his dramas—on the grounds of their superiority. It cannot be questioned, then, that Lyly and his work constitute a most important link in the chain of evidence connecting the work of "Shakespeare" with the Earl of Oxford; only, under the influence of the Stratfordian theory, cause is mistaken for effect.

V

Literary men in the Savoy.

Having presented the relationship of Lyly's work to that of "Shakespeare" as stated by an eminent Shakespearean, we shall now give it as it appears to the leading English authority on the work of John Lyly, Mr. R. Warwick Bond, M.A. (*The Complete Works of John Lyly, now for the first time collected and edited.* Clarendon Press, 1902). This is of such importance as to deserve a section for itself.

> Gabriel Harvey [states] that when *Euphues* was being written, i.e. in 1578, he knew Lyly in the Savoy. . . . A recommendation from an influential friend would procure easy admission [to apart-

---

[151] Lee, *Life*, p. 65.
[152] Sir Sidney Lee, "Lyly, John," *Dictionary of National Biography*, vol. 34, p. 331.

ments in the Savoy [for some temporary period at least, of a needy man of letters or university student. . . . From details in Mr. W. J. Loftie's *Memorials of the Savoy*, it appears that various chambers and tenements in the Savoy precinct were customarily let to tenants, and in 1573 Edward de Vere, Earl of Oxford, is over £10 in arrear of rent to the Savoy for two such tenements.[153]

For what purpose Oxford held these tenements, whether for his own literary pursuits, or for the accommodation of poor men of letters, is not known. So early, however, as 1573, when he was but twenty-three years of age, and two years before his Italian tour, he was evidently associated with the men of letters in the Savoy, amongst whom were included within the next few years, Gabriel Harvey and John Lyly. Burleigh's house in the Strand, where Oxford had been domiciled, was quite near to the Savoy, and Oxford's early and habitual association with this particular literary group hardly admits of doubt.

Lyly receives dramatic impulse from Oxford.

In 1580 Lyly dedicates his work, *Euphues and his England*, to his "very good lord and master, Edward de Vere Earl of Oxenforde" and (to resume our quotation)

here we have the first authentic indication of Lyly's connection with Burleigh's son-in-law, a connection which may have begun in the Savoy, where, as we saw, Oxford rented two tenements. . . . He was engaged as *private secretary to the Earl and admitted to his confidence.* The two men were much of an age [Oxford was, in point of fact, Lyly's senior by three and a half years—a considerable difference in early manhood] and had common elements of character and directions of taste. *From the Earl probably it was that Lyly first received the dramatic impulse.* None of Oxford's comedies survive, but Puttenham, writing in 1589, classes him with Richard Edwards as deserving the highest price [? praise] for comedy and interlude. . . . [Then follow some particulars respecting the activities of "Oxford's Boys"] . . . *Suggestion*, encouragement and *apparatus* thus lay ready to Lyly's hand.[154]

In another place, in describing Lyly's educational advantages, he

---

[153] R. Warwick Bond (editor), *The Complete Works of John Lyly*, vol. I, p. 67.
[154] Bond, vol. I, p. 24. Text in brackets is Looney's. Italics were added by Looney.

mentions specially that of being "private secretary to the literary Earl of Oxford."[155]

The work of Oxford in drama is therefore recognized as having furnished the generative impulse which produced Lyly's work in this particular domain. As private secretary, in the confidence of Oxford, assisting in the actual staging of Oxford's comedies, which without appearing in print had made such a name that they are spoken of, more than ten years after they had ceased to appear on the stage, as amongst "the best,"* Lyly would naturally be more intimate with these "lost plays" than any other man except the author himself. And as it was the holding of this office which led him to the composition of dramas, we are quite entitled to say that it was the plays of Edward de Vere that furnished Lyly's dramatic education; whilst contact with his master is a recognized force in his personal education.

Connection with "Shakespeare's" dramas.

As to the relationship of Lyly's dramas to the work of "Shakespeare," Mr. Bond quotes on his title[page] the words of Mézières: "Ceux qui ont été les prédécessors des grands esprits ont contribué en quelque façon à leur éducation, leur doivent d'être sauvés de l'oubli. Dante fait vivre Brunetto Latini, Milton du Bartas; *Shakespeare fait vivre Lyly.*"[156] This is the theme which runs through Mr. Bond's great work; the justification almost of his immense labours on behalf of Lyly and Elizabethan literature generally. The nature and value of his researches can only be gathered, however, from a study of the work itself, and therefore we shall merely submit a few indicative sentences:

> In comedy, Lyly is Shakespeare's *only model*: the evidence of the latter's study and imitation of him is abundant, and Lyly's influence is of a far more permanent nature than any exercised on the great poet by any other writers. It extends beyond the boundaries of mechanical style to the more important matters of

---

[155] Bond (ed.), *Complete Works of Lyly*, vol. I, p. 398. Original wording does not include the word "literary."

* Looney's note: Meres, 1598.

[156] Bond, *Lyly*, vol. I, title page.

structure and spirit.[157]

> Shakespeare imitates Lyly's grouping and, like him, repeats a relation or situation in successive plays.[158]

> Lyly taught him [Shakespeare] something in the matter of unity and coherence of plot-construction, in the introduction of songs and fairies.[159]

This, then, is the situation represented by the consensus of opinion of two eminent authorities. The dramas of Edward de Vere form the source from which sprang Lyly's dramatic conceptions and enterprises, and Lyly's dramas appear as the chief model, in comedy the only model, upon which "Shakespeare" worked. We are therefore entitled to claim that the highest orthodox authorities, in the particular department of literature with which we are dealing, support the view that the dramatic activities of Edward de Vere stands in almost immediate productive or causal relationship of a most distinctive character with the dramatic work of "Shakespeare." Even if we are unable to extract any further evidence from Oxford's relationships with Lyly we shall have added another very important link in our chain of evidences.

Lyly's apparent inventiveness.

Take now the following passage from the work we have just been quoting: Lyly was

> the first regular English dramatist, *the true inventor and introducer of dramatic style, conduct and dialogue,* and in these respects the chief master of Shakespeare. There is no play before Lyly. He wrote eight; and immediately thereafter England produced some hundreds—produced that marvel and pride of the greatest literature in the world, the Elizabethan Drama. What the long infancy of her stage had lacked was an example of form, of art; and *Lyly gave it.* . . . Lyly was one whose *immense merits and originality* were obscured by the *surface-qualities,* the artificiality and *tedium of his style* . . . [There is] far more dramatic credit due and far more

---

[157] Bond, *Lyly,* vol. II, p. 243.
[158] Bond, *Lyly,* vol. II, p. 285.
[159] Bond, *Lyly,* vol. II, p. 296.

influence on Shakespeare attributable to him than to Marlowe or any other of those with whom he has been customarily classed.[160]

Lyly's lack of inventiveness.

In the world of drama, then, Lyly appears as a great inventive genius, to whose originating impulse is due "the greatest literature in the world." Contrast now with the above passage the following comment upon Lyly's *Euphues*, which appears in the same work:

> The book is artificial, divorced from homely realities. It is deficient, too, in characterization and in pathos; but undoubtedly its chief defect is its *want of action.* . . . The want of action is probably preferable to *poverty of invention.* . . . *Poverty of invention* is discerned in the parallelism of the two parts.[161]

In the writing of his novel, then, Lyly shows a distinct lack of dramatic power, and a noticeable *"poverty of invention."* When he enters his employer's special domain, the drama, he appears as "*the true inventor* and introducer of dramatic style, conduct and dialogue."

Oxford the real innovator.

Only one conclusion, it would seem, can be drawn from these facts, namely that the real inventor of those things, which "Shakespeare" is supposed to have derived from Lyly, was the Earl of Oxford. Whether we examine the poems of the latter, the vicissitudes of his career, or the varied and disturbing impressions he left in the minds of others, with all the mystifying and conflicting personal traits that they suggest, we find ourselves in the presence of an original and self-dependent intellect; just the kind of mind to possess that dramatic inventiveness which is attributed to the plays but which is missing from the *Euphues* of Lyly. The inventiveness and dramatic form and dialogue in Lyly's plays is therefore evidently due to Oxford's participation either direct or indirect. The features of Lyly's work which relate it so intimately with "Shakespeare's" dramas are such as an apt

---

[160] Bond, *Lyly*, vol. I, p. vi, vii.
[161] Bond, *Lyly*, vol. I, p. 162.

disciple might have learnt from a master of forceful and original genius: in the intellectual substance of Lyly's dramas, as in his other literary work, his biographer and editor freely admits superficiality and tediousness. The conceptions, phrases, and dramatic form of the master's work could be appropriated by the pupil; its genius he could not appropriate or imitate. As then Lyly's work, apart from what he might have borrowed from Oxford, marks him as an early type of that literary mind which rapidly catches and reflects the ideas of others, it is almost certain that his works will contain not only much that was in Oxford's writings, but also a great deal of what Oxford thought and said without committing it to writing.

Euphues, Oxford and "Shakespeare."

As a kind of unconscious Boswell to the Earl of Oxford it is more than probable that even his *Euphues* owes much to his intercourse with his patron; for this work consists mainly of such talk and reflections as a man of Lyly's type would gather together from the conversation of the group of young littérateurs in the Savoy. Scraps of ideas gleaned in this way, and dressed up in his own inflated style, might easily pass for a time as solid intellectual matter; the deficiency of genuine substance only being disclosed through familiarity. It is interesting to notice that Mr. Bond gives us no less than nine pages of parallelisms between this early work of Lyly's and the plays of Shakespeare. The difference between the two is mainly that in *Euphues* the passages appear as more or less disjointed and rambling remarks, whereas in "Shakespeare" they take their places as parts of a coherent whole. In a word, in Lyly's work they indicate a mind that reflects the conceptions and imitates the expressions of others; in "Shakespeare" they are the expression of an originating intellect; and were it not for the difficulty presented by the fact that Lyly's work was published some years before "Shakespeare's," no competent judge would have questioned Lyly's great indebtedness to "Shakespeare" even in the writing of his famous *Euphues*.

It is no part of our argument, but it is of some interest from the point of view of Elizabethan literature, that as we get a glimpse of this group of young literary men drawn into association in the Savoy, and realize something of what their relationships would tend to be at the time when *Euphues* was being written, one gets a suggestion that, in accordance with their literary methods, Edward de Vere and Philip Sidney were the chief originals for Lyly's principal characters of Euphues and Philautus. For to the names of the men already given we are quite entitled to add those of both Edmund Spenser and Philip Sidney; since it was Gabriel Harvey under whose influence Spenser had come to London about that time, and it was he, too, who introduced Spenser to Philip Sidney. Shortly afterwards Spenser brought out his first work *The Shepherd's Calendar*, dedicated to Sidney, and containing allusions, as we believe, to both Oxford and Sidney. Later, as we have already seen, Spenser addressed an important dedicatory sonnet to Oxford in first publishing his *Fairie Queen*. All the works we have just named are representations, in varying degrees of disguise, of contemporary life and personalities; and as the Earl of Oxford and Philip Sidney were the outstanding personalities connecting this group of littérateurs with the court life it was natural that Lyly's two chief characters should assume some of their features, even if he had not intended the representation at first. Although Harvey, Lyly, Oxford and Sidney all seem to have come to cross purposes within the next few years, there is no reason to suppose that their relations were other than friendly at the time when Lyly was penning *Euphues*.

"Shakespeare"' dramas a social product.

However these things may be, it is much more feasible that the great "Shakespeare" poems and dramas should have owed their rise to the interchange of ideas, and the stimulation which mind derives from contact with kindred mind, such as would be enjoyed by the young wits and savants in the Savoy, than to the studies of an isolated youth poring over well-thumbed books in an uncongenial social atmosphere. And if this social intercourse were really the source of the Shakespeare literature as we believe it to have been directly, and Sir Sidney Lee and Mr. Bond imply that it was indirectly, we should naturally expect to find, in some outstanding play, such a representation of the chief figures of the group as Spenser, Lyly and Gabriel Harvey were accustomed to make of contemporaries in their own writings. *Love's Labour's Lost* is the play that we have selected in this connection, and dealt with in the opening pages of this chapter. That Lyly is also represented in the play is most probable; we know too little, however, of his personality for purposes of identification. The fact that the authorship we are now urging brings "Shakespeare's" plays into line with the literature of the times, as a dramatic representation of contemporary events and personalities, and at the same time gives the works a firm root, like all the other great achievements of mankind, in the direct social intercourse of men possessing common tastes and interests, is not the least of the arguments in its favour.

Lyrics in Lyly's plays.

If Lyly's works were produced as we suppose them to have been; produced, that is to say, by a somewhat ordinary mind working upon ideas and with apparatus furnished by an almost transcendent genius, we should naturally expect to find marked discordances and inequalities in his work, resulting from the imperfect blending of the two elements. This is just the feature that Lyly's work does present; and in the matter of the songs interspersed through the plays, there is such a superiority to much of the other work as to have raised doubts respecting their authenticity. The first play written by Lyly was *Campaspe*, published in 1584; and on more than one occasion, in speaking of later writings, Mr. Bond contrasts them with the superior lyrics in his first play. Some work he describes as "*a disgrace to the writer of 'Cupid and my Campaspe'*[162] (one of these lyrics). Speaking again of a poetical lampoon by Lyly, entitled *A Whip for an Ape*, he asserts that the "authorship is not disputable," though the notion that the author of *Cupid and my Campaspe* also wrote *A Whip for an Ape* had induced him to regard the latter work as doubtful.

This is not, however, the most interesting or significant fact which the writer brings to light in respect to the songs in Lyly's plays. In the editions of these works published during the author's lifetime and the lifetime both of Edward de Vere and William Shakspere, *the songs did not appear*; their positions alone being merely indicated in the text.

> The absence of the whole thirty-two [except two merged in the dialogue of *The Woman*] from the quarto editions [i.e. the originals] has cast some doubt upon Lyly's authorship: but some of them seem *too dainty to be written by an unknown hand*, there is a uniformity of alternative manners and measures, etc.[163]

The writer then proceeds to offer possible reasons for the omission of the songs from the editions of the plays as first published. The important fact is that these songs are in several cases the best things the plays now contain. For nearly fifty years some of these works were published and republished without the songs (*Campaspe* performed at court in 1582, and published first in 1584). Then, in 1632, that is to say twenty-six years after Lyly's death, twenty-one out of the missing thirty unaccountably reappeared in an edition of Lyly's plays issued by the same publishers and in the same year as the Second Folio edition of "Shakespeare's" work, and within the lifetime of Oxford's cousin, Horatio de Vere, who, as we shall have occasion to show, had probably been entrusted with the task of preserving and publishing Oxford's writings. The remaining nine are still missing. The simultaneous reappearance of so many of

---

[162] Bond, *Lyly*, vol. III, p. 439.
[163] Bond, *Lyly*, vol. II, p. 265.

these songs, after so long an interval, would almost certainly be the work of someone who had been carefully preserving the entire set. The non-appearance of the remaining nine suggests that these had already appeared elsewhere, probably in the pages of "Shakespeare."

The possible reasons advanced for the omission of all these lyrics from the original issue of the plays are such as might apply to the work of any other playwright; yet we can find no other instances of sets of superior lyrics being omitted from the original publication of the works to which they belong. The simplest hypothesis is that these lyrics were not the composition nor the property of Lyly, but, like the lyric work contributed to Munday's play, had been composed by the master of the playwright, the "best of the courtier poets" of those days: and although Oxford could not prevent Lyly's rushing into print with superficial plays, in which he saw his own developments in drama being prematurely exploited, he certainly would resent his own lyrics appearing in them, and was quite able to prevent it if Lyly had been disposed to insert them.

Lyric incapacity of Lyly.

Mr. Bond's statement respecting the quality of Lyly's own lyric work is therefore of special importance:

> Spite of his authorship of two or three of the most graceful songs our drama can boast—*an authorship which if still unsusceptible of positive proof* is equally so of disproof—some of those in his plays, and others pretty certainly his, which I have found elsewhere, stamp him as *negligent, uncritical, or else inadequately practised in the art*; while he lacked altogether, in my judgment, 'those brave translunary things' so infinitely beyond technique, so far above mere grace or daintiness or fancy, of which the true poet is made.[164]

The mere raising of the question of the authenticity of these first-class lyrics in this way, by one who adds to his fine literary discrimination an undoubted admiration for Lyly, affords strong confirmation of the theory that these superior verses were either

---

[164] Bond, *Lyly*, vol. I, p. vii.

written by Oxford for Lyly's plays, or were modelled by Lyly on songs written by Oxford.

Oxford the author of Lyly's lyrics.

It is necessary to keep in mind that Oxford was primarily a lyric poet; that during the years in which many of Lyly's plays were being written the two men were working together, writing plays for the "Oxford Boys"; and that eight of the plays written by Lyly have been preserved, whilst the whole of Oxford's plays have disappeared. Seeing, then, that Lyly displays a marked weakness in lyrical capacity, whilst Oxford is specially strong, most of the songs would almost certainly be the exclusive contribution of the latter, to plays in which there was more or less collaboration between the two men.

"Shakespeare's" and Lyly's lyrics.

We come now to what is perhaps the most vital part of this particular argument. In estimating "Shakespeare's" indebtedness to Lyly, on what we are reluctantly obliged to call the orthodox view, we should have to include his indebtedness to this lyric work with which Lyly has been only doubtfully credited. For a comparison of the two sets of lyrics discloses a marked similarity of lyric forms, with something of the same rich variety. We have made a careful examination of the lyrics that reappeared in Lyly's plays in 1632, and although, until supported by recognized literary authorities, we may hesitate to affirm definitively that they are from the same pen as the lyrics of "Shakespeare," no one who knows the best of them will hesitate to say that they are such as "Shakespeare" might have written. Yet some were *written*, though not published, prior to 1584, the year in which the play to which they belong was published, and before William Shakspere is said to have left Stratford. Those, on the other hand, who hold that William Shakspere, who came to London and began to issue plays about the year 1592, studied carefully and modelled his work upon the published dramas of John Lyly, will find some difficulty in explaining how he could have modelled his work upon lyrics which were not published until 1632, or sixteen years after his own death.

In this connection we shall give but one illustration of the similarity of "Shakespeare's" lyric work to the lyrics attributed to Lyly.

Shakespeare.

Fairies sing:

> Pinch him, fairies, mutually;
> Pinch him for his villany.
> Pinch him, and burn him, and turn him about,
> Till candles and starlight and moonshine be out.
> (*Merry Wives*, published 1602.)

Lyly.

Fairies sing:

> Pinch him, pinch him, black and blue,
> Saucy mortals must not view
> What the Queen of Stars is doing,
> Nor pry into our fairy wooing.
> Pinch him blue
> And pinch him black,
> Let him not lack
> Sharp nails to pinch him blue and red,
> Till sleep had rocked his addle head.
> (*Endymion.* Play written 1585.
> Song first published 1632.)

No one can doubt that these two songs were either from the same pen, or the writer of one of them was indebted to the other. The connection being established, not only for the one song but for the lyric work as a whole, a difficult problem, though, of course, not altogether insoluble, is presented to those who believe that William Shakspere in writing lyrics for *A Midsummer Night's Dream*, *Love's Labour's Lost*, and *The Merry Wives*, was working from a copy of Lyly's Lyrics.

Anomalies disappear.

If "Shakespeare" wrote both sets, or if the writer of the lyrics attributed to Lyly worked upon "Shakespeare's" model, then "Shakespeare" must have been someone who was right in the heart of the literary life of London some years before William Shakspere's supposed entry upon his career. If, on the other hand, "Shakespeare" was working in 1602 on the model of Lyly's work, *he must have had private access to his contemporary's manuscripts*, and have not only exploited the work to an extraordinary extent, but slavishly adopted the lyric forms and mannerisms of his fellow poet. That the greatest lyric and dramatic genius of the age should have so gone out of his way to follow pedantically a single writer of inferior powers to his own, even supposing the whole of that writer's work had been accessible to him—an almost extravagant supposition—would bespeak a kind of infatuation to which geniuses are not usually prone.

All these contradictory and far-fetched implications disappear when the theory of authorship we are now advocating is substituted. Under our theory "Shakespeare," in the person of Edward de Vere, furnishes the model, and becomes the initiating force and leader in the poetic and dramatic movement, and Lyly the follower and imitator of "Shakespeare." The anomalies and "disgraceful" inequalities of Lyly's work receive for the first time a rational explanation, and the mystery of "Shakespeare's" apparent dependence upon Lyly entirely disappears. Lyly's dramas are seen to be, for the most part, hasty productions intended for immediate performance; receiving afterwards such dressing as a "superficial and tedious" writer was able to give them; but which had been modelled upon work of a higher order, and, in their first shaping for the stage, had had the advantage possibly of being trimmed and enlivened by the same hand that afterwards gave forth the supreme masterpieces.

The dramas of "Shakespeare," on the other hand, are seen to be the finished literary form of those plays by De Vere which Lyly knew in the rough, as performed by the Oxford Boys in the days of dramatic pioneering, but which their author, with the feeling and vision of the true poet, had seen were capable of being transformed into something much greater and more worthy of an enduring existence. At the same time the so-called Lyly's lyrics are seen to have been, in the main, a contribution made by Oxford to the plays composed by Lyly to be performed by the Oxford Boys—lyrics which on the one hand he had left, maybe, in too crude a form for publication, being composed originally just to be sung, and which on the other hand he was not willing should be made a present to Lyly.

Composition and publication of dramas.

There is no record of a single play of Oxford's ever having been published, and the lyrics from his pen published in his lifetime are without doubt the work of a man who was most reluctant to commit anything to print that had not been very carefully revised and if possible perfected. With his artistic striving after perfection it was natural that he should work long and laboriously at any literary task he undertook, and that in the process of transforming his plays they should undergo such changes that the original work of Oxford should not have been detected in the finished plays of "Shakespeare." That writers of plays should adopt the practice we have attributed to Oxford of deferring publication is no mere hypothesis invented to meet a difficulty. Even in the case of Lyly, with his evident eagerness for literary fame and deficient sense of literary perfection, the intervals between the production and publication of plays were considerable. *Campaspe*, composed about 1579-80, was first published in 1584. *Gallathea*, composed in 1584, was first published in 1592; whilst *Love's Metamorphosis*, which in a defective form evidently first made its appearance about 1584 was not put into its present form and published until 1601. Between the actual performance of his plays and their ultimate publication there was usually a period of three or four years. With the richer, more elaborate, more highly finished and much more voluminous work of "Shakespeare," a longer interval was naturally to be expected; and it is just in that interval between Oxford's composition of his dramas and the appearance of the

"Shakespeare" work that the dramas of Oxford's private secretary and coadjutor make their appearance, having so striking a resemblance, in everything but genius, to the "Shakespeare" work, that the latter is supposed to have been definitely modelled upon it to a most unusual extent.

Somewhere, then, about the year 1592 these plays of Oxford's we believe began to appear attributed to William Shakspere, and this is the time when Lyly's plays cease to appear (*The Woman in the Moon*, composed 1591-3). In 1598 "Shakespeare's" plays are first *published* with an author's name. Lyly's *Woman in the Moon* had been published the previous year, and after it he only published a revised edition of the old play, *Love's Metamorphosis*. Both in the matter of presenting and publishing plays, the appearance of "Shakespeare's" work put a check upon Lyly's. About the same time there appeared Meres' account of Elizabethan poetry and drama, containing names alike of authors and titles of plays; and, though he gives the titles of "Shakespeare's" works, and accords a foremost place to the name of Edward de Vere as a playwright, he does not give the title of a single play that Oxford had written.

Dramatic connections reviewed.

These are matters which belong more properly to a later period than the one we are now discussing. In respect to Oxford's early dramatic activities, and the connection of his missing comedies with the work of "Shakespeare"—for it is this early period with which we are now concerned—we have undoubtedly a most extraordinary set of coincidences. Two men, and two men only, Anthony Munday and John Lyly, are directly and actively associated with him in his dramatic enterprises. Both men have work attributed to them which is evidently not theirs, and it is this work which specially links them on—in Lyly's case in a remarkable way—to the work of "Shakespeare," thus forming a direct bridge between the "lost or worn out" dramas of Edward de Vere and "the greatest literature of the world." Surely this, along with all the other coincidences, is not merely fortuitous. We may have laboured unduly these connections: their immense importance, we hope, is a sufficient justification.

VI

Apparent inactivity.

After the year 1587 we lose distinct traces of Oxford's dramatic activity, and, in reference to this, we must now draw attention to an important set of considerations in which the poet Edmund Spenser is implicated.

Spenser and De Vere.

In the year 1590, by which time the middle period of De Vere's life may be said to have closed, when though only forty years of age he seemed to have quite dropped from public view, and when William Shakspere, then aged twenty-six, was either establishing himself, or being established by unknown patrons, in the dramatic world, Edmund Spenser published his *Tears of the Muses*. These "are full of lamentations over returning barbarism and ignorance, and the slight account made by those in power of the gifts and the arts of the writer, the poet and the dramatist."[165] In this poem occur some stanzas which Dryden in his day, and Charles and Mary Cowden Clarke in more recent times, have appropriated to William Shakspere, but which, notwithstanding this, have been more or less a puzzle to literary men ever since they were written. Most writers on either Spenser or Shakespeare seem to feel it a duty to say something about them. The matter is therefore of extreme importance as a question of Elizabethan literature quite apart from the Shakespeare problem, and will necessitate a somewhat exhaustive statement. The following are the most important stanzas in the set:

> All these, and all that else the Comic Stage,
> With seasoned wit and goodly pleasance graced,
> By which man's life in his likest image

---

[165] Church, *Spenser*, p. 107.

Was limned forth. are wholly now defaced;
And those sweet wits which wont the like to frame
Are now despised and made a laughing game.

And be the man whom Nature's self had made
To mock herself and truth to imitate,
With kindly counter under Mimic shade,
Our pleasant Willie, ah! is dead of late.
With whom all joy and jolly merriment
Is also deaded and in doleur drent.

But that same gentle spirit from whose pen
Large streams of honey and sweet nectar flow,
Scorning the boldness of such base-born men,
Which dare their follies forth so rashly throw,
Doth rather choose to sit in idle cell,
Than so himself to mockery to sell.

Spenser's "Willie."

First of all the expression "dead of late," it has been remarked by others, means, "not that he is literally dead but that he is in retirement." This reading is not only necessary to make it fit in with what follows—"to sit in idle cell"—but is also supported by other passages in the same writer. The reference is evidently to someone who, having been prominent in the writing of poetry, and in connection with dramatic comedy, had lately not been much in evidence.

Whilst therefore the laudatory expressions are such as could only be applied appropriately to "Shakespeare," the date of publication makes it impossible that they should have any reference to the man William Shakspere. At the same time, the name "Willie" only serves to deepen the mystery. In the year 1590 the Stratford man was only twenty-six years of age and was just making his appearance in the dramatic world. He had therefore no great career behind him from which to retire, whereas the "Willie" referred to in Spenser's poem had evidently already held a prominent position in the world of poetry and drama. Dean Church in his *Life of Spenser* proposes a solution the weakness of which he himself fully recognizes. He mentions that

Sir Philip Sidney had somewhere been spoken of as "Willie" and thinks that the verses may allude to him. To this theory he recognizes two very vital objections. In the first place, Sir Philip Sidney had never attempted anything in the dramatic line except some "masking performances," and to these the laudatory expressions would be, he says, "an extravagant compliment." They would, however, be much more than this: a grotesque distortion of the English language would be a more accurate description.

The second great difficulty of the theory is this: Instead of Sir Philip Sidney being in retirement in 1590 he had already been actually dead for nearly four years. This further difficulty, he thinks, might be got over by supposing that the work had been written some years earlier and had been kept back until 1590. To ante-date the work to such an extent as to make the stanzas applicable to the events of Sidney's life would throw out of gear the whole sequence of the production of Spenser's works and the personal allusions they contain, as well as the relation of his works to the events of his own life. Some other solution of the problem must therefore be sought.

The Shepherd's Calender.

The key to this mystery, we believe, is to be found in a work of Spenser's published in the early years of the particular period of De Vere's life with which we are at present occupied. In December, 1579, Spenser issued his first considerable work, *The Shepherd's Calender.* Now, to those who are not specially students of Elizabethan literature, that is to say to the great mass of English readers, to say nothing of the rest of the world, *The Shepherd's Calender* needs some little explanation. This set of poems is simply a series of burlesques upon prominent men of the day, who appear in the guise of "shepherds," and who express themselves under disguises more or less penetrable. In some cases the names given to them suggest their real names, in other cases there is no suggestiveness about them; in some cases it is quite understood whom they represent, in others they remain as yet undistinguished. Spenser himself appears as *Colin Clout*, Gabriel Harvey as "Hobbinol," Archbishop Grindal as "Algrind." The formation of the last two names from those of their prototypes will be readily perceived.

Looking over the names of the various "shepherds," we find that there is indeed one called "Willie." So that when in 1590 Spenser speaks of the Willie "from whose pen large streams of honey and sweet nectar flow," it is natural to suppose that, in accordance with his practice in other cases, he was carrying forward the same person as the one who had figured in the 1579 poem under that name, but who, in the meantime, had given such a manifestation of his powers that by the year 1590 he was able to speak of him in terms which, as Dean Church remarks, "we now-a-days consider, and as Dryden in his day considered, were only applicable to Shakespeare."[166]

It has therefore been a matter of considerable surprise that notwithstanding the great amount of attention that has been paid by writers on Elizabethan literature to the question of who it was that Spenser meant by "Willie" in the above verses, it never seems to have occurred to anyone to connect him with the "Willie" who appears in Spenser's earlier poems. Yet the very manner in which he casually introduces the name is suggestive of an allusion to his first great work. The question, then, which concerns us immediately is this: what are the probabilities that the "Willie" in *The Shepherd's Calender* was the Earl of Oxford? And if a strong case can be made out for such an identification we shall be entitled also to claim for him the allusion in the *Tears of the Muses*, especially if the later representation of "Willie" fits in with the special circumstances of Oxford at the later date. We shall also have made an important contribution to the evidence that Oxford was "Shakespeare." William Shakspere of Stratford, we point out in passing, was a mere boy of fourteen at the time when Spenser's

---

[166] Church, *Spenser*, p. 107. Only a paraphrase. The original reads, "The effect is described in lines which, as we now naturally suppose, and Dryden also thought, can refer to no one but Shakespeare."

"Willie" makes his appearance in Elizabethan poetry.

A rhyming match.

On turning to the poems in *The Shepherd's Calender* we find that "Willie" figures prominently in two of them. Under the month of March his role is somewhat subordinate; but under the month of August he appears in what is probably the most widely known and the best executed of the series; having found its way into modern anthologies: its superior quality suggesting its being one of the latest composed of the set. This piece is neither more nor less than a verse-making contest between two rival poets named "Willie" and "Perigot." In view, therefore, of the general character of the work, its deliberate representation of eminent contemporaries, taken along with the literary situation at that time, the poetic rivalry between Philip Sidney and the Earl of Oxford, there is, to begin with, something more than a mere presumption that the two rival poets, "Willie" and "Perigot," were Oxford and Sidney. We therefore ask the reader to recall Oxford's verse beginning "Were I a king" and Sidney's rejoinder "Wert thou a king," already quoted in this chapter: verses which, from subsequent developments, must have been written shortly before Spenser's poem was published. Then let him turn to this poem of Spenser's and read it with the other verse-making episode in mind. It plunges immediately by its opening lines into the cause of their antagonism. "Tell me, Perigot . . . wherefore with mine thou dare thy music match?" And this he follows up with a further challenge whether "in ryhmes with me thou dare strive." Then, as if to put the matter of identification beyond doubt, a third party called "Cuddy" is introduced as arbitrator, and he assumes office with the irrelevant remark: "What a judge *were Cuddy for a king.*"

Cuddy's "verses."

If any doubt remained as to whether or not the two shepherds represented Oxford and Philip Sidney it ought to be quite removed by the closing part of the poem. After the competition, Cuddy must needs finish up with some "verses" which he claims to have got from *Colin Clout* (Spenser). These are not even doggerel. In the place of rhymes he simply repeats the same words over and over again, and these, together with other words and phrases that make up the "verses," form but a verbal jumble composed of characteristic words from the poems of the two rival writers. To appreciate all the fun of Cuddy's lines one's mind must have been in some measure steeped in the two sets of poems.

If, however, before reading Cuddy's "verses" the reader will turn to the last stanza quoted in the preceding chapter, and also note the few phrases we subjoin here from Oxford's and Sidney's early poems, he may be able to enter into the humour of Cuddy's "doleful verse."

Oxford:
> The more my plaints I do resound
> The less she pities me.
> The trickling tears that fall adown my cheeks.
> > Help ye that are aye wont to wail,
> > > Ye howling hounds of bell.
> > Help man, help beast, help birds and worms
> > > That on the earth do toil.

Sidney:
> Thus parting thus my chiefest part I part.
> Alas, sweet brooks do in my tears augment.
> A simple soul should breed so mixed woe.
> Love . . . bred my smart.

"Void," "House," "Bred," "Nature," are all words which seem to stand forth in Sidney's somewhat limited vocabulary. Even in the competition itself there is a frequent suggestion of the distinctive expressions of the two men. One example of each will suffice.

From a poem by Sidney:

> Such are these two, you scarce can tell

Which is the dainter *bonny belle.*

Spenser's poem:

I saw the bouncing bellibone
Hey, ho, the *bonnibell.*

From a poem by Oxford:

Patience perforce is such a *pinching pain.*

Spenser's poem:

But whether in painful love I pine
Hey, ho, the *pinching pain.*

An old problem solved.

A careful weighing of this poem can leave but little doubt as to the identity of "Willie" and "Perigot" with Oxford and Philip Sidney: the only question is whether "Willie" is Oxford or Sidney. If we associate the contest in Spenser's poem with Sidney's "matching" of Oxford's verse, as we may very reasonably do, then "Willie" is Oxford; for it is Willie who finds fault with Perigot for matching his music and challenges him on that account to another matching of rhymes.

This, then, is the position: The circumstances of Oxford fit in with and afford a very strong presumption of his being the historic prototype of Spenser's "Willie" in the early poem, *The Shepherd's Calender.* Between the writing of this poem and the writing of the *Tears of the Muses* Oxford had been engaged in just those dramatic activities and had made his name in the precise department, Comedy, in which Spenser's "Willie" had evidently won renown. And at the time when "The Tears of the Muses" was written, Oxford had withdrawn apparently from dramatic activity and was seemingly "sitting in idle cell" precisely as Spenser describes "Willie" to be doing. Are we to believe that all this is a series of meaningless coincidences?

Minor points in corroboration of the theory that Oxford and Spenser's "Willie" are one and the same person may be noticed. The shepherd, "Willie," in the other poem in which he appears, remarks:

> Alas! at home I have a sire,
> A *stepdame eke as hot as fire*
> That duly-a-days counts mine (sheep).

(Day by day keeps a close watch over me and my affairs.) The reference to Oxford's domestic position, to the surveillance exercised by Burleigh, and to the irascible Lady Burleigh is obvious. Then in Spenser's sonnet to the Earl of Oxford, which occupies a prominent position amongst those with which he prefaces the *Fairie Queen*, he puts special emphasis upon Oxford's ancient and noble lineage. We find the same note reflected in the verses in *The Tears of the Muses* referring to Willie, whom he represents as "scorning the boldness of *base-born* men." From this it is evident that "Willie" was not "base-born," but rather a man distinguished for his high birth.

Spenser's testimony.

We have every reason to believe, then, that we have not only solved the long-standing mystery of the "Willie" in *The Tears of the Muses*, but have incidentally secured the testimony of no less an authority than the poet Spenser, that the powers of Edward de Vere were recognized to be such as to justify his being described in terms which are said to be only applicable to Shakespeare. The fact that a solution proposed for one problem furnishes incidentally a reasonable solution to another is additional evidence in its favour. The testimony is also valuable as showing that, notwithstanding the non-appearance of work avowedly from his pen, he had given evidence, not of a falling off, but of such a development of his powers as to create a marked impression in the mind of his great contemporary. It is evidence, too, that he had produced much more poetry than we have under his own name, for the few short lyrics can hardly be described as *"large streams."* The solution of this mystery enables us, moreover, to add another link to our chain of interesting evidence; for we find that some important verses which are supposed by several writers to have reference to Shakespeare are found on examination actually to refer to Edward de Vere, Earl of Oxford; whilst the personal description they give is strikingly suggestive of Berowne in *Love's Labour's Lost*. Finally, the two sets of references, the one appearing in 1579 and the other in 1590, link together the opening and the closing phases of this middle period of his life. The former presenting him as a poet, and the latter as a dramatist, together help to make good the claim we have made for him: that he is the personal embodiment of the great literary transition by which the lyric poetry of the earlier days of Queen Elizabeth's reign merged into the drama of her later years. Thus we get a sense both of the literary unity of the times, and of the great and consistent unity of his own career.

Shakespeare and "Will."

Assuming that we have here the correct interpretation of these allusions, there is every reason to believe that we have their counterpart in the writings of "Shakespeare." The two enigmatical sonnets in which he plays upon the word "will" finish with the striking and emphatic sentence:

> For my name is Will.

Had these words been written by a man whose real name was William, like the Stratford man, they would have been as puerile as anything in English literature. Had they contained a direct reference to his nom-de-plume they would have been only slightly better in this respect. We have good reasons, moreover, for supposing that the particular sonnets were written before the "Shakespeare" mask was assumed (1593). Whether this is so or not, the particular words quoted point, no doubt, to some hidden significance. If, then, we are permitted to suppose that Shakespeare was alluding to the "Willie" in the poems of the great contemporary, we shall have in these words nothing less than a direct confession from the great dramatist that he was none other than the Earl of Oxford.

"Willie" and Sidney.

Before leaving this point we must not overlook the statement made by Dean Church that Sidney had elsewhere been referred to as Willie. No reference is given, but we take it to be an allusion to a poem which appeared in Davison's *Poetical Rhapsody* (1602), another of the numerous miscellaneous collections of poetry in which much of the Elizabethan work has been preserved. There Sidney's death is mourned as the death of Willie. It is only in the first edition, however, that this appears; in later editions this is altered, as though the writer or editors had had their attention drawn to a mistake—a possible misreading of Spenser's earliest work—whilst the following footnote by the modern editor appears: "I cannot recall any other poem in which the name Willie is given to Sidney."[167] Although first appearing in 1602 it is mentioned that the poem had been written a long while ago. Being an obituary work it is natural to suppose that it was written shortly after the death of Sidney (1586). Seeing, then, that the writer of the poem would at that time have only the *Shepherd's Calender* to go upon, the mistake was partly excusable. The publication of *The Tears of the Muses* in 1590 would furnish the grounds for the subsequent correction of the mistake which had evidently been overlooked in the first printing.

"In idle cell."

At the time when *The Tears of the Muses* was published the Earl of Oxford did certainly appear to be sitting "in idle cell." It is not impossible that the poem of Spenser's may have revived his literary activity, or it may have been that he was even at the time deeply immersed in the literary work which was soon to burst upon the country. After such a preparation as he had undergone, we believe that such freedom from practical work, as is implied in the words "to sit in idle cell," is just what was needed for the

---

[167] A. H. Bullen (editor), *Davison's Poetical Rhapsody*, vol. I, p. 67. The correct wording is: "I cannot recall any other poem in which the name 'Willy' is given to Sidney."

production of the Shakespearean dramas; and places that production for the first time on a really rational basis. It remains, therefore, to consider the third or final stage of his career, that which synchronizes generally with the period of the appearance of these works.

In bringing this chapter to a close we would urge the extreme importance of the matter it contains. The chapter in which we deal with the lyric poetry of Edward de Vere, and this chapter in which his dramatic relationships are examined, must, by the nature of the case, form the principal foundations of our constructive argument.

CHAPTER XII

MANHOOD OF DE VERE
(AN INTERLUDE)

BEFORE entering upon a consideration of the third and final period of De Vere's life it is necessary to touch upon a few circumstances belonging to the closing years of the second period, which form a kind of link with the third or last period.

Queen Mary's execution and Sir Philip Sidney's funeral.

In 1587 we get the last indications of Oxford's dramatic activities. Towards the end of the previous year Sir Philip Sidney, after enjoying his knighthood for only three years, died four weeks after the battle at Zutphen in which he had been injured. At the time when Sidney was lying dying the trial of Mary Queen of Scots was proceeding in England, and on the commission appointed to try her was Edward de Vere, Earl of Oxford. Certain dates relative to the two events just mentioned must first be fixed. Mary appeared before the commission on the 14th of October, 1586, and received her sentence on October the 25th. Sidney died on the 17th of the same month; that is to say a week before Mary received her sentence. Mary was executed on the 8th of February, 1587, that is to say three and a half months after receiving her sentence, and Sidney was buried on February 16th, a week after Mary's execution. Roughly, Mary's sentence was pronounced at the time of Sidney's death and her execution took place at the time of Sidney's funeral, from three and a half to four months elapsing between the two pairs of events.

It was, of course, an extraordinary length of time to keep Sidney's body awaiting interment. It is still more extraordinary that this period should exactly synchronize with that during which Elizabeth was hesitating about, and Burleigh and Walsingham were urging, the carrying out of the sentence against Mary. To this must be added the fact that the most determined and unscrupulous agent in bringing about Mary's execution was Sidney's father-in-law, Walsingham, and it was he, too, who was most actively concerned in arranging for the elaborately organized public funeral that was accorded to Sidney; the latter affair entailing a call upon his private purse to the extent of no less than six thousand pounds, an enormous sum in those days, equivalent to about £50,000 of our money.[168] All this hardly looks like accidental coincidence.

We draw attention to these facts because an appreciation of their bearing will help towards an understanding of the times in which Oxford lived, and the personalities with whom he had relationships.

The politicians.

Mary's trial and execution is a reminder of the fears entertained by politicians like Walsingham and Burleigh that a Roman Catholic revival might occur at any time in England, and that the accession of a Roman Catholic sovereign would mean for them ruin and possibly loss of life. Mary's execution was therefore determined on by them upon political grounds. The country generally could not be considered whole-heartedly in favour of this step. The only people who really wished for Mary's execution were the politicians and the extreme Protestants; and therefore much remained to be done after securing the sentence before it could safely be carried out. Burleigh's association with the puritans, his "brethren in Christ," it is quite understood rested on grounds of policy. They represented a serviceable force, and he was not the man to neglect anything that would further his

---

[168] In 2018, the equivalent of £2,200,000, or US$2,906,000. See footnote 14, p. 22.

purposes. As the execution of Mary had become a set purpose with him and Walsingham, the puritans and any party or circumstance, which could be used for the fostering of that public opinion upon which the most despotic of governments ultimately depends, must needs be turned to account.

Sidney's fame.

Now, apart from political considerations, Sidney's sudden transformation into a national hero is one of the most curious of historical phenomena. We are not urging that he was not a worthy young man. We are quite willing to rest his case on the best that his friends have made out for him. Let us grant that he was the perfection of courtesy in his deportment, and that his conversation was attractive. Let us assume that the one chivalrous act recorded of him, the forgoing of a drink of water in the interests of a dying soldier, is true and was unparalleled in its unselfishness. Still, it is not for these things that people are accorded elaborate public funerals and their deaths lamented as national calamities. When it is asked what he actually accomplished in life, we begin to wonder at the great demonstration that was organized for the reception of his body in England, and later on for his interment. Neither in arms nor in statesmanship had he attained such a pre-eminence as is usual in the recipients of such state distinctions, whilst his achievements in literature, had they been as noteworthy as those of Spenser, would not have secured for him one half the national honour that attended his obsequies. We are naturally disposed, therefore, to look for some political motive behind the public demonstration and all the panegyrics that followed on it.

Now Elizabeth's fear that the execution of Mary might result in a revulsion of public feeling against herself was so real as to cause her not only to delay the carrying out of the sentence but also to provide for shuffling the odium on to subordinate agents when the execution should have taken place. Burleigh and Walsingham were therefore not likely to be less sensible of their danger, and they, too, took steps to secure themselves against being saddled with the chief responsibility. Meanwhile a public opinion favourable to their purpose must be fostered by every available artifice. In those days "public opinion" meant to a great extent "London opinion" and in times of crisis this could be systematically stimulated and directed by spectacular displays.

Working public opinion.

As Sidney had been a staunch supporter of the anti-papal policy of Burleigh and Walsingham, a policy including antagonism to the Guises; having somewhat aggressively made himself the spokesman of those who thought they were opposing the Queen at the time when she was diplomatically toying with the idea of marriage with the Duke of Anjou; and as his life had been lost in an adventure in support of the same anti-papal policy, his death, with its power of sentimental appeal, was a valuable asset to his party which Burleigh and Walsingham could not afford to neglect. The projected execution of Mary being part of the same policy which had led to the affair at Zutphen, Sidney's death was capable of being turned to account. His party now had the inestimable good fortune of possessing a martyr, and this must needs be worked for all it was worth.

The elaborately organized obsequies, so out of proportion to any recorded achievement of Sidney's, bears much more the appearance of political strategy than of merited honour: the politicians of any one period being strikingly similar to those of any other. It is the very excess of the demonstration joined to the fact that it did not come spontaneously from any public body but was worked up by interested individuals that places the whole business under suspicion. We cannot recall any other instance in which London went into mourning with the same éclat as it did for Sidney. The matter was well staged and the Sidney-mourning-fashion caught on. No blame can attach to the man himself for all this, but when we are asked to perpetuate the adulation we shall persist in asking, what did he do to merit it all? The fame that he has enjoyed throughout history probably owes much to the factitious send-off that it got at this time, and to the fact that the movement and the party to which he belonged were then, and afterwards continued, in the ascendant.

Oxford and his times.

Oxford, on the other hand, with his strong medieval affinities, was completely out of touch with the ascendant party, and his fame has suffered under a corresponding disadvantage. Indeed we may say that what he stood for remained under a cloud until the middle of the nineteenth century, when, through the combined influence of "Shakespeare," Scott, and Newman, a sense of what was admirable and enduring in medievalism began to revive.

Protestant sectarianism was as contrary to his outlook upon life as it is to the wide genius of Shakespeare. On the other hand we cannot say confidently of Edward de Vere, any more than we can of Shakespeare, that he was an orthodox Roman Catholic. With the exception of the remark which we have quoted from Green we cannot discover any further evidence of his connection with the ancient Church. It is much more likely that his was the Catholicism of a universal Humanity, "with large discourse looking before and after,"[169] taking into itself the culture of Greece and Rome on the one hand, and on the other the visions that belong to a "prophetic soul of the wide world dreaming on things to come."[170] We find no trace of medieval theologism in his poetry, nor any religious pietism such as that we have mentioned as appearing in the poems of Raleigh. Oxford's attachment was probably to the human and social sides of Catholicism and Feudalism, which he saw crumbling away and being supplanted by an unbridled individualism and egoism.

Oxford under a shadow.

We have dwelt at some length upon Sidney's death and Mary's execution not only because Oxford's name and reputation are mixed up with Sidney's affairs, and one of the few recorded acts of his life is connected with Mary, but also because the

---

[169] From *Hamlet* IV.4.
[170] Sonnet 107.

relationship we have traced between the celebrity of one and the execution of the other helps us to focus Oxford's religious and political environment, and to realize something of his relationship to contemporary parties. These things go a long way towards accounting for the obscurity into which the names of Oxford and his immediate associates have fallen as compared with his antagonists. It also accounts for the peculiar fact, which has probably struck most of our readers, that we seldom meet with his name except in connection with opponents, thus giving the general impression of a man at loggerheads with everyone— excepting in certain literary and dramatic contacts. This compels us to examine closely the reputations of rivals and to modify any artificial advantages that they owe in this matter merely to the turns of fortune. Between Oxford and Sidney we see that there lay matters much deeper than the artistic vanity of rival poets. The two men represented opposing social tendencies, and to these are largely due the glamour that has gathered round one name and the shadow that has remained over the other. At the time of the French marriage proposal, which Burleigh, Sidney and their party opposed, Oxford had been one of those who favoured the project. One modern writer sees in this nothing more than an attempt on his part to win royal favour—from all accounts the last thing he was likely to go out of his way to do. Only as we realize his spontaneous hostility to the social and political tendencies represented by Burleigh, Walsingham, Sidney, Raleigh and Fulke Greville shall we be able to judge him accurately or adjust ourselves properly to the Shakespeare problem.

"Shakespeare" and France.

The question which concerns us is whether Shakespeare can he claimed as representing Oxford's attitude to contemporary religious and political movements or the attitude taken by the group of men we have just named. On the religious side we have already seen that their ultra-Protestant tendencies meet with no support in Shakespeare, and in this Shakespeare and Oxford are at one. In continental policy the aim of Burleigh (and Sidney) was to keep open the breach between England and France. Oxford, as we have seen, favoured a policy of amity and alliance between the two countries. That this was "Shakespeare's" view is made quite clear in the closing scene of *Henry V*, where he expresses the wish that the contending kingdoms

> Of France and England, whose very shores look pale
> With envy of each other's happiness,
> May cease their hatred, and this dear conjunction
> Plant neighbourhood and Christian-like accord
> In their sweet bosoms, that never war advance
> His bleeding sword 'twixt England and fair France.
>
> That never may ill office, or fell jealousy
> Thrust in between the faction of these kingdoms.
> That English may as French, French Englishmen
> Receive each other.

In international policy, then, Shakespeare and Oxford are again at one.

Shakespeare and politicians.

How differently might the whole course of European history have unfolded itself if the policy of Shakespeare had prevailed instead of that of the politicians of his time. Oxford's general relationship to those politicians, moreover, is most clearly reflected in the works of Shakespeare where the very word "politician" is a term of derision and contempt.

> That skull had a tongue in it and could sing once; how the knave jowls it to the ground as if it were Cain's jaw-bone that did the first murder! It might be the pate of a politician, one that would circumvent God, might it not?'
>
> (*Hamlet*, V.1)

> Get thee glass eyes;
> And, like a scurvy politician, seem
> To see the things thou sost not.
>
> (*Lear*, IV.6)

We can imagine all his contempt for Burleigh running through the above lines, and the minister's pretended attachment to the growing force of puritanism, his "brethren in Christ," finds a counterblast in the words,

> Policy I hate: I had as lief be a Brownist as a politician
> (*Twelfth Night*)

an expression of contempt for both politicians and puritans. In a word, then, Shakespeare represents the Oxford point of view and not that of Oxford's antagonists.

Queen Mary and Portia.

There can be little doubt as to which side Oxford's sympathies would lean during the trial of Mary; and so, when Burleigh, wishing to furnish himself with substantial authority for going forward with the execution, called together the ten men upon the authority of whose signatures he proceeded, Oxford was not one of the number.

Again, we have nothing to do with the merits of the case in the matter of Mary's trial and execution; but, as we read of her wonderfully brave and dignified bearing, and of her capable and unaided conduct of her own defence, we can quite believe that if the dramatist who wrote the *Merchant of Venice* was present at the trial of the Scottish Queen, with

> ringlets, almost grey, once threads of living gold,
> (H. G. Bell—*Mary Queen of Scots*)[171]

he had before him a worthy model for the fair Portia, whose

> sunny locks
> Hung on her temples like a golden fleece.
> (*Merchant of Venice*, I.1)

Mary's speeches.

Of this trial Martin Hume says,

Mary defended herself with consummate ability before a tribunal almost entirely prejudiced against her. She was deprived of legal aid, without her papers and in poor health. In her argument with Burleigh she reached a point of touching eloquence which might

---

[171] This phrase is not from Henry G. Bell's book. It's from *Sharpe's London Magazine*, May 22, 1847, p. 64.

have moved the hearts, though it did not convince the intellects, of her august judges.[172]

And, in a footnote, he quotes from Burleigh's letter to Davison, "Her intention was to *move pity by long, artificial speeches.*"[173] With this remark of Burleigh's in mind, let the reader weigh carefully the terms of Portia's speech on "Mercy," all turning upon conceptions of royal power, with its symbols the crown and the sceptre.

> It becomes the thronèd monarch better than his crown.
> His sceptre shows the force of temporal power,
> The attribute to awe and majesty,
> Wherein doth sit the dread and fear of kings.
> But mercy is above this sceptred away;
> It is enthroned in the hearts of kings;
> It is an attribute to God Himself;
> And earthly power doth then show likest God's
> When mercy seasons justice.

Now let anyone judge whether this speech is not vastly more appropriate to Mary Queen of Scots pleading her own cause before Burleigh, Walsingham, and indirectly the English Queen, than to an Italian lady pleading to an old Jew for the life of a merchant she had never seen before. Who, then, could have been better qualified for giving an idealized and poetical rendering of Mary's speeches than "the best of the courtier poets," who was a sympathetic listener to her pathetic and dignified appeals?

Shakespeare and the Spanish Armada. Preparations.

In February, 1587, Mary Queen of Scots was beheaded, and this is the year in which we lose traces of Edward de Vere's connection with drama. It was a time of great stress and excitement in the country. The fear of a Spanish invasion lay heavily on the nation and preparations were in full swing to meet the expected Armada. Passing, as we of these days have done, through times of still greater stress, we can now quite see the allusion to England prior to the coming of the Armada in the following passage from *Hamlet.*

---

[172] Hume, *Burghley*, p. 409.
[173] Hume, *Burghley*, p. 409.

> Tell me, he that knows,
> Why this same strict and most observant watch
> So nightly toils the subject of the land;
> And why such daily cast of brazen cannon,
> And foreign mart for implements of war;
> Why such impress of shipwrights, whose sole task
> Does not divide the Sunday from the week;
> What might be toward. that this sweaty haste
> Doth make the night joint labourer with the day?

Oxford, like many others who were out of sympathy with the policy of the government, nevertheless put aside all differences to join in the common cause of resisting the invader. As a volunteer he was permitted to join the navy, and took part in the great sea fight that scattered the Armada and delivered England from the fear of subjugation.

The picture of Spain's immense war vessels sailing grandly up the Channel, flying past the English ships, many of them but small traders that rose and fell with each slight movement of the sea, is familiar now to every English boy and girl. It is worth remarking then that the same play of Shakespeare's which suggests the figure of Mary Queen of Scots contains also a picture suggestive of the contrast between the two fleets.

> There where your argosies with portly sail,
> Like signiors and rich burghers of the flood,
> Or, as it were, the pageants of the sea,
> Do overpeer the petty traffickers,
> That curtsey to them, do them reverence,
> As they fly by them with their woven wings.

The Spanish disaster.

Then as we remember the disaster that befell some of these huge vessels through the Spaniards' ignorance of the shoals and sandbanks round the English coast, we can see the picture of one of them, lying on her side with the top of her mast below the level of her hull, in the lines:

> I should not see the sandy hour-glass run,
> But I should think of shallows and of flats,
> And see my wealthy Andrew, dock'd in sand,
> Vailing her high-top lower than her ribs

> To kiss her burial.

Quite what position the Earl of Oxford might have occupied on board ship it is not easy to imagine; but we can well believe that as an intelligent though inexperienced seaman he would find considerable interest and occupation in

> Peering in maps for ports and piers and roads.

The Earl was not a seafaring man, nor is there anything in the record of his life that suggests a special enthusiasm for the sea. The same is true of "Shakespeare" as revealed in his works as a whole, whilst the passages we have quoted indicate some slight but special experiences of a keen observer, who humanized everything on which his eye alighted; not only the active vessels but even the battered wrecks seeming to him to possess a human personality.

Death of Lady Oxford.

Associated with Oxford's experience of sea life was the death of his wife. During the month preceding the appearance of the Armada Lady Oxford died, June 6th, 1588. What this may have meant to De Vere himself is a mystery which will probably never be quite solved, and which mankind would be content to pass over in silence if the Earl of Oxford were to remain for all time no more than what has been supposed hitherto. If, however, he comes to be universally acknowledged as Shakespeare, interest in the matter is certain to be revived, and we may find that in his role of dramatist he either answers our questions on the subject, or suggests some reasonable conjectures.

Hamlet's sea experiences we observe stand in direct association with the death of Ophelia. It is whilst he is away that she dies. He returns at the time of her burial, and after the graveyard scene resumes with Horatio the discussion of his sea adventures. As, then, the attitude of Hamlet to Ophelia resembles in some particular that of Oxford to his wife, we may hope, at any rate, that, as "Shakespeare," he gives us in the famous graveyard scene a revelation of the true state of his affections: a supposition which even his conduct at the time of their rupture quite justifies.

The death of Lady Oxford, and the subsidence of the national excitement in relation to the Spanish Armada, following, as they do, closely upon the last indications we have of his theatrical enterprises, may be taken as marking the time at which he began "to sit in idle cell," or the beginning of the third period of his life.

CHAPTER XIII

Manhood of Edward de Vere

Final or Shakespearean Period
(1590-1604)

> I THINK the best judgment not of this country only, but of
> Europe at large, is slowly pointing to the conclusion, that
> Shakespeare is the chief of all poets hitherto; the greatest
> intellect who, in our recorded world, has left record of
> himself in the way of literature.[174]
>
> THOMAS CARLYLE, *Heroes.*

Dates.

We have now reached a stage in our argument at which the
study of dates becomes of paramount importance. Indeed, we are
tempted to think that the failure to appreciate the precise
significance of certain dates has gone far towards preventing an
earlier discovery of the authorship of Shakespeare's plays. We can
quite believe that other investigators have actually thought of the
Earl of Oxford in connection with the problem, and have
dismissed the idea because of certain chronological
considerations, which may have been thought to stand in the way,
but which, if carefully examined, would have actually been found
to support and confirm the theory. If, therefore, in this and
succeeding chapters we dwell at some length on the question of
dates, it is because what at first blush might give rise to doubts,
when correctly estimated is found to furnish one of the strongest
links in our chain of argument. When, then, we come to these
chronological matters we ask for them a very close and patient
attention.

---

[174] Carlyle, *On Heroes,* p. 96.

Material difficulties.

In entering upon the final and, as we believe, the most important period in the life of Edward de Vere, we must first describe briefly the position in which he then found himself in respect to certain matters not directly literary. Although we have only the barest indications upon which to work, we judge that for the first two or three years of this period things were not going well with him. It is not improbable that the suspension of his dramatic activities was due, in part at any rate, to the exhaustion of his material resources. His tendency to spend lavishly is unmistakable, and his play-acting and literary associates would provide an almost unlimited field for the exercise of his generosity. His own absorption in these interests must, moreover, have tended to place his financial affairs at the mercy of agents, and to throw them into confusion. To this must be added the almost royal state which he seems to have maintained in some respects. For at one point we get a glimpse of him travelling *en famille* with a retinue of twenty-eight servants. Suggestions of this kind of thing, we note in passing, are found in *The Taming of the Shrew*, treated much more from the point of view of the master than of the servant.

Land-selling.

The need for ready cash must often have been pressing, and this need he seems to have satisfied by selling estates "at ruinously low rates." Like the man with a "trick of melancholy" mentioned in *All's Well*, he sold many "a goodly manor for a song," and possibly at the same time developed that contempt for "land-buyers" expressed by Hamlet in the grave-digging scene. It is interesting to notice that when Iago, who, we have supposed, represented Oxford's receiver, urges upon one of his victims: "put money in thy purse;" he meets immediately with the response, "I will sell my lands." What Oxford's exact financial position may have become we cannot say, but it was evidently very low, for we are told that, after Lady Oxford's death, Burleigh refused to give any further assistance to his son-in-law. The implication is, of course, that Burleigh had been assisting him before this. No particulars of such assistance are given, and we may perhaps be pardoned if we are somewhat sceptical upon the matter. In any case it must always be borne in mind that we depend chiefly upon Burleigh's own account of these things. It is clear, at any rate, that although one of the foremost of the aristocracy, and originally a man of great wealth, he had by the time of which we are now treating found himself in reduced circumstances.

Second marriage and retirement.

Like Bassanio in *The Merchant of Venice* he had seriously

> disabled (his) estate,
> By something showing a more swelling port
> Than (his) . . . means would grant continuance.

And, like Bassanio, he also, in some measure, repaired his fortunes by marriage with "a lady richly left." Whether, like Portia, she was "fair, and fairer than that word, of wondrous virtues" we are not told; but if our theory of the authorship of the plays of Shakespeare is maintained, it is evident that the years he spent with her were to himself years of great productivity, whilst their importance in the history of the world's literature can hardly be overestimated. The exact date of this marriage is not given, but from the context we judge it to have taken place either at the end of 1591 or during 1592.

As Sir Sidney Lee suggests that it is improbable that any of Shakespeare's plays made their appearance before 1592, we may take the marriage of Edward de Vere with Elizabeth Trentham as synchronizing with the advent of the Shakespearean dramas. If, however, we take 1590 as marking, in a general way, their first appearance, he would still have had two years of retirement after the events recorded in our last chapter by way of special preparation for his work; whilst if we take the year of his marriage as the real beginning he had the advantage of four years of retirement, preceded by a probable ten years, and a possible twelve years of active association with the drama—quite a considerable and appropriate preparation for the work upon which he was entering.

Seclusion.

During part of the time immediately preceding his second marriage he was living in apartments in London; an arrangement suggestive of that seclusion which we deem one of the essentials for the production of work of the distinctive character of Shakespeare's plays. For we must state here, what must be emphasized later, that the Shakespearean dramas, as we have them now, are not to be regarded as plays written specially to meet the demands of a company of actors. *They are stage plays that have been converted into literature.* This we hold to be their distinctive character, demanding in their author two distinct phases of activity, if not two completely separate periods of life for their production. And, for the production of such a literature as this, freedom from distractions is a most important condition. The seclusion of De Vere, which we believe Spenser at this very time to have been lamenting in the *Tears of the Muses*, has all the appearance, therefore, of a condition imposed upon himself, as necessary to the fulfilment of his purpose.

An important blank.

Now we must draw attention to what is probably as significant a fact as any we have met. From the time of his second marriage till the time of his death in 1604, the record we have of him is almost a complete blank. In Sir Sidney Lee's account of him one very short paragraph covers the whole of these twelve years. We are told that he was living in retirement: not, however, in the country, but in London or its suburb, Hackney, where, therefore, he would be in direct contact with the theatre life of Shoreditch and that great movement of dramatic and literary rebirth, so aptly described by Dean Church: but of which Spenser in 1590 had evidently detected no promise. Two public appearances alone are recorded of him during the whole of this time. But as even these were in the last two years of his life we have a period of ten years which may be considered void of all important record; and the two events recorded of the last two years involve no appreciable encroachment upon his time and energies.

A vital synchronism.

This then is the position. In 1592 he is placed in comfortable circumstances. He is just forty-two years of age and therefore entering upon the period of the true maturity of his powers. He has behind him a poetic and a dramatic record of a most exceptional character. His poems are by far the most Shakespearean in quality and form of any of that time. His dramatic record places him in the forefront of play writers. Then a silence of an additional twelve years succeeds the four years of apparent idleness, *and this twelve years of comfort and seclusion exactly corresponds to the period of the amazing outpouring of the great Shakespearean dramas.* Unless, therefore, we are to imagine the complete stultification of every taste and interest he had hitherto shown, he must have been, on any theory of Shakespearean authorship, one of the most interested spectators of this culmination of Elizabethan literature, and he himself the natural connecting link between it and the past. Yet never for one moment does he appear in it all. His own record for these years is a blank, and—"no specimens of his dramatic productions survive."

In weighing evidence, in certain cases, what may be called negative evidence is frequently of a more compelling force than the more positive kind. If such a dramatic and literary outburst had had no original connection with De Vere it must inevitably have swept him within its influence. But the very man who had the greatest affinities with this particular type of production, and who, up to within a year or two of the first appearance of William Shakspere, had been amongst the foremost to encourage and patronize literary men, is never once heard of either in connection with William Shakspere or the Shakespearean drama. So far as these momentous happenings in his own peculiar domain are concerned, he might have been supposed to have been already dead.

We have, therefore, a most remarkable combination of silences; a silence as to his own occupations during these important years, and a silence as to any manifestation of interest in a work which, under any circumstances, must have touched him deeply. We can only suppose that he did not wish to be seen in the matter; and the only feasible explanation of such a wish is the theory of authorship we are now urging. As a matter of fact the real blank in his records, so far as any adequate occupation is concerned, is one of sixteen years; from 1588 to 1604. This vast lacuna must now, we believe, be filled in by the Shakespearean literature. For he, who was supposed to be sitting in "idle cell," had already spoken of himself, in an early lyric, as one,

> That never am less idle, lo!
> Than when I am alone.

Residences and theaters.

We would add, at this point, certain particulars respecting his domiciliation and life in or near London, that are not without interest in respect to our problem. He resided for some years at Canon Row, Westminster, and this would put him, by means of the ferry, in direct touch with theatrical activities on Bankside; and thence, by an easy walk with Newington Butts, the scene of many of the dramatic activities of the Lord Admiral's company. This company is associated with the performance of plays by Marlowe, to whom "Shakespeare" acknowledges indebtedness. It also performed in the early years of this period plays bearing titles afterwards borne by "Shakespeare" plays. The following passage from a letter by one Anthony Atkinson, showing us the Earl of Oxford in relationship with the Lord Admiral (Charles Howard of Effingham, Earl of Nottingham: of Spanish Armada fame) has some interest for us:

"The Lord Admiral doth credit Captain Fenner, who excuses Elston and . . . the Earl of Oxenford sent word by Cawley that Elston was a dangerous man."[175] The events do not concern us; it is the mere fact of personal dealings which matters.

Oxford's residence at Hackney, the London suburb immediately adjacent to Shoreditch, then the scene of Burbage's theatrical enterprises and the centre of the theatrical life of London, has already been mentioned. A somewhat more interesting detail concerns Bishopsgate: continuous with Shoreditch towards the south. Although, so far as we know, Oxford never resided in this district, we find him, in 1595, addressing a letter to Burleigh from Bishopsgate (Hatfield MSS.). Evidence points to William Shakspere being resident there at the time, and to his having next year removed to Southwark, which was soon to take the place of Shoreditch as the theatrical centre of London.

Letters and occupations.

Thus we see him moving quite close to the "Shakespeare" work, but never in it. Yet, during these years, his letters show unmistakably the clearness and vigour of his intellect. The published documents do not supply the full text in all cases, but little Shakespearean touches appear.

"Words in faithful minds are tedious," is one expression, already quoted in our *Troilus* argument.

"His shifts and jugglings are so gross and palpable"[176] is another; clearly suggestive of "this palpable gross play" in *A Midsummer Night's Dream* (V.I) or "such juggling and such knavery" in *Troilus and Cressida* (II.3). The letters are, for the most part, formal and businesslike; but the poet's tendency to express himself in similes and metaphors is irrepressible.

Not only is there abundant evidence of unimpaired mental

---

[175] Cecil Papers: March 1602, pp. 1-31.

[176] Paraphrase from Oxford's January 11, 1597 letter to Robert Cecil. The exact wording is "His shifts and knaveries are so gross and palpable . . ." (CP 37/66(b).

power, there is also evidence of his being closely occupied with some work. A letter addressed to him by a member of another branch of the family apologises, in a way which does not seem conventional, for breaking in upon his occupations; so that, whatever his pursuits may have been, he was not regarded, by those who were in a position to know, as a man spending his leisure altogether in amusements or in idleness. Yet, there is no external evidence, with one interesting exception, of his interesting himself in dramatic work of any kind during these years; though curiously enough, Meres as late on as 1598, when Oxford had apparently been dead to the dramatic world for ten years, places his name at the head of those dramatists who were "best for Comedy."

Shakespeare's method of production.

One of the greatest obstacles to the acceptance of our theory of the authorship of Shakespeare's plays will be a certain established conception of the mode in which they were produced and issued; a conception which arose of necessity out of the old theory. William Shakspere being but a young man at the time when the issue of the poems and plays began, and having to write, it is supposed, in order to supply the immediate needs of what has been unwarrantably called his company of play-actors, it has been necessary to assume that each play was begun, finished and staged by itself, in a definite period of time, and that no sooner was this done in respect to one play than the next must be put in preparation. A man with no accumulated reserves, immersed, it is assumed, in all the business of directing his company, and building up his own private fortune at the same time, would be compelled to finish off, and have completely done with, each play-writing task just as it presented itself. This he is supposed to have accomplished in a manner which can only be described as miraculous. And, seeing the large number of plays which are understood to have existed before a certain date, not only could there be no intervals for recuperation and the freshening of his conceptions whilst the flood of dramas was at its height, but there has been a real difficulty in finding reasonable spaces of time for them all to be written. Consequently, the supposition that these plays were written by William Shakspere of Stratford involves the belief in a series of stupendous creative efforts within definitely assignable dates, and this conception of a fixed order of production, with settled dates for the different plays, from 1592 onward, the rapid succession, of which betokened a genius of almost superhuman fecundity, is bound to follow us into the discussion of a theory of authorship to which it does not apply.

Re-integration of facts.

All the mass of data that has been collected with much labour respecting the first appearance of plays or the date of their registration or publication, comes to have a totally different significance, and loses a large part of its value, when severed from the supposed miraculous productivity of the Stratford man. Perhaps its chief value may now consist in illustrating the folly of ever supposing that so prodigious an achievement could have taken place. Such a change in the personality and antecedents of the author as we now propose, alters the significance of all that Shakespearean erudition in which mere inference has been passed off as established fact, and demands a difficult revolution in mental attitude towards the question of the manner and times of the production of the work.

What is necessary, in the first place, is to put aside all mere inference, to look at the facts that have been established respecting the issuing of the plays in the light of the quality and contents of the work, and to determine whether all these taken together are more suggestive of an author working under William Shakspere's or Edward de Vere's conditions; whether the work is suggestive of a hasty enforced production amid a multiplicity of other activities, or of painstaking concentration of mind on the part of a writer relieved from material and other anxieties; and whether it suggests a writer living as it were "from hand to mouth" in the production of his dramas, or of one who began the issue with large reserves already in hand.

Dating the plays.

In dealing with the dating of Shakespeare's plays, apart from the system of inferential dates that has grown up around Shakespearean study, we stand on most uncertain ground.

We have dates of the registration of certain works, dates of printing and publication, dates on which it is known that certain plays were performed, and we have contemporary lists of plays that show us that certain dramas were in existence at the time the lists were compiled; but such a thing as an authoritative record of the actual writing of a play does not exist so far as is yet known. All that the facts bear witness to, is that some of the works existed at certain dates; though whether they had existed five, ten, or twenty years before then is all a matter of conjecture—conjecture which may be made very reliable when it concerns William Shakspere of Stratford, but which may be entirely astray when another author is substituted. Nevertheless, if we accept in a general way the dates that have been assigned, we find that, starting with *Love's Labour's Lost* in 1590 or 1592 (the early years of Oxford's retirement) and finishing with *Othello* in 1604 (the year of Oxford's death), we have in these an overwhelming preponderance of the greatest of the Shakespearean dramas. This is then succeeded by a period in which there is greater uncertainty attached to the suggested dates, and a larger admixture of non-Shakespearean work. For in these later years we are assured that the dramatist had reverted to an earlier practice of collaborating with others.

Rate of issue.

What does seem clearly established, however, is that during the period of what may be called the main Shakespearean flood, two and sometimes three plays appeared in the course of a single year, at the same time that great poems like *Venus* and *Lucrece* were also making their appearance. Meanwhile revised and enlarged editions were appearing of plays that had already been issued. Sir Sidney Lee's statement that Shakspere had no hand in these various publishing operations we accept. The idea that the author had no hand in them we reject entirely, as almost an outrage upon common sense. The two plays which are assigned to the years immediately following the death of Edward de Vere are *King Lear* and *Macbeth*. If, then, we assume that these had not been played before (by no means a necessary concession) we may regard them as being in the hands of the actors when De Vere died. Including them, therefore, in the main period, we find that according to Professor Dowden's list,[177] out of the thirty-seven dramas attributed to Shakespeare all but eight had already been produced, and even this small residue includes such works as *Henry VIII*, *Timon of Athens* and *Pericles*, which, in their present state, we might well imagine the author was not very eager to send forth.

The so-called later plays.

Upon the Stratfordian view it is necessary, of course, to find spaces for the writing of what are called Shakespeare's later plays after the year 1604; for the whole of William Shakspere's time before that was fully, and more than fully occupied, and so we have, what must always have appeared something of an anomaly, the spectacle of the world's greatest dramatist, when but forty years of age, and after producing masterpieces like *Hamlet* and *Othello*, resorting to a practice suited only to his literary nonage, that of collaborating with writers inferior to himself. No such necessity attaches to the supposition of Edward de Vere being the author of these later plays. His work during the years 1590-1604 would not consist entirely, or even chiefly, in the production of new plays for the stage; and he would be under no necessity of working at a breakneck pace. In his case works issued after 1604 might have been not only begun but actually completed many years before; and when we find that certain plays, issued after that date, were completed by other writers, the situation involves no

---

[177] Among Edward Dowden's many books is *Shakspere: A Critical Study of His Mind and Art*, which has a chronological listing of the plays on pages viii-ix.

such anomaly as belongs to the Stratfordian view: that a living writer of first rank could so allow his own creations to be marred. The staging of his dramas would be to him only a secondary, though doubtless a fascinating consideration; but he must have seen that he was doing something much greater than supplying contemporary audiences with a few hours' amusement. To William Shakspere, on the other hand, the provision of plays for *his company* of actors (assuming that he was responsible for its direction) would have made it impossible that he should, at any time, be producing dramas much in advance of their presentation on the stage. In his case, therefore, the date of the actual writing of a play might be inferred with considerable certainty from the date of its appearing.

Writing and issuing.

The writer of these dramas must have known that what he was giving to the world was destined to live primarily as literature, or, more precisely, as poetry. He might, therefore, in pursuance of such a purpose have chosen, except for material considerations, to have had every one of his works published posthumously. This hypothesis enables us to see that in such work dates of publication have no necessary correspondence with dates of writing, and makes us realize how completely all inferences with regard to the years in which the several plays were written may be upset by the substitution of another author for William Shakspere of Stratford. In the case of Lyly's plays, for example, we have seen that in some cases many years, and in all cases a number of years intervened between the writing and the publication.

Rapid issue.

By way of illustrating the strange but inevitable results of attributing the works to the Stratford man, we shall take a particular period and consider the writings assigned to it. Although the Shakespearean dramas had been appearing since 1590 or 1592, it was not until the year 1598 that any of them appeared with Shakespeare's name attached: in itself a curious and suspicious fact. It may have no significance, but we mention in passing that this is the year of Burleigh's death and also the year following the death of James Burbage who had staged the first "Shakespeare" plays. Oxford, we have said, died in 1604. In the six years intervening between these two dates, according to Professor Dowden's classification of Shakespeare's plays,[178] William Shakspere wrote all the following:

1. *The Merry Wives of Windsor.*
2. *Much Ado about Nothing.*
3. *As You Like It.*
4. *Twelfth Night.*
5. *All's Well that Ends Well.*
6. *Measure for Measure.*
7. *Troilus and Cressida.*
8. *Henry IV* (part 2).
9. *Henry V.*
10. *Julius Caesar.*
11. *Hamlet.*
12. *Othello.*

Nor had this followed upon a period of rest; for, according to particulars we have compiled from the Biographical Notes to the Falstaff Edition of Shakespeare,[179] during the preceding year (1597) he had written two new plays and published three others that had been previously acted.

In addition to all the new work produced in these few years the same Notes represent him as having also published for the first time:

1. *The Merchant of Venice.*
2. *A Midsummer Night's Dream.*

There was also published a "newly corrected and augmented"

---

[178] See footnote 177, p. 317.

[179] *The Works of William Shakespeare* (Falstaff Edition), pub. 1896, does not have any biographical information about Shakespeare. *The Complete Works of William Shakespeare* (Dr. Johnson edition), published the same year (1896), does have a "Biographical Introduction" with the information Looney referred to. See pp. lxviii-lxix.

edition of *Love's Labour's Lost*; at least one other edition of *Hamlet*; (which was also revised and augmented); two fresh editions of *Henry IV*, part I; a second edition of *A Midsummer Night's Dream*; a new edition of *Richard II*, two new editions of *Richard III* and a new edition of *Romeo and Juliet*.

A literary miracle.

When every allowance has been made for a fair proportion of those pirated and surreptitious issues which has characterized Shakespearean publication, and also for mere reprints, in which the author may have had no hand, it will still be admitted that the output was enormous.

If he had done nothing more than write the twelve new plays, even supposing they had been mere ephemeral things intended only for the stage, the achievement would have been extraordinary. When, however, we turn from quantity to the consideration of literary quality, it is difficult to understand how such an accomplishment could ever have been credited. Yet all this new creative work is supposed to have been produced *pari passu* with an extraordinary amount of other literary labour in the issue of new editions of former plays, much administrative work connected with the direction of the company, the more material occupations of land and property speculations and litigation, entailing much mental distraction and the consumption of time and energy in journeys between London and Stratford. This, we make bold to claim, constitutes a complete *reductio ad absurdum* of the Stratfordian theory of authorship.

A rational performance.

It is much more reasonable, then, to suppose that what was actually happening in these six years was the speeding up of the finishing-off process, as though the writer were either acting under a premonition that his end was approaching, or the time had now arrived for giving to the world a literature at which he had been working during the whole of his previous life. Everything suggests the rushing out of supplies from a large accumulated stock; and, therefore, instead of seeing any difficulty in the appearing of other Shakespearean plays after the death of

De Vere, it is a matter of surprise that, according to the dates that have been assigned to the plays by the best authorities, so small a proportion of the purely Shakespearean work remained to be presented. (We are not now speaking of its being actually printed: this is another matter which must be discussed later.) At the same time, we are struck with the amount of doubtful and collaborated work which is assigned to the period subsequent to De Vere's death. Certainly the last seven or eight years of De Vere's life are, according to the orthodox dating, marked by an extraordinary output of Shakespeare's plays, whilst his death marks an equally striking arrest in the issuing, printing and reprinting of these dramas.

Dramatic Reserves.

The above considerations ought to prepare us for a complete break-up of the seriatim conception of the creation of the "Shakespeare" dramas. We have laboured the point because of the difficulty of the mental revolution involved. If we assume an author who for ten or twelve years had been actively occupied with theatre work; whose great wealth had been spent ungrudgingly upon it, engaging talented and educated men to assist him and to relieve him of much of the drudgery of theatre management; thus leaving him free to concentrate his distinctive powers upon the literary part of the work; then, with the literary capital he had thus amassed, beginning another period of fourteen to sixteen years of comparative quiet and seclusion, in which to give a higher finish to plays already written, as well, possibly, as to produce new works, the whole aspect of the issue of this literature becomes changed. To all the advantages of education and association with the highest classes of society, Edward de Vere was by this time able to bring to the task, on the one hand these stores of dramas which are supposed to have perished, and on the other hand the maturity of his own mental powers, as well as poetic gifts of a high order that had been amply exercised. Contrasted with the Stratfordian view or any other theory of authorship yet propounded, the supposition that Edward de Vere is "Shakespeare" places the appearance of this literature for the first time within the category of natural and human achievements.

That "Shakespeare" had this faculty of secretiveness and reserve in respect to the production of great masterpieces— holding them back until either they were fit or the time opportune for their issue—is no mere guesswork. He tells us so in the plainest terms. For he had already been putting great dramas before the public when he published the poetic masterpiece which he calls "the first heir of [his] invention." Evidently then, according to his own account, it had lain in manuscript for years before its appearance. William Shakspere is supposed to have produced it before he left Stratford, and, as it was not published until 1593, even he must be supposed to have it by him for a number of years. And as *Lucrece* was published the following year, it too must have been well advanced at the time when *Venus* appeared.

Habits of revision.

Everything points to "Shakespeare" being given to storing, elaborating, and steadily perfecting his productions before issuing them, when his mind was bent on producing something worthy of his powers. *Love's Labour's Lost*, which is placed somewhere between 1590 and 1592, was not issued in its final form until 1598, and every line of it bears marks of most careful and exacting revision. *Hamlet*, too, there is evidence, underwent similar treatment. How it could ever have been believed that the finished lines of Shakespeare were the rapid and enforced production of a man immersed in many affairs, will probably be one of the wonders of the future. Everything bespeaks the loving and leisurely revision of a writer free from all external pressure; and this, combined with the amazing rapidity of issue, confirms the impression of "a long foreground somewhere."

De Vere a precisionist.

Andrew Lang, in his posthumously published work on *Shakespeare and the Great Unknown*,[180] finds an argument in favour of the rapidity of Shakespearean production in a comparison with the literary output of Scott. He ought, rather,

---

[180] Andrew Lang, *Shakespeare, Bacon and the Great Unknown*, p. 91-93.

to have found in Scott a warning example of the consequences of rapid writing; and, by contrast with Scott's verbosity, have found in Shakespeare's compression a clear evidence of the latter's careful and persistent elaboration of his lines. Now this tendency to revert to his work in order to further improve it is typical of Edward de Vere. Variant copies of his small lyrics are extant, and these furnish unquestionable proof that he was accustomed to turn back to poems, even after their publication, in order to enrich and perfect them. He was a precisionist the very ease and lucidity of whose lines was the consummation of an art which hid its own laboriousness. His nicety in speech and that careful attention to details of personal dress which frequently marks the man who strives after exactness, were, indeed, the subject of Gabriel Harvey's lampoon.

Penmanship.

These things may justify us in supposing carefulness in a detail like penmanship. His handwriting is accessible and this surmise may be put to the test. Now we know that Shakespeare's MSS. for the use of the printers were clearly written, and a passage in *Hamlet* points to its being a detail to which the author was attentive. As, therefore, there are some very strange mysteries connected with the Shakespearean manuscripts, it is quite possible that the dangers of his handwriting being recognized may have determined their strict custody until everything was printed, and that then the writings themselves were deliberately destroyed. We shall naturally, therefore, be interested to know whether any of the interpolations into Anthony Munday's play seem to be in the handwriting of the Earl of Oxford.

Stage plays and literature.

The question of the relationship of stage plays to literature is one which touches our problem very closely. That the two things are quite distinct in themselves from a certain point of view is evident on the face of it. When the audience in a theatre wishes to see the unravelling of a plot, with all its entanglements in external circumstances and in the complexities of human nature, the elements of novelty, suspense and surprise must enter very largely into the performance. This need of a continued succession of sensations demands a bold and broad treatment; the deeper effects being attained not by the subtleties of condensed sentences, which rest but a moment in the mind, but by the total and general impression conveyed by whole situations.

It would therefore be an irrational and wasteful expenditure of force to put into a play intended primarily to meet the theatre-goer's demand for recreative novelty and sensation, a large amount of carefully elaborated detail and subtlety of thought, which could only be appreciated after reflection and long continued familiarity. To pack with weighty significance each syllable of a work meant only to amuse or to supply thrills for two or three hours would, moreover, defeat its own ends. On the other hand, the amplified form of statement, so necessary with spoken words in handling novel situations, becomes tedious in printed utterances intended to endure and be pondered over. These considerations by no means exhaust the question of the distinction between mere stage plays and dramatic literature. They are intended merely to emphasize the distinction and are sufficient for that purpose.

"Shakespeare" on the stage.

When, therefore, familiar dramatic literature is staged, as it may very properly be, it owes its interest on the stage to entirely different considerations, and makes its appeal, if not to a different set of people, at any rate to a different phase of their mental activities from what an ordinary stage play does. The true purpose of such a stage setting is to offer an exposition of the literature, to which it is itself subordinate. The frequently repeated remark that "Shakespeare does not pay on the stage," instead of being taken as a reflection upon the public taste, ought to indicate that there is some fundamental difference between Shakespeare's and the other plays with which they are put into competition; and that these great English dramas are being viewed in a wrong light, and sometimes, possibly, put to a use for which they are not altogether suited.

Pre-eminently literature.

The fact is that his matchless lines, crowded with matter and intellectual refinements, demand not only maturity of mind in the auditor, but a willingness to turn again and again to the same passages, the significance of which expands with every enlargement of life's experiences. This is one reason why, in order to enjoy fully the best contents of a play of Shakespeare's on the stage, it is necessary first to have read it; and the more familiar one is with it beforehand the greater becomes the intellectual enjoyment, if the play is at all capably handled. In this case the acting becomes a kind of commentary on the literature; a work of interpretation, bringing to the surface and unfolding its deeper significance. On the other hand, to have read and become familiar with many an ordinary stage play before seeing it would diminish interest in the performance. This implies no necessary slight upon these productions, but is meant merely to draw into clearer light the radical difference between those plays and the plays of "Shakespeare." When writings have taken the form and won the position of the latter, they cease to be the special possession of play-goers and actors, and take their place amongst the imperishable treasures of literature.

Secondarily, stage-plays.

Notwithstanding this fact, it yet remains true that, even as stage-plays, Shakespeare's dramas have been made to do yeoman service, and will no doubt continue to do so. Superb literature though his masterpieces undoubtedly are, they nevertheless rest upon a foundation of real stage play. And when this is brought into prominence, embellished with touches of his literary workmanship, effective results can be secured. It is almost absurd to have to emphasize the fact that the writing of even a very moderate stage play demands something more than literary capacity. The production of such work is a highly technical matter, requiring an easy familiarity with all the mechanism of stage directions, and the adjustments of "entrances" and "exits"; and this would be specially so in those early days of dramatic pioneering.

The combination.

Now, it is the unique combination of this technical and spectacular quality with their supreme literary position, that gives to Shakespeare's writings, one, at least, of their distinctive features. Without unduly labouring the point it will be necessary to determine the relationship which these two elements bear to each other in his most finished productions. Here, however, we may say that mankind has already settled the question for us. For it is upon their merits as literature that the fame and immortality of Shakespeare's dramas rest. Though the writer's first aim may have been to produce a perfect drama for stage purposes, in the course of his labours, by dint of infinite pains and the nature of his own genius, he produced a literature which has over-shadowed the stage-play. It is difficult, therefore, to imagine that the relationship of these two elements in the same work represents a simultaneous product. And if we must choose between the theory of their being literature converted into plays, or plays converted into literature, on a review of the work no competent judge would hesitate to pronounce in favour of the latter supposition.

We feel justified in claiming then that the best of the dramas passed through two distinct phases, being originally stage-plays—doubtless of a high literary quality—which were subsequently transformed into the supreme literature of the nation. We further claim that the man who had the capacity to do this had the intelligence to know exactly what he was doing; and having created this literature he was not likely to have become so indifferent to its fate as he is represented by the Stratfordian tradition.

Plays as poetry.

Keeping in mind that our chief purpose at present is to see to what extent traces of the personality and life of Edward de Vere may be detected in the work of Shakespeare, we shall first summarize the position as it stands from the literary point of view at the opening of this third period. Having in his early years earned the distinction of being "the best of the courtier poets of the early days of Queen Elizabeth's reign," and having then passed through a middle period occupied largely with work in connection with the drama, in which he earned the further distinction of being "among the best in comedy"—which must not be interpreted as meaning that he had confined himself to this domain—he enters in the maturity of his powers upon a third period, the longest of all.

Of this period little is known: but what we do know is that the conditions of his life at the time were precisely those which would lead a poet of such powers to work upon his stores of incompleted dramas, giving them a more poetic form and a higher poetic finish. Are, then, the plays of Shakespeare such as to warrant the supposition of their having been produced in this way? Do they look like the work of one whose chief interest was to keep a theatre business going, or of one who was primarily a poet, not only in the large and general sense, but in the special and technical sense of an artist in words, making music out of the vocal qualities and cadences of speech?

Again, to ask the question is to answer it. It is not only the number and quality of the lyrics scattered throughout the dramas that give to Shakespeare his high position as a poet; it is the poetry of the actual body of the dramas themselves, blank verse and rhyme alike, that determines his position. It is here that we have the poetry which raises its author to honours which he shares with Homer and Dante alone. Several of the plays can hardly be described otherwise than as collections of poems ingeniously woven together; and, to conceive of one such play being written as a continuous exercise, starting with the first scene of the first act, and ending with the last "exeunt," is an almost impossible supposition. Everything is much more suggestive of a poet creating his varied passages out of the multiplicity of his own moods and experiences, and incorporating these into suitable parts of his different plays: afterwards putting them through a final process of adjusting the parts, and trimming and enriching the verse.

The work and the man.

Now of all the men we have had occasion to pass in review in the course of the investigations of which we are now treating, we have met no one who could be considered as in any way fulfilling in his person and external circumstances the necessary conditions for performing such a work at this particular time as does Edward de Vere, Earl of Oxford.

Take the single play of *Love's Labour's Lost*, examine the exquisite workmanship put into the versification alone, and it becomes impossible to think of it as coming from "a young man in a hurry" to make plays and money. Think of it as coming from a man between the ages of forty and fifty-four, working in retirement, leisurely, under no sense of pressure or material necessities, upon work he had held in the rough, more or less, for several years, and there immediately arises a sense of correspondence between the workman and his work. It is not improbable that for the production of such work as he aimed at, he felt the necessity of seclusion, and a freedom from a sense of working under the public eye; and this may have been not the least of the motives that led him to adopt and preserve his mask. Whether this was so or not, there can be no doubt that during these years in which there was the largest outpouring of the great drama-poems, Edward de Vere was placed in circumstances more favourable to their production than any other man of the period of whom we have been able to learn.

Henry Wriothesley a personal link.

Such, then, are the activities which there is every reason to believe filled up the years which are at once the years of his maturity and the years of his retirement. For nine years after his marriage no public appearance is recorded of him, and then the silence is broken in a manner as significant to our present business

HENRY WRIOTHESLEY, THIRD EARL OF SOUTHAMPTON

COPY OF A PAINTING BY DANIEL MYTENS, CIRCA 1618.
REPRODUCED BY PERMISSION OF
THE NATIONAL PORTRAIT GALLERY.

as anything with which we have met. As far back as 1593 "Shakespeare" had dedicated to the Earl of Southampton his first lengthy poem, *Venus and Adonis*. In the following year he had repeated the honour in more affectionate terms in issuing his *Lucrece*. In the year 1601 there took place the ill-fated insurrection under the Earl of Essex; an insurrection which its leaders stoutly maintained was aimed, not at the throne, but at the politicians, amongst whom Robert Cecil, son of Burleigh, was now prominent. Whether Edward de Vere approved of the rising or not, it certainly represented social and political forces with which he was in sympathy. We find, then, that the company of actors supposed to be managed, by William Shakspere, and occupied largely with staging Shakespeare's plays, the Lord Chamberlain's company was implicated in the rising through the Earl of Southampton's agency.

Helping the Essex insurrection.

In order to stir up London and to influence the public mind in a direction favourable to the overturning of those in authority, the company gave a performance of *Richard II*, the Earl of Southampton subsidizing the players. In the rising itself Southampton took an active part. Upon its collapse he was tried for treason along with its leader Essex; and it was then that Edward de Vere emerged from his retirement for the first time for nine years to take his position amongst the twenty-five peers who constituted the tribunal before whom Essex and Southampton were to be tried. It is certainly a most important fact in connection with our argument that this outstanding action of Oxford's later years should be in connection with the one contemporary that "Shakespeare" has immortalized. Considering the direction in which his sympathies lay, his coming forward at that time only admits of one explanation. The forces arrayed against the Earl of Essex were much too powerful, and he suffered the extreme penalty. Sentence was also passed on Southampton but was commuted, and he suffered imprisonment until the end of the reign—now not far off. It is somewhat curious that although *"Shakspere's company"* had been implicated, he was not prosecuted or otherwise drawn into the trouble and his fortunes seem to have suffered no setback.

The first connection.

The special interest of this is that it gives us the first suggestion of a direct personal connection between Edward de Vere and the performance of Shakespeare's plays through Henry Wriothesley, Third Earl of Southampton; for it clearly indicates an interest on the part of De Vere in the very man to whom "Shakespeare" had dedicated important poems. As it was only with difficulty that Wriothesley's friends were able to save his life, it is possible, therefore, that he owed much to Oxford's influence. His liberation immediately on the accession of James I may also have owed something to Oxford's intervention; for the latter's attitude to Mary Queen of Scots must have had some weight with her son, and his position as Great Chamberlain, the functions of which he exercised at James' coronation, would place him immediately into intimate relationship with the king. His officiating at this important function is the last recorded public appearance of the subject of these pages.

De Vere's son and heir.

As in investigations of this kind trifles may prove significant, we may point out that just at the time when "Shakespeare" was dedicating his great poems to Henry Wriothesley, and, in the opinion of many, addressing to him some of the tenderest sonnets that one man ever addressed to another, Edward de Vere's only son was born. Now, we have mentioned that De Vere was proud of his descent, and also that the De Veres had come down in a succession of Aubreys, Johns, and Roberts for centuries almost like a royal dynasty. We should naturally have expected, therefore, that he would have given to his only son one of the great family names. Yet, in all the centuries of the De Veres, there is but one "Henry"; Henry, the son of Edward de Vere, born at the very time when "Shakespeare" was dedicating great poems to Henry Wriothesley. The metaphor of "The first heir," which occurs in the short dedication of *Venus and Adonis* to Wriothesley, would also be specially apposite to the circumstances of the time; and as "Shakespeare" speaks of Southampton as the "godfather" of "the first heir of my invention," it would certainly be interesting to know whether Henry Wriothesley was godfather to Oxford's heir, Henry de Vere. It is not necessary to our argument that he should have been, but if it be found that he actually held that position the inference would be obvious and conclusive. We have discovered a reference to the baptism as having taken place at Stoke Newington, so that it ought not to be impossible to find out who the sponsors were.

If the reader will further examine the sonnets round about the one which makes reference to the "dedication" he will probably be surprised at the number of allusions to childbirth.

Contemporary parties and the insurrection.

As it is part of our task to indicate something of the parties and personal relationships of those days we have pointed. out the spontaneous affinity of Oxford with the younger Earls of Essex and Southampton, all three of whom, having being royal wards under the guardianship of Burleigh, were most hostile to the Cecil influence at Court. On the other hand, we have Raleigh along with Robert Cecil representing the force which Essex wished to oust. Of Raleigh we must point out, in relation to the Essex rising, that so malicious had been his attitude, both at the time of the Earl's prosecution and even in the moment of the latter's execution, that he brought upon himself the odium of the populace. It appears that when Cecil was disposed to relent in relation to Essex, Raleigh was most insistent for his punishment; and when the unfortunate Earl had won the Queen's consent to an execution in private, Raleigh made it his business to be a spectator of his enemy's execution.

The conduct of Francis Bacon, too, had been even more

indecent than had been that of his uncle Burleigh towards Somerset. It is interesting to note, therefore, that the fortunes of the two men whose conduct was most open to censure in this matter suffered complete collapse in the course of the following reign; the publicity of Raleigh's execution being a fitting punishment for his unseemly intrusion upon the privacy of the execution of Essex. It is necessary to point out these things if we are to have a correct judgment of the men with whom the Earl of Oxford had to deal, and upon the strength of whose relationships with Oxford most of the impressions of him met with in books have evidently been formed.

Trial of the Earl of Essex.

Whatever opinions may be held about these things, it is clear, from the point of view of the problem of Shakespearean authorship, that the famous trial of the Earl of Essex assumes quite a thrilling interest. Standing before the judges was the only living personality that "Shakespeare" has openly connected with the issue of his works, and towards whom he has publicly expressed affection: Henry Wriothesley. The most powerful force at work in seeking to bring about the destruction of the accused was the possessor of the greatest intellect that has appeared in English philosophy: one to whom in modern times has actually been attributed the authorship of Shakespeare's plays—Francis Bacon. And sitting on the benches amongst the judges was none other, we believe, than the real "Shakespeare" himself, intent on saving, if possible, one of the very men whom Bacon was seeking to destroy. Some artist of the future surely will find here a theme to fire his enthusiasm and furnish scope for his genius and ambition.

Bacon, Southampton and Oxford.

Before leaving the question of the rebellion and trial of the Earl of Essex we shall barely draw attention to an aspect of it which affects a theory of Shakespearean authorship that we have not deemed necessary to discuss at any length. The conduct of Francis Bacon in respect to the trial of Essex has been discussed *ad nauseam* and is therefore too well known to need describing. Nor is it our business to enter into the ethics of his action. It is wholly incredible, however, that he could have been working secretly as a playwriter hand in glove with the very dramatic company that was implicated in the rising, and that one of his plays should have been employed as an instrument in the business. Again, something is known of the nature of Bacon's previous friendship with the Earl of Essex; but, however cordial it may have been, it is quite on a lower plane as compared with "Shakespeare's" feelings towards Southampton. The terms in which the dramatist addresses the nobleman who was being tried along with Essex are those of personal endearment, and we must hope, for the credit of human nature, that to all the treachery implied in the idea of turning upon a friend whose insurrection had been assisted by his own drama and dramatic associates (according to the Baconian theory) it was impossible that he could have added the heartlessness of prosecuting one, his love for whom he had already immortalized by his poems.

Nor should we like to think that the very man whom he had immortalized in this way could in turn have so delighted in wounding him and in seeking his downfall. For the Earl of Southampton was amongst those who sought and ultimately brought about the downfall of Lord Bacon. If to this we add that most of "Shakespeare's" sonnets are supposed to be addressed to the Earl of Southampton, and that these were put into circulation without protest seven years after the trial, at a time when the feeling of Southampton towards Bacon was very bitter, we have as tumbled a moral situation as it is possible to conceive if we suppose that Bacon was "Shakespeare." The decisive answer to the Baconian theory, therefore, it seems to us, is Henry Wriothesley.

Wriothesley's interest in the plays.

Moreover, Southampton's interest in William Shakspere and the Shakespearean plays suffered no decline as a result of his trial and imprisonment; for we find him immediately upon his liberation arranging for a private performance of *Love's Labour's Lost* for the entertainment of the new Queen; a most unlikely thing for him to have done if its author had been a former friend who had treacherously sought to destroy him. On the other hand, unless the Lord Great Chamberlain—"one of the best in comedy"—who had recently shown an interest both in Southampton and the new occupants of the throne was physically incapable of being present, it is safe to assume, apart from the special theories we are now advancing, that he would be amongst the select party of spectators at the performance in Wriothesley's house. A more striking fact connecting the Earl of Southampton directly with Edward de Vere and the work of "Shakespeare," we reserve for the chapter in which we shall have to review *Shakespeare's Sonnets* in relation to our argument.

"Shakespeare" and Queen Elizabeth's death.

The mention of the change that had taken place in the occupancy of the English throne suggests a most significant fact in connection with our problem. When Queen Elizabeth died, the poets of the day, who had loaded her with most absurd flattery during her lifetime, naturally vied with one another in doing honour to the departed monarch. We have elsewhere remarked that we have no single line of De Vere's paying compliments to Elizabeth, either during her lifetime or after her death; a fact which arouses no great surprise. A similar absence of any word of praise from the pen of Shakespeare has, however, always been a matter of considerable surprise. His silence upon the subject of the Queen's death provoked comment among his contemporaries, and Chettle, the personal "friend" of William Shakspere, made a direct appeal to him under the name of Melicert to

> Drop from his honeyed muse one sable tear
> To mourn her death that graced her desert.

This personal intimacy of Chettle and Shakspere, we remark in passing, is another Stratfordian supposition, for which there is no sufficient warrant; and that Chettle's "Melicert" was Shakspere is only another surmise.

The honeyed muse was at any rate unresponsive, and no "sable tear" appeared. Considering the whole circumstances of William Shakspere's supposed rapid rise and early access to royal favour, it is difficult to account for his silence at such a time on any other supposition than that he did not write because he could not: whilst the man whose instrument he was not disposed to write verses for the mere pleasure of adding to the glory of William Shakspere.

The sonnets.

In another connection we have had to point out that Shakespeare's sonnet 125 seems to be pointing to De Vere's officiating at Queen Elizabeth's funeral. This may be taken as his last sonnet; for 126 is really not a sonnet but a stanza composed of six couplets, in which he appears to be addressing a parting message to his young friend. Sonnet 127 begins the second series, the whole of which seems from the contents to belong to about the same period as the early sonnets of the first series.

If, then, we take sonnet 125 as being the Earl of Oxford's expression of his private feelings relative to Queen Elizabeth's funeral, we can quite understand his not troubling to honour her with any special verses. The argument does not touch William Shakspere in the same way; for the reasons which lead us to suppose that the particular sonnet has reference to Elizabeth's funeral only apply if we assume it to be written by the Earl of Oxford. It is worth noticing, too, that these last sonnets seem to be touched with the thought of approaching death; and when we find that De Vere died on June 14th, 1604, the year following the death of Queen Elizabeth, to which they seem to make reference, the two suppositions we have stated in regard to them seem to be mutually confirmed.

Oxford and Elizabeth's death.

The special sonnet to which attention has been drawn, if it does actually refer to the part taken by the Lord Great Chamberlain at Elizabeth's funeral, shows clearly that the participation was merely formal. It is not necessary to account for Oxford's attitude: the point is that the attitude represented in the sonnet is precisely the same as that represented by the absence of any line from Oxford's pen on the subject of Elizabeth's death, and a similar absence of any Shakespearean utterance on the same theme. In a word, everything becomes "of a piece" as soon as the name and person of the Earl of Oxford is introduced.

There can be no doubt that as Oxford was out of sympathy with the party in power at the time, the success of the Essex rising would, from some points of view, have been gratifying to him; although, as a practical thing, he would probably, at his time of life, have considered it rash and ill-advised. The execution of Essex which had done more than anything else to injure Elizabeth's popularity in her closing years would not leave him unaffected. If, further, we suppose that "Shakespeare," whoever he may have been, retained in 1603 the feelings he had expressed for Southampton in 1593 and 1594, it is impossible to think of him writing panegyrics on Queen Elizabeth whilst his friend was being kept in prison. Chettle evidently did not consider his "friend," William Shakspere, sufficiently interested in the Earl of Southampton to withhold, on account of the imprisoned earl, his "sable tear" from the bier of the departed Queen. Oxford's experience as a whole, however, would indispose him to join in any chorus of lamentation or of praise.

The Hatfield manuscripts and the Domestic State Papers of the time represent him as making efforts to restore the fortunes of his family by an appeal to Elizabeth on the strength of his youth spent at her court, and promise made to him which had encouraged his early extravagance. The Queen had replied with gracious words, but neither the special office for which he was asking, the Presidency of Wales, nor any other appointment was granted to him; and his disappointment with the Queen is clearly shown. He certainly would be in no mood for lamentations over the departed monarch.

Oxford's dramatic reappearance.

We must now go back a year in order to draw attention to another of those particulars which had passed unobserved until after the virtual completion of our argument. After fourteen years of apparent retirement from dramatic activities, Oxford makes his appearance once more, and on a single occasion, in the capacity of patron of the drama. It is a mere glimpse that we are permitted to catch of him, but such as it is it has special relevance to our present purpose. Halliwell-Phillipps, in discussing the question of "Shakespeare's" relation to the Boar's Head Tavern, Eastcheap, tells us that "in 1602 the Lords of the Council gave permission for the servants of the Earls of Oxford and Worcester to play at this tavern."[181] It is of some importance, then, that the place which this tavern occupies in respect to the Shakespeare dramas should first be made clear.

In current editions of Shakespeare's plays, this particular tavern is specified in the stage directions as the scene of some of the escapades of Prince Hal and Falstaff (*Henry IV*, parts 1 and 2). In the Folio Editions, however, the name of the tavern is not given in the stage directions. The text of the play, on the other hand, makes it clear that some tavern in Eastcheap is meant: Falstaff remarking "Farewell: you shall find me in Eastcheap" (*I Henry IV*, I.2) and Prince Hal when they meet at the tavern (II.4) adding, "I shall command all the good lads in Eastcheap."

The Boar's Head, Eastcheap.

In reference to this matter Halliwell-Phillipps states:

> It is a singular circumstance that there is no mention of this celebrated tavern in any edition of Shakespeare previous to the appearance of Theobald's in 1733", but that the locality is there accurately given is rendered certain by an allusion to 'Sir John of the Boares-Head in Eastcheap' in Gayton's Festivous Notes 1654,

[181] Halliwell-Phillipps, *Outlines*, p. 309, 310.

p. 277. Shakespeare never mentions the tavern at all, and the only possible allusion to it is in the *Second Part of Henry the Fourth*, where Prince Hal asks, speaking of Falstaff, 'doth the old boar feed in the old frank'? A suggestion of the locality may also be possibly intended in *Richard II* where the Prince is mentioned as frequenting taverns 'that stand in narrow lanes.' . . . There were numerous other tenements in London, including five taverns in the city known by the name of the Boar's-Head. . . . Curiously enough by an accidental coincidence Sir John Fastolf devised to Magdalen College, Oxford, a house so called in the borough of Southwark.[182]

Sir Sidney Lee connects Falstaff chiefly with the Boar's Head Tavern in Southwark, relegating the Boar's Head, Eastcheap, to a footnote, and ignoring the connection of Falstaff with some tavern in Eastcheap in the actual text of the plays.

Falstaff.

Whatever duplication of associations may have arisen from the connection of Falstaff with Sir John Fastolf of the Boar's Head, Southwark, it is evident from the text of the play, the stage-tradition supported by Gayton's Festivous Notes in 1654, and Theobald's and all modern editions of "Shakespeare's" works, that the "Boar's Head," Eastcheap, is associated with Shakespeare's creation of Falstaff. There is ample justification, therefore, for Halliwell-Phillipps's allusion to Falstaff as "the renowned hero of the Boar's Head Tavern, Eastcheap,"[183] and for Sir Walter Raleigh's remark that "the Boar's Head in Eastcheap has been made famous for ever by the patronage of Falstaff and his crew."[184] It is of more than ordinary interest, then, to find the Earl of Oxford reappearing after an absence of fourteen years from the world of drama at the particular tavern associated with Falstaff, and in the very year that the representation of Falstaff culminated in the *Merry Wives of Windsor*. For it was on January 18th, 1601-2, that "a license for the publication of the play was granted" and "an imperfect draft

---

[182] Halliwell-Phillipps, *Outlines*, p. 309.
[183] Halliwell-Phillipps, *Outlines*, p. 133.
[184] Raleigh, *Shakespeare*, p. 52.

was printed in 1602."[185] What would we not give to know the title of the play or plays that the servants of the Earls of Oxford and Worcester performed at the Boar's Head, Eastcheap, in the year 1602? It is another of those mysterious silences that meet us at every turn of the Shakespeare problem.

Oxford's crest the boar.

Halliwell-Phillipps's connection of Falstaff with "the old boar" has also its special interest to those who may believe that Falstaff is a work of self-caricature on the part of "Shakespeare." For Oxford's coat of arms was the boar, and he himself is spoken of, in a letter of Hatton's to Queen Elizabeth, as "the boar." One of his ancestors was killed by a wild boar, and this would readily suggest to him the theme of his first great poem. It may be worth mentioning that the character of Puntarvolo, in Ben Jonson's *Every Man out of his Humour*, who, some Baconians believe, was Jonson's representation of Bacon, was also one whose crest was a boar. These things are at any rate interesting if not made too much of.

A wild adventure.

Another interesting fact belonging to a much earlier part of Oxford's life connects itself with the particular matters under consideration. The escapades of Prince Hal and his men, in *Henry IV*, part I, involve not only the Boar's Head Tavern, Eastcheap, but also that part of the road near Rochester which connects London with Canterbury. Here the madcap Prince and his associates molest travellers. Now in 1573, the same year as Hatton writes his complaint to the Queen, speaking of Oxford as the "boar," others make complaints about being molested by the "Earl of Oxford's men" on the identical part of the road— "between Rochester and Gravesend"—where Prince Hal had indulged in his pranks. Shooting had taken place, and everything is suggestive of a wildness, similar to what is represented in

---

[185] Lee, *Life*, p. 178.

"Shakespeare's" play respecting the future Henry V. The exact correspondence alike of locality and adventure forms not the least striking of the many coincidences which our researches have disclosed.

The 1602 gap.

A special significance attaches to the particular year in which Oxford makes his reappearance as patron of drama after an absence of fourteen years. In Chapter I, when dealing with Stratfordianism, we had occasion to point out that 1602 is the only year of the great Shakespearean period in which the records of the Treasurer of the Chamber contain no entry of payments made to the Lord Chamberlain's company of players. The company, it would appear, had temporarily suspended official operations. An examination of the records of "Shakespeare" publication reveals a similar gap. There was no new play published with any appearance of authentication; the 1602 publication of the *Merry Wives of Windsor* being, the authorities state, a "pirated" issue. For it is curious that, although Stratfordians affirm that William Shakspere published none of the plays, they nevertheless discriminate between "pirated" and authorized issues: the "pirated" being, it is presumed, made up by publishers from actors' copies, and not from complete versions.

With the Lord Chamberlain's company apparently in a state of suspended animation we are naturally disposed to ask, what company of actors had been playing *The Merry Wives of Windsor?* Certainly the probability that this was the play which the servants of Oxford and Worcester performed that year at the Boar's Head Tavern is strengthened. At any rate the gap itself is a reality, and not a surmise; and this gap exactly corresponds to the complete year that Henry Wriothesley spent in the Tower: a very fair evidence that Wriothesley had been acting as intermediary between "Shakespeare" and others. It is then in the exact year in which "Shakespeare" was entirely without assistance from this agent, that the Earl of Oxford reappears in connection with the performance of some play, at the identical tavern associated with

Falstaff; and publishers get hold of actors' copies of *The Merry Wives of Windsor.*

Oxford and the Queen's Company.

To the interesting chain of evidence presented by Oxford's association with the Boar's Head Tavern in 1602 we have now to add an important link. In the following year there occurred the death of Queen Elizabeth, and, again quoting from Sir Sidney Lee:

> On May 19th, 1603, James I, very soon after his accession, extended to Shakespeare and other members of the Lord Chamberlain's company a very marked and valuable recognition. To them be granted under royal letters patent a license freely to use and exercise the art and faculty of playing comedies, tragedies (etc.) . . . The company was thenceforth styled the King's Company.[186]

Then in a footnote he adds,

> At the same time the *Earl of Worcester's company* [that is to say the company associated with Oxford's at the Boar's Head Tavern] was taken into the Queen's patronage, and its members were known as the Queen's servants.[187]

It will, we believe, be readily acknowledged that, without being actually identified with the company that was staging the "Shakespeare" dramas, the Earl of Oxford has now been brought, through the medium of the Boar's Head Tavern and the Earl of Worcester's company, into very close contact with what is usually styled Shakespeare's company. It is important to emphasize the fact that the special reference to these companies in connection with the "Boar's Head" is not one selected from a number, but is the only reference of its kind in that connection. Similarly, it may be worth remarking that the only dramatic companies in any way associated with the family records of William Shakspere at Stratford were "The Queen's Company and the Earl of Worcester's Company" of an earlier date. For, in the palmier days

---

[186] Lee, *Life*, p. 238.
[187] Lee, *Life*, p. 239.

of Shakspere's father "each [of these companies] received from John Shakspere an official welcome."[188] This is the single piece of information that our search has elicited in any way connecting the Shakspere family at Stratford with the drama of Queen Elizabeth's day. This last fact, however, in the absence of fuller particulars, we are content to put in, not as evidence, but as an interesting and probably accidental coincidence.

Oxford's death.

In 1601, then, Oxford took part in the Essex trial. In 1601 he was associated with what was afterwards the Queen's Players in the performance of some unknown play at the Boar's Head Tavern, Eastcheap. In 1603 he officiated at the coronation of James. On June 24th, 1604, he died and was buried at Hackney Church. Unfortunately the old church was demolished about the year 1790, so that it is improbable that the exact spot where his remains lie will ever be located. This we feel to be a real national loss. We cannot believe, however, that the English nation will acquiesce permanently in the neglect of the place where "Shakespeare" lies buried.

The year of Oxford's death (1604), it will be noticed, is the year in which the great series of Shakespearean dramas culminated. *Hamlet* is assigned to the year 1602. It was first published in an incomplete form in the year 1603, and in 1604 was issued the drama substantially as we now have it. This point we shall have to discuss more explicitly in our next chapter. The tragedy which is universally accepted as the author's supreme achievement belongs, therefore, to the year of Edward de Vere's death; and the last words of Hamlet—the passage we quote at the opening of this series of biographical chapters—may almost be accepted as Oxford's dying words. *Othello*, too, has been assigned to 1604 although it was not printed until 1622; that is to say, six years after the death of William Shakspere, the reputed author.

---

[188] Lee, *Life*, p. 10.

Oxford's character and reputation.

The actual details so far recorded of Oxford's life are of the most meagre description, and hardly furnish materials for an adequate biography; but if what we are now contending respecting the authorship of Shakespeare's works be finally established we shall probably, in the course of time, learn more of him than of almost any other man in history. In his case we shall have not the mere externals of life, which never quite show forth the man, but the infinitely varied play of his very soul in the most masterly exposition of human nature that exists anywhere in the world's literature. Although these things mainly concern the future, there is one thing which must be said at once, and an important claim that must be immediately entered on his behalf.

Many generous pronouncements on "Shakespeare" have already been made in the belief that the Stratford man was the actual dramatist. Now, apart from the writings practically nothing is known of the personality of the one who has hitherto been credited with them. These generous estimates of "Shakespeare," being almost wholly inferred from the plays he has left us, must in all honesty be passed on to Edward de Vere when he is accepted as the author. They are his by right. We cannot go back upon the judgments that have been so passed upon "Shakespeare," simply because it transpires that the Stratford man is not he. By the adoption of his mask the author of the plays has therefore secured for himself a judgment stripped of the bias of "vulgar scandal." He has, by revealing himself in his plays, trapped the world, as it were, into passing a more impartial verdict upon himself than would otherwise have been accorded, and given a signal check to its tendency to hang the dog with a bad name.

The references to him, which we have come across in the course of our investigations, have frequently taken the form of condemnatory expressions, altogether unsupported, or most inadequately tested by facts. All these must now be subjected to a searching revision. Having been for so long the victim of "cunning policy," he has, at length, become entitled to such personal appreciation as sober judgment has pronounced upon "Shakespeare" from a consideration of the writings. What the world has written in this connection it has written, and must be prepared to stand by.

CHAPTER XIV

POSTHUMOUS CONSIDERATIONS

ALTHOUGH Shakespeare's powers showed no sign of exhaustion, he reverted in 1607 to his earlier habit of collaboration, and with another's aid composed *Timon of Athens*, etc.[189]

SIR SIDNEY LEE.

An unfinished task.

We have seen that up to the time of the death of Edward de Vere new Shakespearean plays and printed issues of plays formerly staged were appearing at a phenomenal rate. These we have regarded as literary transformations of what had previously existed as stage plays. Our next question is whether Shakespeare's writings, as we now have them, represent a completed or an uncompleted work. Even under the old supposition of an author who spent the last years of his life in retirement from literary work this question has already been answered, and the answer given has again constituted one of the paradoxes of literature. For we are assured that the greatest genius that has appeared in English literature, when he had reached his maturity, and when there was no sign of failing powers, having lined his pockets well with money, retired from his literary labours, leaving in the hands of stage managers the manuscripts of incomplete plays, that others, at a later date, were called upon to finish. Shakespeare's work is therefore admittedly an unfinished performance.

Unfinished performances of great geniuses are not unknown in the world, but when they appear one explanation alone accounts for them—an utter inability to proceed: usually death.

---

[189] Lee, *Life*, p. 251.

To neither William Shakspere nor to Bacon nor to anyone else whose name has been raised in this connection does such an explanation apply. In all these cases we must assume the deliberate abandonment of the work for other interests. In the case of Edward de Vere alone do we get the natural explanation that the writer was cut off in the midst of his work, leaving unpublished some plays that he may have considered finished, and others published later, either unfinished or as they had been finished by other writers.

Geniuses and their works.

To suppose that "Shakespeare," having attained the highest rank as a play-writer whilst still in the heyday of his powers, should, on approaching his zenith, have reverted to his earlier practice of collaboration with others—the master-hand in the craft returning to the expedients of his prentice days—is to deny to him the possession of ordinary common sense. And to suppose that he was so indifferent to the fate of his own manuscripts as to leave them to drift amongst unknown actors, without arrangements for their preservation and publication, is to suppose him incapable of measuring their value. Yet all this is implied in the Stratfordian view, and much of it in the Baconian.

Under the De Vere theory the whole situation assumes for the first time a rational and commonsense appearance. Prevented by death from completely finishing his task, he had nevertheless been speeding up the issue of his works for some years beforehand, and had friends sufficiently in his confidence to safeguard his manuscripts and to preserve his incognito when he was gone. The admittedly unfinished character of Shakespeare's work we maintain, then, can only be rationally explained by supposing that death, and not retirement, had brought his literary activities to a close. This is the first point to be fixed in the statement of our argument from the posthumous point of view.

"Fell Sergeant Death's" Arrest.

When we turn to examine the issue of Shakespeare's works in

relation to Edward de Vere's death, we find facts of a specially interesting and illuminating character. We have already indicated the tremendous outpouring attributed to the six preceding years. Let us now see what happens immediately after his death.

There are three points of view from which the dating of the plays may be regarded. First, we have the system of conjectural dating based upon the assumption that the Stratford man was the author; secondly, there are the ascertained dates of the first known publication of the plays; and thirdly, we have the recorded dates of the various early issues, including revised editions and mere reprints.

Beginning with the first, that upon which much of the argument in the last chapter is based, we find, in spite of the fact that it is largely guesswork, founded upon the very views of authorship which we are now questioning, it indicates a distinct check in the issues at the time of Oxford's death. Professor Dowden attributes but one play, *King Lear*, to the year 1605, and one, *Macbeth*, to the year 1606: and even this last is treated both by Sir Sidney Lee and by the compiler of the "Falstaff" Notes as very doubtful. At the same time, 1607 is chosen by the former as the year when plays again began to appear in which Shakespeare's work was mixed with that of contemporary writers. Even this hypothetical dating of the plays indicates, therefore, some radical change about the time when Edward de Vere died.

Lear and Macbeth.

As *King Lear* and *Macbeth* are ascribed to the two years immediately following the death of Edward de Vere it has been necessary to examine somewhat closely the data from which such a conclusion has been drawn. Most of this has been brought together in the appendix to the *Variorum Shakespeare*, and the point on which much of the argument is made to turn is the suggested allusions to the union of the English and Scottish crowns, contained in the plays. The rest seem determined by the general scheme of finding reasonable spaces of time in the life of

William Shakspere to get the work done. These allusions to the union of the crowns would be very natural to one who had occupied a foremost position at the coronation, if he happened to be trimming up these particular plays at the time: on the other hand, the general scheme of dating the works does not, as we have seen, apply to the Earl of Oxford.

The most significant fact, however, which the study of other authorities brings to light is that, instead of fixing a definite year for each of these two plays, they assign a period of three years, 1603 to 1606, during which they assert these two plays might have been written. It will thus be seen that even these two may fairly be added to the apparently amazing production of the last six or seven years of De Vere's lifetime.

Of *King Lear*, the *Variorum Shakespeare* remarks that "Drake (in *Shakespeare and his Times*) thinks its production is to be attributed to 1604. . . . I think we must be content with the term of 3 years [1603-1606]; no date more precise than this will probably ever gain general acceptance."[190] The case of *Macbeth* is even more interesting. Several authorities give again the 1603-1606 period, and Grant White affirms, "I have little hesitation in referring the production to the period 1604-1605."[191] With this in mind, the quotations given in the *Variorum Shakespeare* from Messrs. Clark and Wright (Clarendon Press Series) showing that *Macbeth* was a work of collaboration between Shakespeare and another are of great importance. The question of an arranged collaboration versus interpolation is raised, and the following conclusion arrived at:

> On the whole we incline to think that the play was *interpolated after Shakespeare's death*—or, at least, after he had withdrawn from

---

[190] *King Lear*, Vol. V of the *New Variorum Edition of Shakespeare*, p. 380. The first part of this quotation—"Drake thinks its production is to be attributed to 1604,"—accurately conveys Drake's conclusion but is only a paraphrase. The second part—that beginning with "I think we must be . . ."—should be attributed not to Drake but to the editor, Horace Howard Furness. In addition, the word "be" should be replaced with "remain."

[191] *Macbeth*, Vol. II of the *New Variorum Edition of Shakespeare*, p. 386. White's exact statement was "I have little hesitation in referring the production to the period between October, 1604, and August, 1605."

all connection with the theatre.[192]

Had the works been dissociated from the Stratford man, or rather, if they had been avowedly anonymous from the first, the study of these particular plays would have justified a suspicion that their writer had died about 1604: the year of the death of Edward de Vere. This furnishes the second stage in the development of our posthumous argument.

The last plays.

After *King Lear* and *Macbeth* we enter upon the period which begins with *Timon of Athens*, and finishes with *Henry VIII*: the former, according to the passage we have quoted from Sir Sidney Lee, marking the beginning of work in which "collaboration" becomes a pronounced feature, and the latter, in which "Shakespeare" is supposed to lay down his pen, being generally recognized as largely the work of Fletcher. In this period we have great dramas that are no mere "prentice work," in which are passages and dramatic situations revealing this great genius at his highest. Yet it is in this work that we meet with deficiencies of poetic finish on the one hand, and the recognized intervention of strange pens on the other: a state of things to which we cannot imagine even a third-rate writer submitting voluntarily.

With all deference to Shakespearean scholars, we are bound to say that, in respect to the work assigned to this period, wonder and praise seem to have got the better discrimination. There is so much here of "Shakespeare's" best, that there has been a fatal tendency to regard as good what is more than questionable. Even the faults of those who have been called in to finish the work, or possibly even of the author's first rough drafts, have been treated as "Shakespeare's" most advanced conceptions, and as marks of his poetic development. We would specify, in particular, the uneven versification due to additional syllables in the lines, faulty rhythm and "weak endings," which have made so much of the later so-called "blank-verse" hardly distinguishable to the ear from honest prose.

---

[192] *Macbeth*, Vol. II, *New Variorum Edition*, p. 392. The original does not have a dash in the middle of the sentence.

Disguised prose.

Our commentators assure us that this "rag-time" verse shows us the mighty genius bursting his fetters. The real roots of this eulogized emancipation will, however, be readily perceived from a consideration of the following passages from North's Plutarch and Shakespeare's *Coriolanus* (one of these later plays), for which we are indebted to Sir Sidney Lee's work:

> *North's Plutarch* (prose).
> I am Caius Marcus, who hath done
> to thyself particularly, and to all the Volces
> generally great hurt and mischief; which
> I cannot deny for my surname of
> Coriolanus that I bear.

> *Shakespeare's Coriolanus* (blank verse!)
> My name is Caius Marcus who hath done
> To thee particularly, and to all the Volces
> Great hurt and mischief; thereto witness may
> My surname Coriolanus.

At last, then, the secret of this great literary emancipation is out. The people who were "finishing off" these later plays took straightforward prose, either from the works of others, or from rough notes collected by "Shakespeare" in preparing his dramas, and chopped it up, along with a little dressing, to make it look in print something like blank verse. That "Shakespeare," living, could have voluntarily suffered such work to go forth as his is inconceivable. The result of such a method has been the production of faulty rhythm and "weak endings," and these have been hailed by learned Shakespeareans as tokens of a great poetic liberation. On this plan even a schoolboy might conceivably give us an edition of Newton's *Principia* in blank-verse.

Cymbeline (another of these later plays) is also strongly marked by "weak endings" and interpolations; and both Professor Dowden and Stanton recognize in the play the participation of an inferior hand.

Of *Antony and Cleopatra*, Sir Sidney Lee remarks: "The source of the tragedy is the life of Antonius in North's Plutarch.

Shakespeare followed closely the historical narrative, and assimilated not merely its temper, but in the first three acts, much of its phraseology."[193] The case of *The Tempest* we reserve for special examination in the appendix.

The general stamp, then, of this later work is greatness, suggestive of unfailing powers; and defects suggestive of unfinished workmanship and the intervention of inferior pens: a combination which we claim can only be explained by the death of the dramatist.

Dates of publication.

With the Earl of Oxford substituted for William Shakspere much of the guesswork relating to the time when the plays were *written* ceases to have any value: what is of most consequence now is the date of actual *issue*. We have, therefore, compiled a list of the dates when the first printed issues of the plays appeared; and although errors may have crept in, owing to the relatively subordinate position hitherto assigned to this particular group of facts, it will presently appear that their general trend is sufficiently well marked for our purpose. *Venus* and *Lucrece* were published in 1593 and 1594 respectively: an interval of four years passed before the printing of the plays began, and even then the first of the series had not Shakespeare's name attached. *The Sonnets* are included in the following list because of their special importance.

THREE PERIODS OF SHAKESPEAREAN PUBLICATION AFTER
VENUS AND *LUCRECE.*

COMPILED FROM NOTES TO *POCKET FALSTAFF* EDITION.[194]

1st Period (1597-1603).
  1. *Richard II.*
  2. *Richard III.*
  3. *Romeo and Juliet.*

---

[193] Lee, *Life*, p. 254.
[194] *"Pocket Falstaff" Edition of Shakespeare's Complete Works*, vol. 40: "Glossery and Notes," pp. 99-118.

   4. *Love's Labour's Lost.*
   5. *Henry IV*, part 1.
   6. *Henry IV*, part 2.
   7. *Henry V.*
   8. *Merchant of Venice.*
   9. *Midsummer Night's Dream.*
   10. *Much Ado About Nothing.*
   11. *Titus Andronicus.*
   12. *Merry Wives of Windsor* (pirated).
   13. *Hamlet* (pirated): authentic in 1604.

Arrested publication (1604-1607 inclusive).
                    No new publication.

2nd Period (1608-9).
   1. *King Lear.*
   2. *Troilus and Cressida.*
   3. *Pericles.*
   4. *Sonnets.*

3rd Period (1622-23).
   1622 *Othello.*
   1623 (Folio Edition).

   All the remainder, twenty plays in all, including such well-known names as,

   As You Like It.
   Taming of the Shrew.
   Macbeth.
   Tempest.
   Julius Caesar.
   King John.
   Twelfth Night.
   Measure for Measure.
   Two Gentleman of Verona.
   All's Well that Ends Well.

   In the six years from 1597 to 1603 it will be noticed there

were no less than thirteen plays of Shakespeare's printed and published for the first time. Some of these had been staged in previous years, and others were then being both staged and printed for the first time. This brings us to the year before Oxford's death.

The 1604 stoppage.

From 1603 to 1608, according to this record, no single play was printed and published for the first time. Even supposing there are mistakes and oversights in these notes, there is still a large enough margin for us to affirm confidently that the publication of Shakespeare's plays was arrested in a marked degree for several years after the death of Edward de Vere. We may add that this arrested publication is fully borne out by Professor Dowden's table, Sir Sidney Lee's account, and every other record we have seen. This gives us the third and probably the most telling of our arguments from the posthumous standpoint.

If, again, we turn to the issuing of mere reprints, entailing no literary work properly speaking, we find that after 1604 there was nothing reprinted until 1608, except the two popular plays of *Hamlet* and *Richard III*, for which we might judge there would be a considerable demand: and even these were only reprinted once, namely, in 1605. It would therefore seem that all kinds of issues, including even pirated and surreptitious editions, as well as mere reprints, were definitely checked at the time of Oxford's death: a fact which should give Shakespearean scholars "furiously to think" respecting much of the so-called "pirated" work. So complete an arrest of publication at this precise moment is almost startling in its character; the slight resumption which took place after an interval of four years is not less striking.

The 1608-9 revival.

In 1608 and 1609 there was a slight revival of Shakespearean publication involving, however, only three plays and the *Sonnets*. Nothing else was newly published until *Othello* in 1622, and the Folio edition of Shakespeare in 1623, six and seven years respectively after the death of the Stratford Shakspere. Even according to the Stratfordian view, then, most of Shakespeare's works were published posthumously. In the Folio edition no less than twenty out of the thirty-seven, so called, Shakespearean plays were printed and published for the first time—so far as anything has yet been discovered. Of the three plays appearing in this temporary revival one is *Pericles*, which was published in 1609; the same year as the *Sonnets* appeared. Now the manner of the publication of these two, *Pericles* and the *Sonnets*, is as strong a confirmation as could be wished for that the dramatist himself was by this time dead. We shall take *Pericles* first, quoting again the "Falstaff" notes.[195]

Pericles.

Pericles is mainly from other hands than Shakespeare's, probably those of Wilkins and Rowley. It was first printed in quarto in 1609 with the following title: *Pericles . . . as it hath been divers times acted by his Majesty's servants at the Globe. . . . By William Shakspere. . . ."*

This play was therefore issued with the full imprimatur of William Shakspere and the Globe Theatre, although it is mainly from other hands than Shakespeare's. Contrast this with the plays issued during the life of De Vere under the "Shakespeare" nom-de-plume. They are:

1598	*Love's Labour's Lost.*
1600	*Henry IV*, part 2.
	The Merchant of Venice.
	A Midsummer Night's Dream.
	Much Ado About Nothing.
1602	*The Merry Wives of Windsor* (pirated).
1603	*Hamlet* (curtailed and pirated).
1604	*Hamlet* (authorized).

Leaving out of consideration the plays published in 1597 and 1598 without any author's name attached, the important point to notice is the character of the plays which received the Shakespeare imprimatur up to the time of the death of De Vere.

---

[195] *"Pocket Falstaff,"* vol. 40: "Glossery and Notes," pp. 111-12.

No one would venture to say of any one of these that it was "mainly from other hands" than Shakespeare's, whatever opinion he might hold as to the quality or completeness of the play itself. It is of interest, too, that although *Titus Andronicus* was published in the same period it was without the name of "Shakespeare." The natural conclusion is that when in 1609 *Pericles* was published, with all the éclat of a genuine Shakespearean play, the controlling hand of "Shakespeare" himself had been removed. Those who were directing matters may have believed it to have been his: what is more probable is that it was they who had called in assistance to finish a play which he had left unfinished.

The Sonnets.

Take now the issue of the *Sonnets*, a problem that has agitated and puzzled the literary world for so long. We need not at present discuss the question of who W. H. and T. T. may have been, or attempt to clear up the mystery of their association with the publication of these poems; but ninety percent of the mystery of the publication disappears as soon as we suppose a posthumous issue. Indeed the dedication to the *Sonnets* has been telling us for three hundred years, in the plainest of terms, that the writer was already dead. It may be a curiosity of language, but it is nevertheless a fact, that we only speak of a man being "ever-living" after he is actually dead; and in the dedication of the *Sonnets* their author is referred to as "our ever-living poet." Who then was this "ever-living poet"? Surely not the man who, to all appearances, had deserted or was preparing to desert the high interests of literature and drama and attend to his land and houses at Stratford, and who was being completely ignored by those who were issuing the full literary text of what were supposed to be his great personal poems. Neither is it likely that "our ever-living poet" was at that moment discharging the functions of solicitor-general with his eye upon the wool-sack, or planning his "Great Instauration."

A publication absurdity.

To suppose that a set of no less than one hundred and fifty sonnets, many of them of exquisite quality, touching the most private experiences and sentiments of a great genius, whose work proclaims an almost fastidious regard on his part for his productions, could, while he was yet alive, have found their way into print, surreptitiously, with strange initials attached, without his knowledge, consent, signature, or immediate and emphatic protest, is as extravagant a supposition as could be imagined. Yet all this is implied in the Stratfordian theory of authorship. The only hypothesis that adequately explains the situation is that the poet himself was dead and his manuscript had passed into other hands. The dedication itself proclaims the fact, and the simultaneous issue of *Pericles* confirms it.

We shall close the discussion of these two publications with a sentence bearing on each from Sir Sidney Lee's *Life of Shakespeare*.

Pericles: "The bombastic form of title shows that Shakespeare had no hand in the publication" [1609].[196]

Sonnets: "He [Shakespeare] cannot be credited with any responsibility for the publication of Thorpe's collection of his sonnets in 1609."[197]

King Lear and Troilus.

In respect to the other two plays published in 1608-9 it will be enough to give the following quotations from the same work. *King Lear* . . .

> was defaced by many gross typographical errors. Some of the sheets were never subjected to any correction of the press. The publisher, Butter, endeavoured to make some reparation . . . by issuing a second quarto which was designed to free the text of the most obvious incoherences of the first quarto. But the effort was not successful. Uncorrected sheets disfigured the second quarto little less conspicuously than the first.[198]

---

[196] Lee, *Life*, p. 253.
[197] Lee, *Life*, p. 298.
[198] Lee, *Life*, p. 249.

Troilus and Cressida . . .

> Exceptional obscurity attaches to the circumstances of the publication. . . . After a pompous title-page there was inserted for the first time in the case of a play by Shakespeare that was published in his lifetime, an advertisement or preface . . . the publishers paid bombastic and high-flown compliments to Shakespeare . . . and defiantly boasted that the grand possessors of the manuscript deprecated its publication.[199]

This is the particular play which we pointed out in an earlier chapter probably contains the matter of Oxford's early play of *Agamemnon and Ulysses.*

William Shakspere of Stratford was evidently not even the holder of the manuscript in this instance: and certainly the expression "grand possessors" is worth attention. The point that matters, however, is that neither the author himself, nor the owners of the authentic manuscript, had anything to do with this particular publication. And as the same has been shown to be true of the author's relation to the other three issues of this period, all four, without exception, give unmistakable support to the views we are now advocating. This, then, is the position. *We have a flood of Shakespearean plays being published authentically right up to the year before the death of Edward de Vere, then a sudden stop, and nothing more published with any appearance of proper authorization for nearly twenty years,* although the reputed author was alive and active during twelve of these years. We have no hesitation in saying that the simple fact we have enunciated in our last sentence furnishes an argument it is hardly possible to strengthen further.

Hamlet.

Decisive as may appear the fact we have just stated there remains one other consideration which brings us into still closer contact with the actual date of Oxford's death. It will be seen that on either the Stratfordian or the De Vere theory, the last play published with any appearance of proper authorization during Shakespeare's lifetime was *Hamlet.* An examination of the facts connected with the printing of this play is therefore of special

---

[199] Lee, *Life,* p. 235.

importance. We have included it in the 1597-1603 period because a quarto edition of it appeared in the last year of this period. The 1603 quarto edition, however, is described by Sir Sidney Lee as "a piratical and carelessly transcribed copy of Shakespeare's first draft of the play."[200] In 1604 the Second Quarto edition, he tells us, was published "from a more complete and accurate manuscript."[201] He further adds:

> The concluding words of the title-page were intended to stamp its predecessor as surreptitious and unauthentic. But it is clear that the Second Quarto was not a perfect version of the play. A third version figured in the Folio of 1623. Here many passages not to be found in the quartos appeared for the first time, but a few others that appear in the quartos are omitted. The Folio text probably came nearest to the original manuscript.[202]

Now, with an interval of nearly twenty years between the second and third versions of a play which had evidently been subjected to constant revision and development, whilst simple reprints of the second edition had appeared in the interval, what is the natural inference in view of the facts already pointed out? Simply that the author was removed by death whilst actually engaged upon the particular play, at the time when the Second Quarto was published, namely 1604, the exact year of the death of Edward de Vere. We feel quite justified in claiming that 'Shakespeare,' whoever he may have been, died in 1604 almost in the act of revising *Hamlet*, just as at a later day Goethe died almost in the act of finishing his greatest work *Faust*.

First Folio.

Of the first Folio edition of "Shakespeare's" plays (1623) we shall again quote a passage from Sir Sidney Lee,

> John Heming and Henry Condell were nominally responsible for the venture, but it seems to have been suggested by a small syndicate of printers and publishers who undertook all pecuniary responsibility. . . . The dedication . . . was signed by Heming and Condell. . . . The same signatures were appended to a succeeding address. . . . In both addresses the actors made pretension to a

---

[200] Lee, *Life*, p. 231.
[201] Lee, *Life*, p. 231.
[202] Lee, *Life*, p. 232.

larger responsibility for the enterprise than they really incurred.[203]

In a word, they were being employed as a blind, and their part was overdone. It is evident, at any rate, that the initiative did not come from the two actors. As, therefore, they formed the only connecting link between the Stratford Shakspere and the publication of the plays, it is obvious that they had been brought into the business in order to throw a veil over others who did not wish to appear in it. The silence of William Shakspere's will respecting these important manuscripts has already received attention.

The further fact that the plays now published for the first time were not from the curtailed play-actor's copies, such as had furnished the text of several pirated issues, but the full literary text; in some instances, as we have seen in the case of *Hamlet*, even improved versions of plays that had already enjoyed a proper literary publication, has also been considered and ought to dispose completely of the claim that the collection had been brought together by actors from the stores of unspecified theatre managers, or fished up out of the lumber rooms behind the scenes. Such a view does not accord with common sense and would hardly have been credited in any other connection. The only feasible supposition is that the documents had been in the safe keeping of responsible people, and that the death seven years before of the man who had formerly served as a mask rendered necessary the "Heming and Condell" subterfuge, if the incognito was to be preserved. In a word, the resumption of authorized publication after being arrested for eighteen or nineteen years is marked by the same elements of mysteriousness and secrecy, in which everything connecting the man and his work has been involved, and furnishes its own quota of evidence that the master's hand had been removed for very many years.

Shakespeare's retirement and Oxford's death.

Not only does the time of the death of De Vere mark an arrest in the publication of "Shakespeare's" works, it also marks, according to orthodox authorities, some kind of a crisis in the

---

[203] Lee, *Life*, p. 318.

affairs of William Shakspere. Charles and Mary Cowden Clarke, in the *Life of Shakspere* published along with their edition of the plays, date his retirement to Stratford in the year 1604 precisely. After pointing out that in 1605 he is described as "William Shakspere, Gentleman, of Stratford-on-Avon," they continued: "Several things conduced to make him resolve upon ceasing to be an actor, and 1604 has generally been considered the date when he did so."[204] Several other writers, less well known, repeat this date; and works of reference, written for the most part some years ago, place his retirement in the same year: "There is no doubt he never meant to return to London, except for business visits, after 1604."[205]

This is probably the most exact and startling synchronism furnished by Stratfordians. We have elsewhere given reasons for our belief that his actual retirement from London was much earlier than this. The fact that this date has been chosen is evidence, however, that Shakespearean records are indicative of some crisis at this precise time. More recent authorities, finding it necessary probably to give a date more in accord with accepted ideas as to the writing of the plays, and the continuance of William Shakspere's material interests in London, have added eight or nine years to this, during which time his forces are supposed to have been divided between Stratford and London, but during which period he has left no traces of domiciliation in London, and no "incidents." In either case the time of De Vere's death corresponds to the time assigned for William Shakspere's retirement, partial or complete. The latter's work in London was practically done, and he could no longer remain in constant

---

[204] This exact quotation does not appear in the 1866, 1869, 1870, 1874, or 1893 editions of Charles and Mary Cowden Clarke's *The Plays of William Shakespeare*. The closest wording that exists is in "The Story of Shakespeare's Life" in the 1866 edition, which states (p. vii), "1604 is the probable date of Shakespeare's retirement from the stage as an actor; and the lack of his prudence and discretion in counsel was adverse to the company. His control and presence ceasing, the ill effects were felt; but it is probably that at the age of forty, which he had now attained, Shakespeare felt that he had earned a right to enjoy that comparative leisure and withdrawal from the more active bustle of public life, which most men of ardent natures and imaginative temperaments feel creep over them as they advance in maturity."

[205] See footnote 65, p. 60.

contact with the old life without a danger that the part he had played as mask to a great genius should be detected.

William Shakspere's purchases.

It is worthwhile noticing that William Shakspere's first purchases of property extended from the time of the first publication of the plays, in 1597, up to the year following De Vere's death, when, in 1605, he purchased "for £440 of Ralph Hubbard an unexpired term"[206] of the lease of certain tithes; and another important purchase is recorded for 1613, the year following the death of the second Lady Oxford. Not much of this kind of transaction is recorded of the interval between the two events. The only one we have found was in 1610, when he purchased some land adjacent to his estate. This, it will be observed, was in the year following the publication of *Pericles* and the *Sonnets*. His purchase in 1613 of property in London for £140 was "his last investment in real estate."[207]

There is certainly a distinct suggestiveness worth considering about this correspondence of dates, especially as it is reported that on one occasion he received a large sum of money (£1000, it is said) from the Earl of Southampton for the express purpose of buying property. However lucrative theatre shareholding may have been, authorship, at any rate, was not then the road to affluence; whilst an actor, who seems not to have risen above playing the Ghost in *Hamlet*, would hardly be in enjoyment of the plums of his profession.

William Shakspere's role.

Whatever opinions may be formed of William Shakspere on other grounds, we do not wish to suggest any reproach for the part he took in assisting Oxford to hide his identification with the authorship of the plays. The former's role in life was indeed a humble one from the standpoint of literature, and, in view of the glory he has enjoyed for so long, becomes now somewhat ignominious. Neverthess, whatever inducements may have been held out to him he fulfilled his part loyally. His task was to

---

[206] Lee, *Life*, p. 212.
[207] Lee, *Life*, p. 276.

assist a remarkable but unfortunate man in the performance of a
work, the value of which he himself could probably not have
estimated; and though it will be the duty of Englishmen to see
that the master is ultimately put in possession of the honours that
have for so long been enjoyed by the man, it will be impossible
ever totally to dissociate from the work and personality of the
great one, the figure and name of his helper. Such, at any rate,
would be the desire of Oxford, if we may interpret it in the light
of the principle of *noblesse oblige* that shines through the great
Shakespearean dramas. We may even suppose that Oxford had
some hand in defending William Shakspere from Greene's attack.
Chettle's defence of him that he was "civil" and that "*divers of
worship have reported* his uprightness in dealing, which argues his
honesty,"[208] is distinctly suggestive of some such intervention on
the part of Oxford. The terms of the defence are undoubtedly
much more appropriate to a testimonial to a faithful servant than
a tribute to the supreme genius of the age.

Loyal helpers.

That such a work of secrecy could not have been done
without the loyal cooperation of others goes without saying. In
order to maintain our thesis, however, it is not necessary that we
should solve the problem of who his associates were, or of how
they went about their work. It is reasonable to suppose that
Henry Wriothesley was one, and it is natural to conclude that the
wife with whom he was living in evident comfort was another. We
may venture a guess, too, that his cousin, Horatio de Vere, the
eminent soldier, may have been a third.

We should imagine that Horatio de Vere was a man after
Edward's own heart; and, although the former spent much of his
life abroad, he was living in England in the years when the
Shakespearean publication was resumed (1608-9), and also when
the 1623 Folio edition was published. The publication of the
Sonnets in 1609 and the plays in 1623, many of which would
otherwise have perished precisely as Oxford's plays are supposed
to have done, may have been the final discharge of part of a
solemn trust. The publication of the plays ought indeed to have

---

[208] Lee, *Life*, p. 60.

taken place during the lifetime of William Shakspere, whose death probably created a perplexing situation for those entrusted with their publication; a situation from which, as we have seen, they tried to escape by the "Heming and Condell" device. Horatio de Vere's absence from the country during the latter years of William Shakspere's life may account for the fatal delay. This, however, is merely interesting speculation and forms no essential part of the argument.

Henry Wriothesley.

The part taken by Henry Wriothesley first in arranging for a performance of *Richard II* in connection with the 1601 insurrection, and then for a private performance of *Love's Labour's Lost*, to entertain the new Queen in 1603, has already been mentioned. So that, although ten years had elapsed since Shakespeare began to dedicate poems to him, he was still not only deeply interested in, but actively occupied with, the doings of the so-called "Shakspere's company," and the Shakespearean plays. In the autumn of 1599, however, his theatrical interests were so pronounced as to provoke special remark: he is then reported to have been spending much of his time every day at the theatres. In view of the enterprising temperament he subsequently evinced, such a mode of spending his time is not likely to have arisen from mere idleness; it is much more likely to have been connected with some definite purpose. Now, the following year was the most important year in the history of Shakespearean publication during the lifetime of either Edward de Vere or William Shakspere. For in the one year 1600 there were published or reprinted no less than six plays.

1. *Henry IV*, part 2.
2. *Henry V* (probably pirated, however).
3. *The Merchant of Venice* (2 editions).
4. *A Midsummer Night's Dream* (2 editions).
5. *Much Ado About Nothing.*
6. *Titus Andronicus.*

The 1602 suspension.

In 1601 *Southampton was imprisoned, and all publication of proper literary 'Versions of the plays stopped immediately*; only the pirated actors' drafts of *Hamlet* and *The Merry Wives of Windsor* appearing during his imprisonment. It looks as if, at that time, the complete issue of the plays had been decided upon and begun, and that Wriothesley's imprisonment had interfered with the plans. After his liberation it was immediately resumed with an authorized version of *Hamlet*. Then De Vere's death occurred, and all further authorized publication was suspended till 1622 and 1623. Meanwhile Southampton dropped William Shakspere, and took to other pursuits. It cannot be denied, therefore, that there is much to support the view that Henry Wriothesley acted as intermediary between the Earl of Oxford and those who were staging and publishing the dramas. The fact that his step-father, Thomas Henneage, was Treasurer of the Chamber, and therefore responsible for the financial side of all the business, is not without significance. The special relationship between Oxford and Southampton, to be considered in connection with *Shakespeare's Sonnets*, gives to these matters a position of first importance.

After the events connected with Southampton's liberation, including, we are assured on the best authority, a reference in one of Shakespeare's sonnets, Sir Sidney Lee informs us that "there is no trace of further relations between"[209] Southampton and William Shakspere. That is to say, the death of Edward de Vere is followed immediately by the loss of all traces of a personal connection between William Shakspere and the only contemporary whom the poet has directly associated with the issue of his works.

The second Lady Oxford.

With regard to De Vere's widow, the second Lady Oxford, we remark that she died in 1612, whilst 1613 is the later date assigned by some authorities for the final and complete retirement of William Shakspere from the scene of London dramatic and literary life. The substantial fact upon which this conclusion rests is that there is a record of his presence in London in that year, attending to business. Curiously enough this business had nothing to do with either dramatic or literary affairs, but wholly

---

[209] Lee, *Life*, p. 396.

with the taking over of property: "his last investment in real estate."

The series of sonnets closes.

To these general posthumous considerations one remains to be added. The particular sonnet which, according to Sir Sidney Lee and other authorities, welcomed Southampton's liberation from prison in 1603, is one of the last of the series; and,

> Sonnet cvii, apparently the last of the series, makes references to events that took place in 1603—to Queen Elizabeth's death and the accession of James I.[210]

In a word, the death of Edward de Vere brought to a close the series of sonnets that "Shakespeare" had begun some twelve or fourteen years before. Then for five or six years these sonnets lay, without a single one being added to their number, before the complete series was mysteriously given to the world by strangers (1609). And, although the Stratford man lived for yet other seven years, no further sonnets appeared from the pen of the greatest sonneteer that England has yet produced.

No amount of harping upon a point like this can possibly strengthen its significance; and the man who, viewing it in conjunction with the other points urged in this chapter, does not believe that "Shakespeare" died at the same time as Edward de Vere would not be persuaded though one (and only one) rose from the dead.

Résumé of chapter.

The following is a résumé of the various points established in this chapter:

1. The latest plays of Shakespeare, being finished by other hands, indicate that the dramatist had already passed away at the time to which they are allocated.

2. The plays usually ascribed to the years immediately following Oxford's death, especially *Macbeth*, furnish additional testimony that he was already dead, thus making the death of the dramatist synchronize with the death of Oxford.

---

[210] Lee, *Life*, p. 91.

3. The printed issue of the plays came to a sudden stop at the time of Oxford's death, and the slight resumption of issues in 1608 and 1609 furnishes further corroboration of the death of the dramatist.

4. The manner of the publication of the *Sonnets* in 1609 is strongly suggestive of the death of their author: the dedication seeming to testify directly to the fact.

5. Nothing of an authentic character was newly published from the time of Oxford's death till 1622 and 1623; six and seven years respectively after the death of William Shakspere.

6. The way in which the various issues of *Hamlet* appeared affords strong evidence that the author passed away in 1604, almost in the act of revising his greatest work.

7. The manner of the publication of the First Folio edition suggests that Heming and Condell were being used as a blind, by others who had special reasons for not being seen in the matter.

8. The time of Oxford's death marks, according to orthodox authorities, a crisis and definite change in the circumstances of William Shakspere of Stratford, and his partial or complete withdrawal from the dramatic life of London.

9. The time of Oxford's death marks the cessation of Henry Wriothesley's dealings with William Shakspere, and a pronounced change in his interests and pursuits.

10. Finally, the death of Edward de Vere, Earl of Oxford, brings to a sudden and complete close the series of sonnets which "Shakespeare" had been penning during many preceding years.

"Every fact in the universe," says one writer, "fits in with every other." To suppose that all the above considerations are merely fortuitous is to suggest that the very gods had conspired to make the death of "Shakespeare" seem to synchronize with the death of the Earl of Oxford in 1604. In other words our theory seems to be supported by nothing less than the principle of the universal harmony of truth. By way of comparison we therefore subjoin a list of the dates of the decease of the men whose names have at one time or another been brought into this problem, including the special name we have had the honour of introducing.

> Edward de Vere died 1604.
> Roger Manners, Earl of Rutland, died 1612.
> William Shakspere died 1616.
> Francis Bacon died 1626.
> Wm. Stanley, Sixth Earl of Derby, died 1640.

On the other hand, we cannot find a record of the death of any other literary man occurring about the year 1604: the nearest being that of Lyly, which occurred in 1606. And of course he is quite out of the question in such a connection. We have his own plays, and they furnish all the evidence needed.

Finishing a decisive stage.

We thus bring to a close the series of chapters in which an approximate biographical sequence has been attempted, and thus conclude the longest, most difficult, and most decisive part of the investigations we have undertaken. The necessities of argumentation have frequently involved the sacrifice of chronological order, and even the omission of interesting details. This must all be remedied when the biography of the real "Shakespeare" comes to be written. For the present our purpose has been, in accordance with the general plan of research, to proceed from the work, the personality, and the career of Edward de Vere, to the work of "Shakespeare"; and, reviewing the chapters as a whole, we make bold to claim that the mass and character of the evidence they contain will, when duly weighed, ensure the universal recognition of the authorship we would now substitute for the old Stratfordian tradition.

In displacing the Stratford Shakspere by the substitution of Edward de Vere we, no doubt, deprive the thought of "Shakespeare" of one element of attractiveness. It has been pleasant to think of the great dramatist, after all his labours, enjoying the rest and quietness of his retirement in a countryside to which his heart had ever reverted amidst the glory and excitement of his London career. If we lose this suggestion of the idyllic in the close of a great career, we replace it, at any rate, by a vigorous conception of tragic and poetic realism. The picture of a great soul, misunderstood, almost an outcast from his own social sphere, with defects of nature, to all appearances one of life's colossal failures, toiling on incessantly at his great tasks, yet willing to pass from life's stage having no name behind him but a discredited one: at last dying, as it would seem, almost with the pen between his fingers, immense things accomplished, but not all he had set out to do: this, it seems, will have for the manhood of the England that "Shakespeare" most certainly loved, a power of inspiration far beyond anything contained in the conception we have displaced.

CHAPTER XV

POETIC SELF-REVELATION: *THE SONNETS*

SHAKESPEARE is the only biographer of Shakespeare, and even he can tell nothing except to the Shakespeare in us.[211]

EMERSON.

Autobiography of the sonnets.

The line of investigation pursued throughout the greater part of these pages has been to search for indirect and unconscious self-expression on the part of "Shakespeare." Anything like deliberate and complete direct self-disclosure is not to be expected: otherwise there would have been no problem for us to solve. There is, however, between the two a form of what may be called an intentional self-expression and self-revelation, which the writer might, or might not, hope would lead at last to definite self-disclosure. Seeing, then, that we have insisted throughout on the distinction between the poet and the dramatist, and that Edward de Vere began and ended as a poet; a lyric poet at the outset, and in his last years, as we believe, converting his dramas into poems: our first task must be to take whatever poetic self-revelation "Shakespeare" may have given of himself, and see to what extent it may be regarded as a work of self-disclosure on the part of Edward de Vere. Shakespeare's work of poetic self-expression is, of course, the *Sonnets.* The idea that these poems are fantastic dramatic inventions with mystic meanings we feel to be a violation of all normal probabilities and precedents. Accepting them, therefore, as autobiographical, our next step must be to see how these poems, as a whole, stand related to the

---

[211] Ralph Waldo Emerson, *Representative Men.*

authorship theory we are now advancing.

Several points of accord between Edward de Vere and the "Shakespeare" disclosed in the *Sonnets* have already received attention in the course of our argument; these we shall now recapitulate.

Former references summarized.

1. It was from the *Sonnets* that we first of all deduced Shakespeare's personal attitude towards women: that curious combination of intense affectionateness with want of faith. All the passionate tenderness of his nature combined with mistrust runs through the set of sonnets addressed to the "dark lady"; whilst his lack of faith finds an additional expression in the sonnets addressed to the young man, who is

> not acquainted
> With shifting change as is false woman's fashion.

The same passionate affectionateness finds expression in Oxford's verse, whilst the passage just quoted from the *Sonnets* is the particular theme of the whole of the first poem of Oxford's we met with: that on "Women."

2. The writer of the *Sonnets*, notwithstanding the philosophic vigour of the poems, confesses to having "gone here and there and made himself a motley to the view"; which is strictly in accord with the "lightheadedness" and "eccentricity" that are attributed to Oxford, along with the high testimony that has been borne to the superiority of his powers both by contemporaries and modern writers—thus affording a contrast between his actual capacity and his external bearing which had not escaped the observation of Burleigh himself.

3. The *Sonnets* bear unmistakable testimony to the fact that the writer was one whose brow was stamped with "vulgar scandal"; whose good name had been lost, and who, at the time of writing the sonnets dealing with this theme, wished that his name should be buried with his body. That Edward de Vere was a man fallen into disrepute is the one fact about him that seems

to have been grasped by those who are at all acquainted with him. That it was a matter upon which he felt sore, as Shakespeare did, is shown by what is probably one of the most powerful of his poems; one on "The Loss of his Good Name."

4. Edward de Vere's loss, early in life, of home influences, and his being brought up at court: possibly, too, the Bohemian life necessary to the fulfilment of his purposes as a dramatist, all contributed to produce the conditions under which his "name received a brand."

This finds its expression in sonnet 111,

> O! for my sake do you with fortune chide,
> The guilty goddess of my harmful deede,
> *That did not better for my life provide*
> *Than public means which public manners breeds.*

5. That Shakespeare was one who was pursuing a vocation involving, at the outset, concealment of materials from those with whom he was in direct social relationship is evident from sonnet 48.

> How careful was I when I took my way
> Each trifle under truest bars to thrust.

This exactly fits in with the bearing of Oxford's early domestic relationships upon his dramatic and literary enterprises.

6. An allusion to Oxford's functions as Lord Great Chamberlain is probably contained in sonnet 125 beginning,

> Were't aught to me I bore the canopy?

7. As there is strong evidence to support our theory that Oxford was the man referred to by Spenser as "our pleasant Willie," we are able to connect with this theory the cryptic utterance of "Shakespeare" in the "Will" sonnets:

> For my name is Will.

8. In our chapter on Posthumous Considerations we have shown that there is good ground for believing that "our ever-living poet" was dead when the *Sonnets* were published in 1609;

and the fact that, after being penned during many years, the series was brought to an abrupt close, as near as can be judged, just before the death of Edward de Vere, supports the contention that the writer of the *Sonnets*, whoever he was, died at the same time as Edward de Vere.

Starting with these several points of accord, which in their combination certainly represent a remarkable set of coincidences, our next task must be to examine the general situation represented in the *Sonnets*, and see to what extent this, along with the details just enumerated, combine and form a consistent unity, applicable to the person and circumstances of Edward de Vere.

Southampton; "The better angel."

The first and most important set of sonnets is itself divisible into sections, the opening section being a set of seventeen, the main burden of which is to urge the young man to whom they are addressed to marry, in order to secure the continuance of his own aristocratic family and the rebirth of his own attractive personality in his posterity.

> Then what could death do if thou shouldst depart,
> Leaving thee living in posterity?

> Thou stick'st not to conspire,
> Seeking that beauteous roof to ruinate
> Which to repair should be thy chief desire.

> Who lets so fair a house fall to decay,
> Which husbandry in honour might uphold
> Against the stormy gusts of winter's day?
>
>   *   *   *   *   *
>
> You had a father: let your son say so.

We are not told who the particular young man was; but the general assumption is that it was Henry Wriothesley, Earl of Southampton. This is not only a reasonable position, but it would be unreasonable to suppose that it was anyone else; for the following reasons:

1. The personal description exactly fits.
2. The personal situation also fits, for his father was dead, his

mother was living, he was the only surviving representative of his family, and efforts were being made to get him to marry: efforts which he was resisting.

3. The poet addresses him in the same terms of strong affection as in the dedication to *Lucrece*.

4. Direct reference is made to the dedications.

The fact of the young man's father being dead and his mother being still alive is made clear by the separate references to them:

> You *had* a father: let your son say so

and

> Thou art thy mother's glass and *she*, in thee,
> *Calls back* the lovely April of her prime.

The Countess of Southampton.

Such references to Southampton's father and mother are quite befitting a writer who was old enough to have been the father of the youth, and who had been on intimate terms with both parents; for Oxford's former close association with the late Earl is made quite clear in the State Papers dealing with the catholic troubles some ten years before. The reference to "the lovely April" of the Countess's "prime" was natural to one who remembered her in her early years; so that the youth, the deceased father, the Dowager Countess, and the writer, all assume a very intelligible relation to one another and to the poems, as soon as we assume the Earl of Oxford to have been the writer.

On the other hand it is well-nigh impossible to fit William Shakspere of Stratford into the picture, and to think of him at the age of twenty-six speaking with such assurance of intimate knowledge of the Countess's "lovely prime." We may perhaps be excused for reminding the reader again that it was the Countess of Southampton who made the *entry after date* into the accounts of the Treasurer of the Chamber, of the only reference to Shakespeare that these accounts contain. In a letter written later to her son she makes what has always been regarded as a mysterious allusion to someone whom she speaks of as

"Falstaff." This, again, will be interesting to those who may think with Mr. Frank Harris that Falstaff is "Shakespeare's" caricature of himself under particular aspects. We need not pretend, however, to explain Lady Southampton's part in these matters.

Dedication of Lucrece.

The identity of the young man of the sonnets with the one to whom the long poems were dedicated is further attested by sonnets 81 and 82.

> Your name from hence immortal life shall have,
> Though I, once dead, to all the world must die.
>
>   *   *   *   *
>
> Your monument shall be my gentle verse.

As, then, the name of Southampton is the only one which the poet has associated with his verse, not even excepting his own, it is difficult to see how the young man addressed could be any other than he; especially as the companion sonnet proceeds,

> I grant thou wert not married to my Muse,
> And therefore may'st, without attaint, o'erlook
> The dedicated words, which writers use
> Of their fair subject, blessing every book.

In our conclusion that these sonnets were addressed to Southampton, we have the full support of the great majority of authorities on the subject.

W. H. and T. T. in the Dedication.

We desire to avoid as far as possible being drawn into the entanglements of discussing the dedication prefaced to Thorpe's edition of the *Sonnets*. Whether the letters W. H. are the transposed initials of Henry Wriothesley or not, there are no traces of "our ever-living poet" attempting to give "immortality" to any other contemporary; and the man to whom the first of the sonnets are addressed was certainly the "begetter" of the first section in the sense of being their theme and inspiration. It is natural to suppose, therefore, that the "begetter" referred to in the dedication means the person to whom the particular sonnets are addressed. At the same time he was not the "only begetter" in this sense, since others of these poems are just as certainly addressed to a "dark lady." As, however, this dedication is without any "Shakespeare" authority it may have been penned by T. T. before he had read the whole series. At any rate, no conclusive argument can be drawn from a study of the initials alone.

The only argument that really needs attention is to the effect that the use of the letters W. H. shows that, in the opinion of the writer of the dedication, Wriothesley was not the person to whom the *Sonnets* were addressed; that, if concealment was aimed at, the transposed initials device was too transparent to have been used: whilst if concealment was not aimed at, the initials would have appeared in their right order. Decisive as this argument may appear, facts are unfortunately against it; for, in the publication of an important anthology of the time, *England's Helicon*, which contains matter relevant to our present enquiry, though put aside for the time being, the editor appears as L. N., the transposed initials of Nicholas Ling, the publisher of *Hamlet*. W. H. may or may not therefore have referred to Henry Wriothesley; and, as we know nothing of the writer's authority, it evidently does not matter whether they do or do not. In a word, the discussion is perfectly useless, but will probably for that reason continue to exercise a strong fascination for "intellectuals."

So much printer's ink has already been wasted over these initials that a little more will hardly matter. Seeing, then, that others have indulged in guesses about T. T., the favourite theory being that they refer to Thorpe the publisher, we may perhaps be permitted to point out that the name of the father of Oxford's widow was Thomas Trentham, and that if he were alive at the time when Oxford died, he would be the one to whom the widow would naturally turn for assistance in straightening out the affairs. Certainly her brother's name appears more than once in connection with the management of her son's estate. Fortunately the question is not likely to arise as to whether these initials are in their original or transposed order.

Quite apart, however, from this discussion of the dedication, there is ample justification for the belief that the "better-angel" of the *Sonnets* was Henry Wriothesley, Third Earl of Southampton.

The age of "our ever-living poet."

Now, as to the man who wrote the sonnets: for this is really the most important point. Throughout the whole series he assumes the attitude of a matured man addressing a youth. Indeed, in one of the other series he speaks of himself as being no "untutor'd youth," but that his "days are past the best." The following, from sonnet 63, is unmistakable:

> Against my love shall be, as I am now,
> With Time's injurious hand crush'd and o'erworn;
> When hours have drain'd his blood and fill'd his brow
> With lines and wrinkles, etc.

We may even detect an indication of his approximate age in the lines:

> When *forty* winters shall besiege thy brow,
> And dig deep trenches in thy beauty's field.

The next point is the date at which these particular sonnets were written. We find that the first sonnets of the first set are assigned generally to about the year 1590, when Oxford was just forty years of age. The dedication of "Venus" to Wriothesley is dated 1593; and as the sonnet which seems to refer to it is number 83, 1590 may be accepted as a reasonable date for these seventeen opening sonnets. This, then, is the situation represented by the poems. About the year 1590 a matured man "With Time's injurious hand crush'd and o'erworn," addressed to the youthful Earl of Southampton, then only about seventeen years of age, a number of sonnets urging upon him the question of matrimony, and putting in the specially aristocratic plea of maintaining the continuance of his family's succession.

A Stratfordian absurdity.

In respect to these facts we shall first consider the Stratfordian position. In the year 1590, William Shakspere, the son of a Stratford citizen, having become interested in theatres, and thereby acquainted with a young man just home from the university, and having himself by that time attained the patriarchal age of twenty-six, suddenly becomes greatly concerned about the continuance of the youth's aristocratic family, and writes a set of exquisite sonnets urging him to marry. He also assumes the bearing and tone of a man of large and even painful experience, "past his best," with chilled blood and wrinkled brow. We doubt whether a more ridiculous position ever provoked the hilarity of mankind. The position of Bacon in respect to this matter is only slightly better; for he, at that time, was still under thirty years of age, though, as one about the court, his acquaintance with Wriothesley would have been of longer duration and probably more intimate.

Most amusing in connection with the question of the age of the poet is the theory that Roger Manners, Fifth Earl of Rutland, was the author of the sonnets. For in 1590 Roger Manners was only fourteen years of age, and the entire series of *Shakespeare's Sonnets* was brought to a close before he had reached the age of twenty-seven.

Southampton and Oxford.

To get over the inherent absurdity of William Shakspere being the author of these poems, far fetched explanations of his attitude have had to be invented, and the personal contents of the sonnets either passed over as pure enigma, or interpreted in some extravagant metaphorical sense. The substitution of De Vere for the Stratford man alters all this, and makes these verses really intelligible and rational for the first time since they appeared—

over three hundred years ago. In the year 1590 Edward de Vere was forty years of age. Behind him there lay a life marked by vicissitudes in every way calculated to have given him a sense of age even beyond his forty years. He was a nobleman of the same high rank as Southampton and just a generation older. The question of the perpetuation of ancient aristocratic families was to him a matter of paramount interest; an interest intensified by disappointment, for although he had several daughters, that dominant desire of feudal aristocrats, a son, had been denied him.* His only son had died in infancy and he was at this time a widower. The peculiar circumstances of the youth to whom the *Sonnets* were addressed were strikingly analogous to his own. Both had been left orphans and royal wards at an early age, both had been brought up under the same guardian, both had the same kind of literary tastes and interests, and later the young man followed exactly the same course as the elder had done as a patron of literature and the drama.

An important marriage proposal.

Then just at the time when these sonnets were being written urging Southampton to marry, he was actually being urged into a marriage with a daughter of the Earl of Oxford; and this proposed marriage he was resisting, although his mother had sanctioned it, and the parties on the other side were anxious to bring it about. This furnishes the vital connection between the Earl of Southampton and the Earl of Oxford, to which allusion has been made in previous chapters. We shall therefore state the fact in the words of the eminent Stratfordian authority to whom we are under such large obligations.

> When he was seventeen Burleigh offered him a wife in the person of his granddaughter, Lady Elizabeth Vere, eldest daughter of his daughter Anne and of the Earl of Oxford. The Countess Southampton approved the match. . . . Southampton declined to

---

* Looney's note: One authority says two sons.

marry.[212]

Now with this fact in mind, and with a sense of all we have represented of the Earl of Oxford in these pages, let the reader turn again to the *Sonnets*, especially the first seventeen, and ponder them carefully. To have urged marriage as a general and indefinite proposition upon a youth of seventeen, with the single aim of securing posterity for the youth, would have had something fatuous about it. In connection with a definite project of marriage, from one who was personally interested in it, the appeal comes to have, at last, an explicable relationship to fact.

Judge Webb's support.

This had evidently occurred to Judge Webb; for in his work on *The Shakespeare Mystery*,[213] he got so far as to attribute these sonnets to the particular marriage proposal, and even to suggest the idea of their being written by someone specially interested in the lady. How he managed to miss the obvious inference looks like another "Shakespeare mystery" in itself. The Judge surmises that as Bacon was nephew to the lady's grandfather, he might have felt sufficiently interested in the marriage proposal to have penned the *Sonnets* at this time. His Honour's Baconian leanings had evidently disturbed his juridical balance; for not only would a family connection like this be much too remote to call forth such enthusiasm, but, as we have already said, Bacon at the time of this marriage proposal was still under thirty years of age.

Stratfordian support.

Seeing that we have quoted a Baconian in support of the idea that the sonnets sprang from this particular marriage proposal, we may mention the fact that Mrs. Stopes, as a Stratfordian, supports the view, and suggests that Shakspere was urged to write the sonnets by someone who was anxious to bring about the marriage.

No man answering to the description which the writer of the

---

[212] Lee, *Life*, p. 394.
[213] Judge Thomas E. Webb, *The Mystery of William Shakespeare*, p. 159-61.

Sonnets gives of himself could have had better reasons for the peculiar kind of interest expressed in the poems than the father of the lady. To find so reasonable a key, then, to a set of sonnets on so peculiar a theme is something in itself; and to find this key so directly connected with the very man whom we had selected as the probable author of the poems is almost disconcerting in its conclusiveness. The very obviousness of it all makes us pause. For the first time since they appeared we feel entitled to maintain these seventeen sonnets are raised above the absurd and enigmatical, and made into a perfectly simple and intelligible expression of a legitimate desire. The older man who was urging the young one to think of sons, a matter not likely to interest a youth of seventeen, was contemplating his own possible posterity in the shape of grandsons.

Sentiment of the Sonnets.

If, now, we turn from the external relationships represented by the sonnets to the internal sentiments which they express, though we may not be able to bring these yet within the bounds of what we should now consider normal, it is difficult to imagine any other circumstances under which the friendship of one man for another would fit in better with such expressions. All that is necessary is to read through the biographies of these two men, as they appear in the *Dictionary of National Biography*. It will then be realized that in many of its leading features the life of the younger man is a reproduction of the life of the elder. It is difficult to resist the feeling that Wriothesley had made a hero of De Vere, and had attempted to model his life on that of his predecessor as royal ward. When to this striking correspondence in external circumstances and literary and other interests is added the intensely affectionate nature of the elder man, and his comparative isolation at the time, there exist certainly the most favourable conditions for such expressions of attachment as the sonnets contain.

Proposal rejected and "Shakespeare's" interest declines.

With regard to the rate of the output of these sonnets it would be absurd to reduce it to one of simple arithmetic. Even works of poetic genius have nevertheless some relation to number and time. If, then, sonnet 82, which refers to the dedications of the poems, were written about the years 1593-4, when the poems were published, we get an average of between 20 and 30 per year for the initial rate of production. That brings the first I 7, in which the writer is harping largely upon the one string of marriage, well within the year which corresponds, so far as can be judged, to the time when the marriage of Southampton to De Vere's daughter was under consideration. Owing to Southampton's decided opposition the matter seems to have been dropped; and, on turning to the sonnets, we find that although the personal feelings of the writer for Southampton become more intensely affectionate, concern for the young nobleman's posterity altogether disappears: for after these opening sonnets the question is never again raised. The writer of the *Sonnets*, it would seem, cared more about this particular marriage than about Southampton's posterity: a state of things which would have appeared strange by itself, but read in the light of Oxford's own personal interest in the particular marriage proposal which fell through, it is, of course, quite intelligible.

Before leaving the question of this marriage proposal, seeing that we have already introduced the names of two others who have been put forward as candidates for Shakespearean honours, Bacon and Rutland, we may perhaps be excused for referring to the only other whose name, so far as we know, has been raised in this connection, namely William Stanley, Sixth Earl of Derby. He was about the same age as Bacon, and as a matter of fact, actually married the very lady whom Southampton was urged to marry. So that, if our theory of the authorship is correct, Mr. Greenstreet[214] in England and M. Lefranc[215] in France, in putting forward the son-in-law of Oxford as the author, may be congratulated upon having come very close to the right man.

---

[214] James H. Greenstreet, articles in *The Genealogist* (1891, 1892).
[215] Abel Lefranc, *Sous le Masque de "William Shakespeare"* (1919).

The Derby theory.

It may be worthwhile pointing out that, from letters in the Hatfield Manuscripts, it appears that Oxford interested himself more in his daughter Elizabeth than in either of the other two, and this marriage with William Stanley, Earl of Derby, was a matter of very special concern to him. Seeing, then, that the Derby theory arose from the simple fact that in 1599 the Earl of Derby had been occupied in "penning" plays, whilst nothing is known of his composing them, it is not an unreasonable supposition that, as husband to Oxford's favourite daughter, he may have been assisting his father-in-law in the actual penning of "Shakespeare's" plays.

The "worser-spirit" mystery.

The other personal relationship with which these poems deal—"Shakespeare" and the "dark lady," whom he describes as the "worser spirit," and his "female evil"—presents a problem not yet solved, and which may remain unsolved for all time. There is perhaps no particular reason why we should trouble about it except for the purpose of doing justice to the poet. One thing does, however, stand out clearly from the set of sonnets (beginning 127) namely, that to him it was a matter of the heart, of a most intense and sincere character, but to the lady a much more equivocal affair. Nothing but an overwhelming heart hunger could ever have induced any man of spirit to maintain the attitude described.

The crossing of the two series.

Mixed in with this shorter series we find that there are several sonnets which do not belong to it as a special personal series. Nor do those which belong properly to the set appear to be all printed in the order in which they were written. If, however, we take those which refer to the "dark lady" episode in the writer's life, we find that just before the series is abruptly ended it touches upon matters dealt with in sonnets 40, 41, and 42 of the first series. In other words, the events dealt with in the second series (see 133-144) come to an end in the early part, possibly the second year, of the first series. This would bring us to the year before De Vere's second marriage. The events as a whole, then, would seem to belong to a period of about two years in the four years that he was a widower. The intolerable state of affairs which they disclose could not go on, and the words which Shakespeare puts into the mouth of Othello might be taken as an allusion to his own personal affairs.

> Though that her jesses were my dear heart strings
> I'd whistle her off, and let her down the wind
> To play at Fortune."

This is the passage which is exactly paralleled by De Vere in the lines:

> Who would not scorn and shake them from the fist
> And let them fly, fair fools, which way they list.

The sudden closing of the series is at any rate suggestive of such an action, and if we attribute words and action alike to the Earl of Oxford, his marriage, in the following year, would be in harmony with such an act of self-liberation from discreditable bonds. It is to be remarked, however, that it is as "Shakespeare" not as Oxford that we get evidence of this regrettable alliance. In spite of the general accusations made against Oxford, no single definite and authenticated example is otherwise forthcoming.

Peace and retirement.

If, now, we take the whole of the short series as having been written about the same time as the first forty or fifty of the first series, we may resume the examination of the first sonnets at this point with a sense of their now forming an uninterrupted series, with no cross currents from the other set. From this point onwards neither the original theme of the young man's marriage, nor any allusion to the painful episode common to the two series appears. What there is of a painful character arises from personal retrospect, reflection, or passing moods, rather than from contemporary events; which is quite suggestive of a man whose stormiest outward experiences were over. This corresponds to the period when the Shakespeare dramas were being given forth, and when Oxford was, to all appearances, enjoying his retirement after his second marriage.

A hitch in the friendship between the poet and the young man appears about the time of the dedication of the poems (sonnets 80-90), and the particular circumstances that may have lain behind this and other references to passing events, would, of course, be known only to the parties involved. The important point is that all these appear, if not explained, at any rate explicable for the first time, when we suppose them to be written by the somewhat lonely and mysterious nobleman, whose known experiences, joined to those which the sonnets reveal, represent him as one of the most pathetic and heroic figures in the tragic records of genius.

Supplementary details.

As supplementary details we would suggest for consideration the following from sonnet 91.

> Some glory in their birth, some in their skill,
> Some in their wealth, some in their body's force;
> Some in their garments, though new-fangled ill;
> Some in their hawks and hounds; some in their horse;
> And every humour hath his adjunct pleasure.
>
>   *   *   *   *
>
> All these I better in one general beat,
> Thy love is better than high birth to me,
> Richer than wealth, prouder than garments' cost,
> Of more delight than hawks or horses be.

From a man like William Shakspere such an expression would be so palpably a case of "sour grapes," that it is incredible that any poet of intelligence would make himself so ridiculous. From a man in Oxford's position, who had had all of these things, and who had no doubt gloried in them all in turn, the expression is lifted above the childish and placed in a reasonable relationship to facts. It is not too much to claim that every word of this sonnet bespeaks Edward de Vere as its author; for it gives us practically a symposium of the outstanding external facts of his life and his interests. Yet all these things, the advantages of birth, the fame for skill and "body's force," rich clothing, wealth, hawks, hounds and horses, he had proved himself capable of sacrificing to those interests that appealed to his spirit. In every particular, then, the contrast presented by supposing those sonnets to have been written by the Stratford man on the one hand or Edward de Vere on the other, leaves no doubt as to which of the two mankind would choose as the author if the decision had to rest on a consideration of the *Sonnets* alone.

Importance of the Sonnets.

The *Sonnets* stand there for everyone to read, and no arguments could have the same value as an intimate knowledge of the poems themselves viewed in the light of the actual facts of the life and reputation of Edward de Vere. Upon all who wish to arrive at the truth of the matter we urge the close and frequent reading of the *Sonnets*. It is not necessary to believe that all the first set were addressed to the youth or all the second set to the "dark lady." Nor is it necessary to solve the mystery of the dark lady: for it is not in the nature of things for such a man to pass away and leave no insoluble mysteries. Some of the sonnets seem to have no personal hearing and others can hardly be made applicable to the two chief personalities. These things are immaterial. Neither is it necessary to penetrate all the disguises which "Shakespeare" himself, or his executors after him, may have thought right to adopt in respect to these effusions of sentiment and their objects. But we are unable to place ourselves in the position of a reader, who with the facts concerning Oxford that we have submitted, can become conversant with these sonnets without realizing that they reflect at once the soul and the circumstances of "the best of the courtier poets of the early days of Queen Elizabeth."

The inventor of the Shakespearean sonnet.

In conclusion, we must add a word about the technique of the sonnets. Shakespeare's rejection of the Petrarchan sonnet we hold to have been sound poetic judgment, based upon a true ear for musical qualities and acoustic properties of the English language. The Petrarchan sonnet has grown out of the distinctive qualities of the language of Italy, and the attempt to impose its rhyme rules upon the English sonnet, involving so great a sacrifice of sense to sound, has gone far to produce the relative poverty of post Shakespearean sonneteering. However this may be, the Shakespearean sonnet has its own distinctiveness, which bears upon our subject.

The so-called "Shakespeare sonnet," we are told by William Sharp in his *Sonnets of this Century* (19th), possesses "a capability of impressiveness unsurpassed by any sonnet of Dante or Milton."[216] He points out, however, that when Shakespeare used this form of sonnet in the last years of the sixteenth century, he was using a form "made thoroughly ready for his use by Daniel and Drayton."[217] Now, as Daniel was twelve years, and Drayton thirteen years younger than Edward de Vere, and as the last named was publishing poetry at a relatively early age, it is clear that his early lyrics come before those of either of the other two men.

Seeing, then, that we have a sonnet of Edward de Vere's which is obviously an early production, and that this is in what we now call the Shakespearean form, we are entitled to claim, on the above authority, that the actual founder of the Shakespearean sonnet was Edward de Vere: certainly a very important contribution to the evidence we have been accumulating. The *Sonnets*, therefore, which are fundamentally a work of spiritual self-revelation, almost become a work of complete self-disclosure. In submitting the following sonnet of Oxford's mainly on account of its form we would also point out its note of constancy: a theme upon which many of "Shakespeare's" sonnets dwell.

---

[216] William Sharp, *Sonnets of this Century*, p. ix.
[217] Sharp, *Sonnets*, p. lvi.

SONNET BY EDWARD DE VERE.

LOVE THY CHOICE

Who taught thee first to sigh, alas! my heart?
    Who taught thy tongue the woeful words of plaint?
Who filled your eyes with tears of bitter smart?
    Who gave thee grief and made thy joys to faint?
Who first did paint with colours pale thy face?
    Who first did break thy sleeps of quiet rest?
Above the rest in court who gave thee grace?
    Who made thee strive in honour to be best?
In constant truth to bide so firm and sure,
    To scorn the world regarding but thy friends?
With patient mind each passion to endure,
    In one desire to settle to the end?
Love then thy choice wherein such choice thou bind
As nought but death may ever change thy mind.

This, then, may be regarded as the first "Shakespeare" sonnet. It is the only sonnet in the collection of Edward de Vere's poems, and it is composed in the only form employed by Shakespeare, although other sonneteers were then experimenting upon other forms. It is obviously one of his earliest efforts, for it expresses an attitude towards woman only found in one other of his poems, "What Cunning Can Express?"—an attitude belonging to the unsullied ideals of his youth, which later on gave place to the cynicism or bitterness of the De Vere poem on "Women," and of what are now known as the *Shakespeare Sonnets*. From the point of view of evidence of Oxford's identity with Shakespeare its chief value lies in its technique, which is most certainly Shakespearean. It does, however, furnish another link in the chain of evidence which is worth mentioning.

The first sonnets of "Shakespeare's" to appear were those in *Romeo and Juliet*, a play which has already furnished us with important connections between Edward de Vere's poetry and Shakespeare. Now, *Romeo and Juliet,* not only first presents sonnets on this model, *but it is the only play of Shakespeare's which expresses seriously the sentiment of this sonnet* of Edward de Vere's. Shakespeare's comedies treat the theme of man's love for woman in the spirit of comedy; and his great tragedies like *Othello* and *Antony and Cleopatra* give us the vigorous passions of matured men. *Romeo and Juliet* alone, of all the plays, gives us seriously the tender, gentle, idealistic love of young people. And, as we have already more than once pointed out, Juliet was just the age of Oxford's wife at the time of their marriage (about 14 years).

With this sonnet of Oxford's in mind then, turn to *Romeo and Juliet,* and look into the text of the play, especially the parts spoken by, or in reference to, Romeo himself, observing the allusions to sighings, floods of womanish tears, bitter griefs, broken sleep, pledges of constancy, and death. The youthful Romeo in the play is the young Earl of Oxford as he represents himself in the sonnet before us.

So much from the point of view of evidence. We have, however, another purpose to achieve in this work: namely, to assist towards the formation of a correct estimate of Edward de Vere. We ask, therefore, for a careful weighing of this particular poem and the spirit it reveals. Gentle, tender-hearted, supersensitive, idealistic, refined almost to the point of femininity; such is the young Earl of Oxford as he here reveals himself. And as in the light of such a revelation we review the various references to him in modern books, we can only say, without attempting to fasten the full blame anywhere, that he was the victim of a most adverse fate: the many references to which throughout the sonnets stand now explained for the first time, making plain why a Shakespeare Problem, or a Shakespeare Mystery, has happened to have a place in the world's history.

We conclude our examination of the sonnets with a sense of its being marked by the same feature as has manifested itself in every other section of our investigation: namely, that it is not merely in one or two striking points that the personality disclosed coincides with that of the Earl of Oxford; but that everything fits in, in a most extraordinary manner, the moment his personality is introduced. There is surely only one explanation possible for all this.

CHAPTER XVI

Dramatic Self-Revelation: Hamlet

In Hamlet Shakespeare has revealed too much of himself.[218]
FRANK HARRIS.

Shakespeare's contemporaries in his plays.

As the fame of Shakespeare rests chiefly upon his great achievements in drama, it is to these that the world is bound to look for some special revelation of the author himself. Such a revelation, however, it must be expected, will be in keeping with the character of his genius. Cryptograms and anagrams, though they may play a part, especially the latter, as being a recognized feature of the literature of the times, can only come in as supplementary to something greater: the real self-revelation being a dramatic one.

The essential objectivity of Shakespeare's work, with its foundations fixed in observation, is assurance enough that his characters would be taken from his own experience of the men and women about him. Mere photographic reproduction, of course, such a genius would not offer us; but actually living men and women, artistically modified and adjusted to fit them for the part they had to perform, are what we may be sure the plays contain. The fact that these have not been identified before now is no doubt due, in part, to such cunning disguises as we should naturally expect from a mind so profound and complex. The fact, too, that the active life of the reputed author does not fit in with either the time or circumstances of the active life of the actual author has also tended to prevent detection. Another explanation is that "Shakespeare" probably saw contemporary events and

---

[218] Harris, *The Man*, p. 142. The correct phrasing is "discovered too much of himself."

personalities from a standpoint totally different from that taken by Englishmen since his day. If, therefore, the substitution of a new personality, as author, furnishes a point of view which enables us to identify characters in the plays, it will form a very strong argument that the right man has been discovered.

Such a faculty of observation as we notice in him, leading him to fix his attention specially upon those whose lives pressed directly upon his own—inevitable in one so sensitive and self-conscious as the *Sonnets* reveal him—is certain to have made his work much more a record of his own personal relationships than has hitherto been supposed. His special domain, moreover, being the study of the human soul, this faculty of observation must have compelled him to subject his own nature to a rigorous examination and analysis. Consequently, when the author is better known, it will doubtless be found that his works are packed with delineations and studies of his own spiritual experiences. The working out of this department of Shakespearean enquiry belongs largely to the future. Something of this kind has, however, already been attempted in a desultory manner in these pages. Our present purpose is somewhat more definite.

The dramatist in his dramas.

The long-accepted notion that the author has not given us a representation of himself in his plays breaks down completely, as we have seen, under the view of authorship put forward in this work. Already attention has been drawn to the case of Lord Berowne in *Love's Labour's Lost*, and also to a most striking parallel between Edward de Vere and another of Shakespeare's characters, namely Bertram in *All's Well*.

Bertram, a young lord of ancient lineage, of which he is himself proud, having lost a father for whom he entertained a strong affection, is brought to court by his mother and there left as a royal ward, to be brought up under royal supervision. As he grows up he asks for military service and to be allowed to travel, but is repeatedly refused or put off. At last he goes away without permission. Before leaving he had been married to a young woman with whom he had been brought up, and who had herself been most active in bringing about the marriage. Matrimonial troubles, of which the outstanding feature is a refusal of cohabitation, are associated with both his stay abroad and his return home. Such is the summary of a story we have told in fragments elsewhere, and is as near to biography, or autobiography if our theory be accepted, as a dramatist ever permitted himself to go. The later discovery, which we have fortunately been able to incorporate into this work before publication, that the central incident of Bertram's matrimonial trouble has a place in the records of the Earl of Oxford, leaves no doubt as to his being the prototype of Bertram. Still it is conceivable that a contemporary dramatist, knowing De Vere's story, had utilized parts of it in writing the play; and, therefore, if viewed alone, is not entitled to be called a dramatic self-revelation.

The world's choice.

Properly speaking, it is the whole of the dramas that constitutes the full dramatic self-revelation. It is, therefore, as we approach the highest triumphs of his genius, which represent the whole, that his work becomes a special or synoptic self-revelation. This, however, pertains to the inward or spiritual life rather than to its external forms. If, then, to a spiritual correspondence there is added a marked agreement in external circumstances, as evidence of the personal identity of the author, such dramatic work becomes specially convincing. The question, therefore, resolves itself into this: What play of Shakespeare's holds such pre-eminence that we are entitled to regard it as a work of special self-revelation, and how far do its inner spiritual facts, and the outward forms in which they are clothed, warrant the assumption that they constitute a work of self-revelation on the part of Edward de Vere?

On the first point, the choice of play, there is fortunately no need for the exercise of our own individual judgment, nor any uncertainty as to the social verdict; for the world at large has long since proclaimed the play of *Hamlet* as the great *tour de force* of this master dramatist. The comedy of *Love's Labour's Lost* undoubtedly occupies a unique position amongst the lighter plays. It is usually accorded priority in time; it bears unmistakable evidence of the most painstaking labour; and it was the first to be published under the pseudonym of "Shakespeare." The correspondence of its central figure, Berowne, with the Earl of Oxford has therefore a special value, particularly if taken as supplementary to the play of *Hamlet*.

The central figure in the latter play occupies, however, a most exceptional position in relation to the work in which he appears, and therefore stands out as the supreme dramatic creation of the artist. "The play of *Hamlet* with Hamlet left out" has become a proverbial expression for the very extreme of deprivation; and Sir Sidney Lee assures us that "the total length of Hamlet's speeches far exceeds that of those allotted by Shakespeare to any others of his characters."[219] These, again, have so passed into common currency as to justify the well-worn joke about the play being "full of quotations." The play and the character of *Hamlet* may therefore be accepted as being in a peculiar sense the dramatic self-revelation of the author, if such a revelation exists anywhere.

Hamlet and Destiny.

Great as is the mass of printed matter which this particular creation has already called forth, probably exceeding in amount what has been written about any other literary work of similar dimensions outside the Bible, more is certain to appear if we succeed in making good our chief claim. The burden of much that has appeared is to the effect that in Hamlet the poet meant to give us the picture of a human soul struggling with Destiny. We venture to say that he meant nothing so philosophically abstract; but that what he was actually striving most consciously and earnestly to do, was to represent himself; and he, like every other human being born into this world who succeeds in keeping

---

[219] Lee, *Life*, p. 233.

his soul alive, was indeed a soul struggling most tragically with Destiny; refusing to be swept along passively by the currents into which his life was plunged or to surrender to the adverse forces within himself. This is certainly the picture which stands out from that self-presentation of the poet contained in his sonnets; and the fact that the character of Hamlet has been defined in terms that bring it into direct accord with that poetic self-revelation, is one more proof that the play is intended to be a special and direct dramatic self-revelation. It is this personal factor, doubtless, that has given to the drama that intense vitality and realism which makes its words and phrases grip the mind; becoming thus the instruments by which mankind at large have found new means of self-expression.

Hamlet is "Shakespeare."

It is this fact of Hamlet representing the dramatist himself which also makes him stand out from all Shakespeare's characters as an interpreter of the motives of human actions. Into no other character has the author put an equal measure of his own distinctive powers of insight into human nature. Whilst other personages in the play are trying to penetrate his mystery, to discover his purposes and to read his mind, we find Hamlet confusing them all, and, meanwhile, reading them like an open book.

> I set you up a glass
> Where you may see the inmost part of you,

he says to his mother.

All that quickness of the senses which marks alike the work of De Vere and Shakespeare manifests itself in the person of Hamlet. He misses nothing; and everything he sees or hears opens some new avenue to the "inmost parts" of those about him. A man like this is almost foredoomed to a tragic loneliness; for even such a love as he shows towards Ophelia and she towards him cannot blind him to her want of honesty in her dealings. He sees much of which he may not speak. In the play he can express himself in soliloquy or cunningly reveal to the audience what is hidden from the other personages in the drama; but in real life he would become a man of large mental reserves and an enforced secretiveness. Something of this is certainly noticeable in the slight records we have of De Vere: a trait which even Burleigh found disconcerting.

De Vere as Hamlet.

Having decided that *Hamlet* is the play which, by its preeminence, is entitled to be regarded as "Shakespeare's" special work of self-delineation, the next part of our problem is to see whether the revelation it contains has a marked and peculiar applicability to the case of Edward de Vere. In examining the work from this point of view it must be borne in mind that Shakespeare's plots are seldom pure inventions. The dramatist is obliged, therefore, to conform in certain essentials to the original; and it is to what he works into this, and the special adaptations he makes, that we must look for his self-revelation, rather than to the central idea of the plot itself. Naturally, however, his own definite purposes must influence his choice of plot: though it must also be borne in mind that self-disguise is one of his purposes as well as self-expression.

Life at court.

In testing the parallel we must substitute first of all the royal court of England for the royal court of Denmark. For Hamlet, Prince of Denmark, at the Danish court we shall then have to substitute Edward, Earl of Oxford, at the court of England. Oxford, of course, was not a prince of royal blood: but then there were no princes of royal blood at the English court, and the Earl of Oxford, in his younger days, was the nearest approach to a royal prince that the English court could boast. In the matter of ancient lineage and territorial establishment a descendant of Aubrey de Vere had nothing to fear in comparison with a descendant of Owen Tudor. And when it is remembered that noblemen of inferior standing to Oxford were, in those days, contemplating the possibility of sharing royal honours, either with Elizabeth or her possible successor, the Queen of Scotland, for the dramatist to represent himself as a royal prince was no extravagant self-aggrandizement. With the substitution we have recommended in mind, let the reader turn again to *Hamlet* and read the play with the attention fixed, not upon the plot, but upon the characterization. If he does not experience all the elation which comes with new illumination, if he does not feel that every line of Hamlet's speeches pulsates with the heart and spirit of Oxford, either we have failed to represent accurately, or he has failed to appreciate, the character and circumstances of this remarkable and unfortunate nobleman.

We shall endeavour to indicate elements of parallelism and coincidence between the two, but nothing can take the place of an attentive and discriminating reading of the play itself. As, then, we have elsewhere urged that one of the most convincing proofs is to read the *Sonnets*, so now we would also urge those who are interested to read *Hamlet*. Already, in tracing illustrations of the life and circumstances of De Vere in Shakespeare's works, we have frequently had to call attention to analogies with Hamlet, extending to details of private relationships. We may therefore shorten our present task by asking the reader to revert to those chapters dealing with the early and middle periods of Oxford's life.

Hamlet's eccentricity.

Following upon the consideration of his social rank comes the central fact of Hamlet's working out a secret purpose under a mask of eccentricity amounting almost to feigned madness. To have feigned complete madness would not have allowed him to accomplish his purpose, and therefore he assumes just sufficient insanity as is necessary to bewilder those whom he wishes to circumvent, and who are trying to circumvent him. It is a match of wits in which the ablest mind wins by allowing his inferior antagonists to suppose him mentally deficient. Now the records we have of Oxford represent his eccentricity in his early and middle period as being of an extreme character, and if we suppose him to be Shakespeare, we can quite believe that his own secret purposes were being pursued partly under a mask of vagary.

Resistance to interference.

It is to be observed how frequently Hamlet employs this particular stratagem in resisting molestation, especially from those who are trying to penetrate his secrets. This appears in his dealings with Rosencrantz, Guildenstern, Polonius and Ophelia. Now this resistance to interference stands out clearly at the time when Oxford, having returned from abroad, is reported to have behaved in a strange manner towards Lady Oxford; for, in addition to the taciturnity which he adopted, and which one writer calls "sulkiness," he says, in the letter quoted in our *Othello* argument, "neither will he weary his life any more with such troubles and molestations as he has endured."[220] Compare especially with the spirit expressed in this, the interesting scene in which Rosencrantz and Guildenstern are trying to probe and "play upon" Hamlet (III.2).

> You would play upon me; you would seem to know my stops; you would pluck out the heart of my mystery; you would sound me from my lowest note to the top of my compass. 'S blood I do you think I am easier to be played on than a pipe? Though you can fret me, you cannot play upon me.

Comedy in tragedy.

That Hamlet is Shakespeare's representation of himself receives confirmation from another characteristic which the latter shares with Oxford. That remarkable combination of tragedy with comedy, in the ordinary sense of these words, which we find in Shakespeare attains its highest development in the play of *Hamlet*. The only possible competitor is *The Merchant of Venice*. In the latter we have a comedy which may at any moment resolve itself into an appalling tragedy. In *Hamlet* we have a tragedy which, at parts, runs perilously near comedy, and may at any moment break up in absolute farce. Even in times of melancholy

---

[220] See footnote 123, p. 230.

and in the very thick of disaster the wit and subtle fun of the hero never desert him. Over his life there hangs a dark shadow. Impotence, failure and despondency dog his steps. Yet, when things are at their worst he turns rapidly upon his butts, teasing and confusing them with an evident enjoyment of the intellectual fun of the business. The play of *Hamlet*, which may therefore, in this particular, be taken as a compendium of "Shakespeare's" dramas as a whole, is unquestionably symptomatic of the general mental constitution and career of the Earl of Oxford.

Hamlet's father and mother.

The social position and general character of the hero of this play having lent support to the theory that its author was Edward de Vere, we shall find additional and even more surprising corroboration when we turn to the details of personal relationships. The driving force in the play of *Hamlet* is, of course, father-worship; the love and admiration of a son for a dead father who had borne himself in a manner worthy of his exalted station. Such affection and respect are the spontaneous source of ancestor-worship. Although, therefore, we are not told that father-worship was a marked trait in Edward de Vere, we have abundant justification for such an assumption, and might indeed infer it from the fact that ancestor-worship was a pronounced feature of his character.

When, however, we turn to Hamlet's relationship to his surviving parent we are met with a totally different picture. Grief and disappointment at his mother's conduct lie at the root of all the tragedy of his life. With a capacity for intense affection, such as we have already pointed out in "Shakespeare" and in De Vere, Hamlet was incapable of any real trust in womanhood. His faith had been shattered by the inconstancy of his own mother. This curious combination of intense affectionateness with weakness of faith in women is therefore characteristic of all three, "Shakespeare" (in his *Sonnets*), Hamlet, and De Vere.

Oxford and his mother.

It would not be fair to the memory of De Vere's mother to maintain, in the absence of positive proof, that she had furnished by her inconstancy a justification of her son's mistrust. We may, however, draw attention to facts that might account for it, even if they did not justify it. It has already been pointed out that in the short biography of De Vere, from which we have drawn so freely, no mention whatever is made of his mother, and one gets the impression that after his father's death she had almost dropped out of his life, the whole of the circumstances contrasting markedly with those recorded of Southampton and his mother. From the account given of De Vere's father, however, we learn that his widow died in 1568, Oxford being then only eighteen years of age; and that sometime in these early years of his life at the royal court, his mother had married Sir Charles (or Christopher) Tyrell. As, moreover, her death occurred at Castle Hedingham, one of the chief of the ancestral homes of the De Veres, it looks as though Oxford's stepfather had established himself on the family estates, and may have appeared to the youth as having doubly supplanted his father, first in his mother's affections and then in the hereditary domains. This, of course, is the situation represented in Hamlet. Whether, in addition to the central fact, there had also been an unseemly brevity in the widowhood of Oxford's mother we cannot tell; for although the precise date of her death is given, the date of her second marriage is not. We have spent much time in the search for this date; so far without result. It will be interesting, therefore, to learn whether or not it was an "o'er hasty marriage," and whether as Hamlet ironically remarked,

The funeral baked meats
Did coldly furnish forth the marriage tables.

Apart from this, however, there was sufficient in the general situation to cut very deeply into the mind of an imaginative and supersensitive youth, and to have struck a severe blow at that poetic ideal of feminine constancy which was natural to his age and temperament. The important point for our present argument is that we have in Oxford the same moral trait that we have in Hamlet, that we have parallel external circumstances tending towards its production, and that these external circumstances are just such as might lead to all the tragic developments which succeeded in both instances. Faith in motherhood being the fount at which faith in womanhood may be revived when threatened by the failure of other relationships, the man who like Hamlet or Oxford lacks this faith to carry him through crises can have but a hopeless outlook on the most vital and fundamental of human relationships.

Polonius and Burleigh.

The personal relationship in the play which bears most critically upon our present argument is that of Hamlet with Polonius and Ophelia. The chief minister at the royal court of Denmark is Polonius. The chief minister at the royal court of England was Burleigh. Is the character of Polonius such that we may identify him with Burleigh? Again it is not a question of whether Polonius is a correct representation of Burleigh, but whether he is a possible representation of the English minister from the special point of view of the Earl of Oxford. To what has already been said elsewhere in this connection, it will perhaps suffice to quote from Macaulay's essay on Burleigh:

> To the last Burleigh was somewhat jocose; and some of his sportive sayings have been recorded by Bacon. They show much more shrewdness than generosity, and are indeed neatly expressed reasons for exacting money rigorously and for keeping it carefully. It must, however, be acknowledged that he was rigorous and careful for the public advantage as well as for his own. To extol his moral character is absurd. It would be equally absurd to represent him as a corrupt, rapacious and bad-hearted man. He paid great attention to the interest of the state, and great attention also to the interest of his own family.[221]

---

[221] Macaulay, "Lord Burghley and His Times," p. 236.

Burleigh's characteristics.

Hardly anyone will deny that Macaulay's delineation of Burleigh is correct portraiture of Polonius; and, therefore, if Burleigh appeared thus to Macaulay after two and a half centuries had done their purifying work on his memory, one can readily suppose his having presented a similar appearance to a contemporary who had had no special reason to bless his memory. The resemblance becomes all the more remarkable if we add to this description the spying proclivities of Denmark's minister, the philosophic egoism he propounds under a gloss of morality, his opposition to his son's going abroad, and his references to his youthful love affair and to what he did "at the university." All these are strikingly characteristic of Burleigh and most of them have already been adequately dealt with.

Burleigh's maxims.

Probably the most conclusive evidence that Polonius is Burleigh is to be found in the best-known lines which Shakespeare has put into the mouth of Denmark's minister—the string of worldly-wise maxims which he bestows upon his son Laertes (I.3). They are much too well known to require repetition here. With these in mind, however, consider the maxims which Burleigh laid down for his favourite son, of which Burleigh's biographer (Martin A. S. Hume) remarks that though "these precepts inculcate moderation and virtue, here and there Cecil's own philosophy of life peeps out."[222] He then gives examples:

> Let thy hospitality be moderate.

> Beware that thou spendest not more than three of four parts of thy revenue.

> Beware of being surety for thy best friends; he that payeth another man's debts seeketh his own decay.

> With thine equals be familiar yet respectful.

> Trust not any man with thy life, credit, or estate.

> Be sure to keep some great man for thy friend.

---

[222] Hume, *Burleigh*, p. 25.

The whole method, style, language and sentiment are reproduced so much to the life in Polonius's advice to Laertes that Shakespeare seems hardly to have exercised his own distinctive powers at all in composing the speech. The connection of the advice of Polonius with similar precepts in Lyly's *Euphues* has long been recognized. What seems hitherto to have escaped notice is that both have a common source in Burleigh. How much of what appears in Lyly of these precepts was derived through Oxford it would be useless to discuss. The general relations of the two men has already been sufficiently considered.

The ethics of Polonius.

We take this opportunity of remarking, what may not be very material to our argument, that the spirit of the closing words of Polonius's speech, the words beginning, "Unto thine own self be true," seems to us to be generally quite misunderstood. These words bring to a close a speech which, throughout, is a direct appeal in every word to mere self-interest. Is, then, this last passage framed in a nobler mould with a high moral purpose and an appeal to lofty sentiment? We think not. The bare terms in which the final exhortation is cast, stripped of all ethical inferences and reinterpretations, are as direct an appeal to self-interest as everything else in the speech. They are, *"unto thine own self"*; not unto the *best* that is in you, nor the worst. Consistently with his other injunctions he closes with one which summarizes all, the real bearing of which may perhaps be best appreciated by turning it into modern slang: "Be true to 'number one.' Make your own interests your guiding principle, and be faithful to it."

Opportunist moralizing.

This is quite in keeping with the cynical egoism of Burleigh's advice, "Beware of being surety for thy best friends"; but "keep some great man for thy friend." And, of course, it does "follow as the night the day" that a man who directs his life on this egoistic principle cannot, truly speaking, be false to any man. A man cannot be false to another unless he owes him fidelity. If, therefore, a man only acknowledges fidelity to his own self, nothing that he can do can be a breach of fidelity to another. On this principle Burleigh was true to himself when he made use of the patronage of Somerset; he was still true to himself, not false to Somerset, when he drew up the articles of impeachment against his former patron. Bacon was true to himself when he made use of the friendship of Essex; he was still true to himself, not false to Essex, when he used his powers to destroy his former friend.

This philosophic opportunism was therefore a very real thing in the political life of those days. And the fact that Shakespeare puts it into the mouth not of a moralist but of a politician, and, as we believe, into the mouth of one whom he intended to represent Burleigh, serves to justify both the very literal interpretation we put upon these sentences, and the identification of Polonius with Elizabeth's chief minister. Needless to say, one who like "Shakespeare" was imbued with the best ideals of feudalism, with their altruistic conceptions of duty, social fidelity and devotion would never have put forward as an exalted sentiment any ethical conception resting upon a merely personal and individualist sanction. For this admiration of the moral basis of feudalism would enlighten him in a way which hardly anything else could, respecting the sophistry which lurks in every individualist or self-interest system of ethics.

Laertes and Thomas Cecil.

The advice of Polonius to Laertes is given just as the latter is about to set out for Paris, and all the instructions of the former to the spy Reynaldo have reference to the conduct of Laertes in that city. The applicability of it all to Burleigh's eldest son Thomas Cecil, afterwards Earl of Exeter, and founder of the present house of Exeter, will be apparent to anyone who will take the trouble to read G. Ravenscroft Dennis's work on *The House of Cecil.*

The tendency towards irregularities, at which Ophelia hints in her parting words to her brother, is strongly suggestive of Thomas Cecil's life in Paris; and all the enquiries which Polonius instructs the spy to make concerning Laertes are redolent of the private information which Burleigh was receiving, through some secret channel, of his son Thomas's life in the French capital. For he writes to his son's tutor, Windebank, that he "has a watchword sent him out of France that his son's being there shall serve him to little purpose, for that he spends his time in idleness."[223] We are told that Thomas Cecil incurred his father's displeasure by his "slothfulness," "extravagance," "carelessness in dress," "inordinate love of unmeet plays, as dice and cards"; and that he learnt to dance and play at tennis.[224]

With these things in mind let the reader again go carefully over the advice of Polonius to Laertes, and the former's instructions to Reynaldo. He will hardly escape, we believe, a sense of the identity of father and son, with Burleigh and his son Thomas Cecil. One point in Hamlet's relations with Laertes strikes one as peculiar: his sudden and quite unexpected expression of affection:

> What is the reason that you use me thus?
> I loved you ever.

Now the fact is that Thomas Cecil was one entirely out of touch with and in many ways quite antagonistic to Burleigh and his policy. In spite of his wildness in early life he is spoken of as "a brave and unaffected man of action, out of place in court, but with all the finest instincts of a soldier."[225] He was also one of those who, along with Oxford, favoured the Queen's marriage with the Duke of Alençon, in direct opposition to the policy of Burleigh. Thomas Cecil was an older man than Oxford, and they had much in common to form the basis of affection.

Ophelia and Lady Oxford.

It is impossible therefore to resist the conclusion that Polonius is Burleigh, and that Thomas Cecil formed, in part at any rate, the model for Laertes. This being so, it follows almost as conclusively, that Hamlet is Oxford. For, although Polonius's daughter, Ophelia, was not actually Hamlet's wife, she represents

---

[223] Dennis, *Cecil*, p. 81.
[224] Dennis, *Cecil*, p. 79.
[225] Dennis, *Cecil*, p. 92.

that relationship in the play. The royal consent had been given to the marriage, and it was through no fault either of herself or her father that the union did not take place. Hamlet's bearing towards his would-be father-in-law is moreover strongly suggestive of Oxford's bearing towards his actual father-in-law. What points of resemblance may have existed between Ophelia and Lady Oxford it is impossible to say. We notice, however, that the few words the Queen speaks respecting Ophelia harp on the idea of that sweetness which, we have noticed, Lady Oxford and Helena in *All's Well* had in common:

> Sweets to the sweet: farewell! I thought thou should'st have been my Hamlet's wife . . . sweet maid.

Something, too, of that mistrust and peculiar treatment which Hamlet extended to Ophelia has already been remarked in Oxford's bearing towards his wife, along with suggestions of the ultimate growth of a similar affection. We have also observed that the only accusation which Oxford was willing to make against his wife was that she was allowing her parents to interfere between herself and him. This is precisely the state of things to which Hamlet objects in Ophelia. He perceives that Polonius is spying upon him with her connivance, and cunningly puts her to the test; whereon she lies to him. His reply is an intimation to her that he had detected the lie.

> *Hamlet.* Where is your father?
>
> *Ophelia.* At home, my lord.
>
> *Hamlet.* Let the doors be shut on him that he may play the fool nowhere but in's own house.

Hamlet's use of the double sense of the word "honest" in a question to Ophelia—the identical word which in its worse sense was thrust to the front by Burleigh respecting the rupture between Lord and Lady Oxford—is not without significance. Polonius, we take it, then, furnishes the key to the play of Hamlet. If Burleigh be Polonius, Oxford is Hamlet, and Hamlet we are entitled to say is "Shakespeare."

Patron of drama and dramatist.

No feature of the parallelism between Hamlet and Oxford is more to the point than that of their common interest in the drama, and the form that their interest takes. Both are high-born patrons of companies of play-actors, showing an interest in the welfare of their players, sympathetic and instructive critics in the technical aspects of the craft. They are no mere passive supporters of the drama, but actually take a hand in modifying and adjusting the plays, composing passages to be interpolated, and generally supervising all the activities of their companies. Not only in the play within the play, which forms so distinctive a feature of *Hamlet*, but also before the period dealt with, it is evident that Hamlet had been so occupied. In all this he is a direct representation of the Earl of Oxford, and of no one else in an equal degree amongst the other lordly patrons of drama in Queen Elizabeth's reign.

Minor points.

To fully elaborate the parallelism between Hamlet and Oxford would demand a rewriting of almost everything that is known of the latter, illustrated by the greater part of the text of the play. We shall therefore merely add to what has already been said several of the minor points. Hamlet expresses his musical feeling and even suggests musical skill in the "recorder" scene (III.2). In the same scene he shows his interest in Italy. The duelling in which he takes part also has its counterpart in the life of Oxford, and even the tragic fate of Polonius at the hand of Hamlet is a reminder of the unfortunate death of one of Burleigh's servants at the hands of Oxford. Hamlet's desire to travel had to yield to the opposition of his mother and stepfather. His unrealized ambitions for a military vocation are indicated in the final scene, and his actual participation in a sea-fight is duly recorded. The death and burial of Ophelia at the time of Hamlet's sea episode is elsewhere shown to be analogous to Lady Oxford's death about the same time as De Vere's sea experiences. Suggestions of a correspondence between minor characters in the play and people with whom Oxford had to do can easily be detected. Rosencrantz, for example, might well be taken for Oxford's representation of Sir Walter Raleigh, "the sanctimonious pirate who went to sea with the *ten* commandments"—less one of them. If we are right in this guess we have a most subtle touch in Act III, scene 2. Hamlet instead of saying "By these hands," in speaking to Rosencrantz, coins an expression from the Catechism and calls his hands his "pickers and stealers," thus indicating most ingeniously the combination of piracy with the religiosity of Raleigh. Hamlet's next ironical remark that he himself "lacks advancement" helps to bear out the identification we suggest.

Horatio.

That the dramatist had some definite personality in mind for the character of Horatio hardly admits of doubt. The curious way in which he puts expressions into the mouth of Hamlet describing this personality, without allowing Horatio any part in the play which would dramatically unfold his distinctive qualities, marks the description as a purely personal tribute to some living man. Here, however, it is the very exactness of the correspondence of the prototype, even to the detail of his actual name, that makes us suspect the accuracy of the identification we propose. For the introduction into the play of Oxford's own cousin, Sir Horace de Vere (or, as the older records give it, Horatio de Vere) seems only explicable upon the assumption that the dramatist was then meditating—just before his death—coming forward to claim in his own name the honours which he had won by his work; or, at any rate, that he had decided that these honours should be claimed on his behalf immediately after his death, and that Horatio de Vere had been entrusted with the responsibility. Such an assumption has full warrant in the last words with Hamlet addresses to Horatio. Certainly the agreement is of a most surprising character and must not be neglected.

Sir Horace Vere (*as he is also named*) had followed the vocation which had been denied the Earl of Oxford, and in becoming the foremost soldier of his day, and chief of the "Fighting Veres,"[226] had maintained the military traditions of the family. This was the kind of glory which Edward de Vere had desired to win: an ambition which has left distinct marks in the Shakespearean dramas. The passage in which Hamlet describes the character of Horatio ought therefore to be compared with what Fuller says of Horatio de Vere.

Hamlet to Horatio:

> Since my dear soul was mistress of her choice,
> And could of men distinguish, her election
> Hath seal'd thee for herself; for thou hast been
> As one, in suffering all, that suffers nothing,
> A man that Fortune's buffets and rewards
> Hast ta'en with equal thanks; and bless'd are those
> Whose blood and judgment are so well commingled
> That they are not a pipe for fortune's finger
> To sound what stop she please. Give me that man
> That is not passion's slave, and I will wear him
> In my heart's core, ay, in my heart of heart,
> As I do thee.

Fuller's Worthies.

Horatio de Vere had "more meekness and as much valour as his brother [Francis]. As for his temper it was true of him what is said of the Caspian Sea, that it doth never ebb nor flow, observing a constant tenor neither elated nor depressed, . . . returning from a victory [in] silence . . . in retreat [with] cheerfulness of spirit."[227]

Sir Horace Vere was therefore noted amongst his contemporaries for the possession of just such a character and temperament as Hamlet has described to Horatio, in terms that have become classic. And as Horatio was the man selected by Hamlet to "tell his story," the theory we put forward, that

---

[226] This is a reference to Sir Clement R. Markham's *The Fighting Veres*, published in 1888.
[227] Thomas Fuller, *The History of the Worthies of England*, vol. 1, p. 351.

HORACE, LORD VERE OF TILBURY

PAINTING BY MICHIEL JANSZ. VAN MIEREVELDT, 1629.
REPRODUCED BY PERMISSION OF
THE NATIONAL PORTRAIT GALLERY.

"Shakespeare" had instructed his cousin Horatio de Vere to "report him and his cause aright to the unsatisfied," is not without very substantial grounds.

Hamlet and his times.

The religious situation represented in *Hamlet* is peculiar. Though Hamlet himself and his father show distinct traces of Catholicism, we do not find him in contact with the institutions and ministrations of Catholicism, such as are represented in *Measure for Measure* and *Romeo and Juliet;* nor do we find the other characters in the play exhibiting the same point of view. Even Hamlet's most intimate friend, Horatio, evidently differs from him in religious outlook. Hamlet's position, therefore, is very similar to that which an English nobleman of Catholic leanings would occupy in court circles in the days of Queen Elizabeth. On the other hand, Hamlet is not a Catholic of the saintly type. His frankness with regard to his shortcomings is as clear and genuine as that shown by "Shakespeare" in the *Sonnets.* Hamlet confesses "I could accuse me of such things that it were better my mother had not borne me," just as "Shakespeare" confesses in his sonnets.

> . . . . you in me can nothing worthy prove,
> Unless you would devise some virtuous lie,
> To do more for me than mine own desert,
> And hang more praise upon deceased I
> That niggard truth would willingly impart.
>
>   *   *   *   *
>
> For I am ashamed by that which I bring forth.

The applicability of all this to Edward de Vere, so far as the records of him are concerned, is, unhappily, one point over which hangs no shadow of doubt and from which no dispute is likely to arise.

Religious uncertainty.

Nor is the religious faith of Hamlet of the steadfast orthodox kind. His soliloquies reveal a mind that had been touched by the kind of scepticism that was becoming pronounced in the literary and dramatic circles of the latter half of Queen Elizabeth's reign. This again is representative of the mind of Shakespeare as shown by the plays as a whole: for the attenuated Catholicism they contain could hardly have come from the pen of one of the faithful. All this, too, is in accord with the shadowy indications that are given of Oxford's dealings with religion: his profession of Catholicism at one time, the accusation of atheism against him at another. Hamlet's cry, therefore, that "the time is out of joint," points to something deeper than his personal misfortunes and the tragedy of his private life. They are much more like the outburst of a writer, himself suffering from a keen sense of the unsatisfactory character of his whole social environment: one out of rapport with the age in which he lived; an age of social and spiritual disruption incapable of satisfying either his ideals of social order or the poet's need of a full, rich and harmonious spiritual life. All this personal dissatisfaction that the poet expresses through Hamlet is quite what was to be expected from one placed as was Edward de Vere in his relations to the men and movements of his day.

Social and political aversions.

The aversion which Hamlet shows towards politicians, lawyers, and land-buyers has no real connection with the plot of the drama; it is evidently then an expression of the author's personal feelings towards the times in which he lived: to what he calls "the fatness of those pursy times"—times which were glorying in being no longer "priest-ridden," but which, he perceived, had only exchanged masters, and were becoming politician-ridden, lawyer-ridden and money-ridden. These were indeed precisely the middle-class forces which were rising into power upon the ruins of that very feudalism which "Shakespeare," on the one hand, delineates, and Edward de Vere, on the other hand, personally represents. In this again we see Hamlet, "Shakespeare" and Edward de Vere are entirely at one in relation to the times in which the play was written.

Hamlet laments in relation to his time "O, cursed spite that ever I was born to set it right." And yet the setting right has not been achieved though three centuries have passed away since "Shakespeare" penned this lament. Still, if the new order for which the "prophetic soul" of "Shakespeare" looked is to arise at last through a reinterpretation and application to modern problems, of social principles which existed in germ in medievalism, then, "Shakespeare," in helping to preserve the best ideals of feudalism, will have been a most potent factor in the solution of those social problems which in our day are assuming threatening proportions throughout the civilized world. The feudal ideal which we once more emphasize is that of *noblesse oblige*; the devotion of the strong to the weak; the principle that all power of one man over his fellows, whether it rests upon a political or industrial basis, can only possess an enduring sanction so long as superiors discharge faithfully their duties to inferiors. In this task of "putting right," Hamlet or "Shakespeare," who we believe was Edward de Vere, through the silent spiritual influences which have spread from his dramas, will probably have contributed as much as any other single force.

Political events.

Not as an important part of our argument, but as strengthening the feeling of a connection between the play of Hamlet and events in England at the time when it appeared, the rising of the citizens of Elsinor with the cry "Laertes shall be king," is suggestive of the rising in London under Essex, though it must not be omitted that Thomas Cecil, who in some respects resembles Laertes, was chiefly instrumental in putting down the Essex rebellion. Again the change, not only in the occupants of the throne but also of dynasties in Denmark, "the election lighting on Fortinbras," from the neighbouring country of Poland, is suggestive of a similar change in England when, consequent upon the royal nomination, England received the first of a new dynasty from the neighbouring country of Scotland. In this case Fortinbras would be James I, and Oxford's officiating at the coronation might appear as an equivalent to Hamlet's dying vote, "He has my dying voice."

For Oxford would probably be of those who expected from the son of Mary, Queen of Scots, more sympathy with what his mother represented than James actually showed. A comparison of the different editions of *Hamlet* in respect to these political matters might disclose interesting particulars.

Hamlet's dying appeal.

In view of all that is known of Edward de Vere, and of "Shakespeare" as revealed in the *Sonnets*, no other words contained in the great dramas surpass, either in significance in relation to our problem, or in power of moving appeal, than the parting words which Hamlet addresses to Horatio. The more they are dwelt upon the less appropriate do they appear to the fictitious Hamlet, and the more do they sound like a real heart-wrung cry from the dramatist himself for reparation and for justice to his memory. Put Edward de Vere quite out of the question; remember only that "Shakespeare," in sonnets written years before the drama, had spoken of himself as a man living under a cloud of disrepute beyond anything he had merited, desiring for himself nothing more than to pass from life's scene in such a way that his name would drop from the memory of man, then read the dying words of Hamlet:

> Had I but time as this fell sergeant, death,
> Is strict in his arrest, O, I could tell you,—
> But let it be. Horatio, I am dead;
> Thou livest; report me and my cause aright
> To the unsatisfied.
> O good Horatio, what a wounded name
> Things standing thus unknown, shall live behind me!
> If ever thou did'st hold me in thy heart.
> Absent thee from felicity awhile,
> And in this harsh world draw thy breath in pain,
> To tell my story. . . .
>   . . . The rest is silence.

Reparation demanded.

If, therefore, Hamlet may be regarded as an indirect dramatic self-revelation of Shakespeare, so evidently do these dying words link themselves on to explicit statements in his direct poetic self-revelation, that they may be accepted, without in any way straining a point, as a dying appeal of "Shakespeare," whoever he may have been, that his true story should be told and his name cleared of the blemishes that "vulgar scandal" had stamped upon it. The change of attitude was justified by what he had accomplished in the interval. His was no longer the record of a wasted genius. Sitting apparently "in idle cell," he had achieved something which altered the whole aspect of his title to honour. He had created, and offered as an atonement for any short-comings of which he had been guilty—and who, indeed, has not?—the most magnificent achievement that English literature can boast; one of the three greatest achievements in the literature of the world. It is impossible to resist the conviction, then, that these dying words of Hamlet's were intended for some friend of "Shakespeare's," who, from some cause or other, has fallen short in the discharge of the trust with which he was honoured; though the publishing of the sonnets, and of the folio editions of Shakespeare, may have been a partial discharge of this trust.

Although these things are applicable to any "Shakespeare," and any man to whom they will not apply is, *ipso facto*, excluded, it would appear, from all claim or title in the matter, it is to Edward de Vere alone, so far as we can discover, that they can be made to apply fully and directly. When, then, we find that this particular play, although appearing unauthentically in a curtailed form the previous year, was published, much as we have it now, in the year of his death, and then, although no further revision appeared for eighteen years, an edition appeared containing alterations upon which he had evidently been engaged at the time of his death, we can read in these closing passages of the play nothing less than a final call for justice and for the honour he had merited by his work.

A future task.

For three hundred years actors have uttered and audiences have listened to these tragic and pathetic passages, never dreaming that they came out of the inmost soul and the bitter experiences of the writer. Their deep personal significance we claim to be making known now for the first time; and we trust that our own imperfectly accomplished labours may achieve something towards winning that redress for which our great dramatist has so dramatically appealed.

The whole story of his life, as he may have wished it to be told, will probably never be known. To reinterpret the known facts by the light of the Shakespearean literature, in which work we have made the first essay, will doubtless yield larger and truer results when others have taken up the task. There is also the possibility that new data may be unearthed, and this, together with the gathering together and unifying of facts scattered through the diverse records of other men, may bring to light the things "standing yet unknown" which were in his mind. The greatest of the facts "standing thus unknown" is that which is now announced, and its substantiation will go further towards healing his "wounded name" than any other single fact that may in future be laid bare.

———————

On a review of the contents of this chapter, it will hardly be denied that the number of the particulars, and the general unity of the plan, which bring the greatest "Shakespeare" masterpiece into accord with the life and personality of the man whom we selected, on quite other grounds, as the probable author of the play, is not the least remarkable of the series of correspondences that have appeared at every step of our investigations.

CHAPTER XVII

CHRONOLOGICAL SUMMARY OF EDWARD DE VERE AND "SHAKESPEARE"

THE biographical parts of this work are not intended in any sense as a biography of Oxford, nor as an adequate representation either of himself or of the different people whose lives were mixed with his. Everything is treated from the point of view of the main argument, which is concerned primarily with the identification of the author of Shakespeare's plays and in a secondary way with the correction of a false and incomplete conception of the Earl of Oxford that has become established. In the statement of our argument we have been able to preserve only a very general adhesion to chronological order. Events that may have been separated by many years have sometimes had to be stated together owing to their relation to some specific point of evidence. A certain amount of overlapping of the periods and much repetition of facts have therefore been unavoidable. As a necessary corrective we now offer the following summarized statement of events in the order in which they occurred.

Early Period.

1550. Birth of Edward de Vere, Seventeenth Earl of Oxford (April 2nd).

1556. Birth of Anne Cecil (December 5th).

1558. Accession of Queen Elizabeth.

1562. Death of Oxford's father: Oxford becomes a royal ward and an inmate of Cecil's house in The Strand. Arthur Golding (his uncle), translator of Ovid, becomes his private tutor.

1568. Oxford's mother died (having previously married Sir

Charles—or Christopher—Tyrell. Date of
marriage unknown).

1569. Oxford seeks military service and is refused.
1571. Cecil becomes Lord Burleigh.
          Oxford comes of age: marries Anne Cecil.
1573. Arthur Golding enrolled in "Inner Temple Records."
          Hatton writes to Queen Elizabeth of Oxford (as "the
              boar").
          "Oxford's men" indulge in wild escapade suggestive of
              Prince Hal and his men on the identical road
              (between Gravesend and Rochester).
          Oxford asks for naval employment and is refused.
          Oxford has apartments in the Savoy: a literary centre.
1574. Oxford runs away to the continent and is brought
          back.
1575. Oxford visits Italy: Milan, Venice, and Padua.
          (Particulars suggestive of *Taming of the Shrew* and
          The Merchant of Venice).
1576. Returns via Paris. Writes from Paris particulars
          suggestive of *Othello*.
          Temporary estrangement from Lady Oxford.
          Remarkable episode recorded in Wright's History of
              Essex identifying Oxford with Bertram in *All's
              Well*.

Middle Period.

1576. Begins Bohemian association with literary men and
          play-actors.
1576-8. Publication of many early lyrics.
          Letter to Bedingfield.
          Rivalry with Philip Sidney.
1579. Oxford's quarrel with Sidney.
          Publication of Edmund Spenser's *Shepherd's Calender*
              containing probable reference to Oxford's rivalry
              with Sidney: "Willie and Perigot."
1580. Anthony Munday, playwright and theatre manager,

discloses that he is the servant of the Earl of
Oxford. Munday's plays contain passages not written
by himself: passages which "might have rested in the
mind of Shakespeare."

1580-4. Oxford's company (The Oxford Boys) tour in the
provinces.

Lyly, Oxford's private secretary, entrusted with their
management.

1584. Oxford's company visits Stratford-on-Avon.

1584-7. The "Oxford Boys" established in London. They
perform plays written by Oxford.

Oxford Boys perform *Agamemnon and Ulysses.*

1586. Trial of Mary Queen of Scots—Oxford takes part.
Death of Sir Philip Sidney.

1587. Mary executed.

1588. Sidney's funeral.

Death of Lady Oxford.

The Earl of Oxford takes part in the sea-fight against
the   Spanish Armada.

Oxford begins his life of privacy and retirement.

Final Period.

1590. Spenser publishes *Teares of the Muses* with probable
reference to Oxford (as Willie) "sitting in idle cell."

Beginning of William Shakspere's career.

Supposed date of first sonnets.

Proposed marriage of De Vere's daughter, Elizabeth,
to Henry Wriothesley, Earl of Southampton, to
which proposal the first of the sonnets have been
attributed.

1591 or 2. Oxford's second marriage (complete retirement).

1592-1601. Great Blank in Oxford's record.

1592. Date assigned to *Love's Labour's Lost* (containing
representations of contemporary men).

1593. Birth of Oxford's son Henry (Feb. 24th).

Dedication of *Venus* to Southampton.

1594. Dedication of *Lucrece* to Southampton.

1597-1604. Great period of Shakespearean publication.

1597. The great issue of Shakespeare's plays begins.

1598. The name "Shakespeare" first printed on the plays.

1600. Rush of Shakespearean publications (6 in the year).

1601. Rising under the Earl of Essex.

1601. The Earl of Oxford emerges from his retirement to take part in the trial of the Earls of Essex and Southampton.

1602. Date assigned to *Hamlet*.

A notable gap: Southampton in The Tower; Blank in accounts of the Treasurer of the Chamber.

Oxford's servants play at the "Boar's Head" Tavern.

Pirated edition of *Merry Wives* published.

1603. *Hamlet* unauthentically published.

Death of Queen Elizabeth—no tribute from "Shakespeare" or Oxford.

Oxford officiates at coronation of James I.

Southampton liberated—arranges performance of *Love's Labour's Lost* for the new Queen.

Last of "Shakespeare's" sonnets written.

1604. Authentic publication of *Hamlet*.

Date assigned to *Othello*.

Death of Edward de Vere.

Last of authentic Shakespearean issues for 18 years.

William Shakspere's supposed retirement to Stratford. (according to some Stratfordian authorities)

Southampton's connection with William Shakspere ceases.

Posthumous Matters.

1605-1608. Suspension of Shakespearean publication.

1608-1609.   Slight revival.

Publication of three plays and the *Sonnets*, all published unauthentically.

1612. Second Lady Oxford dies.

Date assigned for William Shakspere's complete
retirement from London.

1616. Death of William Shakspere.

1622. Separate publication of *Othello*.

1623. The First Folio "Shakespeare" published.

1624. Death of the Earl of Southampton.

1632. The Second Folio Shakespeare published.
Publication of Lyly's plays by the same firm. There
appears for the first time in these plays a set of
excellent lyrics which had been omitted from all
previous editions of Lyly's work.

1635. Death of Sir Horace Vere (April 2nd).

CHAPTER XVIII

CONCLUSION

WE called Dante the melodious Priest of Middle-Age Catholicism. May we not call Shakespeare the still more melodious Priest of a true Catholicism, the Universal Church of the Future and of all times.[228]

CARLYLE, *Heroes.*

We may now bring our labours to a close with a review of the course our investigations have taken and a summary of their results. Having examined both the internal and external conditions of the old theory of Shakespearean authorship, we found that the whole presented such an accumulation and combination of anomalies as to render it no longer tenable. We therefore undertook the solution of problem of authorship thus presented.

Beginning with a characterization of Shakespeare drawn from a consideration of his writings, a characterization embracing no less than eighteen points and involving a most unusual combination, we proceeded to look for the dramatist. Using the form of the *Venus and Adonis* stanza as a guide, we selected one Elizabethan poem in this form, which seemed to bear the greatest resemblance to Shakespeare's workmanship. The author of this poem, Edward de Vere, was found to fulfil in all essentials the delineation of Shakespeare with which we set out.

We next found that competent literary authorities, in testifying to the distinctive qualities of his work, spoke of his poems in terms appropriate to "Shakespeare." An examination of his position in the history of Elizabethan poetry showed him to

---

[228] Carlyle, *On Heroes*, p. 103.

be a possible source of the Shakespeare literature, whilst an examination of his lyrics revealed a most remarkable correspondence both in general qualities and in important details with the other literary work which we now attribute to him. Turning next to the records of his life and of his family we found that these were fully reflected in the dramas: the contents of which bear pronounced marks of all the outstanding incidents and personal relationships of his career, whilst the special conditions of his life at the time when these plays were being produced were just such as accorded with the issuing of the works.

His death, we found, was followed by an immediate arrest of Shakespearean publication, and by a number of other striking evidences of the removal of the great dramatist, whilst a temporary review of publication a few years later was of such a character as to give additional support to the view that the author was then dead. Finally, we have shown that the sonnets are now made intelligible for the first time since their appearance, and that the great dramatic *tour de force* of the author is nothing less than an idealized portraiture of himself.

Summed up we have:

1. The evidences of the poetry.
2. The general biographical evidence.
3. The chronological evidence.
4. The posthumous evidence.
5. The special arguments:
    (*a*) The *All's Well* argument.
    (*b*) The *Love's Labour's Lost* argument.
    (*c*) The *Othello* argument.
    (*d*) The *Sonnets* argument.
    (*e*) The *Hamlet* argument.

It is the perfect harmony, consistency and convergence of all the various lines of argument employed, and the overwhelming mass of coincidences that they involve, that give to our results the appearance of a case fully and, we believe, unimpeachably proven.

We have by no means exhausted the subject, however. Not only does much remain to be said, but it may be that in taking so decisive a step, involving the readjustment of more than one long-established conception, some statements have been made that later will have to be modified or withdrawn. Working, too, amongst a mass of details, in what was previously an unfamiliar domain, it is possible that serious errors have slipped in. In arguments like the present, however, whole lines of subsidiary evidence may break down and yet leave the central contention firmly and unassailably established.

It would not in the least surprise us, moreover, if particular items of evidence much more conclusive than any single argument we have offered, should be forthcoming, or even if it should be pointed out that we have blunderingly overlooked some vital matter. From experience in the course of our enquiries we have no fear that any such oversight will appreciably affect the validity of the argument as a whole. For the detection of oversights hitherto has but brought additional strength to our position; and so frequently has this occurred in the past that it is difficult to think of its having any other effect in the future. Only one conclusion then seems possible; namely, that the problem of the authorship of Shakespeare's plays has been solved, and that all future enquiry is destined to furnish but an accumulating support to the solution here proposed.

It will be seen that only in a general way has it been possible to adhere, in our last chapters, to the plan of investigation outlined at the start. In tracing indications of the life and personality of Edward de Vere in the writings of Shakespeare, much of the ground mapped for separate succeeding stages of the enquiry has been covered. The sixth stage was to gather together "corroborative evidence," and this is largely furnished by last two chapters in which the poetic and the dramatic self-revelation of the poet are respectively dealt with. The seventh stage, to develop personal connections, if possible, between the new author and the old authorship, including the man William Shakspere, is covered by those biographical chapters which treat of Arthur Golding, the translator of Ovid; Anthony Munday, the playwright; Lyly, Oxford's private secretary and "Shakespeare's only model in Comedy"; and lastly Henry Wriothesley, Earl of Southampton, to whom the Shakespeare poems are dedicated, who is known as the munificent friend of William Shakspere, and in whom the Earl of Oxford manifested a special interest.

The task which we set out to accomplish has therefore been performed in sufficient accordance with the original plan. However unworthy of so great a theme the manner of presenting the case may be, it is impossible not to feel gratified at the good fortune that has attended our excursion into a department that is not specially our own. In the brief moment of conscious existence which lies between the two immensities Destiny has honoured us with this particular task, and though it may not be the work we could have wished to do, we are glad to have been able to do so much.

The matter must now pass out of our hands, and the case must be tried in public by means of a discussion in which expert opinion must play a large part in the formation of a definitive judgment. Whether such discussion be immediate or deferred, we have no doubt that it must come at some time or other, and that, when it does come, the ultimate verdict will be to proclaim Edward de Vere, Seventeenth Earl of Oxford, as the real author of the greatest masterpieces in English literature.

We venture, therefore, to make an earnest appeal first of all to the thoughtful sections of all classes of the British public, and not merely of the literary classes, to examine, and even to insist upon an authoritative examination, of the evidence adduced. The matter belongs, of course, to the world at large. But England must bear the greater part of the responsibility; and her honour is involved in seeing that a question of the name and fame of one of the most illustrious of her immortal dead, the one name which England has stamped most unquestionably upon the intellectual life of the human race, is not given over to mere literary contentiousness. We are bound, however, to make a special appeal to those, whose intellectual equipment and opportunities fit them for the examination of the argument, to approach the problem in an impartial spirit. It will not be an easy thing for Stratfordians or Baconians of many years' standing to admit that they were wrong, and that the problem has at last solved itself in a way contrary to all their former views. To sincere admirers of "Shakespeare," however, those who have caught something of his largeness of intellectual vision and fidelity to fact, the difficulty of recognizing and admitting an error will not prove insuperable, whilst their power of thus aiding in a great act of justice will be immense.

In addition to securing the recognition of Edward de Vere as the author of Shakespeare's works, much remains to be done in the way of lifting the load of disrepute from his memory, and winning for his name the honour that is his by right. "That gentle spirit," as we believe Spenser to have described him and as his own verses reveal him (according so well as the expression does with our "Gentle Shakespeare"), has remained for too many years under the "unlifted shadow."

Whatever his faults may have been, we have in him a soul awake at every point to all that touches human life. All high aspiration and endeavour find their encouragement in his work, and no phase of human suffering or weakness but meets in him a kindly and sympathetic treatment, even when his mockery is most trenchant. "The man whom Nature's self had made, to mock herself and truth to imitate with kindly counter under mimic shade"—the terms in which we have shown Spenser speaks of De

Vere, and which so accurately describe "Shakespeare"—could be no profligate. The irregularities to which the Shakespearean sonnets bear witness are beyond question rooted in sincerity of character and tenderness of heart. We do not condone such, but we are bound to draw a very marked distinction between this and mere dissoluteness. All that Shakespeare has written, and every line of De Vere, bespeaks a man who, even in the lowest depths of pessimism, and in his moments of bitterest cynicism, had kept alive the highest faculties of his mind and heart. No man of persistently loose life can do this; and, therefore, the establishing of the identity of Edward de Vere with "Shakespeare" demands the relinquishing of all those superficial judgments that might have been allowed to pass unchallenged so long as Edward de Vere was supposed to be a person of no particular moment in the history of his country or the world.

Until now the world has moreover seen and known in him only the eccentricity and turbulence of Hamlet. The real Hamlet, tender-hearted and passionate, whose deep and melancholy soul broods affectionately upon the great tragedy of human life, and who yet preserves the light of intellect and humour, whose "noble heart" breaks at last but who carries on his fight to the last moment of life, when the pen, not the sword, drops from his fingers, is the Hamlet which we must now see in Edward de Vere, as he stands before the world as "Shakespeare." The fret and trouble of his objective life in the Elizabethan age have hung around his memory for over three hundred years. All this, we believe, is about to end; and, the period of his purgation passed, we may confidently hope that, entering into the full possession of his honours, a time of still richer spiritual influence awaits his continued existence in the hearts and lives of men.

"The fatness of these pursy times," against which his whole career was a protest, has settled more than ever upon the life of mankind, and the culminating product of this modern materialism is the world war that was raging whilst most of these pages were being penned—a war which has been the most insane gamble for material power that the undisciplined instinct of domination has ever inflicted upon a suffering humanity; threatening the complete submergence of the soul of civilized man. Yet amongst the projects of "after the war" reconstruction that were being set afoot, even whilst it was in progress, materialistic purposes everywhere prevailed. In education, for example, where especially spiritual aims should have dominated, commercial and industrial objects were chiefly considered. And now that the conflict is over the entire disruption of social existence is threatened by material "interests" and antagonisms.

Against this the spirit of "Shakespeare" again protests. His "prophetic soul," still "dreaming on things to come," points to a future in which the human spirit, and its accessory instruments and institutions, must become the supreme concern of man. The squandering of his own material resources, though unwise in itself, was the soul's reaction against the growing Mammon worship of his day: and the fidelity with which he represents in his plays the chivalries of feudalism is the expression of an affection for those social relationships which minister to the finer spirit in man. He stands, then, for an enlarged and enriched conception of spiritual things: a conception embracing the entire range of man's mental and moral faculties, from gayest laughter and subtle playfulness to profoundest thought and tragic earnestness of purpose. He stands for these things, and he stands for their supremacy in human life, involving the subordination of every other human concern to these spiritual forces and interests.

More than ever in the coming years shall we need the spirit of "Shakespeare" to assist in the work of holding the "politician" and the materialist, ever maneuvering for ascendancy in human affairs, to their secondary position in subordination to, and under the discipline of, the spiritual elements of society. We cannot, of course, go back to "Shakespeare's" mediaevalism, but we shall need to incorporate into modern life what was best in the social order and social spirit of the Middle Ages. "The prophetic soul of the wide world" fills its vision, not with a state of more intense material competition and increased luxury, but with a social order in which the human heart and mind will have larger facilities for expansion; in which poetry, music, the drama, and art in all its forms will throw an additional charm over a life of human harmony and mutual helpfulness; in which, therefore, "Shakespeare," "our ever-living poet," will be an intimate personal influence when the heroes of our late Titanic struggle will be either forgotten or will only appear dimly in the pages of history.

His works do not, and can never, supply all that the human soul requires. To satisfy the deepest needs of mankind the Shakespearean scriptures must be supplemented by the other great scriptures of our race; and all together they will only meet our full demands in so far as they succeed in putting before us the guiding image of a divine Humanity. In this work, however, "Shakespeare" will always retain a foremost place. Speaking no longer from behind a mask or from under a pseudonym, but in his own honoured name, Edward de Vere, Seventeenth Earl of Oxford, will ever call mankind to the worship of truth, reality, the infinite wonder of human nature and the eternal greatness of Man.

APPENDIX I

THE TEMPEST

I DO not discern those marks of long practice in the dramatic art and the full maturity of the poet's genius which some have discovered in [*The Tempest*].[229]

HUNTER.

Its place amongst the plays.

Although, as was inevitable, difficulties have arisen in the course of our investigations, the surprising thing has been that they have proved so few and unformidable. Up to the present, the greatest obstacle is that presented by one play, *The Tempest*. If we pass in review the different plays of Shakespeare, in order of the dates assigned to them, we find that this one occupies a very remarkable position. First of all, we notice that the great popular comedies are all attributed to the earlier part of Shakespeare's career, and the best-known tragedies, with the exception of *Romeo and Juliet*, to the later part. These tragedies culminate in *Hamlet* and *Othello*, in the early years of what may be called the tragedy period, and taper off with such mixed compositions as the tragedies of *Coriolanus*, *Timon*, *Pericles* and *Cymbeline*. The great dramatist is supposed to have paid his final respects to the dramatic world he had adorned for so many years, in a play which another man had been called in to finish—the composite and somewhat inharmonious play of *Henry VIII*. Then we have *The Tempest* sandwiched in between the group which contains such a

---

[229] Rev. John Hunter, *A Disquisition on the Scene, Origin, Date, Etc. Etc. of Shakespeare's The Tempest*, p. 65, quoted in the New Variorum edition of *The Tempest*, p. 285.

tragedy as *Pericles* and the nondescript history play *Henry VIII*.

From this point of view it looks like a play that had wandered away and fallen into bad company. Its natural associate, *A Midsummer Night's Dream*, is separated from it by almost as wide an interval as the Shakespearean period will permit. Under any theory of authorship this work occupies an anomalous position. To the views we are now urging it presents a real and serious difficulty: the only formidable obstacle so far encountered, and therefore demanding special attention.

Date of writing.

It will be noticed that it is one of the twenty plays printed for the first time in the 1623 folio edition. Although printed then for the first time there is abundant evidence that a number of these plays were in existence many years before. In relation to *The Tempest* the only authoritative fact seems to be that a play of this name was amongst those performed to celebrate the marriage of the Princess Elizabeth to the Elector Frederick in 1613. There existed, however, a forged reference to it connecting it with the year 1611; and as the 1613 reference almost pushes it outside the Shakespearean period proper, the forged reference seems like an attempt, for some reason, to bring it more within the period. The circumstances are certainly suspicious. There is no record of its having been registered, and no indication of its having been in print before 1623. Facts like these, when connected with such a play as *Timon of Athens*, do not strike us as being at all remarkable. In connection with a stage favourite like *The Tempest* they are not what we should have expected, whoever the author of the play may have been. It bears more heavily upon our own theories, however, than upon the Stratfordian view. It seems incredible that it could have been written and staged in the early Shakespearean period without some trace appearing, and it is very improbable that such a play should have been written and allowed to remain unstaged for many years, seeing that the staging element in it is more pronounced than in any other play attributed to "Shakespeare."

Contemporary events in the play.

In addition to all this, it is held to contain traces of contemporary events of the early years of James I's reign and even to be in part indebted to a pamphlet published in 1610. This fact by itself presents no insurmountable difficulty, seeing that the interpolation of other men's work is quite a recognized feature of the later Shakespearean plays; but, taken along with its more modern character, and, what seems to us the less Elizabethan quality of its diction, it appears to justify the assumption that the work as a whole belongs to the date to which it has been assigned.

We have endeavoured to present the case in respect to *The Tempest* with all the adverse force with which it bears upon the theory of Edward de Vere being "Shakespeare"; and must confess that it appears, at first blush, as if *The Tempest* were threatening the shipwreck of all our hopes and labours in the cause of Shakespearean authorship.

Alternative dates.

The somewhat anomalous position occupied by the play has, however, already given rise to doubts respecting the accuracy of the date assigned to it. The first writer of eminence to raise these doubts was Hunter, who is described in the *Variorum Shakespeare*, as "one of the most learned and exact of commentators."[230] He also has been the first to question its title to the high praise which it is fashionable to lavish upon this composition: the words which we quote at the head of this chapter. Sir George Greenwood, too, has raised doubts as to whether the masking performance is from the hand of "Shakespeare."

Other critics and commentators have given attention to the question of its date, and although the great majority confirm the later date which is usually ascribed to it (1610-1613), we furnish now some authorities for an earlier production.

Hunter.[231]   1596.

---

[230] The New Variorum edition of *The Tempest.*, p. 291. Hunter is quoted many times in that work. See footnote 229, p. 429.
[231] See footnote 229, p. 429.

Knight.[232]   1602-1603.
Dyce[233] and Staunton.[234]   After 1603.
Karl Elze.[235]   1604.

There exists, therefore, some Shakespearean authority both for an earlier date and also for the intervention of a strange hand. Nevertheless, we have not felt convinced by these authorities; and have therefore been indisposed to take refuge behind their findings. The reader who, in spite of the contents of this chapter, may continue to cling to the old estimate of the play may at any rate find comfort in the dates furnished above.

Contrast with other comedies.

We must now ask the reader, who we assume is willing to take some trouble to get at the truth of the matter, to first read carefully some of the earlier comedies like *Love's Labour's Lost, A Midsummer Night's Dream* and *As You Like It*. When he has read these works appreciatively, and has got a sense, as it were, of Shakespeare's force of intellect and wit, the packed significance of his lines, his teeming imagery, the fecundity of his ideas on everything pertaining to the multiple forces of human nature, his incisive glances into human motives, his subtle turns of expression, the precision and refinement of his distinctions, the easy flow of his diction, the vocal qualities of his word combinations: all these well-known Shakespearean characteristics; let him then turn and read *The Tempest*, thinking not so much of the broad situations presented by the stage play, but looking for that finer literary and poetical material that constitute the true Shakespeare work, and he will probably experience a much greater disappointment than he anticipated.

Take, for example, the second scene in the first act, the dialogue between Prospero and Miranda, especially where the

---

[232] Charles Knight, in *Studies of Shakspere: Companion Volume to Every Edition of the Text*, says 1611. I wasn't able to find any other date mentioned in any other of Knight's books on Shakespeare.

[233] The Rev. Alexander Dyce, editor, *The Works of William Shakespeare*, p. 172.

[234] Howard Staunton, editor, *The Plays of Shakespeare*, vol. 3, p. 3.

[235] Karl Elze, "Essay 1: The Date of *The Tempest*," *Essays on Shakespeare*. See especially pp. 9, 15-16, 18.

former is relating his misfortunes to the latter. It seems all right, no doubt, on a first reading, or on hearing it repeated on the stage. It explains a particular situation lucidly, in bold outline, making no special demands upon the mind of the reader or hearer; and, for those who wish to push on with the business of the play and see how things work out, it is just the thing wanted. One does not, however, feel a great desire to read it over again immediately so as to drink more deeply of its poetic charm; nor would anyone seriously memorize its phrases for the purpose of enriching his own resources of expression.

Literary quality.

The situation was, however, eminently suitable for fine poetic treatment; yet the prosy character of the narration, broken by Prospero's harping on the question of whether Miranda was attending to him or not, makes one wonder what there is in it to justify the attempt at blank verse. We use the word "attempt" advisedly; for a close examination of it will reveal a larger proportion of false quantities and non-rhythmic lines than can be found in an equal space in the best Shakespearean verse. Indeed, throughout the play there is a general thinness, so far as first-class literary matter and the figurative language which distinguishes the best poetry are concerned. Our task is to ascertain whether what there is possesses true Shakespearean characteristics.

Its chief passage.

Judging this point, not by its worst, but what is accepted as its best passages, we shall not attempt to select what may appear to us as the best, but take the one passage in *The Tempest* that has been singled out for special notice by others.

> These our actors.
> As I foretold you. were all spirits, and
> Are melted into air, into thin air:
> And, like the baseless fabric of this vision,
> The cloud-capp'd towers, the gorgeous palaces,
> The solemn temples, the great globe itself,
> Yea, all which it inherit, shall dissolve,
> And, like this insubstantial pageant faded,
> Leave not a rack behind.

If our ideas of Shakespeare's style have been formed from studying this particular play, the passage will doubtless seem quite Shakespearean: not otherwise, however. Before discussing it as a whole, however, we ask the reader to notice the word "and" at the end of the second line, as it connects itself with an important point which we shall presently have to consider. To what, then, do these lines owe their popularity? We know to what a speech of Portia's, or a meditation of Jacques', or a soliloquy of Hamlet's, owes its popularity. All these great Shakespearean utterances owe their power, not to the mere grandiloquence that fits them for perorations, but to their direct appeal to the human heart and mind which form their own subject matter. Cosmic theories come and go, but the fundamental constitution of human nature, the nature of man's inward experiences, sufferings and struggles, remains substantially and eternally the same. It is because Shakespeare's theme is ever this enduring spiritual matter that his influence suffers no waning, but grows with the centuries.

Negative philosophy.

In the passage we have just quoted there is not a touch of Shakespeare's special interest. It is simple cosmic philosophy, and, as such, it is the most dreary negativism that was ever put into high-sounding words. Shakespeare's soul was much too large for mere negation. He was essentially positivist. When he handled his own theme of human nature he expounded what he saw and felt, always holding the subject down to its own realities, conditioned by its own essential relationships. In modern terms, he was an experimentalist; or, to use a clumsier, though more accurate, word, an experientialist. On the other hand he was no mere empiricist: his was a vision that "looked before and after," a "prophetic soul dreaming on things to come." Recognizing the limitations of human vision, his mind could yet take in the thought of the great unknown that stretched beyond the range of immediate faculties, but he filled it in with no mere negative, however undetermined his positive may have been.

> There are more things in heaven and earth, Horatio,
> Than are dreamt of in your philosophy.

Stolen thunder.

The philosophy of the passage we have quoted from *The Tempest* is such as we might conceive Hamlet attributing to Horatio, and not that of Hamlet himself. Nor do we believe that it owes its popularity to the outlook it represents. It is rather the awe-inspiring vastness of the conception and its high-sounding phrases that have won for the passage its place in English rhetorical literature. Neither in theme nor in philosophy, however, does it seem to us to be Shakespearean.

Even the terms of the passage are not original to the writer of this much beloved comedy, but are clearly suggested by a passage in a play written in the last years of the sixteenth century (see *Variorum Shakespeare*). Their value as evidence of Shakespearean authorship is therefore negligible. When, however, we come to the closing sentence of the passage we are assured by readers of Shakespeare that here, at least, we have the work of the master:

> We are such stuff as dreams are made on, and our little life is rounded with a sleep.

The stuff of dreams.

Here we find ourselves faced with one of the chief difficulties in discussing Shakespeare: namely, dogmatic assertion based upon literary feeling or instinct, but offering no fixed standard of measurement by which the truth of the claim may be tested. Although, then, we are assured that these words are eminently Shakespearean, we make bold to say that they appear to us as un-Shakespearean as any utterance with which "Shakespeare" has been credited.

When we read that "all the world's a stage and all the men and women merely players," we feel that the writer's mind, in dealing with life, is occupied with clear and definite conceptions, which he imparts vividly to his readers by the crispness and precision of the terms he employs. When the mind of Hamlet works upon the great unknown, the "sleep of death," and the possible experiences after death, "what dreams may come," we have the same definiteness of conception, the same precise relationship of language to thought. We may think that he stops short: that he might have given us more; but we have no uncertainty respecting the part he has given. We move with him in the plane of realities alike of life and death: and when he deals with what he does not know, he knows what it is he does not know. If, then, this mental clarity, this definiteness and precision alike of thought and expression, are not dominant notes of "Shakespeare," we must confess that our understanding of his work has yet to begin.

Muddled metaphysics.

Compare now from this point of view the characteristic utterances of Shakespeare on life and death just quoted with the lines previously cited from *The Tempest*. We may safely challenge anyone to produce another passage from the whole of Shakespeare that will match with the latter in metaphysical vagueness. Abandon for a moment the practice of squeezing into or squeezing out of these words some philosophical significance, and attempt the simpler task of attaching a merely elementary English meaning to the terms and placing these meanings into some kind of coherent relationship to one another. We are stuff: the stuff of dreams: dreams are made on (or "of"?): life *rounded* with a sleep—we will not say that Shakespeare never gives us such "nuts to crack," but we can say with full confidence that they are not characteristically Shakespearean. So far as we can get hold of the general drift of the metaphors, it seems that the present life of man is likened to dreams: "We *are* such stuff, etc.," and that he brings his dreams to an end by going to sleep. In common with Shakespeare and the majority of mankind, however, we are accustomed to associate our dreams with our actual times of sleep.

On its deeper side we would say that the sentence is in flat contradiction to the mind of Shakespeare. To him human life is the one great objective reality. We are not now saying that he is right or wrong in this; but it is this objective pressure of human life upon him 'that has produced the immortal dramas; whether wholesome or vile it is real wholesomeness and real vileness; whether life is spent in earnest or is merely that of "men and women playing parts," his world is peopled by real men; not *dreamy stuff.*

Whether, then, we take the cosmic philosophy of the whole passage, or the touch of human philosophy with which it closes, we maintain that whether written by "Shakespeare" or not, it is not Shakespearean.

Quality of The Tempest.

If we are disposed to deny to the play the possession of first-class Shakespearean work it would nevertheless be folly to discredit the good work, of what might be called the second class, that it certainly does contain. The times were prolific of second-rate work, judged by the standard of Shakespeare; work which, but for this high standard, might have ranked as first class. There seems, indeed, to be in the play indications of a real collaboration between two men, a playwright proper and a poet. The passage quoted, and others, especially the lyrical verse, seem to be from a different hand from the one that wrote the play as a whole; but it does not look like the unfinished work of one writer being finished by another. Our present business, however, is to see whether or not it is Shakespearean.

"Dumb-shows and noise."

Continuing this enquiry we shall first recall certain criticisms in *Hamlet* upon a class of play then coming into vogue.

> There is, sir, an aery of children, little eyases, that cry out on the top of question, and are most tyrannically clapped for it.
>
> *   *   *   *
>
> . . . the groundlings . . . for the most part are capable of nothing but *inexplicable dumb-shows and noise.*

With these remarks in mind let the reader turn over the pages of the great Shakespearean dramas, noticing the stage directions.

For the most part these are little more than the simple expressions "enter," "exit," "aside," "sleeps," "rises and advances," "trumpets," "noise within," and such like. When, as in the case of the dumb-show episode in the by-play in *Hamlet*, directions are necessary, these are limited to mere outline, every particular action indicated being an essential part of the drama, and moreover quite explicable. Now, with *Hamlet's* special animadversion on "inexplicable dumb-shows and noise" in mind, turn to the stage directions in *The Tempest*.

> A tempestuous noise of thunder and lightning heard . . . A confused noise within . . . Thunder (at intervals).

> Enter Prospero, above, invisible. Enter several strange Shapes, bringing in a banquet; they dance about it with gentle actions and salutations; and, inviting the king, etc., to eat, they depart.

Again:

> Thunder and lightning. Enter Ariel, like a harpy; claps his wings upon the table; and with a quaint device, the banquet vanishes.

Again:

> He vanishes in thunder; then, to soft music, enter the Shapes again, and dance, with mocks and mows, and carry out the table.

Further on:

> Enter certain reapers, properly habited; they join with the Nymphs in a graceful dance; towards the end whereof Prospero starts suddenly and speaks; after which to a strange hollow and confused noise they heavily vanish.

And there is still more of this kind of thing. Yet it is supposed that the very man who penned all this had, six or seven years previously, taken up arms against such pantomimic products and entered into his great masterpiece a caveat against this development of "inexplicable dumb-shows and noise."

Un-Shakespearean details.

In the First Folio only six out of all Shakespeare's plays are

prefaced with lists of dramatis personae. Of these *The Tempest* is
one and *Timon of Athens*, an admittedly "collaborated" work, is
another: in the latter work it is done most ostentatiously. As we
shall find the singularities of the former play accumulate, the
exceptional fact just narrated should be kept in mind. Turning to
the list in *The Tempest* we find that one character is described as
"drunken," another as "honest," and a third as "savage."
Although in another of these lists (*The Two Gentlemen*) Thurio is
spoken of as "foolish," in none of them is there so much of it as
in the play we are considering. The whole thing strikes one as
alien to the spirit of "Shakespeare," whose method is naturally to
reveal the character of his personae in the working of the plays. It
is hardly probable that "Shakespeare" had a hand in any of the
lists: they are editorial work; and the character they assume in this
instance helps to emphasize the fact, which others have pointed
out, that exceptional care was bestowed upon the editing of *The
Tempest*. The editor or editors had evidently some special interest
in this particular drama.

Without wit.

Coming now to the question of general workmanship, we
may take any other of the great Shakespearean comedies, and
examine the dialogue throughout, particularly that between
young people of the opposite sexes. What strikes us most is the
constant clash of wit and the subtle teasing that takes place
whenever young men and women meet, together with the playful
cross-purposes in which Shakespeare's lovers invariably indulge.
There is nothing like this in *The Tempest*. In its place we get the
milk and water sentimentality of Miranda and Ferdinand
unillumined by a single flash of intellect. Yet Miranda was no
child ignorant of life: a fact most evident from her previous
conversation with her father. Possibly the dramatist, in
composing this love scene, in which he wished to represent
Miranda in a particular light, had overlooked what he had already
written in the previous scene. Be that as it may, the

character of the intercourse between these two lovers is worth considering. They meet for the first time and spend about five minutes together. In that short space of time they have fallen deeply in love, confessed their sentiments and arranged their first tryst, "half-an-hour hence." All this, of course, is due to Prospero's magic. How interminable that half-hour must have seemed to the young people! And so, when it comes to an end, they meet again, in the presence of Miranda's father, and listen to a lecture from him; but when he leaves them, and they are at last alone together, for the first time as a betrothed couple, in the transports of their new-born love they pour out their mutual affection in a rapturous *game of chess.* Is it possible to conceive of "Shakespeare" representing thus any of the outstanding couples of his plays, like Romeo and Juliet, Orlando and Rosalind, Hermia and Lysander, Valentine and Sylvia, Berowne and Rosaline, Portia and Bassanio, or Beatrice and Benedick? In all these cases the interest centres in the play of dialogue: mind meeting mind; and not upon the play of limelight upon a pretty stage scene.

Coarse fun.

Not only in the kind of intercourse we have just been discussing, but throughout the play the great Shakespearean trait that we most miss is genuine wit, in the proper sense of intellectual refinement and subtlety. The drama depends for its interest very largely upon the spectacular, and is probably for this reason selected in modern times for displaying the skill more of the stage mechanics than of the actors. It has, indeed, been acknowledged by one authority that "there is no wit in *The Tempest.*"[236] Nevertheless its author was solicitous regarding the lighter side of the play; and so when fun and some relief from stage display is sought, the play makes its appeal to the grotesque, coarse, and ludicrous, drawing almost the whole of the laughter it contains from drunken buffoonery. Without its elaborate stage

---

[236] New Variorum edition of *The Tempest*, p. 389, quoting the November 7, 1667 entry in Samuel Pepys's diary.

effects the performance would probably fall very flat; and this fact supports the theory that it is not a true Elizabethan work, but belongs to the period to which it has been assigned, although such plays were evidently coming into vogue in the later Elizabethan period.

On the other hand, to think of it as coming from the greatest Elizabethan dramatist, when to his vast powers had been added the mellowing influence of a still larger experience, increases the mysteriousness in which the work is involved. The fact is that this play has always been looked at with the other dramas as an imposing background. Viewed as supplementary to a monumental literature, the greatness that is in the other writings has been carried forward and added to its account. Separated from the other works, however, it is seen to contain much thinner intellectual stuff than has been supposed.

The Tempest problem.

The effect of these considerations is to raise the question, not merely of whether *The Tempest* contains a large admixture of other men's work, but the bolder and more momentous question of whether it is, in any sense, a work of Shakespeare's.

This is not a question of whether it is a good or a poor production, or whether certain genuine Shakespearean plays are not in some respects inferior to this one. The question is this: Judging from a comparison of the characteristics of this play with the outstanding features of Shakespeare's work, what are the probabilities that it did not come from the same pen as the others?

A play apart.

We have already pointed out that its position amongst the other dramas, from the point of view of date, marks it at once as a work quite by itself. In other respects, too, we shall find that this is so. It is the only play staged with a background of the sea and sea-faring life; the nearest approach to it, curiously enough, being *Pericles*. And it is the only one that has the practice of magic as a dominant element: the supernatural agents in *A Midsummer Night's Dream* not being under human control and direction.

This trinity of singularities constitutes a sufficient impeachment to begin with. We must, however, add to this what is perhaps the strongest general argument against it, that it is the only play attributed to "Shakespeare" which makes any attempt at conforming to the Greek unities. That "Shakespeare" should do this at any time seems highly improbable: it is contrary to the free spirit of his genius, and it is an illustration of that "tongue-tying of art by authority" which he explicitly repudiates. To think of him submitting to such unwholesome restriction at the extreme end of his career would require some extraordinary explanation.

Feudalism.

Take the work now in its bearing upon some of those points according to which we sought to characterize "Shakespeare" at the beginning of our investigations. Although it contains a king and a duke no one can feel in reading it that he is in touch with the social structure of a medieval feudalism. Prospero, the Duke of Milan, represents in no way a ducal dignity, or the functions of a dukedom. He is, first and last, a magician, and it would have mattered little to his part in the play if he had been originally a patriarchal deacon.

King Alonso can hardly be regarded as a personage belonging to the play. In certain important scenes he is only required to stand and ejaculate such expressions as "Prithee peace," or "Prithee be still." He is the most wooden and least royal of all Shakespeare's kings; a part to be relegated to a subordinate member of the company of actors. Prospero's brother, Antonio, the usurping duke, is a very ordinary stage villain, whom the writer of the drama seems almost to have forgotten after the second act, with a most curious result; for, although the anti-climax of the play consists in his undoing, his only part in the final act involving disaster to his fortunes, is to make a single remark—about fish. This is neither feudalism nor "Shakespeare."

Catholicism.

So much for the social side of medievalism. When we turn to its religious aspect, Catholicism, a more curious situation is presented. Whatever "Shakespeare's" personal opinions may have been in respect to religion, there exists no doubt as to his being thoroughly conversant with the Roman Catholic standpoint and quite familiar with its terminology; and all this he introduces frequently and appropriately into his dramas. Now *The Tempest* is a work dealing with Italian noblemen of Milan and Naples, that is to say, belonging to a Roman Catholic society, yet from the first word of the play to the last we cannot find a single term employed suggestive of a distinctively Catholic conception. At the same time innumerable occasions are presented when such touches of local colouring could have been inserted, and when any writer having the material at command would unconsciously have tended to introduce it. We need only cite the call "to prayers," the betrothal of Ferdinand and Miranda, and the serious religious cast given to some of Prospero's intercourse with his daughter.

Whether, therefore, we approach it on its social or its religious side, we may say that the medievalism which "Shakespeare" has, by embodying in his dramas, done so much to preserve in living colours, is almost, if not wholly, absent from this particular play. We are entitled to say that the man who wrote it had neither "Shakespeare's" intimacy with Catholicism nor his vitalized conception of what was best in feudalism.

Woman.

Significant results are again obtained when we apply to *The Tempest* the test of the dramatist's treatment of woman. We shall put aside that definite and peculiar attitude we deduced from the *Sonnets*, which does not appear in the best Shakespearean comedies, and confine our attention to the dramas. Here we find the most frequent and varied references to the characters, disposition, moods, motives and conduct of women. That he had observed women accurately might be questioned, but that he had observed them closely and had a very great deal to say on the subject no one will deny. Consequently the word "woman" is one most frequently in use in his plays. Now, in *The Tempest* the word "woman" never occurs once in connection with such matters as those to which we have just alluded. It will perhaps be a matter of surprise to many that the word only occurs twice in the whole play, and these are most formal and void of character. Miranda remarks that she "no woman's face remembers," and Caliban remarks "I never saw a woman but Sycorax my dam and she." The three occasions on which the plural is used are equally colourless. This is indeed a very poor show for a work that is supposed to have come from the hand of such an exponent of human nature as "Shakespeare."

Horsemanship.

In tracing indications of the life and character of Edward de Vere in the writings of "Shakespeare" we had occasion to remark upon the prominence given to horses and horsemanship generally. We find that the simple noun "horse," leaving out all compound derivatives, occurs about 206 times; an average of about seven times in each of the 36 plays. If we add to these the words that suggest horse-riding, like "horse-back" and "horsemanship," the total reaches nearly 300, not one of which occurs in *The Tempest—the only play attributed to "Shakespeare" of which this can be said.*

The word "colt" does, however, occur, and the passage is most instructive.

> Like unback'd colts they prick'd their ears,
> Advanced their eyelids, lifted up their noses,
> As they smelt music.

We shall pass no comment upon these awkward lines, but ask the reader to compare the passage with the following from *The Merchant of Venice*, which either consciously or unconsciously seems to have suggested it.

> For do but note a wild and wanton herd,
> Or race of youthful and unbandled colts,
> Fetching mad bounds, bellowing and neighing loud,
> Which is the hot condition of their blood,

If they but hear perchance a trumpet sound,
Or any air of music touch their ear,
You shall perceive them make a mutual stand,
Their savage eyes turn'd to a modest gaze
By the sweet power of music.

We are asked to believe that the former travesty of the latter passage was written by the same poet after he had added fifteen years to his experience as a writer. Had the dates been reversed we might have supposed a development of the idea and technical power. As they stand, however, it is outrageous to suppose that any eminent poet could so mutilate his own work.

Sport.

Again, in the matter of falconry terms, in which the vocabulary of Shakespeare is so varied, "hawk," "falcon," "haggard," "eyas," "tercel," "tassel-gentle," "puttock," "pitch," "to seel," "to prune," "to whistle off"; none of these occur in the play we are now examining. We find indeed the same state of things in all other matters relating to sport, the chase and archery (excepting a single reference to Cupid's bow and arrows). No deer, stag or pricket, hare or hound, greyhound, game, slips or trumpet, once appears. These are enough to show that not merely a few odd terms, any one or two of which might be missing from a true Shakespearean work, but whole strata of terms, dealing with the imagery in which the mind of Shakespeare habitually worked, are entirely missing from this play. A mere layman may be excused if his faith in the judgment of Shakespearean experts grows weak.

Human nature.

Shakespeare's special domain being human nature, how does *The Tempest* stand with respect to prominent words of the dramatist in this domain? One of his constantly recurring words is the word "will," and in Mary Cowden Clarke's concordance only when it is used as a noun is it recorded. In this sense it appears no less than 280 times, and out of these only once does it appear in *The Tempest*, in the following phrase, "the *wills above*"; so that, as a matter of fact, the human will, which meets us at every turn in Shakespeare, is never once referred to in this play except in some editions in which the noun "good-will" has been broken into two words. How important a word it is in the vocabulary of Shakespeare will be realized by anyone who will take the trouble to read Sir Sidney Lee's chapter on the "Will" sonnets.[237]

Take again so fundamental a word as "faith," which, with its derivatives, occurs about 250 times. Neither this word, nor any one of its derivatives, "faithful," "faithfully," "faithfulness," once appears in the play. Or, again, the word "duty," not once does it occur, nor any of its derivations, "dutiful" or "duteous," notwithstanding the fact that these words are bound up with the Feudal System, and occur about 200 times. We meet with exactly the same thing in reference to such dominant words as "courage" and "jealousy." The word "melancholy" and the noun "desire," the latter especially representing a most persistent idea in the mind of "Shakespeare," are again entirely absent. In short, many of the terms most essential in handling those problems of human nature with which "Shakespeare" deals are missing from the work which is supposed to represent the matured mind of the dramatist.

General vocabulary.

On the strength of the last group of words alone we should be quite justified in rejecting absolutely any claim that this play was written by the same author as the great Shakespearean dramas. Of minor points we may mention the absence of the "red and white" contrast, and, of course, the "lily and the rose." Indeed, neither lily, rose, nor violet, which we take to be Shakespeare's favourite flower, is once mentioned.

It is difficult to represent how *The Tempest* stands in the matter of general vocabulary. If, however, any Shakespearean concordance be taken, and a number of pages be selected at

---

[237] Lee, *Life*, Chapter VIII, "The 'Will' Sonnets," pp. 432-442.

random from different parts of the book, then closely examined, it will be found that *The Tempest* is more frequently absent than almost any other play from long lists of examples of the recurrence of words which appear in most of the other works. It will thus be seen that it has probably the poorest, as well as the least Shakespearean, vocabulary of them all; not even excepting *Pericles.* Moreover, in reading it with an exclusive attention to this point, one gets the impression that its vocabulary is not only more restricted in range, but is drawn from quite a different stratum of the English language. In addition to this there appears about the language an artificiality and affected archaism suggestive of a later writer trying to compose in Shakespeare's vein.

Scansion.

After all the praise that has been lavished on this particular work it may seem presumptuous to question such a thing as the quality of its versification. If, however, a critical examination be made of the text of the play, the large proportion of bad metre to be found in it will probably occasion some surprise. From first to last its blank verse jogs and jolts in a most uncomfortable way. Such false quantities as occasionally interrupt the even flow in the best Shakespearean verse, so crowd upon one another in *The Tempest* that it is impossible to preserve for any length of time that sense of rhythmic diction which gratifies the sub-conscious ear in the silent reading of the other plays. There is nothing to be gained by rating the work below its true value, but we are bound to say that in many instances the scansion seems to us so wretched that we suspect the writer of building up his pentameters by mechanically counting syllables on his fingers: and counting badly.

"Weak-endings."

In this connection we have already had occasion to draw attention to the blank verse of the first important piece of dialogue in the play: that between Prospero and Miranda in which the former is relating the story of his misfortunes. A minute inspection of this discloses the fact that much of it is not verse at all in the true sense, but merely prose, artificially cut up into short strips: precisely as, in an earlier chapter, we saw was actually done in *Coriolanus*. Versification, which is fundamentally the breaking up of utterances into short pieces, or lines, according to some rule, always implies that, in a general way, the pause formed by the end of the line corresponds to a pause, however slight, in the spoken utterance; the exceptions to this only serving to emphasize the rule. When the connection between the last word of one line and the first word of the next is too close, and such connections become too frequent, the sense of versification is lost and it becomes merely dismembered prose.

Take then the two first lines of this dialogue:

> If by your art, my dearest father, you *have*
> *Put* the wild waters in this roar, allay them.

Auxiliary verbs.

Now, it is hardly possible to get two words more closely connected in spoken utterances than a Principal and an Auxiliary Verb, when no adverb comes between them, as in the case of this verb, "have put." Nor is this the only example of its kind. Broken up in precisely the same way we have the verb,

> "*had* Burnt" (III.1); "*will* Revenge" (III.2);
> "*have* Incensed" (III.3); "*have* Been" (V.1);
> "*have* Received" (V.1); "*must* Take" (V.1)

Taking *Hamlet* as our standard for measuring Shakespeare's style of versification, we do not find a single example of this defect in the great masterpiece.

Continuing our examination of this dialogue, we find, a few lines further on, this passage:

> It should the good ship so have swallow'd, *and*
> The fraughting souls within her.

Conjunctions.

This "and" at the end of lines in *The Tempest* is quite a feature of its author's style. We pointed it out in the passage "*and* Are melted into air." We find it repeated three times in this short dialogue:

> "*and* A prince of power;"
> "*and* She said;"

the third being in the above quotation.

In exactly the same way we have:

> "*and* My strong imagination" (II.1)
> "*and* I'll seek" (III.3)
> "*and* Harmonious charmingly" (IV.1)

Again, not once does this defect appear in *Hamlet*.

We have also instances of the conjunction "but" placed at the end of lines

> "*but* For every trifle" (II.2)
> "*but* The mistress" (III.1)
> "*but* If thou dost break" (IV.1)

Nor does this defect once appear in *Hamlet*.

Examples also occur of lines ending in other Conjunctions, to which may be added Conjunctive Pronouns and Conjunctive Adverbs:—

> "*who* Art ignorant" (I.2)
> "*that* Hath kept with thy remembrance" (I.2)
> "*who* To trash for over topping" (I.2)
> "*that* A noble Neapolitan" (I.2)
> "*that* I prize" (I.2)
> "*for* He's gentle" (I.2)
> "*whom* We all were" (II.1)
> "*that* We say befits" (II.1)
> "*which* Lie tumbling" (II.2)

And so it continues on to end of the play. Yet never once does this form of intimate connection between the end of one line and the beginning of the next appear in *Hamlet*. How it is possible to hold, in face of a comparison of this kind, that the versification of both plays came from the same pen, is most difficult to understand.

Prepositions.

Another peculiar form of connection between the end of one line and the beginning of the next is to split between them simple Prepositional phrases. For example:

> "*upon* A most auspicious star" (I.2)
> "*upon* Some god" (I.2)
> "*at* Which end" (II.1)
> "*of* Our human generation" (III.3)
> "*with* A heaviness" (V.1)
> "*on* The strangeness" (V.1)

The only Prepositions which appear at the end of lines in *Hamlet* are those which belong to the preceding verbs, and do not, except in one case, which has a special justification, enter into the formation of Prepositional phrases.

Shakespearean terminations.

A critical and exhaustive examination of the line terminations in the blank verse of the plays attributed to "Shakespeare" will, we imagine, yield surprising results. We have therefore taken not only the play of *Hamlet*, which we made our standard in examining the blank verse of *The Tempest*, but all the Shakespearean plays which received a proper literary presentation between the publication of *Henry IV*, part I, the first of the issue in 1597, and *Hamlet* (1604), the last of the authentic issues prior to the First Folio, and we have spent some hours in running the eye over the terminations of their blank verse. Not once have we found a line ending in "and," "but," or other simple Conjunction or Conjunctive Pronoun. We will not venture to say that such an ending does not exist in *Richard III, Richard II, A Midsummer Night's Dream, Love's Labour's Lost, The Merchant of Venice, Romeo and Juliet, Much Ado, Titus Andronicus* or *Hamlet*; but if any such termination should happen to be there we have not discovered it; and so extremely rare is it that it would have to be ranked with "Homer's nods" and "Milton's lapses." In the case of *The Tempest* however, there is no need to search for these endings: they obtrude themselves in a most uncomfortable way.

"Weak-endings" and strange pens.

When, however, we turn to the plays which "others were called upon at a later date to finish," a totally different state of things is met with. There is probably not one of these without several "and" and "but" terminations. The play which comes nearest to *The Tempest* in this particular we should imagine to be *Cymbeline*. If we glance over it whilst the contrast between the true Shakespearean terminations and *The Tempest* terminations are still in mind, we recognize at once that the *Cymbeline* terminations belong to *The Tempest* order. "Ands," "buts," and Conjunctive Pronouns are met with frequently; and in versification, at any rate, there is a general suggestion of similarity in the two works. It is interesting, therefore, to note in this play, the sea, the scene before a cave, the thunder and lightning, and the dumb-show "mummery" (which Sir Sidney Lee admits could not have been penned by "Shakespeare"),[238] and even the character of Imogen: all of which are suggestive of the work we are discussing.

If, then, the substance of the play of *Cymbeline* is Shakespearean, everything is suggestive of its having been versified by the writer who composed *The Tempest*. A development of this line of study will probably do much to still further reduce the quantity of pure Shakespearean literature. In so far as the conceptions and general wording of the later plays are recognized as Shakespearean, it will tend to bear out a theory we have developed in an earlier chapter, that these dramas existed first as stage plays with a larger proportion of prose, and were subsequently converted into poetic literature; the later works having to receive their versification from strange hands. In the case of *Cymbeline* it is possible to ascribe the poetic dressing alone to the strangers. In the case of *The Tempest* we believe that the

---

[238] Lee, *Life*, p. 259.

entire drama must be given over to those who were engaged in finishing off "Shakespeare's" plays.

Not Shakespeare's work.

We are prepared to maintain, then, on the strength of the various points indicated, that *The Tempest* is no play of "Shakespeare's." It is not the absence of an odd Shakespearean characteristic, but the absence of so many dominant marks of his work, along with the presence of several features which are quite contrary to his style, that compels us to reject it. If, therefore, it was actually put forward during William Shakspere's lifetime as a genuine Shakespearean play, it furnishes an additional testimony to the previous death of the dramatist, and what was at first a difficulty thus becomes a further support and confirmation of our theory. Who the writer or writers may have been, how the work came to find a place in the collected issue of Shakespeare's plays (the First Folio), why it happens to be accorded the first place in that collection and is also edited with exceptional pains, are, no doubt, problems of considerable interest, which, if solved, might throw some light upon our own problem. Their solution, however, is neither pressing nor necessary, and therefore may be allowed to stand over.

Relation to our problem.

We desire, however, to emphasize the fact that but for the theory that Edward de Vere was the writer of Shakespeare's plays we might never have been led to suspect the authenticity of *The Tempest*. When, therefore, the theory of the De Vere authorship suggests doubts as to the genuineness of this play, and on examination we find such an accumulation of evidence that it is not Shakespeare's work, the discovery brings additional support to the supposition that the author of the genuine work was indeed Edward de Vere. And it is the frequency with which such examples of mutual or complementary corroboration have sprung from our theory that has given to that theory such an air of certainty.

We are conscious that in putting forward these views respecting *The Tempest*, we are probably "cutting prejudice against the grain" as dangerously as in the theory of authorship we are advancing, and also risking the opening up of side issues which may divert attention from the central theme. This is why we have relegated the matter to an appendix. To those whom these arguments do not satisfy we would therefore, for the time being, indicate the earlier dates suggested by Hunter and others, and the general theory of collaboration held respecting "Shakespeare's" latest productions. Meanwhile we make it clear that we do not rest upon these earlier date theories, and that the rejection of *The Tempest* must in our view be incorporated ultimately into the general argument.

APPENDIX II

SUPPLEMENTARY EVIDENCE

ONE of the chief difficulties with which we have had to contend in penning the foregoing pages has been that of keeping pace with the accumulation of evidence and placing it in its proper connections: a very strong testimony to the soundness of the general conclusions. Even after the work was virtually all set up some most interesting evidence, one piece of which will probably crown the whole structure, came into our hands. These matters we can only briefly indicate.

I

THE POSTHUMOUS ARGUMENT

First, we would quote the following passage which we had overlooked in the English Men of Letters series, which gives valuable support to our "Posthumous" argument:

"At the beginning of his career Shakespeare made very free use of the work of other men. . . . Towards the end of his career his work is once more found mixed with the work of other men, but this time there is generally reason to suspect that it is these others that have laid him under contribution, altering his completed plays, or completing his unfinished work by additions of their own."[239]

II

OXFORD'S CREST AND FAMILY MOTTO

An examination of the De Vere Crest in *Fairbair's Crests* (vol.

---

[239] Raleigh, *Shakespeare*, p. 109.

II, plate 40, 2) and in the *De Walden Library*[240] discloses the interesting fact that what Sir Edwin Durning-Lawrence in *Bacon is Shakespeare*,[241] had taken for Bacon's Crest, because it chanced to be in a presentation copy of the *Novum Organum*, is in fact the De Vere Crest. Several families had the Boar as their crest; but the distinguishing mark of this one is the crescent upon the left shoulder of the animal (see *De Walden Library*). This is peculiar to the De Vere Crest, and appears in Sir Edwin Durning-Lawrence's illustration. Whatever value there might be in this writer's argument therefore belongs to De Vere. We shall not, however, discuss that argument at present.

The stars upon the De Vere banner and the family motto:

Vero nihil verius

—nothing truer than truth—are specially interesting in view of Hamlet's poesy to Ophelia:

Doubt that the stars are fire,
    Doubt that the sun doth move,
Doubt truth to be a liar,
    But never doubt I love.

This mode of exaggerating by representing something as being "truer than truth" comes out again in Shakespeare's satirizing of Euphuism, where he represents Don Armado as using the terms of the De Vere family motto:

Thou art . . . truer than truth itself.

III

OXFORD'S PORTRAIT AND THE DROESHOUT ENGRAVING

It is not generally known that there is no Shakespeare portrait before the Droeshout engraving which appeared in the First Folio: that is to say, seven years after the death of the man it is supposed to represent; and it is of a totally different type from the bust of him that was set up at Stratford, where he would be

---

[240] Howard de Walden, *Banners, Standards, and Badges*, p. 257.
[241] Sir Edwin Durning-Lawrence, *Bacon is Shakespeare*, p. 41.

personally known. Droeshout, moreover, was only a lad of fifteen when Shakspere died; he would be only twelve when Shakspere was in London probably for the last time, and was born only the year before Shakspere's supposed retirement in 1604. These facts, combined with the peculiar character of the portrait he produced, has made the question of what he had to work on not the least interesting of the many problems connected with Shakespearean authorship.

It was not until a few months ago that we had an opportunity of seeing a portrait of Edward de Vere in Fairfax Murray's reproductions of the portraits that are in the Duke of Portland's place at Welbeck Abbey, near Worksop, Nottingham.

Certain features in the picture immediately suggested the Droeshout engraving; most particularly the thin dark line which runs along above the upper lip, leaving a slight space between this suggestion of a moustache and the edge of the lip itself. Since then we have looked over a large number of portraits of the time, and have discovered nothing else similar. In addition there were the same facial proportions, the same arching of the eyebrows, the identical pose (three-quarter face), the same direction of gaze, about an equal amount of bust, the chief difference being that one is turned to the right and the other to the left: altogether there was quite sufficient to suggest that, when the two could be brought together, a very strong case might be made out for Droeshout having worked from this portrait of Edward de Vere, making modifications according to instructions. For Oxford was only twenty-five when the portrait was painted, and, of course, it was necessary to represent Shakespeare as an older man. This would explain the peculiar Tom Pinch-like combination of youthfulness and age that is one of the puzzling features of the Droeshout engraving.

We have now before us, however, what may prove to be the most sensational piece of evidence that our investigations have so far yielded. This is a picture known as the Grafton portrait of

Shakespeare at 24. The full particulars respecting it are narrated in a work on the subject by Thomas Kay[242] and published in 1915: the chief aim of the book being to show the connection between this and another portrait from which the Droeshout engraving was conceivably made.

Now, until we can place an acknowledged portrait of the Earl of Oxford alongside of it, we shall defer saying positively that this is actually another portrait of him; but speaking from recollections of the other we would say at first sight that it is so. The eye is at once arrested again by the thin dark line on the upper lip that we noticed in Oxford's portrait; there are all the features which we noticed his portrait had in common with the Droeshout engraving; and in those points in which the older features of the Droeshout engraving differed from Edward de Vere this one agrees with the latter. The probability that it is another portrait of the Earl of Oxford is therefore very strong.

We now come to the startling facts. First of all, although the portrait is that of a young man aged twenty-four, he is dressed as an aristocrat, and Stratfordianism is driven to invent far-fetched explanations. Again under the 4 of his age there had been a 31 and again more explanations have to be invented. Then, under the 8 in the date it looks again as if there had been another 31 and authorities are quoted to controvert it. Now as the Earl of Oxford would be twenty-three in the year 1573 *these two alterations are two out of the three precise alterations which would be necessary to make the age and date in a portrait of Edward de Vere agree with the particulars for William Shakspere of Stratford.*

In a word we have here *probably* (to be cautious for the present) a portrait of the Earl of Oxford with particulars altered to fit the Stratford man: in which case our evidence is about as complete as it could be. The probability is, as a study of the work suggests, that this portrait was placed before Droeshout as the basis for his engraving. We would further add that the numbers were probably altered so that the engraver need not be in the

---

[242] Thomas Kay, The Story of the "Grafton" Portrait of William Shakespeare.

secret. The scrubbing to which the picture has been subjected has brought up the numbers from underneath. That same scrubbing has, unfortunately, obliterated the high lights on the nose of the portrait, thus altering its shape and reducing its value for identification.

This enables us to finish our argument almost in strict accordance with the original plan, the seventh and last step of which was to connect directly as far as possible the newly accredited with the formerly reputed author.

Note.—The Grafton portrait of Shakespeare has now been carefully compared with the Welbeck portrait of Edward de Vere, and when proper allowances are made for evident differences of artistic treatment and skill, and for the denudation of high lights from the former, as well as other disfigurements resulting from ill-usage to the picture, there seems abundant justification for the point of view assumed in the above argument. In our opinion the portrait of the Earl of Oxford has more in common with both the Grafton portrait and the Droeshout engraving than these two have with one another.

LIST OF TEXTUAL CHANGES
(made by editor)

Modernization of format
—Embedded subject indicators have been placed as subtitles and italicized.
—Long quotations are indented, in smaller font, and set off from the main text by half spaces.
—Lines quoted from literary works that were in quotation marks are now indented and in smaller font.
—Titles are italicized instead of being in quotation marks: "Romeo and Juliet" in this edition is *Romeo and Juliet.*
—Act and Scene of dramatic works quoted have been standardized; example: "(V.3)."
—Original inconsistent formatting of the titles of the *Henry IV* and *Henry VI* plays has been left unchanged, as in these two attributions from the same paragraph on page 337: "*Henry IV*, parts 1 and 2" and "*I Henry IV.*"
—Other formatting has been standardized to eliminate inconsistencies.
—The font used is Galliard BT.

Spelling
—The British spelling of words—such as "theatre," "apologise," "labours," and "realise"—have been kept.
—Antiquated forms of words used by Looney—such as "amongst," and "whilst"—have been kept.
—Quotations from Elizabethan era works have been kept in the spelling   used in the 1920 edition.
—In most instances, "any one" has been changed to "anyone" and "some one" to "someone."
—"Worth while" has been changed to "worthwhile."
—"Co-operation" has been changed to "cooperation."
—"More over" has been changed to "moreover."
—"Rôle" has been changed to "Role."
—This edition follows the 1920 edition in capitalizing "Sonnets" when the word is used as a short way of referring to the publication *Shakespeare's Sonnets*, and not capitalizing the word when it refers to individual sonnets or group of sonnets.

Punctuation
—Only one space is used between sentences.
—The blank space between words and punctuation marks have been
    eliminated.
—Smart quotes are used.
—The dash after a colon has been eliminated: ":—" is now ":"
—The 1920 editions' placement of semicolons after end quote marks
    but periods/full stops before them—as in "; and ."—is
    unchanged.
—Superscript footnote numbers follow all punctuation marks except
    dashes.
—"The most" has been replaced by "Most:" "The most of [the
    songs]"has been changed to "Most of [the songs]."

Sources and footnotes
—Quotations are footnoted to indicate their source and page number.
—Looney's indication of the source of a quotation in parenthesis
    following the quote has been moved to a footnote and details
    added.
—Looney's insertions into quotations are now in brackets [] instead of
    parentheses ().
—Where Looney's quotations are only paraphrases, this is indicated in
    a footnote and the correct text is usually supplied.

**Corrections & Completions [noted in footnotes; text is
    unchanged]**

Frederick A. Stokes Edition	2018 Forever Press Edition
Life of Spenser	*Spenser*
Richard Bagehot	Walter Bagehot
Dean Church	Richard William Church
Drake	Nathan Drake
Hunter	Rev. John Hunter
Emerson	Ralph Waldo Emerson
Green's *Short History*	John Richard Green's *A Short History of the English People*
Hume's biography of Burghley	Martin A. S. Hume, *The Great Lord Burghley*
Macaulay says . . .	Thomas Babington Macaulay, "Lord Burghley and His Times"
Ruskin says . . .	John Ruskin, *The Two Paths*, and

	Sesame and Lilies
Stopes's Burbage	Charlotte Carmichael Stopes, *Burbage and Shakespeare's Stage*
Thompson's study of Shakespeare's penmanship	Sir Edward Maunde Thompson, *Shakespeare's Handwriting: A Study*
Judge Webb's *The Shakespeare Mystery*	Judge Thomas E. Webb's The *Mystery of William Shakespeare*

BIBLIOGRAPHY
(Prepared by editor)

PART 1: BOOKS AND ARTICLES CITED BY LOONEY

Bagehot, Walter
  1905   "Shakespeare—The Man," in *Literary Studies by the Late Walter Bagehot*, vol. 1, pp. 37-86. Edited by Richard H. Hutton. London: Longmans, Green and Co.

Bayne, Rev. Ronald
  1907   "Lesser Elizabethan Dramatists," in *Cambridge History of English Literature*, vol. 5, chapter 13, pp. 309-335. Cambridge, England: University Press.

Beesly, Edward Spencer
  1892   *Queen Elizabeth*. London/New York: Macmillan and Co.

Bell, Henry Glassford
  1900   *Life of Mary Queen of Scots*. 2 vol. New York: A. L. Fowle.

Bond, R. Warwick (editor)
  1902   *The Complete Works of John Lyly: Now for the First Time Collected and Edited from the Earliest Quartos*. Oxford: Clarendon Press.

Bullen, A. H. (editor)
  1887   *England's Helicon: A Collection of Lyrical and Pastoral Poems*. London: John C. Nimmo. [1600]
  1890   *Davison's Poetical Rhapsody*, vol. I. London: George Bell and Sons. [Francis Davison, 1602]

Cambridge History of English Literature
  1907-17 Alfred Rayney Waller and William Ward Aldolphus, editors. Cambridge, England: University Press.
          Vol. 4, pp. 107-146: "The Song-Books and Miscellanies" by Harold H. Child.
          Vol. 5, pp. 309-335: "Lesser Elizabethan Dramatists" by Rev. Ronald Bayne.

Carlyle, Thomas
  1888   *On Heroes, Hero-worship and the Heroic in History*. London: Chapman & Hall, Ltd.

Child, Harold H.
1907 "The Song-Books and Miscellanies," in *Cambridge History of English Literature*, vol. 4, pp. 107-146. Cambridge, England: University Press.

Church, Richard William
1879 *Spenser*. London: Macmillan and Co.

Clarke, Charles and Mary Cowden
1866 "The Story of Shakespeare's Life," in *The Works of William Shakespeare*. New York: D. Appleton & Co.

Collins, Arthur
1752 *Historical Collections of the Noble Families of Cavendishe, Holles, Vere, Harley, and Ogle*. London: Printed for E. Withers.

Complete Poetical Works of Robert Burns, The
1874 Edited by William Gunnyon. London: William P. Nimmo.

Complete Works of John Lyly, The: Now for the First Time Collected and Edited from the Earliest Quartos.
1902 Edited by R. Warwick Bond. Oxford: Clarendon Press.

Complete Works of William Shakespeare, The (Dr. Johnson Edition)
1896 Philadelphia: The Gebbie Publishing Co., Ltd.

Courthope, W. J.
1910 *History of English Poetry*, vol. II. New York/London: Macmillan and Co.

Creighton, Mandell
1899 *Age of Elizabeth*. London/New York: Longmans, Green, and Co. [1876]

Creizenach, Wilhelm Michael Anton
1916 *The English Drama in the Age of Elizabeth* [translated from *Geschichte des neueren Dramas*]. Philadelphia: J. B. Lippincott Company. London: Sidgwick & Jackson, Ltd.

Davison's Poetical Rhapsody
1890 Vol. 1., edited by A. H. Bullen. London: George Bell and Sons. [Francis Davison, 1602]

De Walden, Howard
1904 *Banners, Standards, and Badges from a Tudor Manuscript in the College of Arms*. London: The De Walden Library.

Dennis, G. Ravenscroft
    1914   *The House of Cecil.* London: Constable & Co., Ltd.
                [Published in the U.S. as *The Cecil Family.*
                Boston/New York: Houghton Mifflin Company.]

Dictionary of National Biography, 2nd edition
    1898   Sir Sidney Lee, editor. London: Smith, Elder & Co.
                Vol. 34, pp. 327-332: "Lyly, John," by Sidney Lee.
                Vol. 58, pp. 225-229: "Vere, Edward," by Sidney
                Lee.
                Vol. 58, pp. 219-220: "Vere, Family of," by Sidney
                Lee.
                Vol. 63, pp. 140-246: "Wriothesley, Henry," by
                Sidney Lee.

Donnelly, Ignatius
    1888   *The Great Cryptogram: Francis Bacon's Cipher in the So-
                called Shakespeare Plays.* London: S. Low, Marston,
                Searly & Rivington.

Dowden, Edward
    1875   *Shakspere: A Critical Study of His Mind and Art.*
                London: Henry S King & Co.

Drake, Nathan
    1817   *Shakespeare and His Times.* [2 vol.] London: T.
                Cadell and W. Davies.

Durning-Lawrence, Sir Edwin
    1910   *Bacon is Shakespeare.* London/New York: Gay &
                Hancock, Ltd.

Dyce, Rev. Alexander (editor)
    1893   *The Works of William Shakespeare,* 2nd edition. [9 vol.]
                London: Chapman and Hall [1866]

Elze, Karl
    1874   *Essays on Shakespeare.* Translated with the author's
                sanction by L. Dora Schmitz. London: Macmillan
                and Co.

Emerson, Ralph Waldo
    1850   *Representative Men: Seven Lectures* [1850] [There are
                many editions; it's not known which Looney
                consulted.]
    1855   "July 21, 1855 Letter to Walt Whitman." [Letter has
                been reprinted many times; it's not known where
                Looney encountered it.]

Encyclopaedia Britannica
    1910   11th edition. Hugh Chisholm, editor. Cambridge:
              Cambridge University Press.
              Vol. 24, pp. 772-797: "Shakespeare, William"
              Vol. 27, pp. 1019-1021: "Vere"

England's Helicon: A Collection of Lyrical and Pastorla Poems
    1887   Edited by A. H. Bullen. London: John C. Nimmo.
              [1600]

Fuller, Thomas
    1840   *The History of the Worthies of England*. London: T.
              Tegg. [1662]

Furness, Horace Howard (editor)
    1873   *The New Variorum Edition of Shakespeare*, vol. 2,
              Macbeth. Philadelphia: J. B. Lippincott & Co.
    1880   *The New Variorum Edition of Shakespeare*, vol. 5, *King
              Lear*. Philadelphia: J. B. Lippincott & Co.
    1892   *The New Variorum Edition of Shakespeare*, vol. 9, *The
              Tempest*. Philadelphia: J. B. Lippincott & Co.

Green, John Richard
    1886   *A Short History of the English People*, vol. 2. London:
              Macmillan and Co.

Greenstreet, James H.
    1891   "A Hitherto Unknown Noble Writer of Elizabethan
              Comedies," in *The Genealogist*, New Series, vol. 7,
              pp. 205-208.
    1892   "Further Notices of William Stanley, 6th Earl of Derby,"
              in *The Genealogist*, New Series, vol. 8, pp. 8-15.
    1892   "Testimonies Against the Accepted Authorship of
              Shakespeare's Plays," in *The Genealogist*, New
              Series, vol. 8, pp. 137-146.

Greenwood, Sir George G.
    1908   *The Shakespeare Problem Restated*. London/New
              York: John Lane Company.
    1916   *Is There a Shakespeare Problem?* London/New York:
              John Lane Company.

Grosart, Alexander Balloch (editor)
    1872-76 "The Poems of Edward de Vere, Earl of Oxford," in
              Grosart, *Miscellanies of the Fuller Worthies' Library*,
              vol. 4, pp. 351-352, 359, 394-429. London.

Gunnyon, William (editor)
    1874   *Complete Poetical Works of Robert Burns*. London:

William P. Nimmo.

Halliwell-Phillipps, J. O.
    1883   *Outlines of the Life of Shakespeare, Third Edition.*
           London: Longmans, Green, and Co.

Harris, Frank
    1909   *The Man Shakespeare and His Tragic Life-Story.*
           London: Frank Palmer Red Lion Court.

Hume, Martin A. S.
    1898   *The Great Lord Burghley: A Study in Elizabethan*
           Statecraft. New York: Longmans, Green, and Co.

Hunter, Rev. John
    1839   *A Disquisition on the Scene, Origin, Date, Etc. Etc. of*
           Shakespeare's Tempest. London: Printed by C.
           Whittingham. [Quoted from numerous times in the
           New Variorum edition of *The Tempest.*]

Kay, Thomas
    1915   *The Story of the "Grafton" Portrait of William*
           Shakespeare. London: S. W. Partridge.

Knight, Charles
    1849   *Studies of Shakspere: Companion Volume to Every Edition*
           of the Text. London: Charles Knight.

Lang, Andrew
    1912   *Shakespeare, Bacon and the Great Unknown.*
           London/New York: Longmans, Green and Co.

Lee, Sir Sidney (author)
    1898   "Lyly, John," *Dictionary of National Biography [DNB]*,
           2nd ed., vol. 34, pp. 327-332. London: Smith,
           Elder & Co.
    1898   "Vere, Edward," *DNB*, 2nd ed., vol. 58, pp. 225-229.
    1898   "Vere, Family of," *DNB*, 2nd ed., vol. 58, pp. 219-220.
    1898   "Wriothesley, Henry," *DNB*, 2nd ed., vol. 63, pp. 140-
           146.

Lee, Sir Sidney (editor)
    1899   *Dictionary of National Biography*, 2nd ed., London:
           Smith, Elder & Co.

Lefranc, Abel
    1918   *Sous le Masque de "William Shakespeare": William*
           Stanley, Vle Comte de Derby. Paris: Payot & Cie.

Lyly, John
    1902   *The Complete Works of John Lyly. Now for the First Time*

Collected and Edited from the Earliest Quartos. (R. Warwick Bond, editor), 3 vols. Oxford: Clarendon Press.

Macaulay, Thomas Babington
    1889   "Lord Burghley and His Times," in *Macaulay's Essays and Lays of Ancient Rome*, pp. 235-250. London: George Routledge and Sons. [Originally published in *The Edinburgh Review*, April, 1832. Republished many times; it's not known which edition Looney consulted.]

Markham, Sir Clements R.
    1888   *The Fighting Veres.* Boston/New York: Houghton, Mifflin and Company.

Morant, Philip
    1768   *History and Antiquities of the County of Essex.* London: Printed for T. Osborne.

National Encyclopedia: A Dictionary of Universal Knowledge by Writers of Eminence in Literature, Science, and Art.
    London: William MacKenzie.
    1884   Vol. 4: "Shakspeare, William," pp. 607-?. [Pages 615-618 are missing in the only edition available for examination.]

New Variorum Edition of Shakespeare.
    Horace Howard Furness (editor). Philadelphia: J. B. Lippincott & Co.
    1873   Vol. 2: *Macbeth.*
    1980   Vol. 5: *King Lear.*
    1892   Vol. 9: *The Tempest.*

Nichols, John Gough
    1852   "On the Descent of the Earldom of Oxford," in *Archaeological Journal*, vol. 9, no. 1, pp. 17-29.

Nicolas, Sir Harris
    1847   *Memoirs of the Life and Times of Sir Christopher Hatton.* London: Richard Bentley.

Penzance, First Baron – see James P. Wilde

"Pocket Falstaff" Edition of Shakespeare's Complete Works
    1898   [40 volumes.] London: Sands & Company.
    Vol. 40: "Glossery and Notes"

Raleigh, Sir Walter (editor)
    1907   *Shakespeare.* London: Macmillan & Co. [Published in

the *Eminent Men of Letters* series.]

Ruskin, John
    1887   *The Two Paths: Being Lectures on Art and Its Application to Decoration and Manufacture.* New York: J. Wiley. [1859]
    1910   *Sesame and Lilies: Three Lectures.* New York/London: Thomas Nelson and Sons. [1864]

Sharp, William
    1886   *Sonnets of this Century.* London: W. Scott.

Sharpe's London Magazine: A Journal of Entertainment and Instruction for General Reading.
    1847   "Mary, Queen of Scotts." From an Old Manuscript. May 22, 1947, pp. 63-64.

Staunton, Howard (editor)
    1858-60   *The Plays of Shakespeare.* Vol. 3. London: Routledge, Warne & Routledge.

Stopes, Charlotte Carmichael
    1913   *Burbage and Shakespeare's Stage.* London: A. Moring, Ltd., The De la More Press.

Thompson, Sir Edward Maunde
    1916   *Shakespeare's Handwriting: A Study.* Oxford: Clarendon Press.

Walpole, Horace
    1806   *A Catalogue of the Royal and Noble Authors of England, Scotland, and Ireland; With Lists of Their Works.* London: Printed for J. Scott [1759]

Webb, Judge Thomas E.
    1902   *The Mystery of William Shakespeare: A Summary of Evidence.* London: Longmans, Green, and Co.

Wilde, James P. (First Baron Penzance)
    1902   *Lord Penzance on the Bacon-Shakespeare Controversy.* Edited by M. H. Kinnear. London: S. Low, Marston & Co., Ltd.

Winter, William
    1907   *Shakespeare's England.* New York: Grosset & Dunlap Publishers.

Wright, Thomas
    1836   *The History and Topography of the County of Essex.* London: G. Virtue.

PART 2: PAPERS AND MANUSCRIPTS

Calendar of the Manuscripts of the most Honourable the Marquis of Salisbury . . . at Hatfield House, 24 vol.

Calendar of Rutland Manuscripts.

Calendar of State Papers, Domestic.

PART 3: OTHER WORKS CITED IN EDITOR'S FOOTNOTES

Fowler, William Plumer

 1986 *Shakespeare Revealed in Oxford's Letters.* Portsmouth, NH: Peter E. Randall

PART 4: EDITIONS OF JOHN THOMAS LOONEY'S "*SHAKESPEARE*" *IDENTIFIED IN EDWARD DE VERE THE SEVENTEENTH EARL OF OXFORD.*

 1920 First British edition. London: Cecil Palmer.

 1920 First U.S. Edition. New York: Frederick A. Stokes Co.

 1948 Second U.S. Edition. New York: Duell, Sloan & Pearce. Introduction by William McFee. Afterwords by Charles Wisner Barrell.

 1975 Third U.S. Edition, 2 vol. Ruth Loyd Miller, editor. Port Washington, N.Y.: Kennikat Press & Jennings, La: Minos Publishing.

 2018 Centenary Edition. James A. Warren, editor. Somerville, MA: Forever Press.

INDEX

Made in the USA
San Bernardino, CA
16 November 2018